"Not only have Barge and Carlson done something that badly needed to be done, but they have done it with great thoroughness. So there is now detailed guidance for anyone who wishes to follow their lead—controlling health care costs based on modern ideas of quality management."

Harry V. Roberts
Sigmund E. Edelstone Professor of
Statistics and Quality
Graduate School of Business, University
of Chicago

"Management of their own employee health plan ranks among the most significant challenges facing the 1990s executive. The authors explain managed care and outline all the critical associated issues in an uncommonly insightful, nonjargonistic manner. The chapter on the new importance of health care information systems is essential reading."

Brian S. Gould, MD
Senior Vice President
United Health Care Corporation

"*The Executive's Guide to Controlling Health Care and Disability Costs* speaks compellingly about a major national problem in a language that corporate executives and public policymakers will understand. It offers linkage between the total quality philosophies, systems thinking and improvements in employee health."

Joseph F. Kasper, ScD, MBA
President, Foundation for Informed
Medical Decision Making

"Business executives can no longer blame the health and disability cost issue solely on external factors. Just as organizations have improved quality by concentrating on their own management practices, Barge and Carlson clearly present the opportunity to control these costs through active management efforts."

John M. Burns, MD
Vice President, Health Management
Honeywell, Inc.

"Integrated care delivery systems as part of health care reform require a connection with the consumer. Barge and Carlson's systematic approach to proactive employer/employee management of health and disability is the breakthrough needed for creating true health systems in partnership with providers."

Stephen J. Hegarty
President
Massachusetts Hospital Association

"Read this book! It represents a synthesis; bringing together issues that have been apart for too long. The approach employed is a new paradigm—the one needed for creating lasting solutions."

Leland Kaiser
Kaiser & Associates
Health Care Futurist

"This book is an action plan for competitive advantage. It defines the next generation of activity for TQM-driven organizations, shaping the potential for a wide range of higher value-added transactions between buyers of health care services and the professional and institutional providers."

David R. Ott
Vice President—Ambulatory Care
Mt. Sinai Medical Center, New York

"*The Executive's Guide to Controlling Health Care and Disability Costs* applies systems thinking to probably the two most difficult business challenges—health care and workers' compensation. A quantum leap forward for those executives seeking employer-driven solutions to health care and disability costs."

Ray C. Mulry, PhD
Consultant, CEO of American Network
Services

"This book makes health and its improvement everybody's business for business. By unifying language in a systems framework, it provides a sound approach for organizations and their employees to improve both cost and quality for their mutual benefit and health."

Robert W. Hungate
Principal—Physician Patient Partnerships for
Health
Former Manager Government Affairs/
Health Care—Hewlett Packard Co.

"This book's approach is unique because it is both definitive and systematic. The management tools presented allow for continuous improvement in health outcomes without major new investment; ideal for a public agency. Most importantly, measurable results can be achieved within a structure that integrates a large body of data."

Jeffrey W. Ritter
Commissioner, Medical Security
Commonwealth of Massachusetts

"Important and sophisticated, an invaluable guide for executives, managers, and policy analysts. This book shifts the paradigm from short-term cost containment to maximizing value and return on investment, providing a comprehensive guide for organizations who wish to achieve the next generation of health and disability excellence."

Donald E. Galvin, PhD
Director, Institute for Rehabilitation
and Disability Management
Washington Business Group on Health

THE EXECUTIVE'S GUIDE TO
CONTROLLING HEALTH CARE AND DISABILITY COSTS

Strategy-Based Solutions

Bruce N. Barge
John G. Carlson

JOHN WILEY & SONS, INC.

NEW YORK • CHICHESTER • BRISBANE • TORONTO • SINGAPORE

To our wives and our children
for their support

Copyright © 1993 by Bruce N. Barge and John G. Carlson
Published by John Wiley & Sons, Inc.

Library of Congress Cataloging-in-Publication Data

Barge, Bruce N., 1956–
    The executive's guide to controlling health care and disability
costs : strategy-based solutions / Bruce N. Barge, John G. Carlson.
        p.   cm.
    Published simultaneously in Canada.
    Includes bibliographical references and index.
    ISBN 0-471-58497-5 (alk. paper)
    1. Insurance, Disability—United States.   2. Workers'
compensation—United States.   3. Insurance, Health—United States.
4. Managed care plans (Medical care)—United States.   5. Industrial
hygiene—United States.   6. Industrial safety—United States.
I. Carlson, John G.   II. Title.
HD7105.25.U6B37   1993
658.3'82—dc20   93-14655

Printed in the United States of America

10 9 8 7 6 5 4 3 2 1

About the Authors

BRUCE N. BARGE is an organizational psychologist specializing in health and disability risk management and quality improvement. He has published numerous articles and papers and is a frequent speaker on topics linking organizational management, quality improvement, and risk management. Currently, he is an internal quality improvement consultant for St. Paul Fire & Marine Insurance Company, as well as the company's Director of Human Factors Loss Control, a policyholder risk consulting service.*

Mr. Barge has extensive practical experience working with employers to develop and implement management strategies to reduce health and disability costs. He has consulted with a wide range of companies and industries and has provided training and implementation assistance to executives, managers, and employees. He is a member of several health and management-related professional associations, a reviewer for several health and business journals and publications, and holds a Ph.D. in industrial/organizational psychology from the University of Minnesota.

JOHN G. CARLSON is president of RHM Systems, Inc., Marlboro, MA, a management consulting, information services, and training organization addressing organizational cost and productivity issues related to health and disability. He developed the company's systems technology over the prior two years. He has published numerous articles and has spoken at conferences and seminars on application of a systems approach and Total Quality Management principles to health, health care, and disability.

Mr. Carlson has a diverse management background with experience in finance, operations, and general management. He has held senior management positions in the electronics and health care industries, principally with General Instrument Corporation and Learning Services Corporation. His management roles have included vice president, finance and controller of a worldwide operating division, chief financial officer of two developing organizations, and president of a national multilocation organization. These

---

* Mr. Barge co-authored this book on his own time, outside of employment with St. Paul Fire & Marine Insurance Company; the ideas and positions in the book are independent of St. Paul Fire & Marine's positions and policy.

environments have included small and large companies, both domestic and international.

Mr. Carlson graduated from Bucknell University with a degree in political science and received his M.B.A. in finance from the University of Chicago. While involved in a career in management, he developed an interest in writing, contributing to various regional and national publications. An area of personal concern is disability, particularly brain injury. Mr. Carlson has contributed his management insights to survivor and family issues through public speaking and articles written for advocacy groups.

Preface

Organizations have been struggling with the costs of health care and workers' compensation for at least the past 10 years. Despite repeated attempts at cost containment most organizations have continued to experience double digit annual cost increases. This situation places employers at odds with their employees because health care and workers' compensation are seen as a zero-sum game in which one or both parties must lose.

This book was written because our practical experience convinced us that lasting cost solutions can be obtained without sacrificing human values. Leading organizations of all sizes and in all industries have demonstrated such solutions. These organizations maximize their leverage by focusing—not outward on physicians, attorneys, and legislatures—but rather inward on management practices under their direct control. Apart from having well designed and effectively managed programs, employers need to involve employees in being part of the solution. Executives, line managers, and employees can now take ownership and become more personally involved. Senior managers can also extend the successes achieved by leading organizations into broader strategy-based solutions, thereby integrating internal and external management and controlling a previously uncontrollable segment of their cost structure.

Our combined experience has included management and consultative assignments in the employer, provider, and insurer/third party worlds. These experiences have crossed industries and have been at line and staff levels, including senior management. A common thread has been the significant ability of organizations to influence health and disability results. When management focuses directly on health and disability, employers find they can exert considerable leverage over health care and workers' compensation costs within their own operations. Organizations adopting a systems view of health and disability, with supporting comprehensive measurement, can proactively address a wide range of issues affecting costs and ultimately organizational quality.

Health and disability is a business issue. Management strategies and practices applied with success in other parts of the business can and should be transferred to this critical area. This book forms a bridge between the interests of employer line and financial management and the interests of internal and external specialists involved in risk, health, safety, and disability. Solutions from many disciplines are integrated into a coherent, practical, and focused approach for managing health and disability costs. The management mechanisms applied include:

- Systems thinking to interconnect organizational approaches and strategies.
- Quality management strategies and techniques, including continuous improvement, re-engineering, and empowerment.
- Proactive risk management.
- Management of organizational culture to integrate employer programs and performance.
- Financial management strategies and techniques including activity-based costing, return on investment, and portfolio concepts.

Controlling and reducing costs will be most successful when these mechanisms are employed as part of a total systems framework. Organizations can consider a wide range of situations and potential results and then tailor their internal and external management to best meet these cost exposures and employee needs. This is the essence of leverage—focus and flexibility combined with maximum return in terms of both cost and quality. Cost uncertainty and litigation exposure will be similarly reduced.

Employers tailoring and applying these approaches to their situation will significantly lower the direct costs for health care and workers' compensation as well as the indirect and hidden health and disability costs in operations. These include the costs of poor health in reduced productivity and quality, costs of replacement and temporary workers, and administrative and management costs that add little value to the organization. Improving the effectiveness of health and disability management is therefore an important contributor to organizational competitiveness.

This book is organized as follows: Chapter 1 frames the opportunity for employers and should be read by all. Part One (Chapters 2–7) presents executives and the management team with an integrated, strategy-based, management system to address costs comprehensively while managing organizational issues. Utilizing limited, but highly focused information in a systematic manner is the key to such management. The Overview or Part One, "Optimizing Managed Care," provides essential background for understanding the interrelationship of the six chapters.

Part Two presents concrete examples and practical guidance for reducing costs through functional and operational management of health and disability. The overview, "Managing Organizational Culture," identifies the operational framework underlying Chapters 8 through 13. Chapter 14, the conclusion, further develops the systems and culture framework employed throughout this book, with an emphasis on continuous learning as well as continuous improvement. Some readers may choose to read Chapter 14 after Chapter 1 to get a broad view before reading the remaining chapters.

Strategy, systems, and culture are the essence of this book, but what positions the strategy-based solutions so differently is the emphasis on management action. This proactive approach identifies the risk in *not* taking action, rather than in committing to an involved and focused effort. These actions must also maximize return on investment rather than cost containment alone. The book describes prescriptive solutions throughout for deriving the benefit of this management action.

Those organizations managing for health can have it all—lower health care, workers' compensation, and disability costs; lower indirect and hidden health and disability costs; improved health-related productivity and quality levels; the best employment profile; and employees motivated to strive for excellence in personal and organizational goals. This is the competitive advantage inherent in strategy-based solutions. Managing for health can build national health care and regional workers' compensation success, one employee and one employer at a time simultaneously throughout our nation.

Acknowledgments

One of the benefits of writing this book is the feeling of contributing to people, organizations, and a country that have contributed much to us. We would like to thank and acknowledge the executives, managers, and employees in organizations with whom we have worked as fellow employees and as consultants. In particular, we wish to recognize the many dedicated professionals in health, health care, risk management, disability, and safety who have generously shared their ideas and insights in publications, conferences, and conversations over the years.

Bruce Barge would like to acknowledge teachers, mentors, and peers—Mike Billings, John Campbell, Marv Dunnette, Tom Gag, John Kamp, the Michigan Workers' Compensation Advisory Panel, Shelly Wolff, and co-workers at St. Paul Companies and Personnel Decisions Research Institute—who provided insight and opportunity for learning the organizational dynamics affecting health and disability management. Their support of training, management, and consulting experiences helped crystalize the role of an organization's strategy and culture in determining its health and disability performance. Bruce would also like to thank his parents and family and friends for their support, especially that of Carol, Rachel, and Matthew, for their understanding and love.

John Carlson would like to acknowledge the insight into management gained during his career at General Instrument Corporation. Hands-on experience in Total Quality Management was an important early developmental milestone. Much learning about organizational strategy and management systems was gained from a number of senior managers, some of whom acted in mentoring roles. Integration of such business strategies and management practices to health and disability was benefitted by the knowledge gained from managing staff and organizations, from interacting with health care and disability professionals and, most importantly, from listening to the interests and concerns of survivors of brain injury and their families. John would especially like to thank his wife, Nuala, and his children, Sean and Tara, in supporting his total commitment to writing this book.

We would like to thank Nancy Marcus Land and Charlotte Saikia of Publications Development Company of Texas for their enthusiasm, skill, and professionalism during the production of the book. Special thanks to John Mahaney, our editor at John Wiley & Sons, for supporting our vision of the book and helping bring it to fruition.

We hope this book will extend the knowledge and insight of the many with whom we have been associated into a broader organizational context. When employed in this more integrated way, the management of health, health care, and disability can benefit employers and employees alike. Moreover, America can bring a new financial and human impetus to improving its global competitiveness by truly solving our nation's health care and workers' compensation crises.

Contents

1. Employer Control over Health and Disability Costs   1

PART ONE
Optimizing Managed Care:
Linkage with Health and Productivity

2. Integrating Risk Management into a Health and Disability Strategy   33

3. Developing a Quality-Based Health System: Employer-Directed Management   51

4. Managing Health: An Intervention Approach   71

5. Managing Care: A Systematic Approach to Obtaining Value   95

6. Managing Productivity: Integrating Workplace Health and Disability   119

7. Operationalizing Strategy-Based Management through Information: Control, Performance, Investment   145

PART TWO
Managing Organizational Culture

8. Addressing High-Risk Behavior   177

9. Supervision for the New Health Issues   197

10. An Integrated Approach to Employee Wellness   216

11. Fighting the War on Substance Abuse   244

12. Managing Stress and Employee Mental Health   267

13. Innovative Strategies for Workplace Safety   290

Conclusion

14. Conclusion: Achieving the Full Promise of Strategy-Based Solutions   311

Index   335

1

Employer Control over Health and Disability Costs

Right now, from twenty-five cents to fifty cents of every dollar of net profit earned by American corporations pays for employee health, workers' compensation and disability costs. Health care costs alone accounted for 26 percent of corporate net earnings in 1989 and rose to 45 percent in 1990, against the backdrop of the recession.[1] These costs have increased so much faster than inflation over the past decade that they have become a key issue in both global competitiveness and national social policy.

Figures 1.1 and 1.2 show how dramatically the rate of increase has affected U.S. competitiveness. Double-digit annual increases have pushed employee health care costs more than twice as high in 1991 as in 1984. As a result, health care costs in the United States represent a far more significant percentage of gross national product than they do in any other major industrialized country.[2] A Congressional Budget office study projects that health care costs will double again by the year 2000, to an estimated $1.68 trillion and approximately 18 percent of gross domestic product.[3]

These rapid increases have not been limited only to health care costs. As shown in Figures 1.3 and 1.4, workers' compensation costs have followed a similar meteoric rise in both the average medical cost and average indemnity (wage replacement) cost per case. Workers' compensation cost the average employer about 0.5 percent of payroll in the 1950s, 1 percent by 1975, 2 percent by 1988, and an estimated 3 percent in 1993.[4] Countrywide costs for workers' compensation are currently about $60 billion annually and could reach $150 billion by the year 2000 if current trends persist.[5]

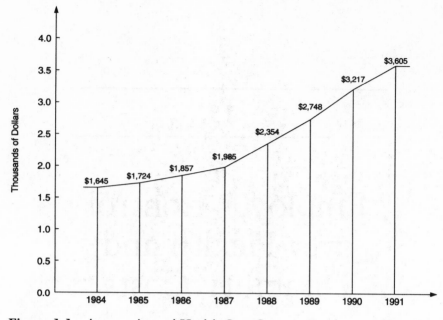

Figure 1.1 Average Annual Health Care Cost per Employee, 1984–1991 (*Source:* Foster Higgins. Used with permission.)

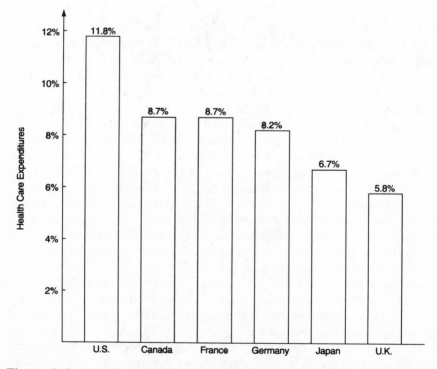

Figure 1.2 American Health Care Costs Compared to Other Industrialized Countries

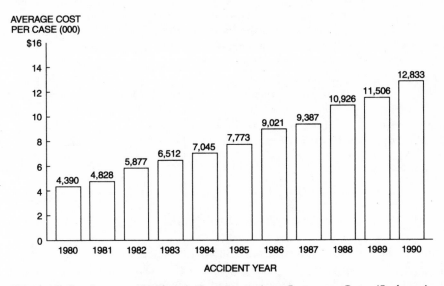

Figure 1.3 Average Workers' Compensation Cost per Case (Indemnity Cost) (Copyright 1993 National Council on Compensation Insurance, Boca Raton, Florida. All rights reserved. Reprinted with permission.)

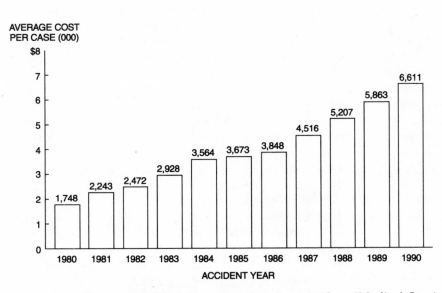

Figure 1.4 Average Workers' Compensation Cost per Case (Medical Cost) (Copyright 1993 National Council on Compensation Insurance, Boca Raton, Florida. All rights reserved. Reprinted with permission.)

Finally, this pattern has also been repeated for short- and long-term disability costs. Costs for long-term disability increased nearly 80 percent from 1980 to 1988, while short-term disability benefits increased 50 percent during this period. The number of American adults drawing disability payments has increased from 4.1 million in 1962 to over 10 million in 1989. Direct costs to American business exceed $10 billion annually.[6]

Health and disability costs—including costs for health care, workers' compensation, and short and long-term disability—have increased so rapidly that they are now one of the nation's most significant economic problems. American organizations' ability to survive and compete require an increased ability to significantly reduce these costs.

The Parallel to Quality

Whereas the explosion of health and disability costs has been getting most of the attention, an equally interesting aspect of the current situation is its resemblance to the state of American manufacturing 10 years ago. As with health and disability costs today, the inferior quality of U.S. products had become a problem that could no longer be ignored. Motorola, for example, found that its manufacturing defect rate was up to 100 times greater than for comparable Japanese products. Xerox found that Japanese competitors were able to sell copiers retail for less money than Xerox's manufacturing cost.

American manufacturers at that time frequently blamed their problems on external groups or macrolevel causes such as unfair foreign trading practices or the incompetence of American workers. In health and disability today, the blame is often directed toward greedy doctors and lawyers or the inefficiency of payment and delivery systems. The manufacturers were no doubt right in some of their criticisms of the competitive environment 10 years ago, just as criticisms of the health and disability system today are also justified. Nevertheless, the quality of American-made products improved only when manufacturers concentrated on their own management practices.

Industry executives, by focusing on the areas over which they had control, discovered major opportunities for improvement. In analyzing their business processes more carefully, they found many operations they had not fully understood or managed effectively. American managers began to realize they had significantly more leverage over product quality and related costs than they had previously believed.

The payoff was significant for the firms that chose to control their own destiny in this way. Motorola reduced its defect rate 100-fold in just four years, with an estimated savings of $1.5 billion during that period. Xerox went from rapid loss of market share to the actual winning back of markets from foreign competitors. Although not all firms have been equally successful, hundreds, perhaps thousands, of companies achieved significant results through greater management efforts to improve quality. One study showed that firms implementing effective quality improvement initiatives have experienced a net advantage of 8 percent gain in market share, 9 percent gain in sales, and 11 percent gain in return on sales compared with firms not taking such actions.[7]

Like manufacturers 10 years ago, employers today possess considerably more leverage over health and disability costs than they typically use. Quality improvement, however, is just one of several management solutions that can be applied to these costs. Executives and managers are also increasingly aware that waiting for the perfect legislative solution to the health and disability problem is not a viable alternative. To control—even reduce—health and disability costs, organizations must begin to manage their own destiny by carefully studying the root causes of the costs; enlisting the cooperation of line managers, employees, dependents, and third-party managers; and finally, integrating management solutions so all parties work in concert.

The world of manufacturing has been changed forever through innovation, technology, and the demands of the marketplace as well as the work force. Some companies, by recognizing these changes and adapting their management practices, have dramatically improved their performance. Similarly, the world of employee health and disability is fundamentally different today from in the past, and it too requires new thinking and revised management approaches. Organizations that identify and capitalize on these changes will likewise gain a significant competitive advantage.

Evidence That It Can Be Done

Throughout the United States, many organizations—from both the private and public sectors, and from large, medium, and small organizations—are successfully controlling their health and disability costs. For all these organizations, the savings have been significant, producing results noticeably better than the national average. Some organizations actually have held costs flat over a period of years and even have reduced certain costs significantly. These organizations demonstrate that managers can regain control over an area that too often is considered uncontrollable.

Table 1.1 describes 10 employers that have successfully controlled health and disability costs while using varying approaches based on their size, goals, and situation. The common thread, however, is an active management effort to tackle the root causes of cost. These 10 organizations are representative of hundreds of firms that are using a wide variety of strategic and management approaches to control health and disability costs. The snapshot summary in Table 1.1 merely introduces the richness of these organizations' efforts and the resulting opportunities for curbing runaway costs. Still, the table does suggest four key conclusions:

1. Health and disability costs can be significantly reduced and controlled.
2. This opportunity exists in organizations of all types and sizes.
3. Many different approaches can be of value in reducing these costs.
4. All successful programs have active management support.

Table 1.1   Companies Successfully Controlling Health & Disability Costs

Organization	Approach	Results
City of Birmingham, Alabama Medium-sized public entity	Active, multifaceted wellness program combined with HMO	Health care costs flat from 1985 to 1990, saving estimated $30 million
DuPont, Inc. Large manufacturing organization	Long-standing tradition of management involvement in safety	Workers' compensation lost workday rate 1500 times better than national average
Standard Telephone, Inc. Small telephone company	Active wellness and employee involvement in health	Spends 8% of payroll on health care costs compared with 13.6% nationally
Johnsonville Foods, Inc. Medium-sized meat-preparation company	Team-based, empowering environment with strong commitment to quality	1991 total health care costs of $1900 per employee, half the national rate
Bank of America Large financial services company	Individually tailored health promotion program for retired employees	Reduced retiree health care costs by 22% in study group vs. 12% increase in control group
Leaf, Inc. Small candy company	Strong employee involvement in quality and safety	Reduced workers' compensation costs by 35% from 1986 to 1991 vs. national increase of 82%
Quad Graphics, Inc. Medium-sized printing organization	Strong culture of encouraging employee involvement and responsibility	1991 health care costs per employee $2350, one third lower than U.S. average
McDonnell-Douglas, Inc. Large manufacturing organization	Strong employee assistance program that tailors treatment to employee	Estimated savings of $15 million for 1987–1989 in lower costs and absenteeism
Weyerhauser, Inc. Large forest products firm	Very active safety, disability management, and return to work program	Reduced workers' compensation costs by 51% from 1984 to 1990, saving over $50 million
Northern Telecom, Inc. Large telecommunications firm	Integrated, cross-functional effort; enhanced use of information, prevention, benefits changes	Reduced cost per health care claim 18% from 1984 to 1988; workers' compensation reduced by 40%

In gaining control of health and disability costs, organizations typically can tap tremendous leverage that managers are not currently using. Even the successful organizations cited in the table can find opportunities for further improvements. These costs are not uncontrollable. In every category of health and disability cost, some companies are doing substantially better than average and others substantially worse. The goal is to learn from the experience of those who are setting the pace.

Comparing Companies: Critical Success Factors

Until recently, little information was available about the organizational characteristics that differentiate health and disability performance. Many managers assumed uncontrollable factors such as industry, size, or geography primarily determined their health and disability results. For example, if an organization's disability rate was higher in its Los Angeles facility than in its Sacramento facility, the difference was attributed entirely to external environmental factors based on location. As a result, the manager would seldom try to control these costs.

Sometimes, differences in size of operation or in the particular tasks performed also were used to explain any differences observed. For example, the manager of a large operation with poor results might explain that the management and coordination of a large operation can involve many complications. Meanwhile, the manager of a small operation would attribute poor results to the lack of health and disability resources at the small site. In this mind-set, any number of external factors could be used to explain why health and disability costs have gone up and why little can be done about the trend.

External factors, however, typically account for a minority of the differences in health and disability performance. The management of the operation, under the direct control of the organization, is far more important. Two recent large-scale organizational comparisons illustrate the importance of management, in both general and specific areas. The factors differentiating the best performing organizations from the worst were remarkably similar across both studies and across hundreds of organizations.

The first study, conducted in 1989 by researchers at the Columbia University Graduate School of Business, tried to identify which organizational characteristics best predicted the number of employee lost time days (due to both occupational and nonoccupational illnesses and injuries). Investigators used existing research, organizational case studies, and data gathered from 77 companies employing 700,000 workers.[8]

Findings showed that some of the variation in disability rates was attributable to external factors such as industry group, occupational mix, age of the work force, and company size. Manufacturing firms, for example, had higher rates of disability than service firms. Firms with more manufacturing employees experienced higher rates of disability than firms with mostly white-collar employees. The key finding, however, was that four management policies and practices significantly differentiated an organization's rate of employee disability regardless of industry group. The following organizational characteristics predicted disability rate across companies and across industries:

1. *Employee Participation.* The researchers constructed an employee involvement index that measured the existence of formal employee involvement programs such as quality-improvement teams, the extent of information sharing with employees, the scope of involvement in

decision making, and the presence of financial gain sharing with employees. Analyses showed that the higher the company's score on the employee involvement index, the lower its rate of employee disability.

2. *Conflict Resolution.* In both case studies and empirical analyses, the researchers observed that two aspects of effective conflict resolution were important in reducing disability. Disability rates were lower when (a) mechanisms existed for getting conflict out in the open, and (b) there were effective avenues for resolving the conflict.

3. *Stability of Work Force.* Disability rates were markedly lower among firms with low rates of employee turnover. In addition, higher rates of disability were found within companies undergoing severe layoffs, reorganizations, or mergers/acquisitions, even among employees not immediately affected by the disruption. Relative stability in the work force was associated with low rates of disability.

4. *Disability Management.* Low rates of employee disability were associated with high organizational commitment to disability policies and programs. This includes early intervention in potentially high-cost cases, job modification for early return to work, training in lifting techniques, employee assistance programs, health promotion programs, and special assistance for persons with a disability.

These findings show that active concern for employee health and provision of opportunities for employee involvement notably reduced the levels of disability claims. These controllable management factors were far more important to health and disability results than external factors that could not be easily controlled.

These conclusions were also supported by the second major study, sponsored by the state of Michigan and including over 5000 Michigan employers. In this study, workers' compensation loss results were used to identify the best and worst organizations within each industry (SIC code). The best and worst were then studied to determine what characteristics may have contributed to their results. Again, the findings are striking.[9]

First, within every industry classification investigated, there were huge differences between the best and the worst firms. The worst employers had *at least 10 times as many claims* as the best. For example, in the Transportation Equipment Manufacturing industry, the best 6 percent of the plants had less than one injury per 100 employees, while the worst 8 percent of plants had eleven or more injuries per 100 employees. This discrepancy between the best and the worst was found in every industry investigated.

Second, the great majority of the difference between the best and worst was attributable to internal characteristics of the firms. External factors did play a role, such as the size of firm (big companies have proportionately lower losses) and the location (some parts of Michigan have higher losses than others). The bulk of the difference, however, related to the companies' management policies and practices, as shown in the following list:

Low-Loss Organizations

- Strong commitment to safety and accident prevention:
    Monitoring and correcting of unsafe behaviors on a systematic basis.
    Safety training for all new and transferred employees.
    Modeling and attentiveness to safe behavior by company leaders.
- Disability prevention and management:
    Provision of wellness programs and fitness resources to promote health.
    Light duty or modified work to help injured workers return.
    Encouragement and monitoring by supervisors to help injured workers return.
    Provision of an employee assistance program.
    Ongoing employee screening for health and disability risks.
- Management climate and culture:
    Profit or gain sharing with employees.
    Employee participation in problem solving/decision making.
    Bottom-up communication as well as top down.
    No employee union, or if union, positive relations with management.
    Longer tenured employees, low turnover.

High-Loss Organizations

- Lower level or absence of safety, health, or disability programs.
- Higher likelihood of negative labor–management relations.
- Bureaucratic, controlling management style and climate.
- Little attempt by management to communicate with or assist employees.
- Higher rates of turnover.

Summarizing these findings, there are large differences between organizations in health and disability costs, including numerous firms that achieved significantly better results than the national average. The best companies had markedly better results than the worst companies in the areas of health care costs, workers' compensation, and disability rates.

Throughout, the most important influences on these costs are under the control of management. Although external factors play a role, they are not responsible for the bulk of the difference, as shown by comparing companies of similar size, in the same industry and same geographic area. Instead, the active efforts of management distinguish the leading companies. These managers, using a strategic and active approach, offer a variety of health and management initiatives to create an environment that prioritizes health.

For the organization seeking to capitalize on this untapped leverage, the cost savings represent a significant competitive differentiator. Reducing health and disability costs by even 10 percent can boost corporate earnings, free up capital for investment, or allow more flexibility in pricing. This advantage is compounded over future years, as the cost levels established one year affect cost baselines and rate of progress in the following years. In addition, employees will usually be healthier, more productive, and more committed to the organization. The opportunity is great for creating a more competitive organization through enhanced management of health and disability.

Identifying the Problems

Organizations have not deliberately set out to generate high health and disability costs. In fact, most organizations have tried hard to stem the health and disability cost hemorrhage with managed care and related techniques. Their progress, however, has typically been limited in two ways. First, despite the annual double-digit percentage increases over the past decade, many organizations have failed to view health and disability as a long-term cost issue requiring senior management attention. Second, most organizations have failed to recognize the extent of change and management opportunity in several core aspects of health and disability.

Why haven't more employers made health and disability management a more visible, integrated part of their strategic and operational focus? In many cases, they simply have not seen the need to change their management approach. Traditionally, costs for employee health care, workers' compensation, and disability seemed small in relation to overall organizational expenditures; many employers believed that existing approaches would eventually get expenses back to a more manageable level. For most executives and managers, health and disability make up an unknown discipline—the domain of physicians and other health professionals. Employers are also reluctant to get involved with something as personal as employee health.

Many organizations have not fully recognized or managed the opportunities created by gradual changes in the health and disability environment over the past decade. Key aspects of this new multifaceted environment are:

1. Strong movement toward levels of self-insurance for health and disability costs.
2. Increased availability and use of sophisticated medical technology.
3. Strong increase in subjective types of illness and injury.
4. Proliferation of management services and information.

Each of these four changes represents a major source of strategic leverage for controlling health and disability costs. As discussed in the following sections of this chapter, organizations can proactively manage these trends to their advantage or can reactively allow them to stifle progress and contribute to even higher costs.

Self-Insurance as a Catalyst for Accountability

The first change—moving toward greater self-insurance—represents a significant departure in accountability for health and disability. Traditionally, many employers were buffered from direct involvement in their health and disability costs by insurance companies or third-party managers. Indemnity insurance was the rule, and even with the advent of managed care, the rates of many health plans were based on the experience of the community rather than the organization itself. In short, many organizations did not perceive themselves to be directly accountable for the health and disability results they achieved.

This has changed significantly with the recent movement to higher levels of financial risk exposure in indemnity insurance and to self-insurance in general. An estimated 65 percent of health care benefits is currently self-insured, and 29 percent of workers' compensation is self-insured.[10] Therefore, employers are now much more directly accountable for a rapidly increasing portion of their organization's costs.

This change presents the opportunity to use self-insurance as a motivator for improved operational performance—not just as an isolated adjustment to risk-financing procedures. Although organizations have rightfully moved to self-insurance to gain improvements in cash flow and tax considerations, they have often limited self-insurance to a purely financial mechanism with little impact on the organization as a whole. Instead, self-insurance should build involvement and accountability among managers and employees throughout the organization by providing an important rationale for working together to address the root causes of cost—because "our money" is directly at stake.

Technological Change: Increased Cost or Opportunity?

A second major change in the health and disability environment revolves around technology. Advances in this area can have both a negative and positive impact on costs. Consider, for example, an employee who is diagnosed with cancer. Because of advances in medical technology and more sophisticated treatment, an employee who would have died will survive, after a lengthy recovery. Although this is undoubtedly a good outcome, the technology will have increased costs. On the flip side, advances in technology may also mean that the same employee could have been successfully diagnosed much earlier, thereby reducing cost while delivering an even better health outcome.

What superior technology has really done is to increase the leverage for effective management of health decisions. In effect, technology raises the stakes. Most health and disability cases follow the Pareto Principle, or the 80–20 rule. The bulk of cost exposures (approximately 80 percent) come from a minority of cases (approximately 20 percent). In fact, some studies indicate that only 10 percent of health and disability cases account for 70 percent of total costs, an even stronger relationship than the typical Pareto.[11] Technology has increased both the likelihood of such cases and the cost associated with not preventing them or not managing them optimally. The reverse is similarly true; the cost/benefit of intervening earlier to prevent future costs and to optimize personal health management and treatment has become increasingly attractive. Through the effective use of technology, health and disability expenditures can be proactively managed at every state—from risk prevention, to early diagnosis and preventive care, and finally, to early intervention in treatment inclusive of rehabilitation. Thus, effective use of technology is key to maximizing the impact of health and disability expenditures.

The potential cost impact from medical technology has also been supplemented by corresponding developments in rehabilitation technology and management information technology which benefit a more active role in personal health management by the individual. As shown in the following list, each of these technologies can affect total health and disability costs:

- *Medical Technology*

    Increased range of diagnostic technologies to identify and address health needs early.

    Increased range of high-cost, acute medical procedures to preserve and enhance life.

    Development of trauma techniques to speed patient access to acute medical services.

    Increased number of survivors with impaired functioning requiring rehabilitation or long-term care.

- *Rehabilitation Technology*

    Increased service options to meet personal needs (inpatient, outpatient, and community and home treatments).

    Increased experience resulting in improved outcomes and a corresponding demand for access.

- *Information Technology*

    Wider variety of health information available, but received by individuals unsystematically.

    Information about treatment options is now becoming available for patient and family use.

    Legal profession applying information to address unmanaged risks, undertreated patients, and malpractice issues.

    Personal computers and cost-effective storage allowing distributed databases and more cost-effective access throughout organizations.

The potential cost leverage around technology is significant, increasing the need for effective decisions in the use of medical, rehabilitation, and information technologies to benefit human health. Few organizations have fully capitalized on these opportunities.

Subjective and Psychological Factors

The third major change affecting health and disability costs is the evolution in societal values about health and the related shift in work from a manufacturing economy to an information economy. People in general are now better educated about health issues, do less heavy physical work, and less often operate dangerous machinery or work in hazardous environments. They generally encounter much safer and less demanding physical conditions than their predecessors decades ago, both at work and at home. Unfortunately, improved physical safety has not always translated into improved levels of health.

Societal and economic changes have significantly reduced the most extreme health and safety problems. In 1911, for example, an estimated 21,000 people were killed in American workplaces, compared with 11,000 in 1986. This reduction in fatalities is even more remarkable because the number of people currently in the work force is triple that of 75 years ago.[12] But while these extreme health and safety problems have diminished, other types of health and disability problems have increased dramatically in the past 10 years. Subjective and psychosocially related illnesses and injuries are far more troublesome today than ever before.

Treatment for mental health and substance abuse disorders is among the most rapidly growing categories of health care costs and is also the category most rapidly being limited by employers.[13] So-called stress claims are the most rapidly growing category of workers' compensation claims.[14] A study by Kaiser Permanante, the large health management organization in California, found that 60 percent of all physician visits were by patients who had nothing physically wrong with them, and another 20 to 30 percent were by patients whose physical illness had a stress-related component.[15] Many of the most common workplace injuries—back pain, carpal tunnel syndrome, and repetitive strain injury—involve worker perception and symptoms that are difficult to objectively verify.

Further complicating workplace health are the issues created by a new generation of survivors from today's advanced medical technologies. Survival after cancer treatment and brain injury has increased dramatically over the past 10 years. Such treatment severely impacts both individuals and families for a short-term period and there are usually life-long implications as well. Besides the physical rehabilitation issues, there are psychological issues requiring other forms of rehabilitation and personal compensating strategies. In the case of brain injury, the physical, speech, and cognitive impairments are often brain-related.

Because these illnesses and injuries cannot be seen in a physical sense and are thus more subjective or psychological does not mean they are without merit. Even though work situations may have become less demanding physically, the psychological demands often seem greater. Time pressure, ambiguity, and rapid change characterize virtually all aspects of workers' lives. Society has exchanged the physical strain of years past for today's psychological stress and strain. The environment is challenging for employers and employees alike in dealing with dependencies or personal and family adjustments in return to work.

Along with this change in the external environment has come a corresponding change in attitudes and lifestyles. People are now much more willing to recognize that psychological factors are important in health, and they understand that supports are needed to change health practices permanently and to respond to post-treatment personal and family situations. Society is more accepting of individuals who seek psychological counseling or take extra time to deal with psychological issues in their lives. There is also greater awareness of the health issues surrounding work and family interrelationships, particularly with the growth of two-earner and single-parent families.

All these changes translate into health and disability problems far different from those in earlier years. In many ways, the health and disability exposure has expanded from being largely in the physical environment to being increasingly inside people's heads. The related health and disability risks affect both work and home. An employee's home life and family situation strongly influence the person's ability to function effectively following illness or injury. Approaches used to manage health and disability years ago no longer seem as relevant.

This shift toward increasingly subjective and psychological health issues provides yet another leverage point for organizations to manage either proactively or reactively. Organizations that continue to manage health and disability as they did 10 years ago will fail to meet their employees' needs and will incur increasingly higher costs, whereas employers that redefine their health management strategy to fit today's health issues will attract employee involvement and will reduce overall costs.

Strategic Information as Leverage

A fourth and final major change affecting health and disability is information capability—the strategic use of information to identify key management opportunities that improve health and control costs. The information age has brought about an explosion of data about health care, workers' compensation, and disability claims. For many organizations, however, the data have not bridged the gap between information and understanding—the gap between knowing what happened and comprehending why it happened. Even more, information should lead the way in focusing limited resources to yield the maximum impact on health and cost.

Employers, therefore, should use the increasingly available data to provide focus, understanding, and commitment among line managers, employees, and even dependents. Distributed information can bring risk management into operations as an accountability for all managers, not just those in human resources or corporate risk management. Bringing the information to this actionable level increases the chances that it will have significant impact. Just as in quality, the goal is to mobilize managers and employees to become involved in ongoing continuous improvement of the system factors responsible for most health and disability cases.

Consider these examples of how health and disability information could be used strategically to improve health and reduce costs:

- A work team studying why back injuries represent such a big percentage of workers' compensation claims could look at demographics and activities of injured workers.

- An organization that has had several expensive premature birth claims could estimate its future risk and determine whether an intervention is needed.

- Cost and quality performance could be assessed for health care providers or particular health procedures.

- Employee health training could be supported by regular information about personal and family health and safety risk factors.

- Line managers could compare the costs and benefits of various prevention, medical, and rehabilitation technologies in tailoring strategies for their units.

In general, information could be in the hands of those who need to manage it, rather than being limited to staff units, insurers, or other external third parties.

For maximum impact, the power of information availability must extend to the way it is used. Again, there is a parallel between analyzing health and disability claims and analyzing manufacturing problems in a quality-improvement framework. In the past, many manufacturers either did not analyze their process performance or perhaps used an anecdotal cause-and-effect approach. Applied to the health and disability area, this anecdotal approach might have the following characteristics:

- Each claim treated as unique, without reviewing similarities across claims.
- Gut instinct used, instead of objective criteria.
- Claim description taken at face value, without interviews or outside data.
- Person involved in the claim is blamed, not organizational systems.

- National or industry averages mistrusted, as not applying to the organization or even to justify inaction.
- Statistically invalid conclusions drawn about cost trends and provider performance.

The handling of health and disability claims has too often been considered a low-level job. Administrative clerks who input information often do not receive much training in interpreting the data. Management staff shy away from in-depth and systematic analysis of root causes. Few companies assign one of their "best and brightest" or a cross-functional team to probe which few causes are driving the majority of costs. In what other part of any organization are $25,000-a-year clerks so strongly influencing $100,000 decisions?

In a nutshell, the tremendous explosion in health and disability information capabilities has not been targeted toward the people with the most opportunity to put them to productive use. Information sharing has often been superficial, rather than being focused on root causes that lead to lasting cost reductions. A simple point, but one with major implications for managing health and disability costs, is that all claims—large and small—should not be managed in the same way. Future risks related to activities or characteristics of the covered population (demographics, geography, or job characteristics) also require a differentiated management response. This level of management effectiveness is only possible with in-depth knowledge regarding claim causes and developing exposures. Information capabilities developed over the past decade hold considerable promise for making such achievements practical and widespread, thereby providing stable health improvements and associated cost reductions.

Multiple Causes of Claim-Related Behavior

The rapid growth of health and disability costs is actually the result of all these changes: It is the unique product of the societal, technological, psychological, and economic factors impacting employees today. Employee behavior is the heart of the matter. Employees (and dependents) are the ones who choose whether or not to practice good self-care, when and how to go to the doctor, and how quickly to return to work following illness or injury. Ultimately, the employees' behavior patterns determine the cost of health and disability for their organization.

Years ago, such behavior was a much simpler enterprise. Societally and psychologically, a stronger and narrower norm dictated how a person should respond to injury or illness. Technologically and medically, there were fewer choices about care. Economically, employees had few incentives to do anything other than return quickly to productive work. Employees' lifestyles away from work were not viewed as health issues for employees or the company to worry about.

Today, however, there are a range of choices in each of these areas. Employees are bombarded with information they must balance according to their own situation to decide the best way to behave. Should they pay more attention to the story in the newspaper about colon cancer or to the advice of their neighbor, whose brother is a doctor? Can they trust their employer to look out for their interests or should they call that lawyer on TV? Does it really pay to make lifestyle changes, especially when it means giving up a favorite activity? Employees can easily find experts or information to support many kinds of behavior.

On the economic front, employees are what economists call "rational consumers." For example, a great deal of research in workers' compensation shows that employees adapt quickly to changes in the benefit payment structure. Employees change their claim-filing patterns in response to the benefits available to them. When it is in their economic interest to keep working (because of high wages), they return from injury more quickly; the reverse is also true if benefits are more attractive than wages or there is a high threat of job loss.[16]

Both attitudinally and economically, therefore, organizations today do not have a lock on the attention or beliefs of their employees (let alone dependents). They must compete in the marketplace of ideas, the contest for perceptions. This is probably more true with regard to health than for any other area of employee behavior. Health and disability are in part financial issues for organizations. For employees, their health and the health of their families are personal issues. The implications of organizational action around health can be extremely emotional and meaningful for employees. This is both a challenge and an opportunity for organizations.

The picture surrounding employee costs for health care, workers' compensation, and disability is a mosaic, interweaving societal trends and individual motivations and behaviors. In addition, major changes over the past decade, have exerted considerable influence on health and disability. Organizations that seek ongoing control of these costs must develop a strategy that addresses the factors affecting employee health today. A successful plan will also reflect the lessons learned from using current cost control approaches.

Lessons from the Cost-Containment Approach

Over the past 10 to 20 years, organizations have made a substantial effort to control rising health and disability costs by developing and implementing a wide variety of cost containment approaches throughout the United States. In general, these approaches, using the present medical care paradigm, have focused primarily on reducing treatment costs through improved administration and efficiency of medical care. The approaches include:

- Reducing coverages or shifting costs to employees.
- Developing managed care networks of health care providers.

- Obtaining discounts and other controls over prices charged for health care.
- Establishing and monitoring practice standards to ensure care is necessary.
- Limiting the length of institutional stay for health care.
- Emphasizing outpatient or noninstitutional forms of treatment.
- Managing transfers through stages of treatment.

Each of these factors has been of some value for employers and will continue to play a role in health and disability management. By themselves, however, these cost-containment approaches have been inadequate to stop the health and disability cost spiral because of the following limitations:

- They reinforce a lack of involvement for line managers, employees, and dependents; instead, health care is the responsibility of providers, third parties, or staff units.
- Emphasis is heavily weighted toward treatment and medical care, rather than toward total health care, including prevention, early intervention, and outcomes plus a focus on health as the ultimate accountability of the individual.
- They take a short-term view of cost control, addressing symptoms and "end-of-the-line inspection" rather than the root causes of health and disability costs.
- Risk is narrowly defined as a financial and liability issue, not as a broad employee and operations issue.
- The goal is to moderate costs, not reduce them based on broadly defined organizational strategies.

Most organizations have recognized the limitations of using such approaches in their business operations. For example, quality of products and services was formerly narrowly defined and was delegated to staff functions or inspected on an end-of-the-line basis. The organization's goal was simply to contain the number of quality problems. Today, however, managers and employees are taking a broader approach and are widely involved in improving cost and quality simultaneously. These organizations understand they cannot "contain away" a structural cost problem in their base businesses.

Similarly, containment approaches must focus on the quality and outcomes produced rather than just the activity. For example, case management can be very useful if it optimizes the cost benefit of the outcome. To do so, however, requires taking a broad view of case management as a means for ensuring optimal value between treatment costs and outcomes achieved, not as a routinized procedure for reducing treatment costs without regard to outcomes. Cost-containment approaches have sometimes added layers of management and layers of activity without achieving commensurate value in outcomes. As a result, cycle times may be lengthened, and costs may be constrained only on a short-term basis with large increases in the following quarters or years.

Organizations must therefore eliminate "containment" as their sole response to health and disability costs. Instead, the goal should be *cost management* consisting of the following elements:

1. Costs are controlled/reduced over a sustained period.
2. Cost predictability is obtained.
3. Maximum value is obtained for the costs expended.

Because third parties often focus on the administrative and treatment processes rather than the root causes of cost, they have not achieved this type of cost management for employers. Control may exist only until the next premium requoting. Predictability is similarly uncertain, whether for near-term claims experience or for premium requoting, particularly with a range of third parties involved. Value as a concept, representing a combination of cost and quality in treatment per total dollar expended, is only starting to be addressed.

Cost management, by contrast, is centered in an understanding that costs can only be reduced when health and disability benefits are considered as an investment as well as a cost. Like any financial investment, returns are not maximized by spending the least amount possible. Instead, the goal is to spend the optimum amount to obtain the greatest return. In this way, employers can balance short-term and long-term costs to obtain predictable cost levels over time. Most importantly, organizations need to ensure value for their investment, focusing their dollars and efforts on solving the root problems that can then eliminate more expensive treatment costs down the line.

Unwittingly, cost containment perpetuated an underinvolved employer relationship in health care issues for another decade. The 1980s operated under the perception that cost containment represented the fundamental change needed to solve the structural problems of health care. Cost containment and managed care have also been promoted as the solution to the workers' compensation crisis. The results show, however, that these costs will not be controlled through containment approaches alone. Organizations can exert considerably more influence on costs by deploying their many points of leverage through an integrated and active management strategy.

The Health Triangle

The triangle shown in Figure 1.5 depicts an approach to managing health and disability that recognizes its complexity and need for integration. This

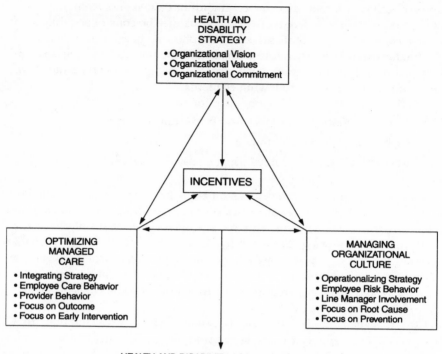

Figure 1.5 The Health Triangle

model shows how organizations can structure their management efforts to achieve lasting control over health and disability costs. The triangle includes three core elements:

1. Health and Disability Strategy.
2. Optimizing Managed Care.
3. Managing Organizational Culture.

Each element is essential to an integrated and strategic approach for reducing cost and improving quality in health and disability. The elements are also closely interdependent, as linked within the triangle.

At the top of the triangle is Health and Disability Strategy, which includes the organization's vision and values for the role of health in the company, as well as its commitment to achieving these goals and objectives. This strategy communicates to employees and managers how health relates to the overall business direction of the organization. Its form, therefore, depends on the organization's needs and future objectives. It could be conceptual and value-driven toward establishing a broad and dynamic vision of national leadership in employee health and well-being. The strategy could also be quite concrete and results-driven, establishing specific activities, accountabilities, and cost or health outcome targets.

The health and disability strategy is the means for ensuring that all parties—managers, employees, dependents, health care providers, and insurers or third parties—are working in the same direction to achieve the same goals. It provides the overall framework for the organization's health policies, programs, and performance measures. The strategy identifies whether health is seen as a line responsibility, staff responsibility, or a shared accountability involving employees and dependents as well. It describes how health fits into the organization's total culture and strategy and how health relates to productivity, quality, and other business objectives. Such a strategy is essential for moving beyond simple cost containment.

The second element in the triangle, Optimizing Managed Care, addresses today's challenge to target a new level of value from the existing managed care infrastructure. This means integrating the organization's strategy in a way that closely links management of employee health and productivity with management of medical care treatment. For optimization of both cost and quality, management must be applied not only to medical treatment, but to the entire spectrum of employee health (including prevention and early intervention). Optimizing managed care means establishing a structure that allows managers and employees to play an active role in achieving the best possible, lasting outcome at all stages of health, not just to temporarily contain treatment costs.

In addition, optimizing managed care means assessing the expenditure of health and disability dollars according to hard-headed and broader assessment of value. Such an assessment studies both quality and cost, as well as the impact of health and disability on productivity. This approach places a premium on preventive care, early intervention, information feedback, and integrated performance accountability. It also reduces the fragmentation and internal conflict within the health and disability system, fully linking workers' compensation into integrated management. Effective use of information and systems for measuring and rewarding performance are particularly important to integrating effort across the strategy.

Managing Organizational Culture, the third element in the triangle, translates the health and disability strategy into operational terms that can be executed by line and staff managers. It includes formal programs: wellness, alcohol/drug, employee assistance, stress management, and safety; and informal management practices: employee involvement, supervisory behavior, and management of change. These influences of the workplace culture have a strong impact on the health-related behavior of all employees and indirectly influence off-the-job and dependents' behavior as well. Managing Organizational Culture is therefore the set of mechanisms for senior management to ensure that strategy has gone beyond concept and is visible in the health and productivity actions of the organization's stakeholders.

Managing Organizational Culture is also a proactive approach to risk management. It enables managers and employees to understand the root causes of health and disability problems and to develop solutions that prevent or minimize them. Embedding these approaches in the workplace culture multiplies the numbers of people—both line managers and front-line employees—who are working to improve health and reduce associated costs and productivity losses.

In the center of the Health Triangle are incentives, such as information, values, or money, that originate in many ways from the core elements. For example, the Health and Disability Strategy can motivate an ambitious manager to get injured employees back to work quickly by emphasizing the links between health, productivity, and organizational success. Or an employee may make greater use of preventive health care in an optimized managed care system because the design of health benefits reward this behavior financially. And because the behavior of supervisors and co-workers in an employer's culture reinforces an orientation toward healthy lifestyles, employees may be more open to participating in an organizational health fair.

These incentives exert strong influence on all stakeholders within the health and disability system, including senior managers, supervisors, employees, dependents, and a range of health and disability providers. In choosing incentives, management must work toward common goals, supporting and reinforcing optimal behavior and reducing waste, mistrust, and poor decisions. Incentives (and disincentives) should not be strictly financial but should also include such nonmonetary incentives as recognition, peer pressure, and timely and meaningful information. Ultimately, incentives have great power in helping to solve health and disability problems.

Many organizations have achieved significant savings by improving their effectiveness in only one of the core elements of the Health Triangle, or even in one aspect of a core element. For example, an organization may have had great success through a wellness program, even though that is just one part of an effective health culture. Or an employer may have developed better accountability in its managed care system while failing to solve other aspects of optimal value for care. Thus, the Health Triangle illustrates the range of options available to management for leveraging health and disability costs.

Over time, the greatest ability to control and reduce health and disability costs comes from close *alignment* of all aspects of the Health Triangle. Such alignment allows optimization, efficiency, and consistency that is not otherwise possible. To develop management solutions that reduce cost and improve quality, organizations look for alignment with customers and suppliers. The most sophisticated organizations pursue this alignment both horizontally (through improved work processes) and vertically (through a shared sense of direction across levels). Similarly, organizations need to work toward alignment in all aspects of the Health Triangle to maximize the value they receive for their health and disability dollar.

The Essence of Health: Systematic Quality

Over the past 10 years, U.S. organizations have made systematic progress in improving the quality of their products and services and in reducing unnecessary costs. During that same period, health care, workers' compensation, and disability management have often seemed to be moving in the opposite direction. Rapidly rising costs indicate that the system is out of control.

Nearly all the past incremental solutions and reforms for health and disability have been rooted in the treatment and administration processes established by regulatory agencies, insurance commissions, third-party managers, and health care providers. At best, the perspectives and needs of the employer and employee have been patched on to existing procedures. What is missing is the essence of a quality system. To obtain real benefits, we must develop quality across a health system that provides an active role for employers, and employees and dependents, as well as providers and third-party managers.

The missing integrating element until now has been health. Instead, attention has been focused on health care—on fixing the symptoms, not the causes. Health care is done to a patient; whereas health requires the active participation of a patient or, even better, of a nonpatient because it is integral to normal work and living activities. Likewise, the focus should not be on disability and its symptoms but rather on health and the integration of functioning capacity into normal work and lifestyle. Employers, employees, and dependents can then integrate quality of life and related productivity as critical elements of health and disability management.

The Health Triangle presents a quality system individualized for each employer's organizational strategy, values, and vision. Companies can create minihealth systems encompassing employees and dependents, employer, providers, and third-party managers. These individual health systems will exercise overlapping points of leverage on health and disability cost and quality. Broader systems can then be developed within industry and regional coalitions of employers, involving all organizations in various forms of managed health networks.

The development of systematic quality through the Health Triangle promises substantial benefits to employers. Already, individual elements of Managing Culture and Optimizing Managed Care have produced evidence of dramatic paybacks. What makes the prospect for cost reductions so compelling is that the results to date have been achieved with individual programs that lack full integration. The wide differences between low-performing and high-performing organizations show that true breakthroughs in costs are possible.

Organizations involved in quality improvement have demonstrated that it is possible to achieve fundamental change in product cost structure while improving quality. The prospect is the same for health and disability, with related benefits in improved cost predictability and increased value from the costs expended. What is required is an employer commitment to developing systematic quality centered in the elements of the Health Triangle and driven by organizational strategy. The payoff for high-performing organizations promises to be a radical transformation of strategic positioning in today's highly competitive markets.

References

1. Foster Higgins & Co. 1992. *1991 health care benefits survey.* Princeton, NJ.

2. Schieber, G. J., Poullier, J. P., & Greenwald, L. M. Fall 1991. Health care systems in twenty-four countries. *Health Affairs,* pp. 23–37.

3. Geisel, J. 1992. Health costs to double by 2000. *Business Insurance,* November 2, 1–4.

4. Venter, G. G. September 21, 1992. Workers' compensation: Are there solutions? *National Underwriter,* pp. 45–55.

5. Calisle, A. K. 1993. Study finds workers' compensation costs may reach $150 billion by 2000. *National Underwriter,* January 25, 2–8.

6. Unum Insurance Company, 1992. *The full cost of disability study.* Portland, ME.

7. Buzzell, R. D., & Gale, B. T. 1987. The PIMS principles: Linking strategy to performance. Free Press.

8. Lewin, D., & Schecter, S. May 1991. Four factors lower disability rates. *Personnel Journal,* pp. 99–103.

9. Habeck, R. V., Leahy, M. J., Hunt, H. A., Chan, F., & Welch, E. M. 1991. Employer factors related to workers' compensation claims and disability management. *Rehabilitation Counseling Bulletin,* 34(3): 210–226.

10. Higgins, A. Foster. November 1992. Survey of 2409 employers, 1991. *Wall Street Journal,* Health Plans are Self-Insured by More Firms, p. B1:3 Nov 11, 1992; Johnson and Higgins. 1992. Self-insurance: Trends and perspectives.

11. Edington, D. W., & Yen, L. 1992. Is it possible to simultaneously reduce risk factors and excess health care costs? *American Journal of Health Promotion,* 6(6): 403–409.

12. Bureau of Labor Statistics, U.S. Department of Labor. 1992. *Employment and earnings.* Washington, DC.

13. Brostoff, S. December 24, 1990. Mental benefit curbs rising. *National Underwriter,* p. 11.

14. Mangan, J. F. March 1991. Stress-related claims: Causes and controls. *Best's Review,* pp. 68–74.

15. Cummings, N., & VandenBos, G. 1981. The twenty years Kaiser Permanante experience with psychotherapy and medical utilization. *National Political Quarterly,* 1: 159–175.

16. Butler, R. J., & Worral, J. D. September 1985. Work injury compensation and the duration of nonwork spells. *Economic Journal,* pp. 34–46.

PART
ONE

OPTIMIZING MANAGED CARE: LINKAGE WITH HEALTH AND PRODUCTIVITY

A dvancing technology, an aging population, a changing legal climate, and evolving medical practice are some of the dynamics confronting employers dealing with health care and workers' compensation issues. In response to these challenges, *Managed Care* has been relied upon as a method to provide increased accountabilities within the system. Performance in terms of both cost and quality measures is being increasingly emphasized in today's information age.

The fundamental issue facing employers is whether Managed Care represents the type of effective management strategies needed to develop lasting cost solutions to health care and workers' compensation. Should employers work toward more advanced generations of Managed Care or is the answer to take an even more active management role? The initial approach has been to manage down on Managed Care organizations or directly on providers, but even then employers are only addressing one aspect of the system—short-term care activities.

Taken alone, Managed Care's contribution in creating increased accountabilities and a performance orientation is not sufficient to address cost problems on a systematic basis. Management today is not penetrating into the causes of costs and the quality of underlying activities. Patients and consumers only sporadically access care; yet health is an everyday concern for individuals and their families. Only employers are confronted by the impact of health throughout their cost structure and organizational productivity. No third party manager or provider is in a position to take this broad perspective. Only the employer can confront the entire range of issues by engaging both management and employees in working toward making the system effective.

This part of the book applies systems thinking to considering the full range of health and disability activities that impact an organization's costs and the productivity of its human resources. Comprehensive measurement allows employers to address a range of costs far greater than the serious issue of health care alone. The full cost opportunity includes:

- Direct and indirect costs of health care, workers' compensation, and disability.
- Indirect and hidden costs of health and disability in operations.
- Productivity losses due to poor health and disability.

Measurement is also the basis for systematic assessment and assignment of accountabilities while reengineering current processes across the broader health system. When viewed in such comprehensive terms, the prime role of employees and dependents and line supervisors in managing health and disability becomes apparent. Employees and dependents are the ones who actually access health and care services, and employees and line supervisors interact daily over a host of health-related matters.

Managing these activities through training, information, and supports provides a major point of leverage over costs that remains relatively untapped for most employers. Provider run programs are not the real answer. Involved employer management is required at every level—from committed and concerned senior management, team-oriented functional management, appropriately involved line management, and involved and empowered employees and dependents.

When an organization is fully engaged in a range of health and disability activities, the effectiveness of health, health care, and disability programs can be continuously assessed and enhanced. Value thus becomes a driving force for optimizing both the cost and quality of internal and external resources. Four levels of value, from the point of direct services up to the strategic intent of expenditures ensures costs are rigorously managed across an organization through:

1. Objective measures of *cost and quality* for all direct health, health care, and disability services.

2. Objective measures of *value added* for all internal and external management services.

3. A comprehensive view of health care that emphasizes preventive care on the front-end of treatment and rehabilitation on the back-end of treatment.

4. A comprehensive program of all health and disability activities and related costs with an emphasis on health and productivity as well as care.

These levels of value are fully developed within a systems approach to health and disability management. Part of the limitation with Managed Care has been that the frame of reference used for assessing value has been too limited to meet the needs of employers. Even if "quality" medical procedures are performed, their value may be dissipated if the human issues involved in rehabilitation are not likewise managed to produce the best possible outcome for patient and family.

Similarly, the value of a well-managed case encompassing both medical and rehabilitation components can be quickly eroded if human productivity is not well managed by line supervisors during return to work. The end result can be a high level of medical costs followed by readmission, continuing care, and disability payouts because the total case is not being managed. Failure to obtain a functional outcome also results in the loss of a trained employee.

A systems approach optimizes value because it brings management to bear at all levels. Even more importantly, it opens up management to considering the total health system encompassing the worlds of home and work as well as care. Both the demand side and supply side for services are thus simultaneously addressed. Movement to a broader view provides the means for optimizing the management of cases, while systematically reducing the need for costly specialty care because line supervisors and employees and dependents are proactively managing health and safety risks. The means for addressing these risks is to focus on activities which create unnecessary risks and related care.

This operations-oriented view of risk places the management emphasis on health instead of care. Health has not been fully effective previously in driving down costs because it has been viewed too narrowly as a set of programs, often tacked onto a medical care plan. The advantage of a systems approach is that health is managed in terms of underlying health and safety risks. It also acts as the overriding goal and ultimate outcome of all activities. Health, health care, and disability can thus become fully linked through a focus on managing the interconnections within the system. This broader view of managing accountabilities and environments is the difference between a care system and a health system.

Traditional Approach	Today's Evolving Approach	Proposed Systems Approach
Cost-Based Care System	Quality-Based Care System	Quality-Based Health System

Even if Total Quality Management (TQM) is increasingly brought to bear among health care providers, only a narrow range of health and disability activities is being managed in today's care system. This can change when organizations begin to manage their individualized health system in cooperation with their employees and in partnership with providers and third-party managers. The potential exists for exerting greater control over a much wider range of costs. Such control comes from systematically managing the activities of all participants, not even from the "programs" themselves. Management thereby becomes a shared responsibility.

Building value into all levels of management is the first phase of management. The second phase involves managing costs through a new strategic framework for categorizing health and disability costs. Once the complete range of direct, indirect, and hidden costs are identified (maybe only initially estimated), costs can be assigned to three categories—health, care, and productivity. Certain health care expenditures are identified between health and care, and workers' compensation between care and productivity. Disability payouts, legal settlements, and workplace health and disability costs are all defined as productivity related. This strategic view of costs arms an integrated management system:

QUALITY-BASED HEALTH SYSTEM

Value-Added Management Third-Party and Functional Management			
Management Tract	Managing Health	Managing Care	Managing Productivity
Prime Accountability	Employee/ Dependent	Provider	Line Management

Instead of patching health and disability programs onto a care system, organizational focus is placed on health and productivity as management issues equal in stature to care. This three-way management system presented in Part One creates specific management accountabilities for employees and dependents and line management for the first time (described in Chapters 4, 5, and 6). In addition, greater direct accountability can be placed on providers as the role of third-party management blends with internal functional management based on value-added criteria (described in Chapter 3).

The need for systematic management across the total health system can be seen in the issue of high risk, high cost cases. Currently, 70 percent to

80 percent of costs are concentrated in 10 percent of the cases[1,2] in health care, workers' compensation, and disability costs.[3] The problem with cost containment alone is that management interventions do not occur until the need for care develops and, even then, may not encompass an outcome that minimizes the probability of future care. Such high dollar users vary by year, and when action is finally taken, a high cost profile of care and related medical and legal exposures has been defined. The way to manage these uncertainties is to proactively and systematically manage health and safety risks and related costs for the entire population in health and disability activities, not just care activities.

By employing integrated management, employers have the ability to manage costs through the same strategic and operational tools employed in other parts of the business. An investment in health can be measured against total costs and cost savings achieved in the cost of care and the cost of productivity. And, at a more detailed level, continuous improvement can be employed in a range of health, care, and productivity activities to systematically reduce costs while organizational health and quality of care is enhanced.

In a global sense, the proof of this systems approach is the result already being achieved by leading employers, further leveraged by these three potential outcomes:

1. Systematic reduction in the underlying causes of costs.
2. Cumulative and continuous cost improvement among a range of cost saving activities while managing total health and disability costs.
3. Investment in a portfolio of activities and related programs to reduce risks and costs.

When these three outcomes are being achieved together, organizations can significantly transform their cost structure and organizational productivity.

As much as a systems approach contains a common framework for organizations to strategically address health care, workers' compensation, and other health and disability costs, the full potential for cost and productivity gains will only be realized when an individualized health and disability strategy is developed (described in Chapters 2 and 3). Every organization has an individualized operating profile reflecting employee demographics, regional locations, industry risk factors, and other characteristics. Employers need to look inward at their health and disability needs before implementing internal or external health, safety, health care, and disability programs. The goal can then be to develop the best possible match between an organization's operating profile and the most focused, quality-oriented, and cost effective internal and external programs to obtain considerable leverage over costs.

The importance of strategy can be seen in the cost and quality leverage points shown here. The size of the up-front investment and the related cost savings are identified for illustrative purposes only. Actual cost savings

Cost-Management Opportunities and Results

Management Techniques	Investment	Cost Savings	
		Current Year	Future Years
Management of financial risk (Chapter 2)			
Avoidance	—	$	$
Levels of self-insurance	—	$	$
Consolidation of programs	—	$	$
Development of a quality system (Chapter 3)			
Program need and effectiveness	—	$	$$
Management effectiveness— internal and external	—	$	$$
Management of health (Chapter 4)			
Health and safety risks	$	$$	$$$
Proactive utilization management based on risk management	—	$$	$$
Health programs	$$	$	$$$$
Primary care	$$	$$	$$$$
Management of care (Chapter 5)			
Value-based approach to care providers	$$	$$	$$$$
Case management on high-risk, high-cost cases	$	$$	$$$$
Management of productivity (Chapter 6)			
Value-based approach to rehabilitation	$$	$$$	$$$$
Closure on cases (disability management)	$	$$$	$$$
Operations issues (employee turnover)	—	$$	$$$

Note: Dollar signs ($) indicate relative investment costs and savings. Actual up-front investments and cost-savings opportunities will depend on individual employer circumstances.

opportunities will depend on individual employer circumstances. The dollar signs ($) do, however, express an indication of the relative leverage available from various cost management techniques identified in Chapters 2 through 6.

A strategy-based cost management effort offers the opportunity to capitalize on near term cost savings while making investments. Some cost areas require relatively little investment; however, an overall program can be linked. One area may pay-off for one employer but not for the next because of different employee participation factors. Instead, the cost savings may take an extra year to be achieved because the organizational culture is not as well developed. And most importantly, some investments complement each other so that the total cost savings cannot be achieved unless an integrated health and disability program is developed.

Return on investment for individual programs and across the total system can thus be used by senior management in decision making about performance as well as in resource allocation. Cost containment becomes a tool for individual cost hot spots, not as the underpinning of cost management strategy.

The strategy-based systems framework identified in Part One emulates the characteristics of an organization. Operating practices and culture are considered in all of the prescriptive solutions. Therefore, the potential for breakthrough cost savings will be compromised by not addressing how employees are managed and how supervisors manage. Forward movement is required at every level. Involved leadership, continuous improvement, and continuous learning are the means defined to place organizations continuously ahead on the management curve.

The key to bringing this proactive energy to health, health care, and disability is an operations-oriented form of risk management that empowers all participants in all their activities. By managing risk systematically, instead of trying to avoid risk, or merely to finance it as a cost of doing business, organizations have the means to fully coalesce these efforts.

The management approach presented in this section, encompassing strategy, systems, programs, and culture, is firmly rooted in operations even as methods are presented to manage providers and third-party managers. Managed Care is very much part of the identified solution; only the issue is presented as one of optimizing, not just managing, Managed Care.

The composition of Managed Care will be determined by both employer and employee self-interests. Such optimization of both structure and performance requires movement toward information age health in which focused information empowers decision making at every level. The end result will be a transition to involved and continuous management—managing activities, not managed programs. This is the basis for transforming an organization's cost structure and health-related productivity. Apart from the cost gains, organizations achieving cooperative management with employees with regards to health have the potential to unlock the most powerful human concern to organizational advantage.

References

1. Schecter, S. M. 1991. Managing health care costs by managing high cost illness. *Human Resources Institute,* pp. 1–8.
2. Garfinkel, S., Riley, G. F., & Iannacchione, V. G. 1988. High cost users of medical care. *Health Care Financing Review,* 9(4), pp. 41–52.
3. Gardner, H. H., & Butler, R. June 1992. Employee health benefits expenditure patterns by Pareto group, Gardner & Associates.

2

Integrating Risk Management into a Health and Disability Strategy

Companies place their strategic focus on developing their product or service in the market. For most young organizations, the strategic leverage is in revenue growth obtained through technology advantage and market positioning. Chief executive officers (CEOs) and general managers therefore concentrate on technology development, product or service enhancement, and sales and marketing. Companies with mature products or services usually give more attention to their cost structure. Regardless, health and disability has generally remained outside the mainstream of senior management priorities.

Health care, workers' compensation, and disability now constitute a major structural cost issue. And for most operating and financial executives, unpredictability of future costs is as troubling as absolute cost levels. In a world of intense competition, both profit and nonprofit organizations need to bring the critical issue of health and disability under control.

One of the problems in controlling health and disability costs is that they have seldom been included in organizational strategy. Employers often perceive workers' compensation as a government entitlement and health care as comprising benefits or insurance issues in the hands of disinterested outside parties. Issues of strategic importance thereby get categorized as administrative matters over which management has relatively little control.

Effective strategy for health and disability has also been hindered by five historical artifacts. Each of these evolved from a fully insured world in which employers relied almost entirely on outside parties to handle health and disability:

1. Organizational accountability for health and disability has been fragmented to fit the insurance carrier model of separate coverages.
2. Personal accountability by employees and dependents for health care and—even more crucially—for health was transferred to deep-pocketed insurers and providers. Today's overriding "benefits" orientation among employers continues to reinforce this perception.
3. Health and disability cost reporting and target setting have been narrowly defined.
4. The difference between "risk" and "insurance" has not been recognized and managed.
5. The difference between avoiding risk and preventing risk has not been recognized and managed.

Together, these conditions have produced a fragmented, narrow response to health and disability. Each of these factors (to be discussed in this chapter) has profound implications for developing an effective organizational strategy for health and disability costs. This strategy, in turn, will determine the sophistication of management approaches used to regain control. Proactive management of health and disability costs demands an updated and effective risk management strategy.

A New Framework for Health and Disability Strategy

In the past fully insured world, the issues of insurance, coverages, and benefits were all rolled into a standard health care program. Employers did not have many choices, nor did they expect many. This pooling of employers in group-rated coverages broke down when some employers realized the advantage of being rated by their own claims experience and not that of a group. And once employers became individually rated, they often decided to absorb part of the financial risk to reduce the costs of insuring financial exposures that they could prudently accept on their own account.

To gain the advantage of proactive management, employers need to separate underlying health and safety risks apart from their financial implications in forms of liability. Such risks can be absorbed cumulatively for years by an individual until they create a financial exposure for employer and insurer as a result of a claim. Underlying health and safety risks can thus be defined as the probability of illness, injury, reduced functioning, and disability due to the uncertainty of human activities.

Exposure to underlying health and safety risks began with experience-rated coverages and has been reinforced by the trend toward self-insuring financial risk to certain levels. This transition to segmenting financial risk apart from health and safety risks while directly connecting risk and cost is still underway. Even employers paying a premium for experience-rated health care may be directly exposed to claims up to a certain defined level although some remain covered under community-rated (group-rated) health care plans offered by health maintenance organizations (HMOs). Others are fragmented between individually rated and group-rated coverages. And even companies that are self-insured to high levels ($200,000 per claim), may have made few changes in managing health care or workers' compensation other than simply contracting with a third-party administrator (TPA) rather than an insurer.

Organizations that accept higher levels of financial risk have a strong incentive to be more proactive in managing health and disability. Reducing health care claims in general and high-dollar claims in particular provides direct cost savings to the employer instead of to an insurer or to a group of employers on a shared basis. Workers' compensation is now replicating these trends.

To obtain the benefits of proactive management, employers need to organize themselves in "Managing Forward" toward health instead of clinging to the reserve-setting and claims-administering orientation of insurance. The past emphasis was on managing illness, injury, and disability after the fact. Managed care perpetuates this uninvolved approach until an employee or dependent becomes a patient being tracked through the treatment continuum (sequential stages of care).

As shown in Figure 2.1, the Managing Forward approach focuses all health, health care, and disability activities toward health. This common focus eliminates fragmented health care, workers' compensation, and disability coverages. The goal is to increase employer control by moving the management emphasis forward or upstream toward health and away from

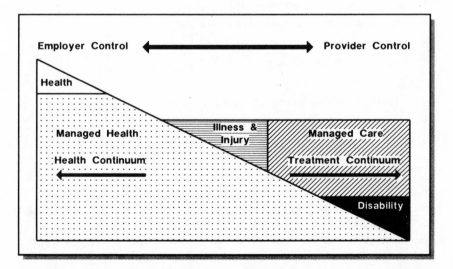

Figure 2.1 Managing Forward: Expanding Employer Control (RHM Systems, Inc., 1993, Marlboro, MA)

back-end treatment stages and potential legal exposures. By eliminating, reducing, and influencing human activities, health and safety risks can be similarly eliminated, reduced, and controlled, often without a care episode ever taking place. This strategy emphasizes health and management interventions by employers and employees themselves instead of treatment interventions by providers with related management oversight.

In a step beyond 24-hour coverage, Managing Forward creates 24-hour management of employee (and dependent) health and safety risks.[1,2] This proactive management can significantly reduce health and disability costs for the following reasons:

- Multiple health risks are the prime cause of serious medical interventions.
- Certain health risks create higher safety risks.
- Cumulative health risks degrade human health over time.
- Safety risks result in accidents which are a serious health issue.
- Disability often develops from health and safety risks, compounding over time into a more serious disability or multiple disabilities.

Comprehensive and systematic risk management can turn these sources of cost exposure into sources of cost leverage when Managing Forward replaces more limited loss control methods. Forward action at the operations level eliminates wasteful delays inherent in today's health care and workers' compensation systems which add to costs in the following ways:

- Health risk not addressed.
- Health risk made more serious.
- Safety risk results in preventable accident.
- Care made more serious.
- Follow-on care made more likely.
- Outcome potential reduced.
- Greater impact on workplace productivity.
- Greater chance of unnecessary care.
- Greater chance of attorney involvement.

A systematic set of health interventions involves more than just a greater commitment to prevention programs; it requires that employees and dependents, line supervisors, and certain areas of functional management are provided with training, information, and supports to utilize the power of health to decrease the need for health care, to optimize the timing and type of health activities, and to intervene early with the best quality care whenever necessary. Addressing health issues earlier reduces the higher costs and greater uncertainties related to back-end treatment. It also protects against legal exposures, particularly by eliminating employee mistrust and restoring confidence.

Managing Forward integrates the health and disability efforts of internal management. Traditional accountabilities have tracked insurance coverages. Depending on the size of an organization, up to six management participants may be involved—Human Resources, Benefits, Finance, Risk Management, Health, and Safety. Human Resources and Benefits traditionally have focused on health care, Finance on costs in general, and Risk Management, Health, and Safety on workers' compensation. Accountabilities have blurred recently reflecting developing potential linkages between management of health care and workers' compensation. The new framework for a health and disability strategy stresses integrated management plus an involved role by line management, as shown in the following two examples:

Example A company has been insuring the exposure on health care claims down to $50,000. After a year of strong profitability and a new bank line of credit, the Chief Financial Officer (CFO) approaches the Risk Manager with the option of raising the company's financial risk exposure. After reviewing past claims, the Risk Manager assesses $150,000 as a reasonable level except for two factors—the mix of future claims in high-cost regions, exacerbated by medical inflation, and the changing mix of the employee and dependent population. Working with Human Resources, the Risk Manager prepares a forecast of major claims for both health care and workers' compensation supporting an enhanced health and safety program from a cost/benefit standpoint. Priority is then placed on initial implementation by the Benefits Manager and Safety Manager working with line management at the company's Los Angeles facility, which has the highest regional medical costs.

Example A fast-growing company has just acquired another company, and the transition team is sorting through the implications. The parent company has been self-insured up to a financial risk exposure of $100,000 per claim with the Risk Manager previously proposing a move up to $150,000. After reviewing the employee and dependent population of the newly acquired company, the Vice President, Human Resources, raises a red flag. He detects a much younger population with a developing pregnancy risk issue, which had been previously discussed for the company at large, but not acted on. Based on an analysis of risk probabilities, a cost/benefit analysis is prepared that strongly supports prenatal care and a proactive program for high-risk pregnancies. This program is subsequently designed with the involvement of key female line managers and is negotiated by the Benefits Manager. The decision to increase to a $150,000 level is deferred for one year to allow for closer analysis of experience.

The financial benefits of Managing Forward are derived in many ways. First, employers can prudently absorb higher levels of financial risk, which will lower current costs. Second, the management of health and disability costs reduces the frequency, severity, and duration of illness, injury, and disability. Moving health events forward compounds costs savings because it prevents subsequent health events. And as activities move toward health and away from health care, employers improve their control over health and disability programs. Similarly, employees and dependents obtain greater control over personal health issues. The result is reduced uncertainty in health and disability costs for future periods, as a strategy rooted in risk management integrates the contributions of all participants.

Establishing the Cost Targets

Strategy-based management ultimately relates to improving mechanisms for managing costs. Yet, for all the concern about spiraling costs in health care, workers' compensation, and disability coverages (currently at least 10–20 percent of payroll for most employers and increasing to much higher levels in higher cost regions and among employers with lower paid staff),[3] the full scope of health and disability costs can be elusive. Most employers develop cost accounting and budgeting systems to track the cost of their product or service. Costs are usually matrixed between fixed and variable classifications and department and natural expense categories. Gross margins, contribution margins, return on assets, and return on equity are focus points for for-profit organizations. They give less attention to productivity and quality measures of performance, and historical accounting ignores opportunity costs.

The underappreciation of health and disability costs needs to be judged in this context. Health care is often captured in employee benefits costs along with short-term and long-term disability coverages. Workers' compensation is frequently included in business insurance as part of a package policy. Many organizations fail to add up health care, workers' compensation, and disability costs.

These are only the direct costs of health and disability. Internal administration generates indirect costs, captured or lost in department budgets. Certain functional staff may be obvious candidates for classification, but what about the increasing time spent by senior management? And line management also needs to assume a more active role in health and disability issues.

Employers may be surprised at the magnitude of their direct and indirect costs of health and disability, but this is only a fraction of the actual outflow. Defining the total cost of health and disability based on a total cost of quality approach reveals that the hidden costs of health and disability are far greater still. Total quality management has shown such hidden costs can exceed the direct costs by a substantial factor. Comparable statistics are not yet available for health, but there is every reason to believe that hidden costs, such as the following, exceed the direct and indirect costs:

- Auto premiums—medical portion.
- Absenteeism.
- Paid sick time.
- Non-pre-authorized vacation time used.
- Overtime to compensate for missing staff.
- Contract staff to compensate for missing staff.
- Recruitment and retraining for replaced staff.
- Lost productivity from loss of trained staff.
- Lower productivity by all staff due to loss of trained staff.
- Lower quality levels.

These are only some of the hidden costs captured throughout an organization's cost structure. Lost productivity is an opportunity cost that can only be approximated. The true costs to organizations also include projects not completed on time or market opportunities not seized. Employers are weighed down by the total cost of health and disability. Staff are paid for not working, either temporarily or for longer periods, while the remaining staff must cover the productivity loss.

Eventually, extra staff may be added on a part-time or full-time basis. The burden of poor health is the "hidden staff"—people being paid who are nonproductive—including staff not present for health reasons, under-productive staff, and staff wasted in administration when they could be more actively managing health, health care, and disability programs. The hidden staff are equivalent to the "hidden factory" in manufacturing[4]—floor space necessitated by inefficient, poor quality practices.

Most employers feel threatened by the rising costs of health care and workers' compensation alone, but by considering the total cost of health and disability, the advantages for integrated management become evident (see Table 2.1).

Accumulation of costs across an organization is important for under-standing the full scope of today's health and disability cost implications, yet this first phase for creating organizational focus remains rooted in tra-ditional lines of separate coverage. Once integrated management has taken hold, a redefinition of costs in the categories of health, care, and produc-tivity can provide a strategic cost management framework as detailed in Chapter 4.

The following are some major opportunities for cost management:

- Effective health programs can reduce costs in health care, workers' compensation, and disability claims.

Table 2.1   Health and Disability: Integrated Cost Management Framework

	Health Care	Workers' Compensation	Disability	Total
Premiums/claims	$	$	$	$
Health, safety, & disability programs	$	$	$	$
External mgt./admin.	$	$	$	$
Internal mgt./admin.	$	$	$	$
Overtime/replacement staffing	$	$	$	$
Absenteeism/paid time off	$	$	$	$
Lost productivity	$	$	$	$
Other	$	$	$	$
Total	$	$	$	$

- Improved management of health and safety issues by employees and line supervisors can result in reduced claims and higher levels of productivity.
- Outcomes achieved in health care (results from medical procedures and rehabilitation) can reduce both health care and disability costs.
- An investment in effective internal or external administration can reduce overall administration costs.
- Effective health, health care, and disability programs can reduce lost work time and other labor-related costs incurred in operations.

The bottom line is that organizations need to galvanize their efforts toward attacking the full cost opportunity.

Risk and Insurance

The terms *risk* and *insurance* are often used interchangeably. This connection resulted from the fully insured, premium-based health care and workers' compensation programs widely prevalent until recently. Such programs insured the financial risk for a one-year period. Some companies remain tied to these forms of coverage through group-rated insurance or community-rated managed care, although some self-insurance exists in 65 percent of current health care programs[5] and 29 percent of workers' compensation programs.[6] Whereas larger employers were the first to self-insure, companies with 100 to 500 employees increased their participation in self-insurance of health care from 26 percent in 1988 to 41 percent in 1991.[7] Even when not self-insured, employers make the connection between underlying health and safety risks and costs through experience-rated health care programs and retroactive billing adjustments in workers' compensation programs.

Risk management in an experience-rated and partially self-insured world is fundamentally different from such management in a fully insured world. Instead of transferring certain risk issues to an insurer, the employer retains many of the associated opportunities and threats.[8] As shown in the Risk Triangle in Figure 2.2, risk management involves exposure management (combining risk assessment and risk control) and financing. An employer can reduce exposure to claims through two strategies—avoidance and prevention. Avoidance is elimination of responsibility for financial liability through coverage limitations. Prevention and early intervention involve eliminating, reducing, and controlling the underlying risk of illness, injury, reduced functioning and disability by managing the activities of the covered population. On the financing side, the emphasis is on funding of claims, cash flows, maximum liability, and taxes.

In the traditional world of fully insured, premium-based health care and workers' compensation programs, risk management was associated with avoiding certain financial risks and financing the rest through the premiums paid. Management directed little attention to the underlying risks because these were personal matters for employees and dependents. And in any case, why should an employer address such risks when the costs and benefits of programs to reduce claims were shared with countless other employers?

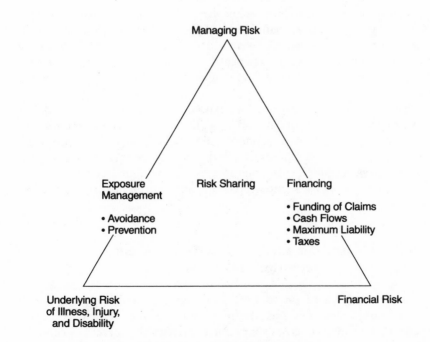

Figure 2.2   The Risk Triangle

Many employers emphasize the financing side of self-insuring health care, workers' compensation, and disability coverages. A one-time cash infusion is derived at start-up from assuming the liability for the runoff of future claims. Another benefit is federal ERISA (Employment Retirement Income Security Act of 1974) status, which eliminates employer exposure to individual state health care insurance differences, thereby potentially reducing costs for certain types of claims, taxes, and administration. In workers' compensation, exposure to the residual market is avoided. Unfortunately, these risk-avoidance features have tended to obscure the cost leverage in prevention. While assuming more accountability for financial risk through experience rating and self-insurance, employers have yet to initiate a parallel movement toward managing the underlying risk related to the uncertainty of human activities, which exists whether or not a claim is filed.

Today's absolute risk exposure extends to the covered population—employees and dependents in the case of health care, and employees only in the case of workers' compensation and disability. It is in the employer's own interest to manage the covered population well. A stable employee population reduces costs since newly eligible participants and others about to leave employment or drop coverage are frequently excess utilizers of health care and workers' compensation. Such employees may be taking care of postponed health needs or may be less familiar with workplace health and safety guidelines, as well as employee health programs in general.

Even more fundamentally, a firm that employs 1500 different employees in one year to maintain an average employee count of 1000 for production purposes will be exposed to far more health and safety risks than a firm that employs 1100 to obtain the same level of production. In these two cases, employee turnover is 50 percent versus 10 percent, respectively, creating 400 percent more exposure to new health and safety risks for the employer with higher turnover and 36 percent more when the total population is considered.

With a relatively stable population, exposure management can be developed through many prevention activities. These can be the prime responsibility of employees and dependents, line supervisors, and functional management, or outside parties involved in health programs, and importantly, primary care physicians. This comprehensive approach to managing underlying risk needs to be integrated throughout the health and disability strategy.

A Broader View of Risk Management—
Prevention versus Avoidance

Risk management based on prevention is fundamentally operations oriented involving employees and line management. Many employers, however, continue to manage costs solely with underwriting practices centered in risk avoidance. Examples of such practices include the following:

1. Coverage eligibility with probationary period for new employees.
2. Coverage limitations, such as policy exclusions and preexisting condition limitations.
3. Incentives to drop coverage.
4. Incentives to remove dependents.
5. Incentives to opt out of coverage.

All these practices may prove effective for insurers because they are party to a financial transaction for just a one-year period and are absorbing only a portion of the possible health and disability costs. Employee productivity does not concern an insurer. Since costs are essentially being managed one year at a time, current cost experience is passed through to the employer in the following period. And there is little incentive for insurers to manage current health and safety risks so as to control or reduce costs in future periods.

The following are typical problems with risk avoidance for employers involved in experience rating and levels of self-insurance:

- Identifying a preexisting condition limitation may save near-term costs, but it does nothing to control multicausal health risks for as long as the individual remains an employee. A preexisting kidney infection may not be covered, but failing to address health in general may generate greater problems. And for every diagnosed preexisting condition, many more undiagnosed preexisting conditions escape detection.

- Time lags in coverage eligibility can compound the severity of the health need when an employee or dependent ultimately receives treatment. For example, a degenerative back problem may require complex surgery and lengthy rehabilitation. In addition, employers feel the impact in employee productivity before, during, and after treatment.

- Removing a dependent or employee from coverage may yield little benefit if he or she is a low utilizer of health care. In fact, payment of cash incentives for dropping dependents who are low utilizers may add to costs.

- Excluding certain health care coverages may multiply costs in other areas. Failure to cover rehabilitation can result in far more costly hospital readmissions or continuing medical treatment. A lack of return-to-work supports can ensure an employee's continued access to health care at a higher rate as well as income supports under both short-term and long-term disability coverages.

Many interdependencies link health care, workers' compensation, and disability coverages. For example, someone injured in a sports accident may become more prone to future workplace accidents. And today's nonphysiological health issues inherently cross over between coverages: Marital problems and job performance problems can both create stress, and these stressors can feed on each other.

Besides the direct costs of health care and workers' compensation claims, many indirect and hidden costs impact employers in such areas as absenteeism, sick time, overtime, and staffing. Using risk avoidance to manage the direct costs of health care and workers' compensation (and the total cost of health and disability) is like trying to produce a high-quality product or service for only those customers who want and expect it.

Risk avoidance perpetuates the insurance-oriented approach of managing the liability, but not necessarily the cost. Insurers, for example, may absorb the costs of diagnostic testing to establish liability between lines of coverage and related carriers or to dispute morbidity issues with previous carriers. These approaches have much less relevance for companies ultimately absorbing the health and disability costs in claims or in operations. Also, such delays raise costs and increase litigation risks because the health problem is not being addressed.

No one can forecast human events, but employers can establish systematic cost management in the areas of greatest risk exposure while basing management of the total covered population on risk probabilities. Consideration of risk on a comprehensive and integrated basis prevents costs managed in one area from billowing out elsewhere. In this design, health, health care, and disability programs are based on the premise that employees are rational consumers who need to be connected into a cost solution. Furthermore, risk management rooted in prevention shows a crucial commitment to employees. An avoidance approach, on the other hand, perpetuates a noninvolved, insurer perspective to health and disability, creating antagonism and barriers with employees and dependents.

Although a certain degree of avoidance is warranted (e.g., a probationary period for coverage of new employees), the real risk management leverage is in prevention. Avoidance concentrates on the small minority of known health risks and on reducing the number of persons covered—a strategy effective only in group-rated, premium-based coverages. If only 5 percent of health risks and 10 percent of the coverage obligations are eliminated, what controls are being exerted on the much greater number of health and safety risks in the remaining 90 percent of the population? This is the opportunity available from the new form of risk management integrated throughout the Health and Disability Strategy.

Proactive Management of Activities-Based Risk

As employers have become more directly involved in health and disability issues, they have made greater efforts to understand claims experience. Frequently, third-party managers are engaged to control provider activities based on developing claims trends. Managed mental health and pharmaceutical programs are examples of such efforts.

Claims information was often unavailable in the past, and some employers still have difficulty obtaining it from health care organizations. Gaining such information represents only an initial step in understanding health risks. Claims experience is a snapshot in time whose significance depends on relating it to the underlying risks of the covered population in terms of normative factors. Two heart surgeries may be good experience if four could have normally been expected, even if none occurred the year before. For this reason, proactive management of risk centers on the health and safety-related activities of the covered population, not just on past claims.

The starting point for these new forms of risk management is development of a demographic profile of the covered population. Age and gender issues allow employers to design health and health care for the areas of greatest risk exposure and employee need. Cardiovascular health can be stressed in a mature population, whereas pregnancy risk and newborn health can take precedence in a younger population. In all cases, the assessment needs to consider risks among the dependent group as well as among employees. Ignoring dependents is a prescription for cost disaster.[9]

Demographics is only a starting point. Risk management can be extended to work and nonwork activities without discrimination or invasion of privacy. Safety risks are reported by the National Safety Council to translate into a wide range of accidents. Medical expense in 1991 totalled more for home accidents at $9.3 billion than for work accidents at $8.7 billion with private and public vehicles usage at $12.3 billion.[10] Employees are paying much of this bill in health care claims, particularly for costly emergency room admissions. Driving safety is a major risk exposure that can be proactively managed for both work and nonwork activities. Home safety is a factor that is often ignored; new parents can be particularly receptive to receiving information on such risks. Even regional living conditions can trigger the need for information on risks related to climate or sports.

To develop programs that proactively manage health and safety risks based on cost/benefit determination, employers must assess living, work, and treatment environments. Prevention efforts can then reduce future costs by eliminating the occurrence of many claims. At the same time claims experience can identify costly patterns of poor health, poor health care performance, and disability. This Managing Forward activities-based approach balances the probability of future health and safety events with the reality of current cost experience. The fundamental challenge for management is to use information to prevent various risks for the entire covered population rather than to avoid the health care needs of targeted individuals. (Chapters 4 and 8 cover these issues in further detail.)

Elements of the Health and Disability Strategy

Risk management is a critical element in a program to address health and disability costs. The starting point is to define a specific health and disability strategy rooted in management of the underlying health and safety risks; it should be separate from the insurance and benefits strategies. As shown in Table 2.2, each strategy addresses a different issue requiring different information for management.

Insurance Strategy

The focus of the insurance strategy is management of an organization's exposure to financial risk. Prudent exposures are determined by examining the firm's financial strategy and related profitability goals and capital structure, or in the case of non-profit organizations, their funding patterns and endowment resources. Although financial risks also need to encompass the uncertainties of underlying health and safety risks and the employer's degree of control over them, these considerations can be isolated from the two other strategy elements until integration of the entire program.

An added advantage of independently developing an insurance strategy related to health and disability is integrated management of insurance issues. Often employers are absorbing financial risk up to $100,000 per claim in health care while taking little financial risk in short-term or long-term disability coverages. Or employers are providing disability coverage for employees who are not covered for health care under their program. An assessment of health and safety risk probabilities and diversification of self-insured financial risk across health care, workers' compensation, and disability coverages can produce major cost savings for employers while breaking down the walls between internal management of health and disability. Experience rating and self-insurance can be the impetus for integrated forms of proactive cost management.

Benefits Strategy

Development of a benefits strategy centers on an employer's management of employee compensation versus industry and regional factors related to hiring and retention goals. A competitive benefits program will cover issues ranging from life insurance, health care and disability, to deferred compensation. The goal is current and future financial well-being which is why

Table 2.2   Strategies for Managed Cost Solutions

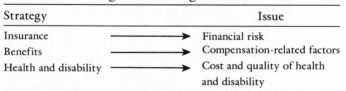

Strategy	Issue
Insurance	Financial risk
Benefits	Compensation-related factors
Health and disability	Cost and quality of health and disability

health care becomes merged into benefits. These benefits programs usually reflect the interests of the employee group. However, despite inclusion in the benefits equation from a relative compensation standpoint, health care and disability costs cannot be effectively managed unless the employer addresses them directly through a separate strategy.

Health and Disability Strategy

Leverage over health and disability costs does not come through the benefits funded, but through the health, health care, and disability programs supported by an employer—and their effectiveness. Employer management of programs permits stressing integrated management of health and safety risks and the obtaining of value added from providers and third-party managers involved in health and disability issues.

Employers need to concentrate their attention toward programs as part of a comprehensive health and disability strategy. For example, employers may decide to fund rehabilitation for return to work in their health care plan based on a cost/benefit analysis although adding such a "benefit" may be of little interest to the majority of employees. In practice, employers may use different return-to-work models, such as work hardening or job coaching, depending on the tasks involved and potential disability incurred. These approaches will make the benefits aspect transparent to employees.

Just as a product strategy is centered in understanding the market, a health and disability strategy is developed from the profile of the covered population as well as the operating profile of the employer, including work activities, locations, and organizational culture. Programs can be put into place as these elements are developed.

Summary of Strategies

Insurance Strategy
- Assess the organization's financial profile.
- Identify appropriate financial risk exposure in health and disability issues.
- Optimize the financing decision.
- Integrate financial risk exposures between health care, workers compensation, and disability.

Benefits Strategy
- Assess the organization's benefits profile.
- Define the organization's benefits goals.
- Develop a focused benefits program.
- Adjust benefits program as necessary based on internal and external factors.

Health and Disability Strategy

- Assess the organization's health and disability profile.
- Identify comprehensive cost targets and related accountabilities.
- Define the organization's health and disability goals.
- Establish programs based on individual employer circumstances.
- Manage overall program effectiveness based on involvement of all participants.

One of the advantages of the separation of insurance, benefits, and health and disability as strategic issues is that it creates a framework for managing health and disability as an investment issue. Programs can thus be based on cost/benefit assessment in the current period and return on investment encompassing future periods. Resources can be placed in the areas of greatest need from both a cost and quality standpoint.

Part of the problem in combining insurance and health and disability is that the financing decision is merged with the investment decision. Premium-based insurance coverages combine these two elements, a condition that has remained unchanged despite the advent of experience rating and self-insurance. Separation of financing and investment decisions is a fundamental finance principle[11] which is necessary for effectively managing health and disability costs.

An emphasis on financial risk can mistakenly identify the investment issue as one of measuring funds used in risk financing against a corporate rate of return hurdle. Regardless of alternate uses of such funds, risk financing always remains a financing issue. The investment side is picked up in health and disability strategy where the funding of proactive management and effective programs earns a return on investment through cost savings in a wide range of areas.

Comprehensive strategy does not imply complexity. Identifying financial risks apart from underlying health and safety risks allows organizations to maintain the size of their financial risk pool to their strategic advantage. Then employers can assess the level of uncertainty in self-insured financial risks per individual and aggregate claims they can absorb based on their financial profile. (Chapter 7 provides more detail on managing uncertainty.) Once this has been determined, a health and disability strategy based on risk management can be developed to address costs. And finally, the design of benefits can be based on compensation considerations.

Interrelating these three strategies is critical to the effectiveness of the overall program. For example, when beginning to manage health and disability costs more directly, the employer may keep the level of financial risk relatively small, at $100,000 per claim. After establishing more visibility into health and disability issues and verifying control over costs, the employer may then raise the level of financial risk. The result is an overall program that optimizes all issues to the advantage of the employer and ultimately to the advantage of employees themselves.

Integrating Health and Disability into Organizational Strategy

Organizations manage their operations through strategy whether it is well defined or in a founder's head. The advantage of organizational strategy is that it commands a common focus and is backed by communications and shared information. Generally, the emphasis has been on technology development, product or service enhancement, and sales and marketing. And recently, quality has begun to receive direct attention as a strategic issue with major competitive implications.

Part of the power of a well-developed quality strategy is that it matrixes across traditional accountabilities while creating linkages between departments and facilities. Activities are thus integrated through a commitment toward a higher organizational purpose. Health offers the same potential advantage; only instead of relating to a product or service, activities relate directly to employees and dependents as people.

This connection between employer and employee is essential to full implementation of a health and disability strategy. Once a health commitment is in place, employers can leverage costs through proactive risk management emphasizing health and related management interventions. Related programs will evolve as will the underlying health and disability strategy itself.

Risk is central in human activities and behaviors. Without risk management, the human trade-offs in personal health and disability matters are controlled by policies and providers, not by employees and dependents themselves. In addition, proactive risk management allows employers to control trade-offs between cost and quality by involving all participants through incentives and risk sharing. Thus, risk management can link employer and employees and dependents in mutual self-interest, which underpins a quality-based health system.

Creating such individualized management requires an employer-specific health and disability strategy. How this strategy fits into an organization's management practices will vary. Much depends on what is currently in place. The goal is not to create excess strategies even though the current health care and workers' compensation crises demand an overriding emphasis on health and disability as a strategic cost issue.

Organizations with a fully developed quality strategy and related programs could add a complementary health and disability strategy. Those without a well-developed quality strategy might consider the opposite tactic—using health to bring quality management into an organization at the most personal level. This interconnection between health and quality has been indirectly recognized by Dr. W. Edwards Deming, who identifies excess medical costs for employee health care as number six of his Seven Deadly Diseases.[12] The difference with health and disability strategy is that health has now been elevated to functional equivalency with quality. Health directly represents the quality of an organization's human resources.

Although implementation of health and disability strategy will vary by organization, one common dimension needs to be an emphasis on risk management. Risk, viewed in both a financial and operating sense, has taken on strategic importance. Proactively managing such risks is critical for building quality into a product or service, and into an organization. Senior operating and financial management will need to increasingly rely on a strategically minded risk manager working closely with risk knowledgeable line management in these uncertain times. Building a team approach among functional management is also essential.

In the final analysis, strategy is only effective when operationalized. This result requires a management framework supported by information. When these conditions exist, management becomes systematic and continuous, reflecting the full promise of a health and disability strategy.

References

1. Issues report, 1991—A summary of issues influencing workers compensation. 1991. *Building a framework for the future.* National Council on Compensation Insurance, Boca Raton, FL.

2. Parry, A. E., Jones, Linda F. March 1992. It's time to consider 24 hour care. *Public Risk,* pp. 3–5.

3. Data Watch, March 1992. *Business & Health,* p. 18.

4. Miller, J. G. & Vollmann, T. E. September–October 1985. The Hidden Factory, *Harvard Business Review,* p. 142.

5. Higgins, A. Foster. November 1992. Survey of 2409 employers, 1991. *Wall Street Journal,* Health Plans are Self-Insured by More Firms, p. B1:3 Nov 11, 1992.

6. Johnson and Higgins. 1992. Self-insurance: Trends and perspectives.

7. Higgins, A. Foster. November 1992. Survey of 2409 employers, 1991. *Wall Street Journal,* Health Plans are Self-Insured by More Firms, B1:3 Nov 11, 1992.

8. Ellis, S. 1991. Making the most of self-insurance. *Risk Insurance.* 2(8): 16–18.

9. Winslow, R. May, 1, 1992. Infant health problems cost business billions. *Wall Street Journal,* B1, B12.

10. Cost of accidents by class, 1991. Accident Facts 1992 Edition, National Safety Council.

11. Miller, M. H., Modligiani, F. 1958. The cost of capital, corporation finance and the theory of investment, *American Economic Review,* Volume 48, #3 pp. 261–297

12. Walton, M. 1990. *Deming management at work.* New York: Putnam.

3

Developing a
Quality-Based
Health System:
Employer-Directed
Management

Organizations face the never-ending challenge of generating enough revenues to cover their costs while providing for capital growth through internal cash sources or access to capital markets. The greatest challenge is to
balance the short and the long terms; as any senior executive knows, a good
long-term strategy is meaningless without a near-term plan to survive and
thrive.

The same challenges exist in health and disability. The advantages of a
competitive employee benefits plan must be balanced with an employer's
ability to pay. Employers sometimes draw the line at a certain level of costs,
passing future increases onto employees. This method of containment does
not focus on the causes of health and disability costs and certainly does not
address the workers' compensation issue.

Simple coverage limitations appear on the face to be a good short-term
solution to cost control. Unfortunately, spending generally continues un-
abated for preventable illnesses, injuries, and disability, making for disjointed and ineffective health and health care programs. Such passive funding for coverages can result in ever-increasing costs, whether borne by
employer or employee, while true investment in health remains minimal.

Undercapitalized and undermanaged health, health care, and disability programs cannot hope to solve health and disability cost problems.

Employers with unacceptable current levels of health and disability costs may find it difficult to consider investing in health. The typical viewpoint is that expensive health programs must be appended to already costly health care plans: Who can afford to wait for the eventual cost savings benefits of health? There is merit to such reservations. The real problem with many of these approaches, however, is that patching health programs onto a medical care plan for illness and injury will not create a well-integrated health and health care program. In addition, most employers fail to capitalize on the natural operations linkage in health and safety issues. Disability can be an afterthought, particularly for cases created by medical interventions rather than by workplace accidents.

Solutions to the health and disability crisis have been lacking because of an overall lack of integrated and effective management. In fact, the transition to managed care perpetuated an underinvolved role for many employers and employees and dependents, who believed that management had been fully and effectively brought to bear on health and health care issues. True management is being constrained by a different set of historical artifacts, some of recent lineage:

- *Confusion between Administration and Management.* "Management" by third parties often simply means administration against process standards (e.g., lengths of stay in treatment) rooted in claims.

- *Overriding Emphasis on Costs.* There is far less consideration of value as a combination of cost and quality.

- *Underemphasis on Comprehensive Management of Workplace Health and Safety.* Safety programs may be lacking or, because of narrow definition, may miss today's workplace health risks, which often develop cumulatively, not through an accident.

- *Lack of Operational Involvement by Employers and Third Parties.* Employer efforts often stop at the plan design level as though the plan itself could control costs. Third-party attention often concentrates on care as though care delivery alone could manage health and disability.

- *Confusion between Cost Sharing and Risk Sharing.* Employees are expected to change their health and health care behaviors based on cost sharing. Risk sharing refers to personal involvement in health, health care, and disability issues based on knowledge of personal health and safety risks, and then reinforced by incentives.

These conditions have often combined to produce disjointed and ineffective management responses. In addition, many employers continue to stand at the water's edge even though they can provide much of the needed management solution.[1] This chapter presents a systems-based management framework for operationalizing a health and disability strategy based on individual employer circumstances. Through a value-added approach, a range of internal and external management (including managed care) can be accessed to produce excellence in cost and quality performance. This type of management will produce lasting cost solutions.

The Essence of a Quality-Based Health System

Employers and third-party managers continue to focus most attention on care alone. All manner of controls have been placed on providers, yet costs continue to rise because the users of services have not received equivalent attention. A broad consideration of the health system requires that three additional participants in the system—employees and dependents, line supervisors and management, and employer functional management—receive full accountability for their role in individual and organizational health:

Care System	Health System
Prime Accountability	*Prime Accountability*
Providers	Providers
Third-party managers/insurers	Third-party managers/insurers
	Employees and dependents
Secondary Accountability	Line supervisors/management
Employees and dependents	Employer functional
as patients	management
Employers as payors	

This inclusive health system manages the interconnections between all participants rather than just individual care activities. Such interconnections exist not only between providers, but also between the worlds of care, work, and home. Management of health is thus a shared accountability, whereas management of care will always involve a measure of control by providers and third parties.

A systems approach defines the full scope of the employer's health and disability issues by identifying and dealing with costs comprehensively based on the total cost of health and disability. Once accountabilities have been defined and a management structure is in place, employers can gain lasting cost solutions through the following mechanisms:

1. A closed loop system that simultaneously addresses control, performance, and investment to reduce costs while improving quality.
2. A system of management that stresses value at every level.
3. A system of management that identifies the need for information for all participants at every stage of the health continuum.

When these mechanisms are in place, management becomes individualized for employees and dependents as well as the employer. This movement away from standardized industrial age medicine to individualized information age health represents the full potential of a quality-based health system.

Management Based on an Employer-Specific Strategy

Although managed care has not yet become the ultimate cost solution, significant positive developments have occurred. A system of accountability backed by measurement has begun to be put in place nationally. New treatment and management services have developed, and these specialized services enable employers and networks to develop individualized management solutions. Managed care thus encompasses a breadth of new services as well as broad-based networks.

Management in health care and workers' compensation is only in its infancy. The information age has been slow to penetrate into treatment and administration, but the pace is quickening. Some of the major developments offering management advantage for employers include:

- A wide array of treatment services in such areas as return to work, catastrophic care, home care.

- A wide range of management services to develop individualized employer health and disability programs or to complement a broad managed care network.

- Increased flexibility by managed care networks in terms of customized employer services.

- Direct access by providers and provider networks to employers through direct contracting, leading to greater consideration of employer interests.

- Increased availability of information about health, health care, and disability to support informed employer and employee roles, backed by the availability and low cost of distributed information and decision-making supports.

Management requires information. Is it any wonder that the initial wave of managed care ended up creating another layer of administration when information did not flow from providers about clinical performance? The early crude attempts to predefine clinical behavior in terms of both cost and quality failed to influence employee and dependent behavior because information for employers and care users remained almost nonexistent. These conditions are beginning to change, creating a major management opportunity.

Because an external infrastructure is now available, employers can develop management systems to support an individualized health and disability strategy integrating health care and workers' compensation issues. Effective employer-directed management connects an employer's operating profile to internal and external programs through strategy. The "management cube" in Figure 3.1 expresses this approach.

The fundamental change in employer-directed management is that health and disability begins with an assessment of employer needs and only then considers external resources. An employer's operating profile represents geographical distribution, employee and dependent demographics, health and safety risks, employee turnover, and other factors. An example of an internal program is employee education and training in personal health management, whereas the Employee Assistance Program (EAP) is an external function.

When considering the management cube of operating profile, strategy, and programs, the variables critical for one employer will differ from those of another employer. Differing needs will create a matrix of programs. This is why different sections of the cube are shaded and others are left unshaded. Employers need to determine which variables are critical for their circumstances and how they can be best controlled even as they assess health and disability on a total systems framework.

Ultimately, the issue is one of leverage. Employers can best control health and disability costs by focusing internal and external management attention as well as related resources on the most critical variables, or leverage

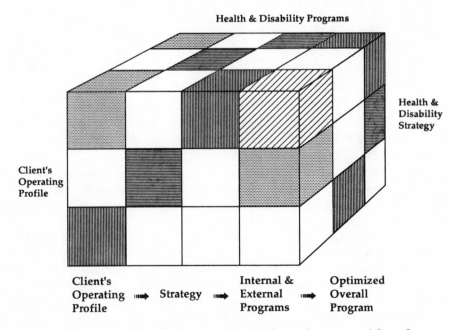

Figure 3.1 The Management Cube: Linking Strategy with a Systems Framework (RHM Systems, Inc., 1993, Marlboro, MA)

points. The advantage is not only in proactively targeting management efforts, but in being able to measure program effectiveness in both cost and quality terms. A company's wellness programs may be effective as a whole; but if there are wide differences between regions, addressing these variances could produce significant cost savings.

Specialized managed care services and provider networks can complement involved employer management, but ultimately employers need to assess and manage continuously, in terms of their own requirements. Even when many program blocks are filled by external programs managed by third parties (particularly for small employers), there is still a need for overall employer management based on ongoing performance assessment. This constructive pressure for verifiable measures of cost and quality performance assures a value-added management approach that reflects an employer-specific health and disability strategy.

Value-Added Considerations

Defining Employer Involvement

The employer's role in health and disability is changing significantly because many organizations formerly beholden to insurers, including Alcoa, Southern California Edison, and Allied Signal, have developed individualized health and health care programs.

The progression of employer involvement is as follows:

Level	*Involvement*
1	Select and assemble generic health care plans (requote and rebroker process).
2	Specify and negotiate features within health care plans (request for proposal process).
3	Build health, health care, and disability programs based on employer-specific strategy and related needs of covered population (strategy emphasis).
4	Manage integrated health and disability strategy and related programs based on regular information to benefit understanding and communications (information emphasis).

A strategy-based approach allows employers to develop integrated management solutions, rather than patching around current problems. As employers move up the management curve, they require a much higher level of value added from third-party managers such as managed care provider networks. Although they may have needed value added in the past, that approach was not commonly used in managing health and disability.

Value added is a frequently discussed concept. Simplistically stated, it is a service worth more than its component parts. To determine relative worth, employers should assess both cost and quality when selecting and monitoring the performance of third-party managers. Table 3.1 defines different levels of value-added contributions: An exceptional organization will be quite developed in terms of value added, whereas a less developed organization may provide only a few levels of value added.

Third-party manager organizations are not yet performing at the highest levels of value added; determining their capabilities requires a rigorous qualification and monitoring process. Complexity and mounds of paper are not the answer: A series of probing questions followed by on-site assessment of management systems can provide a much higher level of understanding. After identifying the third-party organization's levels of value added, employers can develop relationships with those groups most committed to true management of health, health care, and disability. Such groups need to have verifiable financial strength and stability as well as independence from conflicts of interest.

Value-Added Assessment and Development

Before accessing any third-party management services, employers need to stand back and evaluate what is currently in place. Companies often add management and administrative features incrementally over the years. The end result can be management that does not produce cost savings at least equal to its costs. More frequently, management can represent a significant portion of the direct costs of a health and disability program. A common example is a managed dental program that pays low benefits to employees.

Employer self-assessment requires answers to some difficult questions. How much is the company spending on management and administration of

Table 3.1 Progressive Levels of Value Added

Administrative capabilities

Immediate cost advantage (e.g., discounts)

Absorption of some level of financial risk

Knowledgeability about providers

Responsiveness to both the employer and employee/dependent

Information for employee/dependent

Information for employer

Enhanced decision making based on value—quality as well as cost

Discipline over providers, in both cost and quality terms

Accountability for critical decisions

Provider behavior optimized

Employer-specific programs

Strategy and systems in place to manage cost and quality systematically

Verifiably better cost and quality performance

Health issues measured and managed systematically

health and disability, both internally and externally? And where is the firm concentrating its management resources? Many employers will be surprised to find the mismatch between management efforts and the cost leverage points for their individualized health and disability profile. Moving past prior claims experience to assessing the cost/benefit ratio of today's risks is critical. An employer may be spending little on well-focused health and preventive care features in health care coverage and managed care approaches despite having a maturing population and a stable work force. Or even more fundamentally, a firm may spend relatively little on disability management despite a poor return-to-work history for both health care and workers' compensation cases.

To achieve true cost management, employers must invest their efforts and related costs in the areas with the greatest payback potential or cost exposure. Activity-based costing is a mechanism for this direct cost type of strategic cost management.[2] Hours and related costs invested in management activities can be analyzed against the cost opportunity or cost exposure of those activities.

As shown in Table 3.2, activity-based costing can be applied to health and disability management by identifying costs by program; individual program features can then be broken down into administrative costs, management costs, and total direct costs that represent claims and a forecast of potential future costs. Both administration and management can be further segmented into internal and external efforts (including managed care). This may require some estimating of internal efforts, which are often rolled up into general overheads. Value measures encompassing quality as well as cost can then be applied to each activity.

Table 3.2   Health and Disability: Activity-Based Analysis

	Program				Related Program Feature		
	Total Direct Costs	Admin. Cost	Mgmt. Cost		Total Direct Costs	Admin. Cost	Mgmt. Cost
Health awareness	$$	$	$	Employee education	$	$	$
Health and safety	$$	$	$	Wellness	$	$	$
Self-care	$$	$	$	Family information	$	$	$
Primary care	$$	$	$	Incentives	$	$	$
Specialty care	$$	$	$	Case management	$	$	$
Rehabilitation	$$	$	$	Return to work	$	$	$
Long-term care	$$	$	$	Home care	$	$	$

An analysis of management activities commonly underscores the following opportunities for improvement:

- A mismatch between activities of employer and third-party managers and cost management opportunities.
- Limited activities in many critical areas, with more costs spent in administration than management.
- Parallel internal efforts in health programs for health care issues and safety programs for workers' compensation issues with nonintegrated management of health and safety risks.
- Some managed care features that cost more than they save.
- Heavy internal attention to insurance and benefits considerations, but far less to management of health, health care, and disability programs.
- Underappreciation of time and related costs of changes to health, health care, and disability programs, particularly employee productivity loss caused by education and training requirements.

Once employers have completed an activities-based analysis, they can reprioritize internal accountabilities, sometimes between departments and sometimes through task consolidation. Internal accountabilities can then be assessed against those of external management organizations, and in all cases, value added can be used as a criterion for funding the activities. The goal is to align management to achieve the following benefits:

1. An overall understanding of management activities.
2. Optimal deployment of management to strategic issues.
3. Utilization of management based on two value-added criteria: relative expertise of participants and cost/benefit of activities.
4. Ongoing assessment of management effectiveness.

Companies often lack qualitative assessment criteria for selecting and managing third parties. The organization responsible for case management may have been selected because of its hourly rate and costs per case when the real cost management leverage lies in the quality of the services and in the total costs of the cases themselves, including ultimate outcomes such as return to work. When choosing third parties to manage critical cost issues, employers must seek the highest amount of value added for themselves—ideally, well above the cost of the management services.

A value-added approach allows for continuous learning by employer functional and line management. As skills and confidence grow, management can undertake a wider range of activities to optimize the value added from health, health care, and disability programs. Improving the span of control of the employer's management team requires support through comprehensive and timely management information.

Optimizing Managed Care
Based on Employer Interests

Although employers need to be directly involved in managing health and disability, third-party managers can take responsibility for interfacing with a diverse group of providers. Health care practice varies by region of the country, and medical technology advances daily. Such challenging conditions limit self-administration and self-management to the largest organizations. The Washington Business Group on Health estimates that only 8 percent of employers are involved in self-administration.

In contributing verifiable value added, management services must move past pure cost factors to the rigorous consideration of quality. Unfortunately, early forms of managed care emphasized costs with little impact on quality issues. The term *cost containment* itself connotes that broader issues within the medical system are only being monitored, not addressed. A costs-only approach by a managed care network has the following limitations:

- Discounts alone achieve little value added.
- Discounts can give nonoptimal incentives to providers (e.g., a 20 percent fee reduction to a physician handling a high-risk pregnancy).
- When quality is not simultaneously addressed, cost containment can be an inherently reactive form of control based on inspection.
- Leverage over providers may not be as great as providers' leverage over the network (e.g., the need for a rurally based medical center in a health maintenance organization [HMO] network).
- Emphasis is on medical care per state regulatory standards, not on health care (e.g., rehabilitation is not covered).
- Health features often are neither comprehensive nor seriously emphasized (e.g., a health club benefit does not necessarily translate into an aerobically oriented health effort).

Despite these limitations, managed care networks often have reduced traditional health care costs because of the lower negotiated fees, the movement away from fee-for-service billings, and the control provided by a prequalified network. Control is established for an employer by increasing the percentage of the covered population within the network, increasing the percentage of treatment within the network, and increasing the percentage of treatment managed under negotiated pricing arrangements. A cost-containment feature such as a primary care gatekeeper can then be used to control high-cost specialty care. These controls, however, have proven to be only temporarily effective unless fundamental improvements take place in employee and dependent health practices and in the quality of providers' care: It is essential to control costs in future periods by taking a proactive stance in current periods. These are the fundamental challenges confronting managed care.

Unless employers deal systematically with the issues of health and quality, organizations that join or develop a managed care network—after an initial cost improvement—will continue to experience year-to-year cost increases. Leadership in developing this new level of managed care is coming from employers themselves as well as from some of the networks.[3] Specialized management services have enabled employers to develop individualized managed care to meet the needs of their covered population.

A host of alternatives, such as preferred provider organizations (PPOs), are complementing predefined networks (e.g., HMOs) by contracting directly with employers or through third-party administrators (TPAs). Direct contracting by employers with individual providers has also developed. All these approaches are defining preferred networks with preferred provider fees. Managed care networks can thus take many forms.[4]

Even as managed care organizations have developed regionally and nationally, leading firms have recognized that no one network can provide all the solutions. National employers must continuously monitor regional differences in cost and quality performance. In fact, management solutions are becoming quite employer-specific with a composite of managed care networks forming employer-directed managed care systems. The following are specific examples of such approaches:

- A large national chemical company replaced a self-insured, indemnity insurance program with a self-insured, managed care system. The role of one national TPA was replaced by three separate regional managed care networks serving the geographic areas of the company's major facilities and corporate headquarters.

- A major regional power company had fragmented its health care program into 23 options including indemnity insurance and managed care networks for both unionized and nonunionized employees. Consolidation reduced the options to 8 organizations, and the employer negotiated one combined, self-insured financial risk pool.

- A national health care organization replaced an experience-rated indemnity insurance program and local HMOs with a national TPA in which separate indemnity and managed care options linked into one financial risk pool.

Size obviously is beneficial when developing individualized alternatives and negotiating leverage, but employers with only 200 employees may be surprised by the management features they can develop. Often such employee populations are in one region and are further concentrated in adjacent facilities. Depending on commuting patterns, direct contracting with a few local providers or a regional preferred network of providers is thus a possibility. Coalitions of employers can further increase an individual employer's level of management and related leverage over costs.

Development of employer-specific managed care systems reflects a recognition that creating management solutions is the real issue. Employers are seeking answers in the following areas:

1. Optimum management of the financial risk.
2. Provider geographical coverage versus employee and dependent needs.
3. Cost levels and related cost-containment features.
4. Value-added management by third parties.
5. Provider performance—excellence in terms of cost and quality.
6. More involved role for employees and dependents.

Most attention has been on the first three issues as employers, while retaining adequate coverage, eliminate past problems caused by fragmented health care plans such as the loss of critical mass for managing the financial risk, excess administrative costs in interacting with a wide number of organizations, and a lack of standardized information.

Even as health care plans are restructured to improve cost control methods, employers' efforts are inherently limited by the medical care orientation of managed care organizations. Relatively little is being done on the front-end in terms of health and on the back-end of treatment to return care users to health. For this reason, the full opportunity of managed care systems to solve health care cost problems and the broader costs of health and disability requires a managed health approach.

Employers need to focus on value-added management by third parties, superior provider performance, and a more involved role for employees and dependents. An overall health and disability framework can complement managed care with appropriate programs added on or "carved out;" developing synergies between health care and workers' compensation programs. For example, return-to-work efforts directed by a physiatrist (doctor of rehabilitation medicine) can benefit someone covered under a health care plan. Integrated solutions to managing health, health care, and disability are presented in Chapters 4, 5, and 6.

A key part of a systems approach is the creative use of competition. Instead of locking employees and dependents into a managed care network, employers increasingly allow a choice to opt out of network on a point of service basis. Usually a cost differential exists, but increased flexibility by employers in health care plan design and by managed care provider networks in the future will allow competition to occur continuously, rather than on an annual requoting cycle. Such competition can extend to quality as well as cost issues so that employees and dependents can engage in health and health care decision making continuously, not just in plan selection during open enrollment. Information can then address quality-of-care issues as well as coverages, reinforcing both choice by care users and competition among providers.

Many professionals, in proposing extensive reforms, have recognized the lack of integrated health care systems.[5] Establishing interconnections on the supply side of care is vitally important for employers; however, integrated care represents only a portion of the solution. Direct exposures by employers to health and safety risks, return to work, and health and disability management require integrated and effective action on the demand side in the form of broader based health systems. Such flexible systems promise to be the value-added management solution for health care and workers' compensation cost problems in the 1990s and beyond.[6]

Involving Employees in a Systems Solution

Health care conveys the image of physicians and other highly trained clinical professionals. Workers' compensation conveys the image of physicians, vocational rehabilitation specialists, and attorneys. Common to both of these issues, however, is an often neglected participant—the employee.

In the search for a management solution to health and disability cost problems, experts have devoted far less attention to the actions and behaviors of employees and dependents than to those of physicians and other involved caregivers. With the focus on care rather than on health, providers assume a dominant role and employees and dependents are thought of only as patients.

An alternative approach is to define a health system consisting of employer, employees and dependents, providers, and third-party managers. In this quality system, the role of employees and dependents takes on strategic importance. Whereas employers may not directly utilize health care, employees and dependents are direct users. Because of this circumstance, employees can be considered the protagonist in workers' compensation issues, and dependents, if not employees, can be the protagonist in health care issues. If employees are not considered part of the problem, they are usually not considered part of the solution either. The cooperation and involvement of employees and dependents, however, largely determine the employer's degree of control over costs. Unity of purpose in management between employer and employee is necessary because the employee acts as the employer's proxy in interactions with providers.

Unity of purpose is possible when employers focus on health as the reason for their health care and workers' compensation programs. A Managing Forward approach can then be developed for employees and dependents as well for internal and external management activities. Table 3.3 shows the leverage available from this approach. Empowerment replaces dependency to the degree that employers support employees and dependents in efforts to manage their personal health forward toward health and away from care.

The overriding goal is to move choices forward, enabling employees to manage risks and to make decisions as consumers rather than as patients,

Table 3.3 Managing Forward: Employee and Dependent Health Activities

Levels of Empowerment
Selection of a network
Selection of cost-sharing features
Selection of coverages
Selection of a group practice
Selection of physician as an individual
Access to treatment in terms of time and place
Coinvolvement in the treatment plan, most critically in decision making
Involvement in self-care, while healthy and after treatment
Access to health programs
Knowledge of health and safety risks in personal activities and behaviors
Knowledge of health and safety risks in work activities and behaviors

and when healthy, rather than when unhealthy. This is the essence of true quality in health care.

The following examples demonstrate the practical benefits for both employer and employee:

- A woman knowledgeable in early detection of breast cancer self-diagnoses a problem and obtains treatment using less evasive procedures, reduced drugs, and a faster recovery, benefiting her return to work.

- A 35-year-old man with a high-risk lifestyle that includes smoking and overeating is receptive to a lifestyle change on the birth of his first child. The company's wellness program now pays off as he eliminates his high-risk status through one year of aerobic and nutritional activities.

Movement from a dependency health care culture toward an empowered health culture requires an employer commitment to employee education and training because there are few role models and many employees and dependents cannot fathom being informed and empowered consumers. Even low-cost access to primary care as a managed care network feature can create dependency on physicians unless it is supported through education in personal health management and self-care.

The emphasis, therefore, needs to shift to an entirely new line of information directed at employee and dependent self-interests:

- Most people prefer to be healthy rather than unhealthy.

- Few people enjoy hospital stays or admissions through the emergency room.

- Most people with a disability want to recover lost functioning.

- Most people want an end point to treatment.
- People want access to health care services but do not necessarily want to utilize them.
- People want the best quality health care.

The degree to which employers progressively tap into these self-interests will determine the extent to which employees and dependents are incorporated into an employer-directed management solution as part of a health and disability strategy.

Addressing Employee Interests in a Systems Solution

The relationship between employer and employee is being subjected to a wide range of conflicting messages regarding health and disability. In general, employees have been exposed to increased cost sharing and coverage choices. Now they are confronting such issues as incentives for good health and flexibility in the benefits themselves.[7] Benefits such as child care may be added even while a portion of the covered population cannot afford basic coverage for health care. The Families USA Foundation reports that employees paid 23 percent of the cost of employer sponsored health care coverage in 1991, rising from 18 percent in 1980. At the same time, family health care spending as a percentage of income rose from 9 percent to 11.7 percent with the percentage at 13 percent to 14 percent in 12 states.

Benefit changes come at great cost. Such efforts may require engaging many outside consultants; in addition, internal staff time is diverted in revising and changing the plan. Although some program changes are helpful, a treadmill of plan changes has hardly affected the core issue of health itself. Employers may shift costs while doing nothing to alter health and safety risks in either work or home environments. And high contributions for health care often act as an incentive for employees, who want to get back what they have paid for. Even health incentives are often structured to pay employees for participating, rather than for achieving positive results.

Employers need to stand back from this maelstrom, assessing health and disability from the ground up. Where are they expending current efforts-to explain coverages on a topside basis or to train employees in personal health management and optimal access of health care? Do communication materials describe incremental plan changes in insurance or administrative language or explore issues from top to bottom based on real life case examples? Are employees constantly being reinforced in an entitlement mind-set by an overriding benefits orientation instead of being offered a health perspective that identifies mutual accountabilities? And finally, do employers project to employees that good health practices and informed use of health care can reduce costs?

Dealing with costs comprehensively and systematically requires a health perspective rather than a benefits perspective. It is essential to assess whether any cost/benefit is derived from plan changes and from flexible benefits features. With a total cost of health and disability approach, employers can assess a wide range of cost factors in the current and future periods. The assessment should include a careful review of the demographics and socioeconomic factors that motivate employees and dependents. Surveys are a good tool, but employees cannot assess unfamiliar or poorly understood health program features. For this reason, education and training procedures should anticipate health and health care program changes, as well as the surveys themselves.

When a rigorous cost/benefit analysis is applied to employee interests based on risk probabilities, it will usually show that the greatest cost leverage is in optimizing health and health care decision making rather than in shifting costs. Therefore, health, health care, and disability programs need to be based on these priorities:

- Health and health care decision making.
- Coverage impact on health and disability management.
- Flexibility in plan features.
- Incentives.
- Cost sharing.

Although it is essential to involve employees in cost sharing, high levels of contributions and low copayments encourage high utilization. Likewise, anyone questioning the negative influence deductibles can have on personal health management should discuss the matter with line supervisors who witness employees living from payday to payday and running out at lunchtime to cash their paychecks. Unless the need is severe, are these same persons and their families candidates for visiting the doctor's office at a $50 out-of-pocket cost per visit? High deductibles are a strong disincentive to primary care and an incentive to excess utilization of specialty care through delays in diagnosis and treatment. Lower paid employees not electing coverage or exposed to high first dollar coverage payments, can opt to file a workers' compensation claim for nagging, non-acute heath issues. General low levels of out-of-pocket costs, however, can further remove employees from being prudent consumers of specialty care.

One electronics manufacturer has achieved regular single-digit cost increases in its indemnity health care plan through a concerted effort in optimizing the plan for employees and dependents. Apart from incentivizing the right type of care and maintaining reasonable costs for first-dollar coverage, the employer provides incentives for detecting billing errors, and employees receive training in being prudent consumers based on cost and quality issues. Although employees are exposed to out-of-pocket costs to higher levels, they can be reimbursed through coverage credits accrued both before and after treatment over a number of years.

The best course to a cost-effective health care plan and a lower total cost of health and disability is to focus on the mind-set of employees and dependents themselves, not on that of higher paid management. A core group of coverages can optimize employee and dependent health behavior (inclusive of health-related productivity issues explained in Chapter 6). Once a solid health base is established, discretionary features can be added in areas such as deferred income, life insurance, and tax savings.[8] Flexibility is essential for meeting the diverse employment market of the 1990s, but cost and quality solutions need to be fully implemented first.

Incentives and Risk Sharing

One of the most surprising factors in the health and disability cost crisis is that few employees understand the full extent of the problem. Most employees have been sheltered from considering the full costs of care. Bills often go directly to the managed care organization, insurer, or TPA, and in any case, employees are paying little of the cost when incurred.

To obtain effective solutions, senior management must present the full scope of the problem to employees. It is important, however, to present this information in the middle of a plan year when employees are not reacting to overall changes. Employers tend to jump employees with bad news rather than to engage them in creating solutions. Tangible areas where employees can make positive contributions include:

- Self-care instead of an immediate trip to the doctor (including use of common nonprescription drugs).
- Office visits instead of the emergency room.
- Detection of billing errors.
- Questioning of added tests.
- Questioning of rate increases.
- Negotiation of rates with providers.
- Use of generic drugs when appropriate.

Empowering employees in care activities prepares them for the more personal issues involved in health activities and behaviors. When initiating any employee-centered education effort, employers must stress an overriding commitment to accessing quality care. A perception that cost, not quality, is the overriding concern can alienate employees and dependents.

An incentivized health emphasis can turn this general concern about access and quality care to an employer's advantage. Health is an inherent positive value if measured fairly and consistently. Once employees have learned the purpose of a health commitment, the employer can present the Managing Forward approach to personal health management. Employees need reassurance that their rights to lifestyle choices and quality care are being respected, even if certain behaviors will cost more up front. Instead of restricting "choice," the goal is to vastly increase employee control by moving decision making forward toward health.

Health incentives are frequently undermined by presenting a factor that is a positive for most employees as a negative, just because some employees will be feeling the cost impact of personal health risks. Bridging this gap in perceptions is critical. Employees respect fairness. If health risks come with increased costs, then the organization needs to give sufficient time before passing through the costs. Also, employers need to support financially any employee efforts to reduce health risks, such as a smoking cessation program.

Eventually, new employees and existing employees should be on their own, but initially, change must be carefully managed. True risk sharing occurs only when employees and dependents have been fully trained in personal accountability for health and safety risks, not just hit with cost sharing. (Part Two reviews program issues and related incentives in detail.)

Alignment—Integrating a Quality-Based Health System

Incentivized health ultimately aligns employer interests with those of employees and dependents. Creating such common goals is one of the most important breakthroughs in helping an organization reduce health and disability costs. As such, communications about health should be a normal part of an organization's culture.

Management does not stop with the "managers"; employees and dependents must be fully engaged as part of the management solution. Employers can develop an involved and informed consumer frame of reference as the critical missing link in a quality system that encompasses all participants. This focus on a comprehensive health system, not just health care or workers' compensation networks, capitalizes on employee and dependent selfinterests. Incentives and risk sharing promote the cost and quality benefits of this systematic approach to Managing Forward.

Creative alignment must also be extended to providers and third-party managers. All too often, these key participants operate on their own set of interests or do not completely understand employer goals. Employers can realign such interests by negotiating the terms and conditions of performance, with a contract that places a predefined amount of money at risk based on both cost and quality performance targets. Incentivized health can thus be extended to all participants, as shown in Table 3.4.

The following issues need consideration in an incentivized health program:

- Are the activities and behaviors of providers and third-party managers directed toward the interests of the employer?
- Has the employer tapped into the self-interests of employees and dependents?
- Are cost-sharing features limited so as not to undermine optimal health management by employees and dependents?

Table 3.4   Employer Incentivized Health Program

Participants	Incentives
Employees	Performance measures
Dependents	Cost sharing
Line management/supervisors	Financial rewards
Functional management	Current period
Providers	Future period
—Primary care	Non-monetary rewards
—Specialty care	
Third-party managers	

- Are objective performance measures directly tied to the financial incentives?
- Are financial incentives established at a level that achieves a positive cost/benefit ratio for the employer?
- Are financial incentives structured to balance short-term and long-term behavior by providers and third-party managers as well as employees and dependents?

Incentivized health is a tangible expression of an employer health culture. This type of culture provides the "glue" for the management cube presented earlier. Strategy relates an employer's operating profile to internal and external health and disability programs, whereas management and a supportive culture integrate all activities.

When viewed in terms of a quality-based health system, the elements of employer-directed management include:

- Health, health care, and disability managed as an integral element of corporate strategy.
- Defined system of accountability involving all participants.
- Expectancies concerning performance.
- Objective measures of cost and quality performance.
- Information feedback on a regular basis to support decision making.

The benefits of an integrated health and disability approach are improved cost and quality. These gains are obtained through focused management in three strategic directions:

1. Managing Health: An Intervention Approach
2. Managing Care: A Systematic Approach to Obtaining Value
3. Managing Productivity: Integrating Workplace Health and Disability

All the direct, indirect, and hidden costs of health and disability are encompassed in one of these three management tracts. These issues form the basis of Chapters 4 through 6 and provide a framework to manage costs and quality based on continuous improvement in areas of defined accountability. The organizational goal is excellence in both cost and quality management measured in terms of costs controlled/reduced for a sustained period, improved cost predictability, and improved value for the costs expended.

When cost and quality are systematically managed with an overriding emphasis on health, an organizational commitment can be translated into integrated management solutions.

References

1. Belk, H. D., Harris, J. S., & Wood, L. W. 1991. A strategy for employer health care value management. *Journal of Occupational Medicine,* 33(3): 386–389.
2. Cooper, R., & Caplan, R. S. May–June 1991. Profit priorities from activity-based costing. *Harvard Business Review,* pp. 130–135.
3. Schecter, S. M. November/December 1991. The expert provider organization, *Chief Executive,* 47–48.
4. Alexander, R. D., Criteria for evaluation of PPOs. April 8–11, 1991. *The common ground in managed care, reference guide.* National Managed Health Care Congress, pp. 37–44.
5. American Hospital Association, American Medical Association, Catholic Health Association of the United States. *Proposals for National Health Care Reform.* AHA; AMA; CHA., 1992.
6. Washington Business Group on Health. *A Vision of Future Health Care Delivery System: Organized Systems of Care, Executive Summary.* Washington, DC: Washington Business Group, October 1992, pp. 22–28.
7. Logan, D., & Lipsman, S. June 1991. Rethinking employee benefits: The flex complex, CFO special report. *CFO,* pp. 27–41.
8. Health Spending: The Growing Threat to the Family Budget. A Report by Families USA Foundation, December 1991. Supported by a grant from the Henry J. Kaiser Foundation, p. 4.

Resources

Juran, J. M. 1989. *Juran on leadership for quality: An executive handbook,* New York: Free Press.

Schmidt, W. H., & Finnigan, J. P. 1991. *The race without a finish line: America's quest for total quality.* San Francisco: Jossey-Bass.

Senge, P. M. 1990. *The fifth discipline: Mastering the five practices of the learning organization.* New York: Doubleday/Bantam, Doubleday Dell.

4

Managing Health:
An Intervention Approach

Developing systematic management of health, health care, and disability starts with health. Traditionally, employers have viewed health narrowly as a set of programs or as an uncontrollable human condition. Most of their attention has been on care activities and providers, resulting in relatively poor cost and quality results.

Health is the overriding quality measure—the primary goal and the ultimate outcome of care activities. Health relates to the overall state of mental and physical functioning of an individual and an organization. Such a broad definition can relate the activities of all participants to health. Employees and dependents are accountable for managing their personal health, whereas line supervisors must encompass health issues in the way they manage. Providers respond to the results of health choices, but employees' choices can be influenced up front through interactions with health counselors and primary care physicians. Health is also a derivative of the performance of the health care system.

Developing a common strategic focus on health activities is necessary to gain the organizational leverage over costs envisioned by Managing Forward toward health. As organizations develop a health and disability strategy and related management system, they need an index of effectiveness from related activities. To show the whole range of value, this index must cover both quality and cost. Utilization represents such an index since it indicates the level and type of health activities that employees and dependents have undertaken as well as the care they have consumed.

Utilization is a critical measure because it provides multiple pieces of information. First, participation in health programs is an important indicator of the breadth and depth of health activities within a covered population. Second, the incidence of illness, injury, and disability fundamentally determine employees' utilization of health care services, and occasional related legal counsel. The types of utilization by employees and dependents offer valuable insight into how health care dollars are spent. Does most treatment occur late in the illness, injury, and disability cycles? Or is utilization heavy on low-cost preventive measures, minimizing the potential for later, more expensive care?

The importance of utilization can be seen in its relation to the health continuum of health, injury and illness, and disability, which is part of the concept of Managing Forward. Figure 4.1 shows the health continuum for two different utilization profiles. The current profile is heavily skewed toward injury, illness, and disability, whereas the targeted profile is oriented toward health. Managing Forward toward health enhances employer control while reducing costs.

This chapter presents an intervention approach for systematically achieving major cost and quality improvements. Utilization as an indicator of organizational health is analyzed in terms of root causes such as health and safety risks. Various methodologies are then presented for determining the cost/benefit of an investment in health.

The fullest measure of an employer's leverage over costs can be obtained through strategic application of return-on-investment analysis. Health is the investment with the cost savings being achieved in the cost of care and the cost of productivity. In this way, health is an investment that employers make financially and employees and dependents make in their activities and personal behaviors. The payoff is not only in personal and organizational health and related costs, but also in personal and organizational productivity.

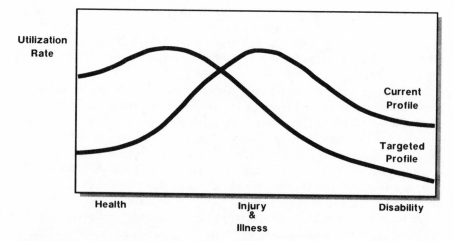

Figure 4.1 Utilization Measured along the Health Continuum (RHM Systems, Inc., 1993, Marlboro, MA)

Defining the Health Opportunity

Now that the exaggerated promise of managed care has faded, many experience-rated or self-insured employers are taking a hard look at the issue of health. Compounding cost levels and ever more complex and expensive medical technologies create a compelling case for a healthy work force. Defining the full scope of this strategic cost opportunity is important for senior management considering an investment in health.

To transform their health and disability cost structure, employers need to manage their utilization forward toward health. The factors causing utilization can be assigned to one of four categories, as shown in Figure 4.2. Health risk and health care are matrixed against each other.

With both preventable health risk and preventable health care estimated at 50 percent, the amount of necessary utilization only equals 25 percent of the amount currently occurring. For the other 75 percent of preventable utilization:

- The health care was nonpreventable, but the health risk could have been prevented.
- The health care was preventable, but the health risk was nonpreventable.
- The health care and the health risk were both preventable.

Although Figure 4.2 uses arbitrary percentages for illustrative purposes, preventable utilization of 75 percent approximates the 70 percent estimate generally assigned to America's health care system. Although precise verification of this prevention opportunity is difficult to obtain, it is corroborated by combining an estimate of preventable health and safety risks, uninformed care

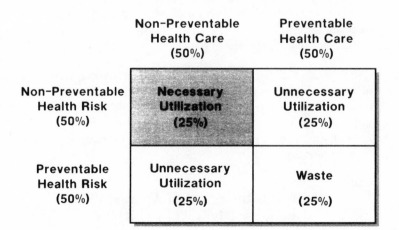

Figure 4.2 Factors Causing Utilization (RHM Systems, Inc., 1993, Marlboro, MA)

access, and poor diagnosis and treatment. The Federal Center for Disease Control estimates preventable health factors as 53 percent for lifestyles, 19 percent for environment, 18 percent for heredity, and 10 percent for health care. This 10 percent figure is on the low end of estimates for unnecessary and inappropriate procedures; speculation among health care industry watchers ranges up to 30 percent.[1] Actual potential will vary by individual employer circumstances for preventable health risk and preventable health care. What the figure graphically demonstrates is that preventable health care feeds off preventable health risk.

Obtaining control over preventable utilization does not require a reduction in health risks equally across a covered population. Many health risks among a limited number of people provide a high degree of leverage to drive down costs. When someone has several health risks, the risk exposure for the individual and employer increases on a multiplicative, not an additive basis. Without considering the significance of individual health risk factors, the implications are that a person with 2 health risk factors has 4 times more risk exposure than someone with just 1, and the exposure from 4 health risk factors is 16 times greater exposure than the effect of just 1.

The cost implications for employers are:

- Health risk behavior change among a limited group of individuals is not just a numbers issue. Reducing the percentage of high-risk individuals will achieve benefits at a much higher rate proportionately than reducing risks for the general population.

- Multiple health risks can overwhelm the importance of one health risk such as family history, making proactive management beneficial in all cases.

- Multiple health risks overwhelm the importance of age in considering employer cost exposures. Actuarial tables present average costs by age when costs are concentrated in a limited number of cases. The critical issue is multiple health risks, with age being only one factor.[2] Aging is a cumulative risk indicator.

Safety risks at work and at home feed off the health risks. Alcohol use and stress both cause higher levels of accidents. Health and safety risks thus trigger many illnesses, injuries, and disabilities. Addressing these key cost leverage points requires an integrated response encompassing health and safety programs as well as proactive management of employee health and safety issues in operations.

A Health Intervention Approach— Doing the Right Things, Right

At first glance, employers may think the concept of health is a bit "soft." In a "hard" world of costs and cash, health can seem a little like mom and apple pie—something to fight for. A comparison between health and quality, however, indicates the rigor that can be brought to an intervention approach. Objective measures of quality such as process control limits may at first appear to be a bit obscure, but over time, statistically oriented quality measures are far more precise than financial measures. Generally accepted accounting principles (GAAP) provide considerable latitude in recognizing revenue, accruing expenses, and depreciating assets to name just a few areas.

When the Managing Forward approach is defined as a health continuum, health interventions supplant treatment interventions. This approach emphasizes "Doing the Right Things, Right": Health represents the first part—doing the right things—which is so often ignored; health care represents doing things right, that is, providing quality in care activities.

Health interventions early in the health continuum allow care to remain under control of the individual and in a normal living environment. As shown in Figure 4.3, up-front interventions such as health awareness, health and safety programs, self-care, and primary care have a large prevention potential. Three of the most common reasons for a physician office visit—the common cold, lower back pain, and tension headache—exemplify the leverage available from improved self-care. On the other hand, the use of primary care for necessary purposes requires increased emphasis.

As more serious care needs develop, control passes to providers in costly treatment environments. Management then concentrates on early intervention to resolve treatment quickly. At the same time, a focus on outcomes can ensure the completion of treatment in a quality manner. In all cases, the goal is timely and effective intervention to restore a person to optimal health.

An intervention approach links directly with incentivized health. Information is the key for Managing Forward toward health, yet it currently

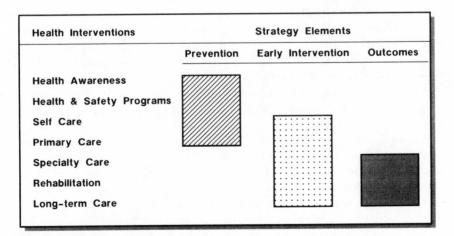

Figure 4.3   Managing Health: The Leverage Points (RHM Systems, Inc., 1993, Marlboro, MA)

represents only 0.5 percent of health care spending[3] (possibly zero in work-ers' compensation). Even when information is provided, it is oriented toward plans and a topside view of coverages, not personal management of health and optimal access of health care. Through employee-centered information backed with the right incentives and forms of risk sharing, employees and de-pendents can actively and continuously target the following results:

- Management of health and safety risks.
- Management of personal health.
- Participation in low-cost health programs, rather than utilization of high-cost health care (e.g., health counselors are far less expensive than physicians).
- Optimal access of health care in terms of time and place with an em-phasis on self-care and primary care.
- Self-regulation of unnecessary and unwanted diagnosis and treatment, including overmedication.
- Coinvolvement in critical treatment decisions so as to consider possi-ble less invasive alternatives.
- Ability to advocate for personal goals in the case of a disabling condition.
- Ability to obtain value from individual professionals and providers.

Supportive employer culture is the best way to help empower employees in risk and care behaviors. Consequently, an intervention approach involves operations. Line, not staff, management are the key to translating health into a way of managing, even though initial education and training are es-sential. Line management should encourage employees to report a health or safety problem for themselves or as an exposure for the entire group. Retri-bution, whether direct or subtle, should not be tolerated by senior manage-ment. An early warning system oriented toward health is the best means to prevent claims for health care and workers' compensation, plus reduce other health and disability costs.

Instead of relying solely on either on-site or off-site health programs, employers need to implement an integrated set of health and safety activi-ties rooted in operations. This strategic focus anticipates health, health care, and disability issues, thereby breaking down the walls between health care and workers' compensation. Table 4.1 shows some examples of proac-tive management in operations that can be directed toward health.

Proactive management removes the loss control and damage control men-tality so widely prevalent with health, health care, and disability issues. Break-ing the information logjam for employees and dependents and line supervisors requires small dollars and yet has one of the greatest potential paybacks. Through informed and empowered line supervisors and employees and depen-dents, common concern can translate into joint action. In the case of workers' compensation, supportive interventions on known health issues will disarm

Table 4.1   Health Management in Operations: An Intervention Approach

Issue	Management Mechanism
Workplace health and safety risks	Suggestion box to facility manager Quality improvement teams
Employee and dependent health feedback	Quarterly meeting to discuss health and health care programs Survey of best and worst quality providers
Employee and line supervisor, education and training	Video display terminal (VDT) usage and health Back self-care at work and home
Management support for health issues	Active management support for utilizing health programs (i.e., eliminate stigma issues) Comp. time used after peak work periods Work assignments adjusted to provide breaks from continuous VDT usage Flex time promoted for personal primary care, child primary care, active personal health program, and supports for a dependent who is disabled Extended lunch period for those in active personal health program Environmental issues such as air quality and temperature and lighting receive on-going consideration
Workplace accidents or other health issues	Immediate access to prequalified health care providers
Return to work	Phone contact by line supervisor soon after any leave for health care or workers' compensation issues Flexibility in hours worked and scheduling during transition period Use of transitional task assignments Predefined range of access and workstation accommodations and related productivity aids

litigation, sharply reducing costs. Any health issue addressed under health care coverage instead of workers' compensation likewise saves on both fronts.

When care moves into provider hands, health interventions do not necessarily stop. Patient and family, backed by appropriate employer staff, need to advocate for the best possible care to return to health. This may mean goal-oriented rehabilitation including return to work through a job coach's support. And sometimes what an employee and his or her family need most is only a phone call to show someone from work cares. All participants must continuously consider "Doing the Right Things, Right"—the first time.

Integrated Health and Safety Programs

The starting point in reducing health and disability costs is to raise employees' awareness of underlying health and safety risks. This information effort must be systematic and continuous, linking employees and line management into an overall health and disability strategy to address root causes of utilization. Then internal and external programs need to be integrated toward a common goal—health.

Often employers develop a disjointed group of programs including a medical care plan oriented toward illness and injury. Primary care may receive little attention, particularly for retirees and persons with a disability, and may, in fact, be undermined through high costs for first-dollar coverage (deductibles). Even when these disincentives are eliminated, not all employees will make use of mammographies, colorectal screening, Pap smears, and other routine physicals. The problem lies in perpetuating a care culture rather than building a health culture. Solutions must come from the integrated efforts of all participants, not from the health care plan itself.

Many companies are looking carefully at health risk management, and some are responding to the cost differentials in annual claims costs, as shown in Table 4.2.[4] The issue is not to identify the health problems associated with smoking and other health risks, but to chart a cost-effective solution. Paying employees to participate in health programs does not necessarily yield results. And changes in health risk behavior benefit the individual and the employer only when they last. Voluntary behavior change is more likely to be permanent than coerced behavior change pointing out the need for managing cultural issues.

Culture effects day-to-day living and working activities plus controls initial participation, effectiveness and continuation of personal health programs. The need to influence all of these factors to obtain lasting cost/benefit identifies the importance of managing the total group, not just to target obvious high risk individuals. Social behavior influences are so strong that a medical researcher concluded that the benefit of controlling large numbers of relatively low risk individuals through volunteer groups may actually increase program efficacy and decrease costs rather than vice versa.[5] And this conclusion only related to heart disease, not to the impact that culture can wield over a wide range of health and safety behavior at work and at home. Similarly, costs can be saved by influencing activities, not just investing in programs.

Table 4.2   Dupont's Experience: Annual Costs per Employee

	With Health Risk	Without Health Risk	Annual Cost Savings
Smoking	3971	3011	960
Alcohol	3672	3233	439
Excessive weight	3530	3130	400
High cholesterol level	3565	3195	370
High blood pressure	3584	3241	343

Source: R. L. Bertera. 1991. The effects of behavioral risks on absenteeism and health care costs in the workplace. *Journal of Occupational Medicine*, 33(11): 1119–1124.

Proactive management of information is the key to a profound change in an organization's health and safety risk exposure. Before rushing into development of health risk management as another "program," employers should establish an integrated health and safety program across the health continuum of work and home activities, not just the physical symptoms of employees. In designing a health culture, employers can target investments to combine short-term and long-term payback opportunities as follows:

- Address both work and home safety proactively; 25 percent of disabilities[6] and a substantial portion of both health care and workers' compensation costs are due to accidents. Safety gains can be realized quickly.

- Cumulative health conditions—stress, back problems, carpal tunnel syndrome, and indoor air—are the new occupational health plague.[7] An employee's back injury seldom results from one lifting incident or even accumulated lifting experiences, but rather from a wide range of risks caused by personal activities affecting the back. It is estimated 80 percent of workers will experience back problems in their lifetimes, with 90 percent of these being recurring.[8]

- Health and disability conditions do not accumulate in a single risk dimension; instead, they interact and multiply to degrade health, causing the need for care while compounding the level of disability.

Even with a strong internal health commitment, employers must integrate health into primary care. Annual physicals are not the real issue. The quality of the primary care provided by physicians is critical to supporting company health programs. A study of primary care practices in 1988 showed a developing trend among physicians toward understanding behavioral risk factors and the related need to modify those factors.[9] The problem centered on carrying out the interventions. The constraints were the physicians' lack of confidence in knowing how to intervene effectively and their perception that patients are unreceptive, unwilling, or unable to change. In the meantime, the Office on Smoking and Health reports only 30 percent of smokers do not see a physician at least once during a year and those 70 percent seeing a physician average 4.3 visits per year.[10] Yet, most primary care physicians provide little or no counseling about smoking unless a smoking-related disorder is present. Effectiveness in health efforts is undermined when such highly regarded experts do not address health fundamentals.

To obtain a major reduction in health and safety risks for a covered population, employers need to move past coverages and even programs, although the benefits of various programs are becoming well documented. And pumping money into primary care will not necessarily have an impact either, if physicians are not providing care based on a health commitment. Instead, an integrated health and safety program combines the following elements:

1. Health and safety management in operations with an emphasis on education and training.

2. Internal and external health and safety programs, including wellness, that integrate into an employer's operating practices and culture.

3. A health care plan that is truly health oriented in its coverages.

4. An emphasis on primary care closely linked with involved physicians to support employee and dependent health goals.

5. Incentivized health to support participation and reinforce adherence to personal health programs.

Financial paybacks, not mere existence, testify to a program's effectiveness.

Measuring Program Effectiveness—
Utilization as an Index of Health Value

Employers spend a great deal of time, money, and effort in managing their financial health, yet they generally fail to address organizational health. Organizations have two methods of measuring health for individuals and for a group:

1. *Indirect Measures.* Participation in health programs and utilization of health care services.

2. *Direct Measures.* Health risks such as blood pressure, cholesterol screening, and smoking.

Direct measures, such as health risks, have received a high degree of attention.[11] Employers are beginning to tie financial incentives to reducing personal health risks or to maintaining a good personal health risk profile. Such a direct approach, however, has problems: Hereditary and aging issues affect the health risks of individuals, swings in personal health can distort measurements on a daily basis, and confidentiality remains an ever-present issue.

Instead of focusing on personal health risks, employers could focus instead on the health risk profile of the covered population. In this approach, all employees have their health risks measured, but the feedback goes to employees on an individualized basis whereas the employer receives an overall report. For example, blood pressure levels can be represented as a group average and mean, a dispersion plot from low to high counts, and an exception analysis of problem blood pressure levels factoring in age and gender. The normalization thus created by a portfolio of individuals in a group limits the uncertainties inherent in data collection.

Health risk, an up-front indicator of health, provides a proactive means for addressing utilization. Utilization itself, however, measures the results of all health activities. As employees and dependents become more empowered and informed consumers, utilization becomes a more direct indicator of health activities and less an expression of sheer benefits consumption.

Traditionally, employers have done little to manage utilization proactively as they considered health care to be a personal matter. Instead, companies have reviewed utilization annually, at the time of health care plan requoting, or they have contracted with a third-party manager for utilization review and have placed some controls over patterns of excess utilization.

The fundamental weakness with this view is its binary aspect: Some utilization is bad, no utilization is good. It is a claims perspective transferred to employers from the world of insurance risk. Employers moving into direct experience rating and self-insurance need to question the applicability of certain insurance practices. A classic example is deductibles. Raising deductibles for vehicle and property insurance makes sense because an employer can cover the financial risk while still retaining insight into the nature of the claims. When it comes to health care, however, deductibles eliminate the submission of key claims data, thereby reducing utilization information. The exclusion of data limits insight into employee and dependent health patterns.

Cost-shifting trends and risk avoidance strategies have undermined employer control over health and disability costs. As employees' health care contributions have increased, more uncovered employees are working for organizations. And family deductibles ranging from $500 to $1000 eliminate claims for primary care. Often, employees submit claims for one year and then none in the next. The employee with this year's major medical problem may be someone who has been covered but has not submitted a claim for 18 months. Is the person who is not utilizing health care necessarily healthy? (Often nonutilizers are those in the worst health.) And even if care has been received, there is no motivation to submit a claim if repayment will not ensue. The end result is less consistent utilization data for a small percentage of employees and dependents, primarily for high-cost specialty care. Because of these factors, many employers are developing a health care coverage profile for employees that resembles the one shown in Table 4.3.

To control health and disability costs with a health intervention approach, employers need to stress utilization as the integrating information

Table 4.3 Employee Profile: Health Care Coverage

Status of Employee	Percentage of Employees
Employed, but not yet eligible	5
Eligible, but covered by another employer	5
Eligible, but opted out of coverage (may be uncovered)	5
Covered, but no claims submitted due to deductibles	25
Covered, but claims being submitted on a lag basis	40
Covered, claims being submitted in a timely manner	20
	100

mechanism. By eliminating barriers such as deductibles, complete and timely utilization data can be examined in many different ways: by provider, by procedure, by individual, and most importantly across the health continuum for types of general care (health programs, primary care, specialty care, rehabilitation). With this information, employers can develop utilization as an index of health value for the following factors:

1. Percentage of employees covered.
2. Percentage of covered employees and dependents utilizing care.
3. Average utilization per covered employee and dependent.
4. Percentage of utilization for specialty care not receiving primary care over prior year.
5. Percentage of utilization for specialty care not involved in health programs.
6. Percentage of employees and dependents receiving primary care.
7. Number and percentage of readmissions on specialty care.
8. Percentage of employees and dependents participating in health programs.

By focusing on the covered population, rather than on targeted individuals, employers can identify their employee and dependent health patterns and assess health and disability expenditures, targeting areas for improvement. It is essential to pinpoint the triggers for the care related to illness, injury, and disability. Internal and external programs can then be designed to solve critical utilization issues. Only when employers develop utilization information as an indicator of health value received will they gain control over all related costs.

Attacking the Root Causes of Utilization

Even with incomplete information, employers can still achieve considerable leverage over costs by addressing their current utilization patterns. Many organizations manage health care through plan design changes and the addition of specialized managed care services. Managed mental health and managed pharmaceuticals are two of the latest examples. Such approaches have some advantages, but the real need is to address causes.

Solutions to utilization problems require a focus on health itself that directly encompasses employees and dependents, line management, and providers. Identifying accountability for cause is the first level of analysis, as shown in Figure 4.4. Once accountability has been assigned, the next level of analysis is to separate preventable and nonpreventable causes. Finally, the preventable causes can be identified as recurring (for employees, dependents, line supervisors) and as readmissions (for providers).

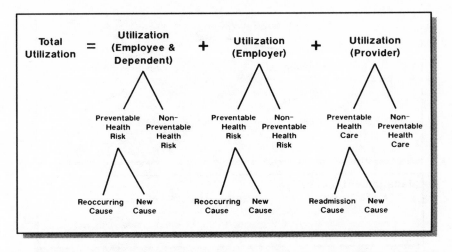

Figure 4.4   Health Care Utilization: Addressing Cause and Effect (RHM Systems, Inc., 1993, Marlboro, MA)

The initial response to this management approach will probably be that everything is in the hands of someone else, most especially providers. Once the employer reinforces the concept of personal accountability for health, cause and effect will more likely be traceable to employees and dependents themselves. For example, a poor rehabilitation outcome may have been attributed to a provider, but quite possibly the patient did not cooperate in the treatment plan. Non-compliance in the use of medications alone is a major source of waste. Also, there are many multicausal health issues.

To analyze utilization needs in depth, employers should first focus on high-risk, high-cost cases. As shown in Figure 4.5, management leverage is concentrated in these cases. Based on a general figure of 70 percent for preventable utilization and 70 percent for high-risk, high-cost cases, almost 49 percent of the direct costs get assigned to preventable high-risk, high-cost claims. And even the remaining 21 percent is a candidate for effective management. These figures will vary based on employer circumstances, but they do point out the cost leverage available from a limited number of cases.

An earlier referenced analysis of high-risk, high-cost smoking cases shows that the general savings from nonsmoking ($960 per employee) are not across the board. Rather a limited number of cases exhibit much higher costs, corroborating the profile of the major cost savings opportunity identified here.[12] Claims administration practice may cause employers to miss this opportunity. No claims may appear above a certain dollar threshold because of submitting multiple claims for the same case. For example, mild brain injury results in a hospital admission and $15,000 in charges. The individual is then discharged with a diagnosis of facial lacerations and a concussion. On the employee's return to work, problems develop; then the individual enters psychiatric care because of marital difficulties. Another

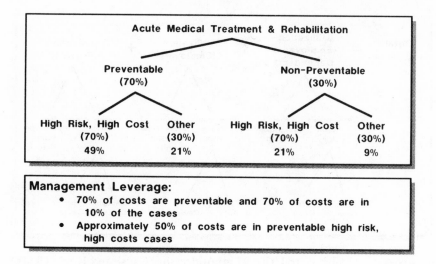

Figure 4.5 Health Care Utilization: Focusing on High-Risk, High-Cost Cases (RHM Systems, Inc., 1993, Marlboro, MA)

$15,000 is expended on a separate claim. In the meantime, the individual incurs $5,000 through the family physician for continual tests about lower back pain. All these costs, already totaling $35,000, relate to the undiagnosed and untreated brain injury. For this reason, multiple sequential claims need to be closely analyzed and included as a high-risk, high-cost opportunity. The high cost linkage between health care, workers' compensation, and disability also needs to be considered.[13]

Even with rigorous claims analysis, current activities may escape full evaluation on a risk management basis. Claims only provide a framework for addressing past utilization patterns—not even today's. Therefore, it is essential to assess activities that might potentially involve employees and dependents, line management, and provider. Proactive risk management has to occur before claims are submitted.

A major benefit of integrated risk management through health intervention is that the orientation toward health and the root causes of utilization naturally leads to health and safety risk and personal accountability. The goal then can be to integrate external health programs to support this accountability, a very different matter from acquiring another "program" on the care side to solve the latest problem.

Optimizing Health through Continuous Improvement

The cost/benefit of Managing Forward in terms of utilization can be expressed through an index of health value. The health continuum from health to illness and injury to disability can be weighted from 0 to 1.0. In Figure 4.6, an employer with a utilization profile of 0.8, heavily weighted

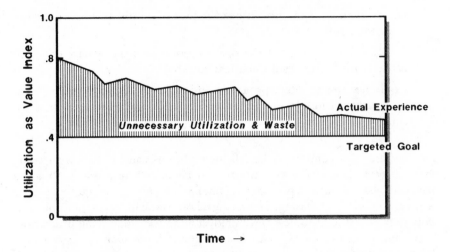

Figure 4.6 Continuous Improvement in Utilization (RHM Systems, Inc., 1993, Marlboro, MA)

toward treatment, decides to target improvement at 0.4, heavily weighted toward health.

As with any investment in operations, returns are not obtained from broad strategic plans, but are achieved one step at a time. Some of the gains will come quickly and others over time. The key is to galvanize and focus organizational commitment in the right strategic direction within a management framework that encourages systematic and continuous savings.

Traditional utilization review looks at care as the issue and then adds management programs to contain problems. Utilization based on risk management through health intervention provides, instead, an optimal index of health value. Improving utilization from 0.8 to 0.4 does not mean eliminating care, but rather developing the right health activities including the most timely and best possible care.

There is no perfect index of health value as health and care activities will depend on the characteristics of the covered population. Are employees and dependents in good or bad health? Are they dependent or empowered in workplace and nonworkplace behaviors? Such factors will influence the pattern of utilization even as the goal is to manage health forward along the health continuum.

The questions asked in a traditional utilization review—"Is this appropriate?" and "Is this medically necessary?"—may be essential for some cases, but such questions are inadequate because they are inherently reactive. In contrast, the health intervention approach frames the following questions:

- How can health be better managed?
- Did health care and management produce an optimal outcome?

- Did treatment of the health need reduce or eliminate the probability of future care?
- Did health care occur at the optimal point or could it have occurred earlier with better results and less costs?
- Could health and safety programs and management supports have anticipated the causes with relevant information and services at the right time?

The advantage of continuous health interventions can be seen with rising pharmaceutical costs. The traditional, and beneficial, response is to add a managed pharmaceutical program to obtain the cost advantage of generic drugs and volume purchasing. The savings, however, will represent a one-time reduction in cost levels unless the employer addresses underlying utilization.

An intervention approach based on employee interests involves reducing drug usage in general. As part of personal health management, employees and dependents require information that all drugs involve risk, most notably in terms of side effects. Medications serve many useful purposes, but the inherent need can be reduced by taking a broader perspective. For example, certain drugs for blood pressure have documented cost/benefit for reducing health risks and related health care costs. The real cost savings, however, come from reducing the health risks themselves through diet and exercise. Long-term drug usage is extremely costly for employers and harmful for some employees and dependents. The connection between this health risk effort and substance abuse problems in the workplace should not be underestimated.

Emergency room admissions illustrate a continuous health intervention involving providers. When an employer experiences an increase in the cost of such utilization from $200,000 per year to $400,000 per year, the traditional approach is to place cost penalties on such admissions. The message employees receive from this type of control is that employer and third-party managers are not concerned about quality care.

An alternative response would be to optimize such admissions through continuous improvement so that the emergency room is used only for true emergencies. Usage patterns may indicate admissions are mostly for young dependents during evenings and for male employees who do not have a primary care physician. In reviewing the dependent care issue with employees, it becomes apparent there are really two problems: child illness that can only be handled during nonwork hours and a high rate of home injuries involving children. So what originally appeared to be an uncontrollable health care problem begins to have solutions. With a largely single-parent work force, the employer initiates flextime, identifying the child health care issue as one of its purposes.

Quality treatment through a primary care physician is then stressed as one of the valid uses of early morning and late afternoon flextime, for parents with children. The intervention continues with follow-up education and training on home safety, personal health management, and optimal use of health care. As a result, emergency room utilization is reduced from $400,000 to $180,000 per year with $30,000 spent for primary care (an emergency room admission is conservatively six times more expensive than an office visit). And employees have now received a strong message that quality care matters and that it is inextricably linked to personal health.

By stressing a continuous improvement approach to the health of individuals and the covered population, employers can manage both cost and quality effectively. Proactively managing utilization toward health requires attention in the following areas:

- Health and safety risks.
- Effectiveness of health programs.
- Costly patterns of poor health.
- Costly patterns of poor health care.
- Effectiveness of health care and disability programs.
- Costly patterns of disability.

The benefit for organizations will be systematic achievement of cost savings by involving all parties in the management solution.

Cost of Health

Many factors can complicate paybacks from health investments including the following common problems:

1. The covered population fluctuates both in terms of absolute participation and intensity and longevity of participation.
2. A generalized health program may not meet the specific needs of an employer's covered population.
3. Health programs run by providers can splinter the covered population. Also, assessing program effectiveness can be affected by different provider methodologies.
4. Causes not controlled by the health programs may influence utilization decision making.
5. Random health events can distort analysis over short-term periods.
6. Health program effectiveness may be compromised by a health care plan that does not promote health as a goal in care activities (e.g., it covers only medically necessary procedures).
7. Cost-sharing features may undermine incentives to up-front health interventions.

8. Line supervisors and work colleagues can connote a stigma to accessing health programs.

This assessment of health programs suggests that programs alone are not the answer. Few employers can fully forecast next year's health risks as employees are hired, fired, and retired. The solution is to develop a strategically focused, yet broad-based and ongoing effort that influences the health activities of employees and dependents, line management, providers, and even third-party managers as involved parties.

Before considering paybacks, employers need to identify the total cost of health activities. Companies usually have some obvious programs such as health risk management and proactive management of high-risk pregnancies. Other health activities may take place but are not currently classified as health related. Health features are embedded within health care coverages and disability management programs. Other activities may be supported through human resources or even risk management. Encompassing all health activities into a cost of health allows an organization to bring an integrated commitment to health as a corporate value and an investment priority. The activities or programs in the cost of health include:

- Wellness, employee assistance program, mental health, and safety.
- Education and training in health awareness, self-care, and optimal use of health care.
- Health and safety risk management.
- Certain health care coverages—annual physical, health club fitness benefit, and primary care.
- Disability management features—return to work.
- Loss control programs—back and repetitive motion issues.

It is necessary to review the components of all internal and external programs and assignments of line and functional management. Many are health related but unfortunately are approached in terms of negative compliance or damage control. "Controlling losses" in risk management presents the same negative perspective to employees and line management as does "containing costs" in health care. Greater organizational commitment is possible when improvement of health is presented as a common concern.

When developing the total cost of health, the emphasis need not be on accounting precision. Some costs can be identified through normal financial reporting mechanisms, but at first, many others will need to be approximated. The purpose is to develop an understanding of health activities and related costs to optimize this investment. Some redundant efforts may be occurring while some obvious gaps may become apparent. Often programs are funded at a level to make them operational, but not truly effective.

Building upon the total cost of health and disability concept, costs can be realigned away from traditional lines of coverage into a strategic cost management framework consisting of the cost of health, cost of care, and cost of productivity. As shown in Table 4.4, the cost of health encompasses all the health, safety, and disability efforts within an organization whether done internally or externally. Certain features in health care coverage need to be placed in this cost category. The remaining health care costs plus the care costs included in workers' compensation make up the next category, the cost of care (fully presented in Chapter 5, Managing Care). Finally, the cost of productivity consists of disability pay-outs and settlements in both workers' compensation and disability plus all the health and disability costs in operations (fully presented in Chapter 6, Managing Productivity). When organizations are experience-rated or self-insured, they have an ability to manage total health and disability costs strategically.

Obtaining a payback from a health investment requires an integrated mechanism to define all the health-related activities influencing employees and dependents and line management. By separating costs into health, care, and productivity elements, return on investment can be identified and used for management. The critical difference is that the investment is in health— a goal that can unite all within an organization.

Return on Investment—
The Cost/Benefit of an Intervention Approach

The benefit of an intervention approach lies in the broad range of activities defined along the health continuum. In addition to participating in health programs, employees and dependents are engaged throughout the whole continuum as are line management in certain areas. Where employers have achieved compelling paybacks, the common message appears to be that an organizational commitment to health and safety is driving the benefits of the overall program. Certainly, individual efforts to stay within cultural norms directly influence participation and level of commitment.

Table 4.4 Health and Disability Strategic Cost Management Framework

	Health	Care	Productivity	Total
Premium/claims	—	$	$	$
Health, safety, and disability programs	$	—	—	$
External mgt./admin.	$	$	$	$
Internal mgt./admin.	$	$	$	$
Overtime/replacement staffing	—	—	$	$
Absenteeism/paid time off	—	—	$	$
Lost productivity	—	—	$	$
Other	—	—	$	$
Total	$	$	$	$

Simple comparisons of programs for an intervention approach do not capture the full cost/benefits because they are essentially three dimensional. When health activities are moved forward, each intervention translates into a reduction in subsequent health and care activities. The actual movement of activities forward will vary.

For one person, increased health awareness may eliminate unnecessary visits to a family physician. For another person, a new relationship with a primary care physician may provide the impetus for joining a wellness program, preventing serious heart and stress problems. And for another person, an awareness of self-care results in active participation in a goal-directed rehabilitation program avoiding a drawn-out rehabilitation effort.

Each time a health event is moved forward, the probability of future care decreases, with individualized cost savings that reflect personal health circumstances. Savings are thus derived from a change in severity and duration at each stage as well as from a reduction in frequency. Figure 4.7 shows these cumulative benefits.

An intervention approach optimizes the health investment while reducing potential care and related productivity losses along the health continuum. This combination translates into three critical direct benefits:

1. Lowered frequency, severity, and duration of illness, injury, and disability.

2. Optimized utilization of health, health care, and disability programs throughout the health continuum.

3. Emphasis on up-front health interventions versus back-end medical care interventions.

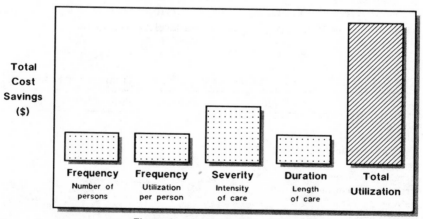

Figure 4.7 Health Interventions: The Results of Strategy-Based Management (RHM Systems, Inc., 1993, Marlboro, MA)

By assessing health and care activities along the health continuum, an organization can manage health through return on investment (ROI), which is the basis of a strategic cost management framework. Defining the cost of health for an organization separates the total health investment from the care and productivity implications. (Chapter 6 reviews ROI application for rehabilitation. Return on Investment is further developed as a management tool in Chapter 7.)

The groundwork is thus established for analyzing health programs, first based on value added to optimize their effectiveness; and second, based on the related return on investment. Investing in health does not just represent new dollars for new programs. The employer must take a hard look at all existing internal and external programs in terms of need and effectiveness, as shown in Table 4.5.

Cost savings can be identified as a reduction in the costs of care and productivity. Specific accountability can be established by program and/or program feature and then tracked over time. The purpose is to develop an overall program meeting the employer's most important needs while obtaining the greatest degree of effectiveness, based on return on investment in health. For example, an annual physical might be dropped until employees are trained in obtaining a health benefit from this program. An on-site testing program might replace physicals until the implementation of quality primary care.

By ranking both current and potential programs and related management, the employer develops the optimal overall health and disability program. The result is to leverage spending in the areas of greatest cost exposure and cost savings opportunity. Certain individual programs, however, may be essential to the overall program so their paybacks may need to be assessed in terms of the total effort.

Table 4.5 Strategic Cost Management through Health Investment

Program or Program Feature	Investment in Health	Cost Savings Current Period	Cost Savings Future Periods
Current			
Program 1	$	$	$
Program 2	$$	$$	$$
Program 3	$	$$	$$
Program 4	$$	$	$
Program 5	$$$	$$	$$$$
Program 6	$$	$$	$$$$
Potential			
Program 1	$	$	$$
Program 2	$	$$	$$$$

Table 4.6 shows how this investment-oriented approach can be further developed into a strategic cost management framework patterned after the total cost of quality employed in total quality management.

The goal is to optimize the health investment while reducing the cost of poor health. Although the cost of care can decline significantly, the strategy is not reduction per case, but optimization through a value approach. Productivity losses are another major cost savings target. The end result is an organization achieving major savings throughout its cost structure with an integrated view of all its health activities.

Health—The Fullest Expression of Systematic Quality

A large measure of the long-sought-after solution to health care and workers' compensation costs relates to restating the problem. Whereas managed care alone may have once been the answer, the greatest degree of leverage over both costs and quality can now be gained by managing health. Proactive interventions move employers forward on the health continuum ahead of a health care system oriented toward late-stage treatment for illness, injury, and disability and complex treatment interdependencies. Increased employer control over costs is the result in a system in which 10 percent of the cases create 70 percent of the costs,[14,15] and only 1 percent of the population generates 30 percent of all costs and 5 percent generates about 50 percent.[16]

Greater control over health events results in greater control over health care and workers' compensation utilization. Less frequency, less severity, and shorter duration mean less chance of unnecessary care and possible litigation. Similarly, the probability of future care declines as the number of transactions decline and intensity of each transaction diminishes. This systematic methodology for managing utilization based on risk management provides improved cost predictability while controlling and eventually reducing costs.

Systematic management of health involves continuous improvement of both cost and quality of care. This health approach creates a direct employer–

Table 4.6 Health in Total Cost of Quality Terms

| | Cost in Dollars | | |
	Current	Targeted	Strategy
Investment in health:			
Cost of health	$ 1,500	$1,700	Optimize
Cost of poor health:			
Cost of care	4,000	3,200	Optimize
Cost of productivity	4,500	3,500	Optimize
Total cost of health and disability	$10,000	$8,400	Reduce

employee bond that becomes the means for addressing the seemingly intractable health care and workers' compensation problems. Health is the basis for increased personal and organizational productivity and quality levels, and ultimately, for reduced costs.

$$\begin{matrix} \text{Organizational} \\ \text{Health} \end{matrix} \rightarrow \text{Productivity} \rightarrow \text{Quality} \rightarrow \begin{matrix} \text{Reduced Health and} \\ \text{Disability Costs} \end{matrix}$$

$$\begin{matrix} \text{Personal} \\ \text{Health} \end{matrix} \rightarrow \begin{matrix} \text{Personal} \\ \text{Productivity} \end{matrix} \rightarrow \begin{matrix} \text{Personal Quality} \\ \text{of Life} \end{matrix} \rightarrow \begin{matrix} \text{Reduced Contribution} \\ \text{for Health Care} \end{matrix}$$

Employers have much of the leverage over health and disability costs in their own hands. But they must link organizational health and personal health to fully involve employees and dependents in achieving the long-awaited solutions.

References

1. Brook, R., RAND Fellow. June 9, 1990. In Chambliss, L., & Reier, S., How doctors have ruined health care. *Financial World,* pp. 46–52.

2. Lynch, W. D., Teitelbaum, H. S., & Main, D. S. 1992. Comparing medical costs by analyzing high cost cases. *American Journal of Health Promotion,* 6(3): 206–213.

3. Webb, J. 1992. Commercial Corporation Fitness Management Program, California Polytechnic State University at San Luis Obispo.

4. Bertera, R. L. 1991. The effects of behavioral risks on absenteeism and health care costs in the workplace. *Journal of Occupational Medicine,* 33(11): 1119–1124.

5. Kottke, T. E. January 1992. Commentary: The "Intervention Index": Insufficient Information, *Journal of Clinical Epidemiology,* 45(1): 17–19.

6. Schwartz, G. E., Watson, D. S., Galvin, D. E., & Lipoff, E. Fall 1989. *The disability management sourcebook* (p. 35). Washington Business Group on Health's Institute for Rehabilitation and Disability Management (reference to Mutual of Omaha Insurance Company, 1988).

7. NIOSH Director Millar speaks out on trends in the health and safety industry. October 1992. *Occupational Health and Safety,* pp. 26–27.

8. Mulry, R. 1992. Five steps to controlling back injury costs. *Professional Safety,* December 1992, pp. 24–26.

9. Eriksen, M. P., Green, L. W., & Flutz, F. G. 1988. Principles of changing health behavior. *Cancer,* 62: 1768–1775.

10. Ibid.

11. Milliman & Robertson, Inc., 1987. *Health Risks and Behavior: The Impact on Medical Costs,* a joint study by Control Data Corporation and Milliman & Robertson.

12. Lynch, Teitelbaum, & Main. Comparing Medical Costs.

13. Gardner, H. H., & Butler, R. June 1992. Employee Health Benefits Expenditure Patterns by Pareto Group, Gardner & Associates.

14. Schecter, S. M. 1991. Managing health care costs by managing high cost illness. *Human Resource Health Institute,* pp. 1–8.

15. Garfinkel, S., Riley, G. F., & Iannacchione, V. G. 1988. High cost users of medical care. *Health Care Financing Review,* 9(4), pp. 41–52.

16. Light, D. W. Spring 1992. Excluding More, Covering Less: The Health Insurance Industry in the U.S., *Health/PAC Bulletin,* 22(1), pp. 7–13.

Resources

Bardwick, J. M. 1991. *Danger in the comfort zone: From boardroom to mailroom how to break the entitlement habit that's killing American business.* New York: AMACOM.

Harrington, H. J. 1987. *The improvement process: How America's leading companies improve quality.* New York: McGraw-Hill.

Matejka, K. 1990. *Why this horse won't drink: How to win—and keep—employee commitment.* New York: AMACOM.

5

Managing Care: A Systematic Approach to Obtaining Value

Managed Care remains an elusive concept. Before care can be managed, organizations require a definition of care itself to understand the full array of potential activities and related accountabilities. Care is defined here as the sum total of treatment and living activities to recover or maintain health, performed by providers (professionals), employees, dependents, and employers. Living represents the broad spectrum of work and home issues such as transportation, diet, safety, and fitness.

With this understanding in place, organizations are in a position to obtain value for services based on a system of management. For some time, management has been the watchword in health care, and now workers' compensation is getting the same type of attention. Controlling costs involves a wide variety of managed care networks and specialized management services. However, management can be quite unsystematic despite all these controls.

Most organizations operate based on a system of controls. The strategic plan and the operating plan define broad-based performance objectives and internal resource allocations, whereas budgets define the related commitments for departments and project teams. Even then, internal approvals provide further control over expenditures throughout the cash disbursement cycle.

Similar performance goal setting backed by controls does not exist for broad system issues related to health care and workers' compensation. Coverages and procedure codes operate as licenses to spend while costs are "contained" through the efforts of third-party managers. And the most important participant in the care transaction—employee or dependent, as patient—often is uninvolved in closing the control loop, either by verifying the services or assessing the quality of care.

Systematic management of both health care and workers' compensation becomes attainable when employers move past a reliance on "plans" and "programs" for cost solutions. Cost containment rooted in the concept of the budget as a grant to spend can give way to the concept of the budget as a baseline for improving performance. Optimization of performance in cost and quality terms can thereby be addressed as a strategic issue.

This chapter presents a systems approach to controlling costs that emphasizes managing the linkages between health, health care, and disability programs and on the interconnections within the system. Managed care tends to stress the stages of treatment as measured by procedure codes and lengths of stay. Real leverage over costs, however, requires managing the quality of the interconnections on a case basis with an emphasis on total costs and ultimate outcomes. Otherwise, all the intervening stages of treatment may be monitored and produce "good" outcomes, yet the final result is poor—the patient does not return to independent living activities or productivity at work.

A value-based approach to cost management complements this case orientation. Using a systematic set of factors to assess services and providers ensures management of all aspects of cost and quality. Underlying this value approach are the health intervention strategy elements of early intervention and outcomes, combined with quality care. As a result, Managing Forward does not stop when treatment begins.

An empowered health consumer thus becomes an empowered patient with major benefits enabling the employer to manage costs while providing for the best quality care. This health emphasis drives the cost and quality benefits of a value-based approach to Managing Care.

Implementing a Systems Approach to Managing Care

Employers who use up-front management interventions sometimes think controlling health care and workers' compensation activities is impossible once an employee gets into the "system." They tend to believe the only hope then is to employ cost containment to control the medical processes employed. This valid concern can be overcome through systematic management.

A systems approach to Managing Care includes the following steps:

1. Develop an overall system encompassing care activities through the specification and use of information (see Chapter 7).
2. Define a strategic profile of optimal care expenditures and then identify methods for reaching that goal based on continuous improvement mechanisms.
3. Optimize coverages with an emphasis on prevention and rehabilitation. Formulation of coverages is where a strategic analysis of risks

and cost/benefit can promote the benefit of utilizing various forms of preventive care and rehabilitation across a covered population. Similarly, experimental medical procedures and related drugs can be assessed in advance based on appropriate expert advice.

4. Ensure that quality local and regional services back up the coverages based on performance standards. Develop quality services for workers' compensation cases as well, promoting availability to employees.

5. Measure and manage performance on a case basis, not a claims basis, utilizing information proactively.

6. Utilize a value-based approach to cost management that emphasizes linkage between health and health care.

7. Fully engage patients in co-managing treatment through a proactive form of risk management.

Quality management services from third parties are essential to obtaining and maintaining employer control, but even more crucial is the role of employees and dependents in managing their personal health and in optimally accessing health care. In addition, employers need to drive the system toward quality by rewarding provider excellence. In this way, care can move toward a new performance level based on value representing a combination of cost and quality.

The Health Continuum as a System for Linking Health and Care

Care is often managed as a discrete event—as if there was no prior health history and would be no future follow-on care. Providers of acute medical care focus on stepping down treatment to an end point, generally a discharge home, and devote relatively little attention to the patient's health status at this end point. Such patients may vary widely in their state of health despite having similar surgical outcomes. The health care delivery system assumes health is an input and care is the output. In fact, the opposite is true. To achieve value, care must be the input and health, the output. This perspective places present and potential patients at the center of the health system.

The health continuum can then supplant the treatment continuum as a closed loop system. In Figure 5.1, all health and care activities are oriented toward maintaining someone in or returning that person to a normal healthy state. Visualizing health care as a closed loop tied to health underscores the cause-and-effect relationship between health and health care (and disability). Prevention and early diagnosis through personal health management, self-care, primary care, and health and safety programs keep employees and dependents from incurring the personal trauma and related costs of acute medical treatment and rehabilitation. Optimized treatment

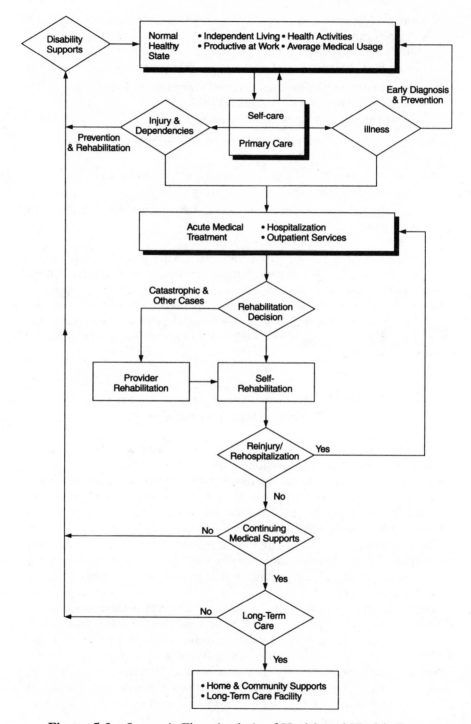

Figure 5.1   Strategic Flow Analysis of Health and Health Care

returns individuals to normal living and away from rehospitalization, long-term care, and dependency in general.

Conceptualizing the health continuum as a system permits easier identification of early intervention and outcome strategies. Treatment activities have value when they return someone to a healthy state and from patient to nonpatient status. And optimizing outcomes and health status in general involves comprehensive health interventions by all participants. Both health and health care are thereby linked in the same manner as in the earlier representation of utilization as an index of health value.

The critical cost pressure points in Figure 5.1 create the justification for a return on investment strategy. Up-front health interventions such as timely annual physicals as part of primary care can reduce the probability of costly treatment, thereby creating cost savings. The internal loops of continuing care in the figure graphically depict situations that do not result in a return to a healthy state.

At the time of overall program development, it is necessary to have an investment approach that strategically commits funding at the critical cost leverage points. Competent internal or third-party management also needs to be engaged at each stage of the health continuum. Information feedback can then provide the basis for ongoing management. Also critical are supports and incentives for employee and dependent participation in up-front health interventions.

Return on investment analysis brings all the cost management elements together. The goal is to invest in health through activities that prevent, intervene, and produce outcomes matching the generalized needs of an employer-specific population. Apart from investing, reductions in costs may be possible through continuous improvement mechanisms and utilization of optimal service environments such as inpatient, outpatient, community, and home environments.

Accountabilities also need to be identified for providers of all types of health, health care, and disability services. Those who do not perform, as evidenced through information, should be replaced systematically; those who do should be rewarded through risk-sharing mechanisms.

When adopting a systems approach, one other critical cost issue stands out—the interconnections in the health continuum. Health status and the quality of care depend on many interconnections:

- Primary care is the linchpin of overall care management and a means for reinforcing health behaviors with patients.[1] The primary care physician should be a facilitator, not a gatekeeper.
- Provider performance at a particular stage of treatment may depend on the performance of earlier providers (e.g., a poor surgical outcome can limit the outcomes targeted in rehabilitation).
- Provider performance at a particular stage of treatment can compromise the performance of later providers (e.g., a poor rehabilitation outcome can mask the outcomes achieved in acute medical treatment).

- The actions and behaviors of the patient can compromise provider performance (e.g., a surgical outcome can be undermined by poor patient physical and mental condition at the time of surgery and by a lack of self-care follow-up such as personal rehabilitation).
- Provider performance may depend on the patient history and clinical documentation provided by other providers.

These factors are critical to both managing cost and quality of care. Understanding and dealing with the quality of interconnections within the system represents a major management opportunity. A flexible, fluid system requires smoothly moving patients through cooperative provider efforts. A static network incurs excess costs throughout all the interconnection points and compromises responsiveness to the patient and family.

Optimizing Coverages—The Real Plan Design Issue

With self-insured health care plans, employers can develop integrated, health-oriented coverages. Freed of the burden of imposed state coverage requirements, employers can integrate health, health care, and disability programs; yet many do not. Coverages often represent only medical care because prevention and rehabilitation fail to meet a "medical necessity" standard for inclusion in coverage.[2, 3, 4]

Even within medical care coverage, group-rated policies have tended to include more exclusion clauses for preexisting conditions or for eliminating a wide range of health issues. So even as rates have increased, the value of coverages being purchased are declining.[5] Some of these coverage practices transfer to the type of coverages included in experience rated and self-insured plans offered by insurers and TPAs. Many health care plans do not fully meet modern health issues, providing limited medical care coverage only. Workers' compensation basic coverages tend to follow trends in medical practice. Restricting payment to treatment only is a prescription for continual cost increases.

Past coverage limitations conversely create a cost reduction opportunity.[6] A well-managed investment in prevention, rehabilitation, and other coverages can drive down the costs of acute medical treatment, as shown in Figure 5.2.[7] The figure shows a consumer-oriented health care system. Employers, employees, and dependents, as consumers, need comprehensive and integrated coverages. Also, an investment in prevention and rehabilitation transforms technology into a proactive force to enhance health, deemphasizing its use in acute medical treatment because there is less need. Strategic coverage of technology should be based on the cost/benefit assessment of varied prevention applications, as well as productivity supports in return-to-work programs for employees with a disability.

Coverages frequently receive attention only when cost problems develop. Mental health and substance abuse services have reached 10 percent of

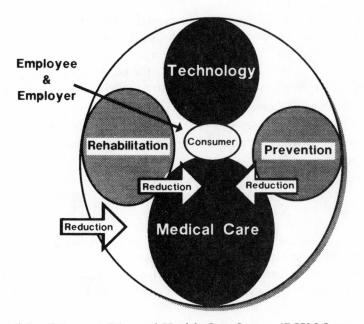

Figure 5.2 Consumer Directed Health Care System (RHM Systems, Inc., 1993, Marlboro, MA)

health care costs, so many employers are now reacting by capping benefits at lower levels in terms of dollars or lengths of stay in a facility.[8] So just when employees and dependents may be needing certain services, coverages are cut. A more effective approach is to assess and manage utilization based on continuous improvement to health. A problem in one area often means there are problems in other areas: Excess mental health utilization may be a reaction to staff reductions, a major change in work scheduling, or a reduction in hiring standards for an extra shift; or the problem may relate to new employees in general, not to well-tenured employees. What appears to be a trend may be a temporary aberration that merits an operational response, not a change in coverage.

Managing the causes of health and disability costs and the quality of underlying activities needs to take priority over coverages. Even without frequent coverage changes, a plan may be difficult for most employees to understand. As a result, decisions between health care coverage options often focus on first-dollar coverage and the lack of claims forms, not the serious issues of specialty care and rehabilitation. Employers must assess these issues carefully in designing coverages and discuss the options thoroughly when open enrollment occurs. Knowledge about coverage can reinforce the importance of personal involvement in health risks as well as in cost sharing, thereby directing employees firmly into better personal health management.

Employers need to assess coverages in the following areas:

- Identify gaps or limitations in coverage by tracing a flow of the most common and expensive cases (not claims) through the system on a prospective basis.

- Specifically consider disability issues for health care coverage (e.g., the use of vocational rehabilitation to support return to work).

- Analyze the impact of regional cost differences on the relative value of all coverages (for employers operating in multiple regions).

- Compare existing or alternate health care plans based on coverage differences.

- Assess the cost/benefit of changing or adding coverages, such as workers' compensation issues or a carve-out or add-on to an existing managed care plan.

Once well-formulated coverages are in place, employers should try to keep health care plans intact. Frequent changes are costly; there is a far greater cost/benefit in concentrating funds and communication time on training employees in personal health management and optimal access of health care.

Developing Services and Networks

Many new health care services have developed during the past 20 years to decrease inpatient treatment of acute medical conditions. Outpatient hospital and clinic care are widely used alternatives for surgical procedures. Even hospitalized patients are stepped down to a subacute facility when their condition stabilizes but their care needs remain complex. The cost differentials for these alternate care environments vary by medical procedures and by region of the country, but a cost differential of 2 or 3 times can exist between inpatient and outpatient care, inpatient and sub-acute care, and acute and postacute rehabilitation.

In a rush to capture cost differentials through a step-down form of cost containment, there has been a tendency to ignore the fundamental issue as to whether acute medical treatment in total is being controlled. Between 1988 and 1992, inpatient procedures were slightly down from 12.4 million to 12.0 million, whereas outpatient procedures increased from 9.5 million to 11.5 million. In total, the number of procedures still increased 1.6 million or 7 percent over those 5 years. Now, home care is being promoted.

In the meantime, costs have continued to rise. Among a large group of community hospitals totaling $217.1 billion in annual operating expenses in the latest reporting period, inpatient expense rose $25.3 billion or 18 percent from 1988 through 1990. At the same time, admissions dipped slightly and surgical operations increased only 3 percent. Outpatient visits, however, increased by 10 percent. A review of a longer time frame for the entire decade shows that inpatient days declined initially, but leveled off by 1988 with the underlying costs unaffected thereafter by efforts to control spending.[9] Essentially, any benefit of reducing admissions and lengths of stay had been exhausted. How are health care costs going to come down with this type of utilization pattern and cost control? The only way to attack this issue is to manage an organization's total care profile through a systems approach.

Table 5.1 summarizes the range of services making up the treatment continuum. The generalized treatment environments are acute medical treatment, acute rehabilitation, postacute rehabilitation, home treatment, and long-term care. Despite many new services, health care is just beginning to move away from a facilities-oriented view of treatment and long-term care because services have developed within and around such facilities. Many are extensions of hospitals, and nursing homes have responded similarly, taking younger patients with varying long-term care needs such as brain injury or stroke. Rehabilitation therapies are often tacked onto hospital or nursing home treatment programs. Much of the treatment has collected around facilities with certificates of need (CON) authorizing them to handle medically dependent patients. Funding sources using medical necessity as a funding criterion combined with a one-year policy perspective perpetuate this facility-based, medically oriented approach.

Even though patients are stepped down in treatment intensity away from hospitals, the orientation remains mostly medical. Outpatient care may save on the cost of room and board, but the treatment is still in a facility and medical necessity is the treatment criterion. This approach has advantages for medically oriented procedures, but when the care includes rehabilitation, facility-based treatment can be inherently limited. Patients require

Table 5.1   The Treatment Continuum

Acute Medical Treatment	Acute Rehabilitation	Postacute Rehabilitation	Home-Based Treatment	Long-Term Care
Inpatient hospital	Inpatient rehabilitation hospital	Outpatient rehabilitation hospital	Continuing medical treatment	Skilled nursing facility
Outpatient hospital	Inpatient hospital program	Outpatient hospital program	In-home rehabilitation program	Attendant care in home
Outpatient clinic		Residential program— group home	Hospice	Supported & assisted living—group home
Subacute facility		Residential program— apartment		Supported & assisted living— apartment
		Day treatment program		

treatment goals that emphasize individual functioning, not medical necessity, and that encompass environmental issues as well as physical ones. Better management of this interconnection between acute medical treatment and the world of living and work is a key cost leverage point. (Chapter 6 covers this issue in detail.)

Home (or a long-term care facility), the end point to treatment, is being reached in less time than in the past. Cost containment emphasizes transfers between alternate treatment environments to move a patient quickly to home. From 1980 to 1990, lengths of stay in hospitals have declined by 0.9 days or 12 percent. However, mix factors in the totals disguise declines of 2.6 days or 27 percent for heart disease and 1.0 days or 26 percent for child delivery.[10] Day and percentage change reductions are even greater for acute rehabilitation employed for serious care needs which often result in a disability. Patients are coming home faster, creating major implications for employers exposed to costs for more than a one-year policy period. Experience-rated or self-insured risks must look at the total costs per case. A transfer home is no end point if the patient ends up being readmitted or continues to access treatment. Services are often utilized on a piecemeal basis (e.g., physical therapy) without a goal-oriented treatment plan. Costs are rising today because of these undermanaged cases and nonoptimal outcomes.

Employers must understand and manage these service issues to achieve excellence in cost and quality. The following factors are critical:

- The increased availability of services identifies the need to manage cases, not just to deliver medical procedures. Advantages of a managed case approach include starting treatment in the lowest cost, clinically appropriate environment, and then accessing subsequent care in the optimal environments. Flexible management can involve bypassing stages of treatment while increasing the time and intensity of care in other stages. This is a better value-added form of management than just shortening inpatient stays at each stage of treatment.

- The complexity of the treatment continuum points out the increased importance of managing the interconnections within the system. Smoothly coordinated transfers between facilities and to home prevent wasted treatment time and are critical in achieving an optimal outcome.

- The drive to get a patient home is implicitly assumed to save money because each step of treatment is less costly. However, managing the financial obligations to the discharge home is not the same as achieving an outcome. Employers funding costly acute medical treatment often do not receive the full benefit of ending care needs combined with a return to work.

- Home itself now demands increased attention. Because of working spouses and an increase in unmarried persons in the work force, fewer patients have natural long-term home supports. Resolving care needs on high-risk, high-cost cases requires management of these issues. A critical distinction is the difference between delivering medical services to the home and developing an integrated care plan that supports a patient at various levels and with nonmedical services, often through community resources.

- The concentration of costs in the treatment continuum and the related management issues indicate the advantage of preventing the need for acute medical treatment and subsequent rehabilitation. The fundamental goal is to prevent illness and injury so as to eliminate the need for any type of "bed." Employers cannot be liable for costs if services are not accessed in the first place.

These are the issues causing so much of today's health and disability costs in a system in which 10 percent of the cases represent 70 percent of the costs.[11,12] Turning this cost threat into a cost opportunity requires a strategic approach to managing care based on the following step-by-step process:

1. *Coverage.* Develop an integrated health, health care, and disability framework.
2. *Services.* Develop a range of services to meet a comprehensive view of potential care needs.
3. *Network.* Ensure integration of coverage and services, backed by a well-managed group of quality providers.
4. *Standards.* Establish terms and conditions in relationships with third party managers and providers which emphasize performance.

The importance of quality care can be seen in the attention now beginning to be given to improving access to primary care. Obtaining quality in primary care is not simply a matter of reallocating funding or eliminating disincentives. Many persons now receive primary care from a specialist, not from an internist or family practitioner. Also, patients can be screened from developing a personal relationship by a nurse practitioner gatekeeper. Excess testing and less feedback on health issues are a natural outcome from such relationships. Employers therefore need to probe into the underlying quality of care activities as they systematically develop services.

Once this structure is in place, employers can focus on procuring value-added management services with care goals that include final outcomes. This will allow the clinical professionals to manage their areas of accountability while employers establish a standard of value from the beginning.

Achieving Accountability for Performance— Managing Cases, Not Claims

To obtain performance, it is necessary to stand back and assess current care practices, but employers first need to establish a system of control. An important way to gain some control is to involve employee and dependent in verifying receipt of services through an incentive mechanism for detecting billing errors. Even then, funneling funds into a system solely based on premiums or claims paid does not provide effective controls over spending. Third-party managers often review utilization and cost levels by studying after-the-fact claims; if the review is on a prospective basis, treatment is generally already underway. There are often no mechanisms to establish expectancies for types of treatment and related spending on a case basis. Instead, controls are placed over an individual procedure, thereby monitoring a discrete event at one point in time with limited control over interrelated treatment activities.

Controlling health care at the point of a claim is really no control at all. Generally, health has been left unmanaged until care is necessary. Treatment has then already occurred when a claim is submitted. Generation of a claim is based on a physician's signature, and other than a diagnostic code and reasonable and customary charges, methods for assessing it may be limited. By the time treatment is underway, a provider's clinical expertise has already influenced the patient. Even cost containment through third-party review involves after-the-fact inspection by similarly trained medical staff. Is it a wonder that almost all second surgical opinions are confirming?

Claims management is a critical link in today's management of health care and workers' compensation. Unfortunately, claims are viewed as a point of control rather than as a point of information. True control only comes in the actions and behaviors of both provider and patient. For this reason, employers need to consider claims in terms of the quality of the overall claims system and related transactions. More important is whether a system of control exists to ensure timely quality data. (Chapter 7 covers information issues in detail.) In addition, interactions with employees and dependents must be based on an overriding customer service orientation. Problems with claims often jeopardize the employer–employee relationship—and provide a natural breeding ground for poor employee perceptions and even litigation.

Establishing control over treatment requires Managing Forward toward health so that treatment decisions can be made when the individual has a greater range of choices. These increasing levels of control can be defined as follows:

1. At claims submission.
2. Across the treatment continuum.
3. At access of treatment.
4. At time of diagnosis (unhealthy condition).
5. At time of diagnosis (healthy condition).
6. Through participation in health programs.
7. Through education and training in health and health care.
8. Through health awareness.

Developing health-conscious employees and dependents has a direct benefit in controlling treatment activities. Health knowledge and appropriate training transfer into care knowledge.[13,14] The fundamental task is to deal with the underlying health and safety risks that extend throughout treatment as follows:

1. Health risk management.
2. Safety risks—work and nonwork activities.
3. Self-care.
4. Early diagnosis.
5. Least evasive forms of treatment.
6. Understanding of drug side effects.
7. Self-rehabilitation.
8. Supports in living and work in cases of disability.

Risk management is the key to moderating demand for care services at every stage of the health continuum. The personal issue needs to be framed as one of risk/reward, not cost/benefit. Cost alone only suppresses demand temporarily if health behavior remains unchanged.

Involved and empowered patients and related family members are critically important for the effective management of these risks while a case perspective is brought to the point of direct care. The goals need to be a return to health and a level of individual functioning, not just access to services. Employees need to understand this distinction because it moves the issue away from advocacy of care in general to that of the right type of care, including performance from providers and value for services. In a sense, individuals are always their own personal case manager responsible for optimizing treatment.

When the severity of a case dictates, a third-party case manager is often engaged for individual cases, but this can create a new form of dependency. Instead of transferring accountability for case management between physician and case manager and then cutting the patient off after transfer home, the individual (and family in catastrophic cases) needs to be involved in case management from the beginning. Trying to empower patients and families at the point of a transfer home is too late. Effective empowerment must be nurtured by an employer as part of a health culture and then further developed by a third-party case manager on individual cases.

Managing on a case basis provides the greatest leverage point on individual transactions while still balancing cost and quality on a personal patient level. Instead of considering costs to be an inherent negative, a broader case perspective identifies the optimal way to manage a case. Delays in starting treatment or in providing treatment can be costly. Conversely, failure to provide the right type and amount of treatment can result in suboptimal outcomes, with immediate and long-term cost implications.

Table 5.2   Current Costs and Opportunity Costs of Poorly Managed Cases

Current Costs	Opportunity Costs
Unnecessary testing	Continuing care—poor outcomes from acute medical treatment
Misdiagnosis	Continuing care—poor outcomes from rehabilitation
Least evasive procedure not utilized	Readmission—poor outcomes from acute medical treatment
Excess treatment—frequency of care	Readmission—poor outcomes from rehabilitation
Excess treatment—intensity of care	No follow-up training in self-care on treated, high-risk patients
Excess treatment—duration of care	No follow-up case management on high-risk expatients
More costly treatment environment than required	No training in personal case management for high-risk expatients
Excess evaluations due to poorly coordinated transfers	Rehabilitation not utilized
Unnecessarily institutionalized in long-term care	
Excessive medications—type, dosage, and duration of use	

Table 5.2 identifies the disadvantages of a poorly managed case. Current costs are those costs incurred in treatment, whereas opportunity costs will be incurred in the future because of current undermanagement of the case. Employers can incur the dual penalty of wasted spending combined with results not achieved because the right spending did not occur. This result frequently occurs despite cost containment mechanisms, because attention is being placed on discrete measures such as length of stay and daily rate instead of total costs per case. And even with effective care, failure to engage a patient in personal health issues before, during, and after treatment reduces the value of treatment services.

A case-managed approach to care can be accomplished systematically through a continuous improvement mechanism. The task is not to find a case management organization that "solves" current problems. Nor is it to define the ultimate way to manage. Instead, the goal is to engage all participants—particularly employees, involved functional management, line management (in return-to-work issues), and third-party managers—in continuously improving case results. Prospective and retrospective review is combined with excellence in ongoing management.

A 5-Point Program for Managing Cases

1. Educate and train employees and dependents in personal case management as part of health awareness and self-care programs.

2. Assess past performance for cases by third-party managers (managed care network and case management organizations) for the 10 most common and/or expensive specialty care procedures.

3. Specify and negotiate quality case management services based on value-seeking criteria, linking health, health care, and disability issues and cycle times of treatment stages to total costs. Ensure that case managers have full accountability for performance on their cases and are not overridden by claims management.

4. Conduct ongoing prospective and retrospective review of cases with third-party managers based on cost and quality performance. Third parties need to be managing based on total costs and pre-identified outcome goals.

5. Identify specific cost and quality improvement opportunities including coverage, services, provider performance and connections between providers; then work with third-party managers in achieving continuous improvements.

Excellence in managing cases as well as in case management is the key to obtaining leverage over costs.

A Value-Based Approach to Cost Management

Managing Care encompasses two critical components—health care and workers' compensation. The cost of care thus encompasses all the direct health care claims costs plus management and administration. Previously, primary care has been added to the cost of health, but until achieving good visibility in this area, employers may want to continue to identify this cost as part of the cost of care. Excluded from workers' compensation are the costs of income supports and legal settlements (included in the cost of productivity, explained in Chapter 6).

Some major opportunities in cost management include:

• Obtain the benefits of self-insured risks to eliminate unnecessary insurance and administration costs while developing an integrated program to address costs proactively.

• Optimize the costs expended in management and administration of health care and workers' compensation programs.

• Achieve comparability between the direct costs of health care and workers' compensation through the Managing Forward approach (workers' compensation costs were 140 percent higher than health care costs for the same diagnosis in one study).[15]

• Utilize certain cost-containment features, such as negotiated fee schedules, to control costs. Attention should include providers who are not part of normal utilization patterns (e.g., care needs while an employee is traveling or a dependent is at college).

- Obtain economies of scale in purchasing services through a managed care network, individualized contracting, or a coalition approach with fellow employers.

- Implement a value-based approach to cost management that systematically addresses cost and quality on a case basis.

Movement toward a value-based approach to care cost management includes a fundamental reassessment of compensation for providers and third-party managers. Discounts and rates are relatively meaningless unless costs are being managed in total and other elements of value added are being provided. Bed and board rates may be negotiated, but then hidden charges in the form of ancillary services can make the effective rate higher (currently 25 percent of hospital costs for standard speciality care, but potentially higher for large dollar, catastrophic cases).[16] And the rate for a medical procedure may pale against the costs of badly managed follow-on treatment plans and a poor treatment outcome that results in a readmission or unresolved continuing care.

The problem with many cost-oriented approaches to managing care is that little is being controlled except the current price. Quality of care, as well as the actual services obtained, may vary widely. The result is often a movement toward the lowest common denominator of services and providers strictly in terms of price. Even superior outcomes can be dissipated by providers who do little to involve the recovering patient in follow-on care including rehabilitation.

In managing the costs of care, employers can require a new accountability by providers and a new approach to management by third-party managers. An overall pricing framework is essential to obtain competitive but fair rates from providers based on a value ratio of cost and quality while ensuring cases are managed optimally on an individualized basis. Table 5.3 shows such a value approach encompassing quality as well as cost.

A value-based approach cuts through the confusion of differing prices and differing services. Again, the goal is not perfect knowledge at the start. Continuous learning about value can move an employer in the right direction toward working with quality-committed but cost-conscious providers and third-party managers. This type of strategic positioning is the basis for lasting cost solutions.

Obtaining Quality Care

Major changes in the quality of health care are underway. Continuous quality improvement (CQI) is being utilized by hospitals based on a Joint Commission on Accreditation of Healthcare Organizations (JCAHO)

Table 5.3   Cost of Care: A Value-Based Approach to Cost Management

Management Issue	Approach
Overall management	Link with 5-point program for managing cases
Pricing	Obtain preferred rates based on inclusion in a network of quality providers (HMO, TPA-based PPO, or direct contracting)
	Obtain full disclosure of rates for comparable services (per procedure and for case) with emphasis on ancillary services
	Obtain comprehensive rates based on a total fixed price approach
	Utilize centers for excellence for specialty care and rehabilitation for high-risk, high-cost cases
Service content	Obtain full disclosure by providers of all services provided
	Ensure provision of necessary services and exclusion of unnecessary ones
	Assess portion of direct care in the rate and in total costs by provider
Quality of care	Obtain planned and well-managed transfers between providers and programs
	Utilize best quality providers based on measurable criteria, such as clinical outcomes, health status, patient satisfaction
Flexible management of care	Optimal treatment period at each stage of treatment (e.g., length of stay)
	Optimal service environment at each stage of treatment (e.g., hospital outpatient, home)
	Optimal treatment intensity at each stage of treatment (e.g., type and hours of rehabilitation therapies)

requirement.[17] Action is needed in a care system in which one-fourth of hospital days, one-fourth of procedures, and two-fifths of medications are unnecessary.[18] And then there is the issue of inconsistent quality of treatment, resulting in both unnecessary deaths and limited or impaired functioning after needless or improper treatment. A patient's health may be affected for a lifetime, and employers are paying the price for a care-dependant population.

The JCAHO requirement and other quality initiatives link up with the continuous improvement mechanisms identified in this book. Employer-directed management of a health and disability strategy, however, can bring effective consumer pressure for quality on hospitals and other health care organizations by equalizing the consumer–provider relationship. Even more significantly, this pressure helps providers realize that the broader health system has the greatest potential for quality gains.

Understanding of quality in health care has in many ways mimicked the traditional American approach to assessing quality by individuals and institutions. The common quality criteria have included:

- Professional training.
- Licensing.
- Continuing education.
- Specialty training.
- Certification.
- Accreditation.

These are important factors, but they really indicate only whether a professional or provider is qualified to practice. This mind-set confuses knowledge and technology with quality when the real issue is performance. Discrete measures are inherently limited snapshots in time. A physician passes his or her boards or a hospital or rehabilitation program becomes accredited, but ongoing quality will depend on the person's actual clinical performance or the facility's day-to-day staff capabilities. Staff turnover can severely impact performance potential, yet is not considered in any of these common quality criteria.

An orientation toward meeting minimum standards can persist even though continuous quality improvement approaches benefit from the consistency of performance measurement plus the availability of continuous information feedback.[19, 20] Involved consumers, however, can shift the emphasis to health as well as care. This development allows employers to move to the true breakthrough level—managing based on best practices—which involves pursuing quality as a major leverage point. Waiting for providers to work through care issues in their facilities has limited potential because the broader health issues of workplace productivity and individual functioning require consumer involvement. Current provider quality efforts can emphasize "hospitality" as the means for satisfying the customer, as though catering to patients in care activities is the same as empowering them in health. The focus with providers and third-party managers needs to be on the 3 "Cs":

1. *Quality of Commitment* (responsiveness)
   Follow through on stated commitments.
   Timeliness of corrective action.
2. *Quality of Caring* (service)
   Systematic approach to ensuring human values.
   Customer satisfaction.
3. *Quality of Care* (treatment)
   Outcome per procedure.
   Outcome per case.
   Health status measures.

The service and responsiveness issues are critical for the optimal effectiveness of health, health care, and disability programs with employees and dependents. In assessing treatment, there can be confusion as to what represents quality. Much of the emphasis in managed care is on appropriateness, yet after-the-fact inspection approaches are having limited success in addressing this issue. When quality is viewed in a health context, a broader framework can identify appropriateness as just one element of outcomes. Health status becomes the ultimate measure.

The four elements of an optimal outcome are:

1. Timeliness and correctness of diagnosis.
2. Appropriateness of treatment.
3. Effectiveness of treatment.
4. Patient's participation in and adherence to a care plan.

Through a health systems framework, employers can zero in on timeliness and correctness of diagnoses by ensuring quality primary care plus an informed and empowered patient and consumer. A risk management perspective and ongoing education are essential.

To deal with the appropriateness and effectiveness of treatment, employers can use benchmarks for assessing the incidence of certain types of treatment and for judging outcomes per procedure and per case.

These issues can become overcomplicated. Detailed outcome studies are important, but in the interim, employers can assess providers' credentials, their programs in employee education and training, and relative work-force stability. Feedback on customer satisfaction can come from periodic surveys of employee groups regarding provider performance. And employers can gain valuable insight by monitoring three discrete performance measures:[21]

1. Readmission.
2. Continuing treatment.
3. Return to work.

Outcomes without readmission or continuing treatment, combined with return to work, indicate functional success in clinical care—a direct expression of quality.

Leverage on High-Risk, High-Cost Cases

Physicians and patients have been unhappy with some so-called management services for health care and workers' compensation. Administering coverages per policy terms for fee limits, care, and predefined lengths of stay are administrative oversight, not management. Health care often operates by trying to put square pegs in round holes; even when pegs and holes are the same shape, few of them are the right size.

Except for surgical interventions, standardized process in hospital settings or generalized treatment programs can create waste in some cases and overlook treatment opportunities in others. The human condition requires flexible management of time as well as other variables to achieve individualized outcomes.

Although there is a universal need for individualized treatment, there are limits to its cost-effective delivery. This issue becomes critical with high-risk, high-cost cases. Case management provides the means to manage costs, quality, and risks proactively for employer, patient, and related family members across a range of highly specialized treatment services in differing environments.[22] When managed well, a cost exposure can be turned into a cost leverage point through the achievement of individualized outcomes. In addition, case management acts as a bridge between the patient and family and the complex world of acute medical treatment, rehabilitation, and long-term care. Ultimately, effective case management must be patient-directed, a relationship revolving around constant communications and advocacy for quality services to optimize human health.

Qualification of a third-party case management organization is important. Many employers rely on a TPA/insurer to perform this activity as part of a comprehensive managed care offering. Although this approach can be acceptable, employers need to closely assess capabilities and potential conflicts of interest since they require aggressive, outcome-directed oversight from a case management organization. A better solution might be to assemble a team of independent third-party managers to avoid conflict of interest. This may mean contracting with two strong regional case management organizations while utilizing a national TPA.

Qualification devices for case management organizations can be drawn from the value-added criteria in Chapter 3 and from the performance measures provided in this chapter. In addition, employers must assess experience/expertise in relation to their risk profile, based on demographics and activities, as well as anticipated case load. Some case management organizations and/or case managers, however competent, may lack experience in handling the clinical and related cost and risk issues of a technically dependent newborn or catastrophically brain-injured adult. Some may be experienced in medical management, but have limited experience in rehabilitation in general, and vocational rehabilitation in particular. In fact, a lack of experience may translate into a bias against or even a professional fear of prescribing and managing certain types of treatment.

This matching of experience/expertise is critical to obtaining the best quality case management. The use of multiple case management organizations may provide the best profile of capabilities to manage the anticipated case load. Placing the most highly qualified and independent management on high-risk, high-cost cases is an important way to manage, not just contain costs.

These cases are costly because they involve care of catastrophic or chronic conditions, sometimes of a degenerative nature. An experienced case manager will probably have managed a greater range and number of cases in his or her areas of experience/expertise than many physicians, except specialists associated with a major medical center.

After initial assessment, employers need to ensure that staff is tenured because turnover can be a debilitating problem in third-party management organizations. The next step in qualification is a review of how cases have been managed in the past while targeting how they will be managed in the future. Some critical criteria for management include:

- Does the organization provide a high degree of management intensity and expertise on each case as measured in terms of case load and verifiable qualifications?

- Is management based on functional outcome goals (e.g., ability to perform work functions, not just increase arm range of motion) by identifying them in advance, not after the fact?

- Does the organization aggressively, but appropriately, manage cost and quality based on value for services and total cost approaches (e.g., not just length of stay and daily rate)?

- Do case managers have the requisite professional competence and confidence to appropriately question physicians and other on-site professionals?

- Does the organization assess and contribute to the latest knowledge through involvement in education and training, publications, and public speaking?

- Do case managers personally contact their patients and families; do on-site visits rather than exclusive telephonic case management?

- Does the organization challenge outcomes on current and future cases based on a continuous improvement approach?

- Is risk assessed and managed on a risk/reward basis throughout case management?

- Do case managers develop comprehensive supports in the community encompassing family and work to ensure a lasting outcome?

This line of questioning transitions a customary focus on costs into a greater awareness of the role of risk throughout treatment. Too often, risk is considered only in financial liability terms, a historical perspective with high-risk, high-cost cases. To fully benefit from case management, employers need proactive management of health and safety risks throughout treatment. Case management focused on outcomes instead of "process" goals, can identify individual risks before treatment.

Linking cost/benefit analysis with risk/reward analysis ultimately benefits the patient. For after all, "recovery" from treatment to the level of prior functioning requires the assumption of certain risks, whether they are extending one's arms, driving a car, or crossing a street.[23]

The key to managing risk is to involve all participants in the targeted outcome. Patient and related family members, with their case manager's support, are the ultimate decision makers. By supporting risk taking, an employer benefits from a managed versus an unmanaged risk, no small issue on high-risk, high-cost cases.

Putting It All Together— Systematic Management of Care

Employers' fear of clinical issues makes them tenuous about becoming involved in the management of care and leads to overreliance on third parties. With systematic management, providers and third party managers can be made more accountable even as employers become more involved.

Obtaining a higher level of management from all participants requires a systems approach that ties all activities into a closed loop of accountabilities. When combined with regular information, quality becomes built into the system. Thus, employers will never deal directly with personal clinical issues, but if performance is determined to be poor based on various means, then that provider or third-party manager does not have to see another case. At the same time, employees and dependents can be linked into care issues based on an overriding health orientation.

Although employers have a powerful lever over costs through health interventions, care will sometimes be required. The key to obtaining similar control is to emphasize early interventions and outcomes in treatment. Even then, a case-oriented approach to care, especially for high-risk, high-cost cases, will achieve the best cost management breakthroughs. When combined with a value-based approach to negotiating and managing provider services, employers can truly lead a transformation to quality care based on optimized health.

References

1. Polzer, K. October 1990. Rationing by choice. *Business & Health,* pp. 60–64.
2. Hahan, H. 1985. Toward a politics of disability: Definitions, disciplines and policies. *The Social Science Journal,* 22(4): 87–103.
3. Trieschmann, R. B. 1990. Sickness treatment or health care: Implications for head injury. *Journal of Head Trauma Rehabilitation,* 5(1): 57–64.
4. Gelb, B. D. March–April 1985. Preventive medicine and employee productivity. *Harvard Business Review,* pp. 12, 16.

5. Light, D. W. Spring 1992. Excluding more, covering less: The health insurance industry in the U.S., Health/PAC Bulletin, 22(1): 7–13.

6. Winslow, R. Dec. 1, 1992. Experts try to gauge mental health care, *Wall Street Journal,* pp. B1, 12.

7. Managing care and costs: Strategic choices and issues, an environmental assessment of U.S. health care, 1991–1996, Deloitte & Touche and Health One Corporation, contained in *Health Care Strategic Management,* June 1991, p. 23, copyright the Business Word, Inc.

8. Selected community hospital statistics: 1988–1991, American Hospital Association: National Hospital Panel Survey Reports, contained in *Health Care Financing Review,* Fall 1991, 13(1): 133.

9. Schwartz, W. B., & Mendelson, D. N. April 11, 1991. Health cost containment in the 1980's: Hard lessons learned and prospects for the 1990's, *The New England Journal of Medicine,* 324(15): 1037–1042.

10. Division of Health Care Statistics, National Center for Health Statistics: Data from the National Hospital Discharge Survey, U.S. Department of Health and Human Services 1991: Health USA 1991 & Prevention Profile (General), short stay hospitals.

11. Schecter, S. M. 1991. *Managing health care costs by managing high cost illness.* New York: Human Resource Health Institute, pp. 1–8.

12. Garfinkel, S., Riley, G. F., & Iannacchione, V. G. 1988. High cost users of medical care. *Health Care Financing Review,* 9(4), pp. 41–52.

13. Winslow, R. February 25, 1992. Videos, questionnaires aim to expand role of patients in treatment decisions. *Wall Street Journal,* B1, B3.

14. Dr. Wennberg on outcomes research: What does it really mean? 1991. *Managed Medicine,* 2(1): 7–16.

15. 1990 Minnesota Department of Labor, Study of Health Insurance versus Workers' Compensation Claims.

16. Metropolitan Life-Insurance Company, Statistical Bulletin, Vol. 72, No. 4, October–December 1991, pp. 28–33.

17. Eubanks, P. June 5, 1992. The CEO experience: TQM/CQI. *Hospitals,* pp. 24–36.

18. Brook, R., RAND Fellow. June 9, 1990. In Chambliss, L., & Reier, S., How doctors have ruined health care. *Financial World,* pp. 46–52.

19. Brook, R., Elwood, P., & Berwick, D. August 1990. Accessing quality of care: Three different approaches. *Business & Health,* pp. 27–42.

20. Burke, M. March 5, 1993. Clinical quality initiatives: The search for meaningful—and accurate—measures. *Hospitals,* pp. 26–36.

21. Evans, R. W., & Jones, M. L. 1991. Integrating outcomes, value, and quality— An outcome validation system for post-acute rehabilitation programs. *Journal of Insurance Medicine,* 23(3): 192–196.

22. Papistrat, L. A. July 1991. Saving lives—and saving money, too. *Best's Review,* pp. 44–46, 99–100.

23. Emener, W. G., Vash, C. L., & Hahan, H. Oct./Nov./Dec. 1991. Empowerment in rehabilitation. *Journal of Rehabilitation,* pp. 7–20.

=================== **Resources** ===================

Foundation for Informed Medical Decision-Making, Joseph F. Kasper, ScD, President, PO Box C-17, Hanover, NH 03755.

Sloan, M. D., & Chemel, M. 1991. *The quality revolution and health care: A primer for purchasers and providers.* Milwaukee, WI: ASQC Quality Press.

Boland, P. (ed.) 1990. *Making Managed Healthcare Work: A Practical Guide to Strategies and Solutions.* New York: McGraw-Hill.

6

Managing Productivity:
Integrating Workplace
Health and Disability

Linking health and care is a critical step in establishing employer control over costs. There is still a missing link, however, in the strategic management of health and disability: productivity.

Without a focus on health, it is difficult to make a connection with productivity. Viewing health care and workers' compensation as issues unto themselves ignores the interrelationship between workplace and nonworkplace health and, even more importantly, between health itself and productivity.

Evidence of employers' productivity losses is everywhere. Substance abuse is now costing $144 billion annually,[1] and mental health, $148 billion annually.[2] The annual costs of disability are more than $140 billion and $200 billion if workers' compensation costs are included.[3] Possibly, these big numbers are part of the problem; they have not been effectively related to the individual employer's cost structure. Even more fundamentally, companies need efficient management tools for dealing with workplace health and disability based on productivity measures and on optimization of the value of rehabilitation.

In developing a health and disability strategy and related management system, organizations need to relate the value of health and disability expenditures to work force productivity. Poor health and disability retard both the quantity and quality of worker outputs. Lost labor hours and less than fully productive labor hours directly impact an employer's bottom line, so relating these losses to health and disability creates a major cost leverage point.

Productivity related to health and disability can be used as a value index in the same way that utilization is used as an indicator of health value. The principal difference is that utilization directly relates health to employee interests, whereas productivity directly relates health to employer interests. In both cases, providers involved in prevention and rehabilitation are connected to the value being received.

Managing productivity involves optimizing the health of the work force. The goal is to reduce the losses from poor health and disability by promoting health, intervening appropriately, and supporting return to work. Management of productivity requires balancing an investment in workplace health against the cost savings from reduced time off for illness, injury, and disability. Critical in this form of management is an awareness of new health issues such as stress and substance abuse. Building a highly productive work force means eliminating the walls between the workplace and the clinical world (dominated by an acute medical orientation and exacerbated by restrictive coverages) because they only add to employer costs.

Productivity, the final management tract in a quality-based health system, operationalizes health and disability strategy in the environment in which adult workers spend most of their waking hours. This chapter addresses health-related productivity issues in operations, fully integrating disability with mainstream management practices. This framework optimizes health-related productivity while simultaneously requiring functional outcomes from care providers, addressing both the benefits of reducing health and disability costs in operations and the operating factors driving the costs of health care and workers' compensation. Performance and culture are thus integrated in a health context.

Defining and Measuring Health-Related Productivity

Productivity measures can often be quite simplistic. Outputs versus inputs may relate revenues versus total labor dollars or units of production versus direct labor dollars. These gross numbers fail to identify the direct costs of health care and workers' compensation and the costs of health and disability in operations. Even when all these costs are added together into the total cost of health and disability, the issue of productivity remains only partially addressed. The opportunity cost of production lost due to poor health and disability is another cost leverage point in the systematic management of health and disability.

Part of the problem in identifying this cost opportunity has been an organizational focus on care, not health. In the meantime, health or the lack of it, impacts organizations whether or not care is received. Employees can be fully productive, underproductive, temporarily unproductive, or permanently unproductive depending on their health condition (Table 6.1).

Health-related conditions determine the quantity and quality of labor inputs. Just as importantly, poor health creates uncertainty in staffing.

Table 6.1   Health-Related Productivity

Work Status	Health-Related Conditions
At Work	
Fully Productive	Healthy personally
	Healthy dependents
Underproductive	Poor health personally
	Poor health of dependents
	Time spent in health programs
	Return-to-work transition
	Person with a disability not accommodated, nor managed optimally
Away from Work	
Temporary	Treatment for illness and injury
	Recovery from illness and injury
	Absenteeism and sick time
	Disability
Permanent	Disability

Excess costs develop from temporary staff, overtime, or compensatory staffing. An organization experiencing absenteeism, sick time, leaves of absence, or other lost work time incurs direct, indirect, and hidden costs. Productivity is reduced either because excess health-related costs are incurred to achieve the same outputs or outputs decline because fewer productive human resources are available.

These health-related costs are embedded in the cost of doing business, only drawing attention when productivity takes a direct hit during a flu epidemic or a maternity leave for a key employee. In the meantime, organizations are taking the hits almost daily. Substance abuse and smoking have both been shown to correlate with higher absenteeism. Back injuries are causing 34 percent of the disabilities[4] and an even higher percentage of claims dollars, yet the productivity losses often are missed. More subtle are the numbers of employees not fully productive due to the same or other health issues. Recovery from illness and injury usually occurs on the job, not just at home.

Health-related productivity can be assessed for individuals, departments, and facilities; either on a periodic or ongoing basis. When optimal productivity without health-related losses is set as the goal, a value index can be developed for departments, facilities, and organizations in total. Figure 6.1 shows a snapshot of productivity losses, with optimal health-related productivity set at 1.0.

This figure makes the cost of workplace health and disability tangible for line management, but the initial reaction may be, What can we do about it? Segmenting controllable from noncontrollable factors is a start. Addressing some of the controllable factors means that line management,

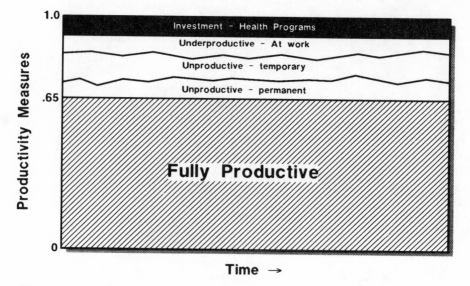

Figure 6.1 Health-Related Productivity (RHM Systems, Inc., 1993, Marlboro, MA)

like the parent organization, must make an investment in health. It may take the form of lost productivity caused by a health fair, employee participation in health programs, or quarterly discussions about health and health care. More direct is compensatory time after a stressful work period or the use of one employee as a job coach to aid another in return to work.

The challenge is to balance this investment against the health-related productivity losses. Managing health and safety risks is an accountability of line management as well as employees. Certainly one of the biggest gains can be made by preventing or reducing work hours lost to disability or recovery from illness and injury. Line management also must recognize that "recovery" often involves the development of temporary or permanent compensating strategies by the affected individual.

Line management needs to tackle the two sides of productivity: (1) labor hours and resources in terms of work outputs, and (2) the health-related productivity of those human inputs. Through continuous improvement, health-related losses can be driven down to produce direct cost savings. Figure 6.2 shows this form of management, indicating that an investment in health, representatively targeted between .95 and 1.00 at the top of the figure, is always necessary and that some random fluctuations in health that create productivity losses are to be expected.

Organizations that manage health-related productivity do far more than control certain costs. In addition, they create a health culture that has direct meaning for line management, and the effectiveness of health, health care, and disability programs becomes apparent to all.

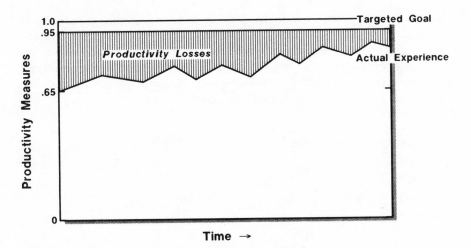

Figure 6.2 Continuous Improvement in Health-Related Productivity (RHM Systems, Inc., 1993, Marlboro, MA)

Managing for Productivity—Optimizing Health

Despite the advent of the information age, many organizations continue to utilize industrial age practices. Productivity as a measurement is no exception. The quality of the work force was not as important when physical outputs were the measurement criteria. Production was production, and not a lot of time and effort was spent in managing the quality of the human inputs. Health and disability costs were a fallout of these practices—not something to manage directly.

Despite the quality revolution and the rise of services in place of manufacturing, many of the management tools remain the same. Organizations attempt to control workplace productivity by defining policy and procedures for sick time and paid time off. In reality, days in the office hardly qualify as a measure of productivity unless shift coverage issues are involved. Staff can be quite underproductive even though they are present, and poor health directly impacts quality levels as often evidenced in the "Monday syndrome" in manufacturing operations.

Part of the past problem in managing health-related productivity was that line supervisors managed departments, not individuals. Output of the collective whole was important, not the value added by individuals. This approach provided little incentive to hire well and to search out and address the underproductive few weighed down by health problems. Nor was there incentive to support those returning to work. As long as the group met its collective goals, line managers did not have to bother with such burdens.

The world has now changed. Rising health and disability costs demand attention by line management, and the Occupational Safety and Health

Administration (OSHA) and The Americans with Disabilities Act (ADA) have raised the ante considerably. But more importantly, employers can manage for productivity when they focus on employees as individuals. Instead of applying an industrial age standard of being at work or absent, managers can define work schedules that optimize the productivity of the individual. Examples of such practices include:

- Flextime.
- Compressed work weeks.
- Part-time work.
- Job sharing.
- Accommodations for those with a disability.
- Leaves of absence.

All these flexible work practices can merely cover hours on a schedule board or can obtain greater health-related productivity from individuals and from a group. The key is to determine individual value added based on optimum health or individual functioning for those with a disability. Line supervisors can then utilize this standard in allowing employees to comanage their own workplace scheduling and to take care of personal and dependent health needs. Management of disability simply becomes a normal part of flexible work practices through this approach. Also, there is a concerted effort to make all scheduled time, productive time.

Optimizing health-related productivity requires individualized management of paid time off as well. Vacation, holiday, and sick time can be rolled into one paid time off allotment. For example, employees might have 30 days off per year of which 20 days have to be used for health and personal reasons.[5] With these management tools, line supervisors and employees can work cooperatively to optimize productivity by meeting personal work goals and protecting group productivity from lapses in work schedule commitments.

When organizational flexibility encompasses individualized health issues, both at work and at home, employers can fully optimize health-related productivity. The reinforcement provided by line management practices will also create spillover effects that increase the effectiveness of up-front health and safety programs. In this way, health, care, and productivity are managed simultaneously to reap mutual gains from improvements in any one area.

Comprehensive Cost Targets—Completing the Cost Management Framework

Health-related productivity can be expressed in terms of costs as well as a value index. Both have different advantages. Many nonlabor costs related to health and disability can be included in the total cost of productivity. An example would be the costs expended to recruit a replacement for an employee who is permanently disabled and does not return to work. This cost measure does not include the opportunity costs from poor health and disability. The advantage of a value index is that time and employee value added are directly managed, not costs.

The cost of productivity is an important component of the total cost of health and disability. After separating out the cost of health and cost of care discussed in Chapters 4 and 5, a group of costs remain that relate more to operations. Some of these direct, indirect, and hidden costs are identified in Table 6.2 in terms of the strategic cost framework introduced earlier.

By identifying disability as part of the cost of productivity, a statement is made that a wide range of disability-related costs need to be managed. Management of disability is thereby normalized as part of day-to-day line accountabilities. Much of today's disability costs can be considered pure waste from a lack of proactive management interventions and ineffective health, health care, and disability programs. Line management involvement can address four critical issues:

- Systematically reduce health and safety risks in the workplace while supporting employees to do the same in home and work activities.
- Reduce time out of work on health care and workers' compensation cases.
- Increase return-to-work success on all cases.

Table 6.2 Cost of Productivity: Health and Disability in Operations

Cost Category	Relative Amount
Premiums/claims	$$
Disability coverage	
Disability payouts	
Workers' compensation settlements	
Workers' compensation payouts	
External mgt./admin.	$
Legal costs related to health and disability issues	
Other expertise employed in health and disability	
Internal mgt./admin.	$
Compliance training programs	
Line management involvement in health and disability	
Overtime/replacement staffing	$
Overtime to compensate for missing staff	
Recruitment and retraining for replaced staff	
Lost productivity	$$
Absenteeism and sick time paid	
Loss of trained staff	
Time spent in health programs	
Other	$$
Quality losses due to health and disability issues	—
Total Cost of Productivity	$$$

- Ensure employees access health and health care services when needed (e.g., most workers' compensation claimants continue to work).

These are the leverage points for making profound change in a wide range of costs. Even organizations with effective return-to-work programs often underemphasize the importance of systematically managing time out of work. Proactive communication including offering an accommodation reduce employee worries and create an immediate discussion about return. Showing flexibility also signals acceptance of an employee's condition at varying levels of recovery. These are the means to preempt attorney involvement, one of the fastest means for reducing costs.

As if direct productivity and quality losses are not enough, organizations wanting to place even more direct accountability for health and disability costs in operations might charge certain staff-related costs to the appropriate department. An example is the legal costs related to disability. Establishing comprehensive cost targets is essential because line management needs to understand the health and disability costs in operations as well as in health and care programs. These costs can be directly related to individual facility and/or department budgets and related incentives. For example, a facility with a high level of workplace accidents needs to be assigned accountability for the cost of temporary or longer term disability payments, compensatory staffing costs, and the cost to return the employee to work.

This approach helps line management recognize the real cost of disability payments and compensatory staffing, which in the past have been hidden in general labor fringe factors and recruitment budgets. Unless these up-front costs are factored into operating performance and related incentive considerations, there is a tendency to look only at the tail end of the issue—the cost to put someone back to work. As a result, managers have felt little organizational pressure to proactively address health and safety risks and to support timely and effective return to work.

Cost attribution should avoid unnecessary and costly reporting. In many cases, employers can use estimates instead of creating separate accounting mechanisms. A failure to return a person to work might cost $30,000 in total for lost productivity, recruitment, and retraining. The average cost of just one on the job injury was estimated at $16,800 in 1988 by the National Safety Council, whereas Du Pont estimates it costs more than $13,000 when a worker loses one day because of a disabling injury.[6] The key is to tie into a total view of the cost of productivity related to health and disability.[7] Comprehensive cost targets are needed for line management unfamiliar with health and disability as critical issues within their span of control.

Operations Issues—The Hidden Cost Opportunity

Managing health-related productivity requires a reorientation toward health and away from seeing health care and workers' compensation as being outside employer control. In addition, operations issues affect the direct costs of health care and workers' compensation.

When risks were fully insured, employee turnover and, in most cases, regional differences in the cost of health care were unimportant. Actuaries did not consider employee turnover in cost projections because it was embedded in costs themselves and there is no way to forecast turnover nor to fully understand it when deductibles and risk avoidance strategies confuse the picture. With experience-rated and self-insured health care plans, however, employers feel these cost factors directly instead of sharing them with many others.

Employee turnover shows the pivotal role of operations in cost management of health and disability, even before managing health-related productivity. High turnover causes the following effects:

- Newly hired employees (and dependents) are often higher utilizers of health care, particularly if they never had coverage previously. This impact is even greater when turnover is prevalent at a facility in a high-cost region.
- When staff turns over rapidly, an employer is more likely to absorb coverage for undiagnosed preexisting conditions and other health issues for the same number of employed staff at any one point in time.
- Newly hired employees have less on-the-job training, which can result in greater levels of workplace accidents and resultant workers' compensation claims.
- Rapid turnover in staff dissipates the value of training employees and dependents in health, health care, and disability issues.
- Undertrained staff may be harder to assist in return-to-work situations resulting in higher and more costly workers' compensation and disability claims.
- Departing employees often plan health care coverage issues well in advance, taking care of elective health care needs and completing final dental visits before leaving employment. Workers' compensation claims sometimes happen for similar reasons.
- Departing employees continuing their health care coverage under Consolidated Omnibus Budget Reconciliation Act of 1985 (COBRA) eligibility cost $633 or 24 percent more in 1991[8] than regular employees.

Operations management is totally involved in several areas of health and disability costs besides risk management. Some major cost leverage points related to operations issues alone include:

- Employee retention (the back-end issues of turnover).
- Employee hiring quality (the front-end issues of turnover).

- Regional employment mix—regional cost differences in health care and workers' compensation.
- Full-time or part-time employment status.

These cost factors can sneak up on employers until suddenly a facility in one region compares poorly with another facility elsewhere. Relative workers' compensation costs are fairly obvious because they are rated by state, but health care can also vary widely between regions. Health care costs in Los Angeles are 131 percent higher than in Charlotte, North Carolina.[9]

One operations response to such differentials and to high costs in general has been to use part-time employment as a way of avoiding paying certain benefits. An employer with group-rated coverages will obtain savings immediately, but an experience-rated or self-insured employer may not. More fundamentally, any cost savings showing up in a local performance center may be more than offset by higher workers' compensation claims and productivity and quality losses when a total cost of health and disability perspective is taken.

Health and disability costs that are fully identified and charged to operations are more manageable. Operating management can strive for higher levels of overall productivity in higher cost regions and attack the causes of health and disability costs in general. A regional index of relative costs might be used, not actual claims experience, which fluctuates. Unfortunately, many organizations seem to have been caught unaware by the operating implications of self-insurance and direct experience rating. One-time charges and facility consolidations are extremely costly ways to deal with health and disability costs and do not provide the organization with a lasting solution.

Reconsidering Compliance—Best Practices versus Minimum Standards

Health and disability involve a host of compliance challenges. The Employment Retirement Income Security Act of 1974 (ERISA), COBRA, OSHA, and ADA are just the major ones. Every two to three years, a new regulatory opportunity seems to arrive for attorneys and consultants, and most certainly those in the seminar business.

If there ever was an example of a productivity loss, compliance stands at the top of the list. Organizations are continuously reacting to new federal regulations, while state legislatures are hard at work recrafting 50 versions of workers' compensation. Staff are diverted to learn and apply all these new laws. Consultants are paid fees that could be more productively invested in business operations. All in all, employers have been struggling to stay on top of all the new regulations in the health and disability arena. And the prospects are for further changes in health care and workers' compensation laws at both the state and federal levels.

After 20 years of incremental changes, employers need to stand back and review what a compliance orientation has done to management of health and disability. Has management turned to administration among a host of functional departments and third parties? And have employers allowed themselves to become fragmented based on an insurance and regulatory model of separate coverages?

Instead of continuing to react to compliance issues, employers should apply a quality-based health systems approach to the management of employees. Government regulations are naturally disjointed because they deal with one issue at a time. Interconnections between federal laws are nonexistent, and they certainly do not exist between federal and state laws.

These frayed and missing interconnections are the breeding ground of litigation and a full employment environment for attorneys. What is problematic is that employer management often mimics these broad-based problems. There is no smooth flow in how an employee is to be optimally managed. Costs are raised all over from management based on minimum standards rather than best practices.

One of the most recent examples is the Americans with Disabilities Act. Many organizations approached ADA in terms of complying with the regulations rather than in building excellence into their employee management practices. A health systems approach to ADA would show the cost/benefit of accommodating existing employees as a group to be more beneficial than that of hiring new employees.[10, 11, 12] If good human resources practices are in place, an existing employee should be a proven performer having been trained and already adapted to the employer's workplace environment. The implication is for employers to be proactive in accommodating existing employees, with a predefined framework to guide line management even as the actual accommodation relates to individual circumstances. It is extremely costly to determine accommodations on a one-by-one basis without guidance when the involved line and functional management may deal with the issue only occasionally. It also delays return to work. Often there is an exclusive orientation toward workers' compensation cases when many employers are faced with more ADA exposure (and opportunity) under their health care plan.

Just as quality is being brought to the management of a product or service, it can be designed into optimal management of employees' health and disability. The starting point is to define health as the overriding value and then to manage toward health-related productivity. The goal is to establish best practices for all employee issues by viewing them as a transactions flow of recruitment, hire, training, job functioning, time off for health and disability issues, return to work, and end to employment.

Designing an optimum employee pathway permits all health and disability issues to be considered along the way. The training of managers and supervisors then stresses functional policies and procedures for this pathway based on health-related productivity that ultimately connects line manager and employee in an ongoing learning process. Quality standards can guide behavior, but health needs change due to family circumstances and life cycle issues. And when accessing rehabilitation, employees need supports in the reacquisition and reapplication of skills in work and living environments.

Focusing on compliance issues is critical in a best practices approach so that line management can become proficient in managing them from both a cost and a legal standpoint. This will eliminate management gaps and systems disconnections. In addition, red flag areas can be identified for obtaining fall-back expertise before pursuing an action with employees. The following resources can provide such expertise:

- Functional management in Human Resources, Benefits, Risk Management, and Safety.
- In-house legal counsel or organizational counsel.
- Prequalified medical and rehabilitation professionals.
- External consultants in health and disability.
- External legal experts in health and disability.

Proactive management of compliance can reduce costs. Besides building it into employee management procedures, employers can bring in experts to provide specialized information to both line and functional management. Comprehensive review of compliance issues can then take place periodically through limited in-house audits by functional management. Operations-oriented compliance translates Managing Forward into line issues. A health intervention approach orients line management as well as employees in the right direction by focusing on the total cost of productivity and on productivity as a value index. This orientation replaces "leading the witness" toward entitlements with leading employees toward health in the workplace.

Family and Dependents—A Productivity, Not Just a Benefits Issue

The work force has undergone a major change during the past 20 years. More than 50 percent of married women are employed outside the home, and two-income families are the norm. Single-parent families now represent 15 percent of the total,[13] while 30 percent of employees are single adults.[14]

These changes in the composition of the work force raise a serious question about employee benefits. In the days of one working spouse in a family, there was little potential of duplicate coverages. In addition, health care was a normal employment pattern with insurers underwriting coverage on a group basis. Connecting productivity directly to health was difficult, and the accepted practice was to view health care as an employer-provided benefit.

In response to the dynamics of a new family environment, some employers have moved toward flexible benefits. Unbundling the benefit choices can produce cost savings for employers while better serving individual needs. Unfortunately, the direct evidence of cost savings appears to exist only for group-rated, premium-based coverages for the next plan year. A host of accompanying changes in cost sharing, managed care features, and coverages confuse most cost/benefit analyses of flex benefits. When employers are direct-experience rated or self-insured to certain levels, flexible benefits do not necessarily translate into lasting cost savings. The real issues are managing health, care, and productivity.

The fundamental question here is, why do employers offer health care coverage before addressing the issues of family and dependents? When the focus moves to health and productivity instead of just care, it creates the framework to cost-justify encompassing family and dependents into employer concerns. The related health and productivity issues are as follows:

- Dependents account for 60 percent of the average employer's health care costs.[15] As such, drawing dependents more fully into the health intervention approach is a major point of cost leverage.

- Spouses can be generally fairly independent in health matters unless unusual circumstances develop. The health of children, however, is a shared parental responsibility. Even more pressure may fall on single parents. Normal health concerns for children are, therefore, major factors in care costs and may affect employee productivity.

- Illness, injury, and disability change the equation substantially. In such cases, a spouse may comanage health with or for a husband or wife. The impact can be twofold, an employee may have to be involved with his or her spouse or a spouse may provide important supports for an employee. The child–parent relationship usually involves parent or parents taking care of a child, but an older employee often reverses the roles. Such health problems may continue for days, weeks, or years seriously impacting employee productivity.

Companies are not avoiding health and disability costs by ignoring the dependents issue. The costs are embedded throughout an employer's cost structure in direct, indirect, and hidden health and disability costs. Parents often use emergency rooms, instead of office visits, for dependents' primary care. Health care is often delayed and made more costly because of work scheduling constraints. Employers also incur the impact in unanticipated days off due to absenteeism, sick time, and unplanned use of vacation time. Part of the problem is a general failure to legitimize dependent health as an important employee productivity issue.

Instead of allowing the issue to remain a serious hidden cost while drifting into the status of another benefits entitlement, employers can treat the matter as a productivity issue involving joint management by employees and line management. With proactive and cooperative management, even parental leave can take on a whole new light.

When considered in terms of the total cost of health and disability, family and dependent health issues impact costs in the following areas:

1. Dependent health—health care.
2. Dependent health—workplace productivity.
3. Dependent disability—workplace productivity.
4. Employee disability—family supports.
5. Employee health—family supports.

These impacts will vary depending on life cycle issues. Child health may be a concern, and then very quickly employees may need to care for aging parents. According to the Gerontological Society of America, employees assisting elderly parents spend 11 hours per week in such activities.

This cycle seriously neglects the unexpected impact of disability, which can involve much more intensive supports. Although disability can be caused by progressively degenerative conditions, it is more often the result of injury and illness throughout the life cycle. And this cost relationship is not always flowing productivity outside an employer's operations as family supports are critical in making an employee healthy and productive. The impact is more apparent in disability cases, but the most significant relationship exists in targeting health, especially preventable health and safety risks, as a family goal.

Ignoring these issues will generally increase the cost of care and cost of productivity. Reorienting the dependents issue toward health and away from a benefits fixation involves a two-way commitment—employees have a responsibility for personal and family health at the same time that their employer provides certain supports. Small employers can capitalize on this health-directed flexibility in work-force management practices as an advantage in hiring and retaining the best staff.[16]

Managing time out of the work force for health issues of employees and dependents has become a critical cost exposure. One out of five of today's workers will die from cancer,[17] and workers have a 30 percent chance of being disabled once for 90 days during their careers.[18] Treatment for cancer and heart disease impacts a substantial portion of the work force. These are only the employee impacts, not the dependent impacts, which are also significant over an employee's lifetime. Those employers who manage family and dependent issues as part of health-related productivity will achieve significant competitive advantage in cost structure as well as in the employment market.

Information-Age Health versus Industrial-Age Medicine

Organizations have traditionally understood that health and disability have an impact on operations, even if an integrated, proactive management response has generally not been the rule. Companies frequently appoint a medical director, an occupational health nurse, and/or a vocational rehabilitation professional to provide either on-site or off-site support. Overall, employers have brought medical care to the workplace, transferring certain accountabilities to the professionals in the same way that they have handled health care and workers' compensation in general.

A medical care model may have worked effectively in the industrial age of large-scale, on-site manufacturing operations with workers deployed in narrowly defined job tasks. Clinical experts could manage work-specific health issues, usually after the need developed, and assist in return-to-work activities based on the constraints of workers' compensation statutes and collective bargaining agreements.

Much has now changed in the workplace. Job content is less likely to directly involve physical functioning because workers are involved in processing information. Task interdependencies and demands for performance have increased. Employment is more likely to be in a service organization, not in a manufacturing operation, and in small or medium-sized companies or at least in decentralized organizations.

And finally, even today's health issues have changed. After undergoing treatments that involve advanced medical technology, employees are more likely to return to work with limited or impaired functioning, while the challenges of modern society have created psychological/social/behavioral issues as major sources of lost productivity for employers.

In the medical care model, the involved professionals act as care gatekeepers. The orientation is toward:

- Symptom-based diagnosis.
- Medical necessity approach to treatment.
- Discrete procedure orientation.
- Limited accountability for benefiting individual functioning.

Treatment is reactive—based on symptoms—when many of today's health conditions can be asymptomatic. These conditions instead require individual involvement in assessing changes in personal health status continuously. Stress and mental health problems are apparent to the aware individual long before they translate into heart problems, aggravation of an asthmatic condition, or an attack on the immune system with detectable physical symptoms.

Proactive attention to stress may even prevent a serious workplace accident potentially affecting co-workers. This first line of defense remains underutilized because information is concentrated among the caregivers, who emphasize treatment, not health. Instead, employers need the support of health care professionals who push the issue back to employees for current and future self-management on a case basis, while remaining a source of support and a facilitator of appropriate health-related services as well as medical care.

Information age health can break down the walls between health and disability. The perception of disability is a difficult issue. Some employees are returning every day to work after cancer treatment, with a measure of impaired or limited functioning. At the same time, other employees, who are injured on the job, may have less impaired functioning but be unable to return to work. Part of this discrepancy relates to an employee's perception of a limitation, which is colored by family and work colleagues' attitudes about the value of work in general and about the particular job being done. In a case of potential disability the attitudes of those directly involved are even more telling—the input of medical staff, rehabilitation staff, lawyer, and especially supervisors and work colleagues carry great weight.

The following three examples show this difference between a care orientation and health orientation.

Example *Care Orientation* Medical staff show little interest in the individual's future, saying he has lost 60 percent range of motion in his arm and will qualify for a disability based on their diagnosis. In fact, a staff member questions the patient about work when he "used to be" a heavy equipment operator.

Health Orientation Medical staff indicate the individual has lost 60 percent range of motion, but they know many who have recovered up to 80 percent of their prior arm movement through rehabilitation and are successfully back at similar jobs.

Example *Care Orientation* Rehabilitation staff express a high degree of concern about the individual not being able to recover full range of motion. They even begin to complain about the health care coverage not funding this outcome after many months of treatment.

Health Orientation Rehabilitation staff immediately assess range of motion against the functional requirements of the individual's current job and ones that he might aspire to. They express confidence in achieving a successful outcome if their client fulfills his side of the treatment plan through self-rehabilitation.

Example *Care Orientation* A supervisor does not call an injured worker after her injury because he is fearful of becoming involved in care matters. He complains about carrying underproductive workers and is visibly bored in company training sessions about ADA. Work colleagues relay this information to the injured worker.

Health Orientation A supervisor calls the injured worker immediately after the injury, expressing his concern about her and her family. He speaks to the employee as a "member of my team," not as an injured worker or former employee and asks her to drop by and review return-to-work issues as soon as she is ready. He expresses the company's commitment to structuring individualized accommodations once the employee is ready.

These wide-ranging responses underscore the importance of controlling the attitudes and behaviors of as many of the participants as possible through a health intervention approach. Depending on prior practices and employer culture, the interaction with an employee might involve an occupational health nurse, but line supervisors should not abdicate their direct role. Having an actively involved employer, even if only in terms of communication, is critical at all times.

If these disparate influences can occur with a physically manifest injury, what greater range of influences need to be controlled in a nonphysically manifest injury or illness? Psychological/social/behavioral issues do not always precede an injury and illness. Many are reinforced or developed as a result of an episode, including the actions and behaviors of caregivers. Personal goals for "recovery" can be limited right from the start, particularly on workers' compensation claims where the emphasis may be on forensic medicine, not health.

Employers cannot afford to place workplace health and disability solely into the hands of caregivers. Today's health issues require an integrated approach. To gain the right accountabilities for performance and the right supports for employees, companies must use an integrated approach that includes the following steps:

1. Assess the specific health issues for the covered population.

2. Qualify and select support from appropriate health, health care, and disability providers with a range of skills, ensuring an overriding health orientation in workplace health and safety issues.

3. Engage workplace health professionals, including the company medical director, as members of the organizational team developing health and disability strategy and related programs. However, total accountability should not be delegated to such professionals.

4. Monitor the quality of provider activities by engaging employees in appropriate feedback.

5. Motivate employees to utilize the best possible preselected care for workers' compensation care needs, including providers handling stress, back, and carpal tunnel issues.

6. Integrate recovery from injury and illness on both health care and workers' compensation cases into health programs for wellness, substance abuse, mental health and stress to anticipate potential disability due to aggravated psychological/social/behavioral issues.

7. Train line supervisors and functional management in personally managing health and disability issues and in interacting with providers.

The bottom line is that employers need providers who deliver the best clinical care and who strive to improve the health of the employee group through a prevention and early intervention commitment, not just through treatment services.

Managing Disability—The Role of Rehabilitation

Employers are spending a great deal of money on acute medical treatment. Yet for all this spending, what are the results? Are patients functioning at a higher level than similar patients were five years ago? Are costs being reduced by the step-down approach to treatment, or do readmission and continuing care persist? And more fundamentally, are the cost-containment methods used by insurers for a one-year policy period relevant for self-insured employers who technically own the risk as long as the individual remains an employee or remains covered under the health care plan?

This different risk perspective creates an opportunity to utilize rehabilitation more proactively after acute medical treatment.[19] Except for workers' compensation cases with long-term exposures, insurers and third-party managers have generally managed rehabilitation in the same manner as acute medical treatment. The determination for use has been medical necessity, not restoration of lost functioning. Restoration encompasses individualized compensating strategies as well as gains in personal functioning capacity. Outcomes thus have different meanings in these two different worlds.

Although outcomes are important in acute medical treatment, the treatment process (e.g., surgery) equates to an outcome (e.g., removal of an appendix). This is not the case in rehabilitation as the treatment process (e.g., hours of therapy) does not necessarily relate to an outcome (e.g., full extension of a person's leg). In addition, control over time in acute medical treatment based on length of stay involves recovery after surgery, not the time in surgery. Similar controls over length of treatment in rehabilitation go right to the heart of clinical value, potentially removing accountability for performance unless outcome goals are negotiated from the start.

Improved management of rehabilitation is an opportunity that exists in most health care plans. Employers need to increase their attention to the back end of treatment, because the benefits of rehabilitation have increased for a number of important reasons:

- Advanced medical technology has increased the absolute number of survivors from medical interventions.
- Shortened hospital stays and alternative surgical settings are resulting in more outpatients with reduced functioning who require rehabilitation follow-up.
- Patients are going home to a less supportive environment as more individuals live on their own or raise a family on their own.
- Primary care needs for persons with a disability are greater and often not addressed effectively.[20, 21] Even without physical issues, patients are bringing with them a range of care issues related to stress and substance abuse that further complicate recovery. Substance abuse is significantly higher among persons with a disability.[22, 23]

- Most patients are involved in more complex job situations involving communications, not just physical functioning.

These conditions create a high probability of functional limitations and permanent disability unless managed. Moving a patient quickly home can be appropriate from medical stability and medical necessity standpoints, but little may have been done to prepare the patient for a return to normal functioning. Rehabilitation often only encompasses physical or speech therapy on an outpatient basis with little integration into home or work activities. These family and work issues, including both temporary or long-term supports, may be unaddressed. The result can be an individual who is functionally disabled under either health care or workers' compensation coverages because of unmanaged environmental factors rather than physical ones.

The total employee environment may sound too global and a bit intimidating to employers. In reality, everyone's functioning capacity can be isolated into a limited number of critical, individualized environmental factors. This represents a health systems framework extended to disability.

Efforts in this regard are being made today by the physician who assesses family history and current family dynamics in a diagnosis, by the discharge planner who considers family issues in a transfer home, or by the vocational rehabilitation specialist who assesses prior job history and current work activities in personal goal setting. The problem with many of today's approaches is that the organized plan of care does not clearly identify environmental factors and develop necessary supports. Provider-centered care systems, not consumer-centered health systems, are the common approach, and health care coverages do not usually include transition back to the workplace.

When employers emphasize individual functioning instead of medical necessity, the role of environmental factors in management of disability becomes clear. Disability is not just a physical condition; it also relates to external factors, which are environmental in nature, as identified in the following examples.

Example   A person living in a remote area of New Hampshire and commuting to a Boston suburb may become functionally disabled due to an inability to commute after a stress-related leave of absence. Another individual, who lives near the job site and has access to public transportation, may return to work successfully, even if in another position.

Example   A person recovering from brain surgery may be striving to recover certain physical skills, but be temporarily unable to drive to work. This condition may require the creation of certain compensating strategies over a 6-month period. In the meantime, the employee's wife obtains her employer's support in adjusting her arrival and departure times from 9:00 A.M. and 5:00 P.M.

to 10:00 A.M. and 6:00 P.M. so that she can assist her spouse in commuting and obtaining access to the facility in difficult winter conditions. Another person without a supportive spouse, family in general, and employer may be deemed functionally disabled for the long term not just temporarily.

By addressing the environmental factors that determine individual functioning, employers obtain functionally based outcome criteria for the process of rehabilitation while expanding the range of compensating strategies. Goal setting can then be individualized for management on a case basis, with attention to cognitive and psychological/social/behavioral issues as well as physical ones. The locus of rehabilitation thereby moves to the workplace and home, and away from the clinical world. The potential benefits include:

- Optimized personal productivity.
- Increased probability of lasting outcomes.
- Case closure based on human values.
- Managed risk in transfers, acting as a bridge between care and the worlds of work and home.

These are the elements that provide return on investment for employers.

The Value of Rehabilitation—Return on Investment

Many studies have identified the compelling cost/benefit of rehabilitation. One insurance study showed the average payback to be 30 times the amount invested.[24] Why then has funding remained so heavily concentrated in acute medical treatment and so inconsistent in rehabilitation? Some of the reasons include:

- Procedurally oriented treatment by physicians who lack training in a case orientation and the value of rehabilitation.
- A traditional one-year perspective in health care plans that emphasizes containing current year spending, not managing total costs or targeting cost savings.
- Funding of rehabilitation based on medical necessity, which limits its value. Rehabilitation needs to be functional.
- No connection between outcomes on health care and workers' compensation cases and the total cost of health and disability.
- A failure by many rehabilitation providers to present rigorously prepared outcome studies justifying their services.

- Poor identification of rehabilitation as a separate cost category in claims data.

Employers can overcome these problems because coverage of rehabilitation is often not mandated. The recommended approach is to manage rehabilitation and related spending separately from acute medical treatment. A program with the following elements can optimize the value of rehabilitation:

- Implement an overriding health intervention approach that requires a rehabilitation phase on all cases involving acute medical treatment.
- Specify the following goals of rehabilitation:

  Case closure as represented by a lack of readmission and continuing treatment, and reduced levels of disability.

  Personal productivity as measured by return to work and independence at home.

  Return on investment measured for a group of cases.

- Identify continuing costs and cost/benefit trade-offs for those requiring continuing supports (e.g., attendant care, adaptive equipment), proactively managing services on high risk, high cost cases.
- Utilize rehabilitation in the following manner:

  Provide fee-for-service funding only for cases of single functional limitations not involving prior specialty care (e.g., physical therapy for sports injury).

  Require rehabilitation after all specialty care as part of a plan of care (e.g., self-rehabilitation after heart surgery). Negotiate inclusion in fees for specialty care or identify separate follow-on requirements.

  In cases of multiple functional limitations after specialty care (catastrophic cases), utilize case management with specific outcome goals. Employ per diem rates for services.

- Incorporate the following elements in management of rehabilitation:

  Base the individualized plan of care on predefined outcomes.

  Include self-rehabilitation in all plans of care.

  Consider environmental issues encompassing activities, supports, and risks in a treatment plan for multiple functional limitations.

  Involve line management in return to work.

- Utilize a value-based approach to cost management (see Chapter 5).

Systematic management can use rehabilitation proactively with less waste and much more consistency than in the past. Simultaneously, increased leverage over future costs is possible because rehabilitation represents prevention on cases with known care needs. The goal is to obtain a return on investment, as shown in Figure 6.3,[25] by prudently investing in treatment to reduce future costs.

The challenge in managing rehabilitation is to maximize the net cost savings by obtaining the best possible outcomes. Each of the curves in Figure 6.3 shows a highly individualized situation and related outcome potential. Individualized treatment is critical because the human condition is involved. Even time needs individual management because one person may need six months to reach the same goal that someone else attains in three months. For this reason, arbitrary length-of-stay guidelines can undermine a return on investment. Outcome 3 in the figure shows the problem with limited investment; the best outcomes require a greater initial commitment of funds before the cost savings are achieved.

Managing based on return on investment does not mean pouring funds into treatment. Instead the goal is to optimize current costs by flexibly managing the type of therapies, the intensity of therapies, the treatment environment, and the days of treatment per week. In this way, total costs can be closely managed while outcome goals are achieved. The future cost savings from achieving each of these outcomes should also be a consideration.

Obtaining consistent funding for rehabilitation has been a problem because of the uncertainty related to achieving targeted outcomes and the potential for outcome regression. Employers can combine portfolio management with a health intervention approach to address this concern. The benefits of the cost savings achieved in the cases with positive outcomes offset the costs invested in the cases with inferior outcomes, as shown in

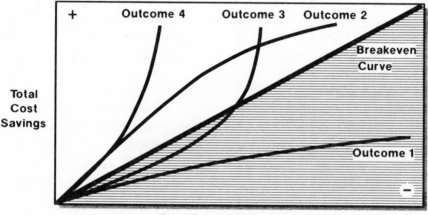

Figure 6.3 Rehabilitation Value Curve (RHM Systems, Inc., 1993, Marlboro, MA)

Figure 6.4. In the meantime, some important human needs have been met, regardless of outcome.

The dynamics of this simplified rehabilitation diagram indicate that a total of $10,000 needs to be spent on each rehabilitation case to save a potential $60,000 per case. By investing $200,000 on 20 cases, cost savings of $840,000 is achieved on 14 cases producing a net cost savings of $640,000, despite no savings on 6 cases. Outcome regression on 4 cases, however, reduces this savings by $240,000 to $400,000.

The investment of dollars and the distribution of cases can be tailored to individual circumstances, but the example demonstrates some important factors:

- An outcome focus is essential for managing rehabilitation based on return on investment.

- Achieving the best possible outcomes necessitates a focus on obtaining excellence in rehabilitation while supporting these activities in return to work and personal productivity in general.

- A well-managed investment in rehabilitation requires combining portfolio management with a health intervention approach.

- Taking the health intervention approach one step further, any small efforts or investment needed to prevent outcome regression can significantly enhance overall returns (e.g., case management follow-up on the highest risk cases as a form of outcome maintenance insurance).

Case management responsibility is first and foremost the individual's as part of a plan of care. A third-party case manager may be employed on more serious care issues. On the employer side, different case management accountabilities exist. The line supervisor is the de facto employer case manager in workplace health and disability issues with a direct accountability in supporting return to work. Appropriate information and supports from

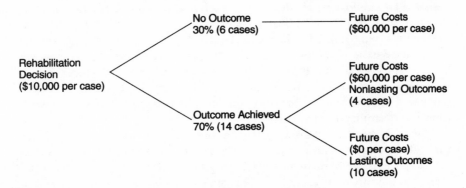

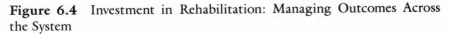

Figure 6.4 Investment in Rehabilitation: Managing Outcomes Across the System

disability management professionals, such as internal and external staff, provider staff, or community sources, can aid even the smallest employer.

When the care issues are more involved and long term, not allowing return to work, this accountability transfers to functional management for direct ongoing management with outside professionals. (Catastrophic and chronic care are reviewed in Chapter 14.)

In summary, well-managed rehabilitation can provide significant leverage over current and future health and disability costs. It can also help optimize personal and organizational productivity in both health care and workers' compensation cases.

Integrating Workplace Health and Disability to Achieve Productivity

Health and disability are no longer just a staff matter, a benefits issue, or the responsibility of third parties. The determinants of costs are very much rooted in employer operations. This connection was always an underlying issue, but its importance has changed significantly with experience-rating and self-insurance.

To gain the needed organizational focus among management, a separate management tract—Managing Productivity—has been developed. Tangible measures of performance include health-related productivity as a value index and the cost of productivity. With this direct accountability, line management can take a leadership role in an issue that has traditionally been outside their domain. While systematically addressing disability, line energy can move the orientation toward proactivity by focusing on human resources practices that create excess health care and workers' compensation costs. Time out of work and return to work can then gain the direct connection with line management that they require and care providers can be held accountable for achieving functional outcomes.

By focusing on health, line management can operate on a best practices basis for all employees. Health issues receive legitimacy at the line level so that potential health and safety risks can be addressed for individuals and for the group in total. Disability classification becomes a consideration only for the legal experts, because the line manager is accountable for respecting individual rights and for intervening at the right time to prevent a crisis and to accommodate someone in a return-to-work situation. This raises productivity to a higher standard based on fully productive work hours. Lost work time and disability-related turnover can receive similar direct attention.

Managing health and disability means optimizing employee productivity through an emphasis on prevention, rehabilitation, and flexibility in organizational management practices. An organization's productive potential is built one individual at a time. This approach identifies poor workplace health and disability practices as counter to organizational success. Both employee and supervisor can thereby be motivated to prevent poor health practices from developing and to work together on time out-of-work and return-to-work situations. Organizational response thus becomes proactive and managerial instead of reactive and administrative; *line* directed instead of *staff* directed.

Success in health and disability management can be best achieved when health, health care, and disability issues are linked to operations. This optimal approach moves beyond compliance training and disability programs to build these issues into the flow of line supervision. Organizational responsiveness is thus developed in the knowledge and motivations of line management and an employee's work accountabilities. Productivity is the natural outcome when information backs an integrated health commitment.

References

1. Rice, D. P., Relman, S., Miller, L. S., & Dunmeyer, S. 1990. *The economic costs of alcohol and drug abuse and mental illness.* San Francisco: University of California, Institute of Health and Aging.

2. Rice, D. P. December 1992. *Estimates of economic costs of mental health,* 1985 and 1990 (unpublished table). University of California, School of Nursing, Institute for Health & Aging.

3. What disabilities cost employers, *Business & Health,* May 1990, 28.

4. Farrell, G. P., Knowlton, S. K., & Taylor, M. C. 1989. *Second chance: Rehabilitating the American worker.* Minneapolis: Northwestern Mutual Life Insurance Company, 1–8.

5. The best companies to work for—What it takes. November 1992. *INC.,* 105–113.

6. What disabilities cost employers, *Business & Health,* May 1990, 28.

7. Polakoff, P. L., & O'Rourke, P. F. 1990. Healthy worker—Healthy workplace: The productivity connection. *Benefits Quarterly,* 6(2): 37–57.

8. Huth, S. A. 1991. COBRA coverage. *Employee Benefit Plan Review,* 46(4): 14–25.

9. *Survey of 1050 U.S. cities shows wide rate variation,* November 16, 1992. New York: Milliman & Robertson, Inc.

10. Kilborn, P. T. July 27, 1992. Company invests in human assets: Disabled employees in regular jobs. *New York Times,* A8.

11. Bernstein, A. 1992. A giant loophole called the Disability Act. *Business Week,* 93–94.

12. Try a new approach to workers comp. (Editorial). October 19, 1992. *Business Week,* 122.

13. U.S. Bureau of the Census, Statistical abstract of the United States: 1992 (112th Ed.). 1992. Reports 56, (p. 46) and 62, (p. 51). Washington, DC: U.S. Government Printing Office.

14. U.S. Bureau of the Census, Statistical abstract of the United States: 1992 (112th Ed.). 1992. (Report 48, p. 43, and 618, p. 387). Washington, DC: U.S. Government Printing Office.

15. Edington, D. W., & Yen, L. 1992. Is it possible to simultaneously reduce risk factors and excess health care costs? *American Journal of Health Promotion,* 6(6): 403–409.

16. Lee, P. M. August 1989. Dependent care options for small firms: The Employee Benefit of the 1990s, *Small Business Reports,* 66–71.

17. National Cancer Institute. December 1992. Despite advances, cancer still claims 1 in 5 Americans. *Boston Globe,* Nov. 29, 1992, 1, 5.

18. Henry, W., Jr., Smoller, B. M., & Rodgers, J. W. December 1991. Uncovering the hidden costs of long-term disability. *Risk Management,* 44.

19. Scheer, S. J., Ed. 1990. *Multidisciplinary perspectives in vocational assessment of impaired workers.* Rockville, MD: Aspen.

20. National Institute on Disability and Rehabilitation Research. 1991. Rehab Brief: Bringing research into effective focus. *Staying fully alive: Can people with disabilities find high quality primary health care in the U.S.?* XIII(9). Office of Special Education and Rehabilitative Services, Department of Education. Washington, DC.

21. Burns, T. J., Batavia, A. I., Smith, Q. W., & DeJong, G. 1990. Primary health care needs of persons with physical disabilities: What are the research and service priorities? *Archives of Physical Medicine & Rehabilitation,* 71: 138–143.

22. Rehab Brief. *Alcoholism as secondary disability: The silent saboteur in rehabilitation.* 5(6): 1–4. Washington, DC: Department of Education, 1982.

23. Greer, B. G. 1986. Substance abuse among the disabled: A case of too much accessibility. *Journal of Rehabilitation,* 52(1): 34–38.

24. Farrell, Knowlton, & Taylor, Second chance, note 4.

Resources

Carbine, M. E., Schwartz, G. E., & Watson, S. D. July 1989. *Disability intervention and cost management strategies for the 1990s.* Washington Business Group on Health's Institute for Rehabilitation and Disability Management.

Jamieson, D., & O'Mara, J. 1991. *Managing workforce two thousand: Gaining the diversity advantage.* San Francisco: Jossey-Bass.

Kravetz, D. J. 1988. *The human resources revolution: Implementing progressive management practices for bottom line success.* San Francisco: Jossey-Bass.

Miller, K. D. 1989. *Retraining the American workforce.* Reading, MA: Addison-Wesley.

Olmstead, B., & Smith, S. 1989. *Creating a flexible workplace: How to select and manage alternate work options.* New York: AMACOM.

Schwartz, G. E., Watson, S. D., Galvin, D. E., & Lipoff, E. 1989. *The disability management source book.* Washington Business Group on Health's Institute for Rehabilitation and Disability Management.

Smith, D. M. 1991. *Kin care and the American corporation: Solving the work–family dilemma.* Homewood, IL: Business One/Irwin.

7

Operationalizing Strategy-Based Management through Information: Control, Performance, Investment

Managing health and disability is no different from managing other organizational issues such as a marketing or product strategy: Information is required to manage toward defined goals and to react to contingencies. Otherwise, there is no baseline for allocating and reallocating resources, measuring performance, and determining investment alternatives. In the absence of information, management of health and disability—which should have been evolving, forward directed, and continuous—has instead been static, retrospective, and annualized.

Obtaining information was often impossible in the past. Group-rated health care coverages did not provide employer-specific claims experience, a problem that continues with community-rated managed care networks such as HMOs. Health care information, however, has become generally more available with experience rating and levels of self-insurance. Workers' compensation experience data has been more commonly available. The issue is now moving to a higher plane—employers' access to data is being supplanted by a need for usable information to manage health and disability more advantageously.

Current attention still lies at the claims level. Employers are obtaining insight into the medical care activities of those employees and dependents who happened to submit a claim. Yet much more is happening in health than what is commonly being reviewed. For example, workers' compensation claims are occurring simultaneously with health care claims, not just in the same year but crossing between policy years. Multiple claims often relate to a complex case. And employee time out of work for sick time, leaves of absence, and even vacation are pieces in the pattern of employee and even dependent health issues. When the focus turns to health itself, employers have access to a vast array of information resources, much of which can be found in house.

Despite all the costs organizations are incurring in administration, they are spending relatively small amounts on health and disability information. Line supervisors receive little training and guidance in managing complex health issues. And employees usually are exposed to coverage issues and nondirected health communications in the mail from managed care organizations, but receive little meaningful information about personal health issues. It should be no surprise then that spending on information is less than 0.5 percent of health care costs.[1] This figure represents a major opportunity for organizations incurring much higher percentages on management information to run their base businesses.

Information technology presents powerful capabilities to integrate and use health and disability data cost-effectively. Employees, line management, and functional management can all tap into a systems solution. Before investing more money in computer hardware and software, however, employers should think through their health and disability problems on a systems basis. Line supervisors fully engaged in a health-directed solution probably have the best insight into an organization's health and safety risks. When a health perspective replaces a benefits orientation, employee surveys can also provide input for programs. What is critical is to consider information as two-way communications between all participants, not just a matter of data and reporting.

The management approaches developed throughout this book are all information-based. The power of information to eliminate waste and to create value can be seen in the following simplified transactions flow of current under-managed care issues:

- Health and safety risk preventable.
- Uninformed care access.
- Poor diagnosis and treatment.
- No follow through on care plan.

Estimates of these issues run anywhere from 25 percent to 50 percent each. When compounded sequentially and across a total population, the amount of waste and non value is massive. Yet as much as diagnosis and treatment is basically a provider issue, the other three issues involve consumers and can be addressed directly by employers through the systematic availability and use of information.

The strategy-based information management approach in this chapter includes these elements:

- Testing assumptions about health and disability cost levels.
- Relaxing constraints in thinking about sources of costs.
- Ensuring high-quality data for decisions.
- Establishing information-based controls—quality assurance.
- Setting targets and managing performance.
- Managing uncertainty—the truest test of management.
- Making decisions based on return on investment.
- Leveraging the system through focused information.
- Integrating the health system through information.

The full power of information operationalizes strategy-based management of health and disability. Control, performance, and investment are simultaneously brought to bear on each of the three management tracts: Managing Health, Managing Care, and Managing Productivity. In this way, control, performance, and investment are optimized in each area and then across the system. Figure 7.1 shows this fully integrated quality-based management system.

In addition to achieving excellence in cost and quality, employers benefit from information in the following ways:

- Understanding the significance of what is presented.
- Understanding the effectiveness of all involved.
- Understanding trends over time.
- Being able to project going forward.

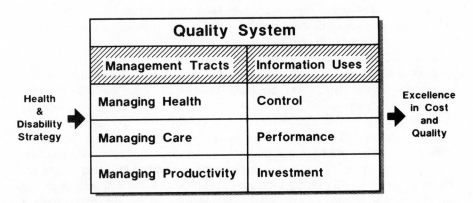

Figure 7.1   Operationalizing Strategy-Based Management: The Role of Information (RHM Systems, Inc., 1993, Marlboro, MA)

This type of management can be achieved when employers escape the self-imposed limitations of a cost-based care system. With information, a quality-based health system can reach its fullest potential in providing strategy-based cost solutions for employers.

Testing Assumptions about Health and Disability Cost Levels

Everyone knows health care and workers' compensation are major problems for organizations, but perceptions of the problem can vary widely within management ranks. Chief executive officers identify the cost of health care and workers' compensation as critical threats to the future of their organizations, probably because they focus on external sources of information. Internal managers can be similarly concerned, but sometimes they rationalize their organization's cost performance against others doing worse. Acceptance can creep in when all that has been accomplished is to slow the rate of cost hemorrhaging. The 1992 average increase in health care costs was 10.1 percent and even higher for workers' compensation.[2] What organization would consider even high single-digit inflation in wages or material costs to be a sign of success?

Much of the initial hurdle lies in testing common assumptions. Organizations often focus on absolute cost levels. Comparisons of health care costs on a per capita basis may show that the organization is in the fiftieth percentile of companies in its industry. The implication may be that the company is dealing adequately with an intractable national problem. Lost in such topside data is that absolute cost levels do not factor out plan design differences, the mix of regional costs between employers, and the underlying health and safety risks of the covered population.

A company in the fiftieth percentile, in reality, may be in the eightieth percentile when recognition is given to its operation in regions with relatively low health care costs. Detailed benchmarks of absolute cost levels are useful for assessing a competitor's cost structure for pricing or investment decisions, but they indicate little about the cost opportunity available from managing health and disability better internally.

A more common basis for assessing health care costs is the rate of annual cost increase. Organizations operate on annual budgets, and health care and workers' compensation coverages have traditionally been underwritten for one-year policy periods. Open enrollment election of health care coverages and various types of related administration further reinforces an annual perspective. Because of operating on an annual basis, many organizations assess their performance in health and disability in terms of the rate of cost increase over the prior year's cost levels versus that experienced by other organizations. Achieving a 13 percent increase in health care costs may be considered good versus an industry or regional experience of 20 percent, particularly if the rate of increase declined from the prior year's rate as well. This approach, unfortunately, has lost much of its relevance with a move away from group-rated and community-rated coverages.

By limiting assessments to such topside comparisons, an organization is essentially indicating that it lacks information for understanding and addressing the health and disability cost problem. The employer is making assumptions that need to be tested. The problem usually is that those directly involved in health care and workers' compensation have a narrow, specialized perspective with no control over broad organizational strategy issues. And those with control over strategy do not have the technical background to systematically address health and disability problems.

The answer to this challenge is to place the accountability on operations: It is necessary to get immersed in health care and workers' compensation problems from the employee level up while line management and functional management work together in assessing all aspects of their organization's health and disability programs. Only when this type of joint action team develops a bottom-up understanding of the cost problem can an employer begin to test fundamental self-limiting assumptions such as (1) that health and disability costs must rise, and (2) that quality will degrade if costs are reduced.

Relaxing Constraints in Thinking about Sources of Costs

Testing assumptions often involves questioning why major improvements in performance cannot be achieved. Initially, this can create some important breakthroughs. Instead of accepting certain accident rates in a facility, a new level of performance might be targeted. For example, the best performing facility in a company may have a tolerance for accidents that is inappropriate regardless of what other facilities are doing. If the workers' compensation rate of California is involved, this further improvement may have a greater cost/benefit than improvements targeted in the poorer performing facilities in some other states.

By itself, however, the assumption-testing process is inherently limited because the rethinking remains within traditional bounds. Results might include eliminating redundancies in internal efforts and creating improved communications. Members of a joint action team may believe they are achieving great breakthroughs, but in reality they may be making an inherently flawed system more efficient. Instead there is a need to reengineer processes across the total system.[3]

Real gains only become possible by relaxing constraints.[4] This is the greatest challenge to achieving significant cost breakthroughs in health and disability. Often the problem lies in a lack of information. A quality-based health system may offer great benefits, but both employer and employees and dependents require training in how to take full responsibility for problem solving. For example, claims data might identify drawn-out workers' compensation cases as a key cost problem. Instead of considering the issue unsolvable because of rapacious lawyers and a flawed state system, management must look at its own operations.

When investigation involves a team of current employees who have successfully returned to work, the problem takes on a whole new light. The real issues may relate to line supervisors who are afraid to interact with out-of-work employees and families because of legal concerns. Other barriers may include a company medical director untrained in the broad array of return-to-work issues and an ineffective hospital-based work hardening program that has no connections with the employer's culture and social environment.

An employer can become quite proactive with such information. Once return to work is addressed for workers' compensation cases, many of the same approaches can be utilized to improve the organization's response to health care cases. The company thereby turns a systemic problem into an operations-oriented solution. Viewing health and productivity as integral to the care issue makes the need for cooperation between operations and functional management more apparent.

Give and take between line management and functional management is essential for relaxing health and disability constraints. Line management usually better understands the causal factors behind claims, but may feel helpless in addressing the problem due to self-imposed limitations regarding personal health matters. Conversely, if functional management has been oversold on the benefits of the traditional cost-based care system, the employer may rely on managed care alone to solve problems. When supported by the right information, management can move to challenge some critical constraints holding back progress. A new set of realities can develop, as shown in Table 7.1.

Assumptions and constraints about these issues may seem insignificant compared with the big picture systemic issues in health care and workers' compensation, but they form the real leverage points of addressing the causes of costs. A health intervention approach is predicated on using the power of information to support new forms of risk and quality management, driving health awareness and decision making forward.

Managing Forward is in the mutual interest of employer and employee when balanced with the right incentives—informational, cultural, and financial. Information is also critical in Managing Care and Managing Productivity to optimize results. With integrated management through an employee-specific strategy, the most important constraint can be relaxed— that employers have limited control over health and disability costs.

Ensuring High-Quality Data for Decisions

The information age is starting to impact health care and workers' compensation, but one of its dangers is to confuse data availability with usability.

Table 7.1   Considering New Realities

Assumptions/Constraints	New Realities
Confidentiality prevents accessing information.	The sensitivity of confidentiality changes when risk prevention for the covered population in total is stressed instead of risk avoidance for targeted individuals.
Coverage limitations are effective for managing risks.	Employees are rational consumers who will find a way to get the care need covered, and providers know how to work around coverage limitations.
Employees and dependents have an inherent interest in accessing care.	More often, the opposite is the case, employees, particularly men, tend to delay care needs until problems become acute.
Nonwork activities are impossible to influence.	There is a transference of activities and behaviors between work and home. Back self care and safe driving are just two examples.
Dependents are impossible to influence.	Control over an employee can directly influence dependent behaviors. A smoking cessation program is an example. Also, high-risk employees often reside with high-risk dependents so addressing risk factors can multiply benefits.
Older employees are inherently more costly than young employees when it comes to health care.	This may not be the case when dependents are considered. Also, multiple and cumulative risk factors determine health care utilization more than the aging process itself.
Employee turnover makes doing anything about managing health care and workers' compensation nonworthwhile.	Any employee creates an exposure in a wide range of health and disability issues. Turnover is more likely to add to costs, not save on them in a world of experience-rated and self-insured risks.

Garbage in translates into garbage out, a maxim that rings true in health and disability as well as in other organizational issues. For example, companies seldom apply the controls over health and disability data that they do for cash receipts and cash disbursements. There is a tendency to accept at face value the data supplied by providers, at least when submitted by managed care organizations.

Ensuring quality of data submission is an essential building block in developing an information-driven strategy and related set of management responses. Some of the mechanisms that can be used include:

1. Negotiate a standard for data quality in the terms and conditions of agreements with third-party organizations.
2. Assess the methods used by third parties to ensure data quality by providers and within their own operations.

3. Identify delays in data submission past a certain standard as a cause for management review of related claims (this is another reason for eliminating deductibles).

4. Involve all participants in data quality through incentives, particularly employees and dependents in red flagging unsubstantiated or inflated claims. Create a watch list of providers who develop a history of such practices feeding this back to third-party managers for changing future relationships.

5. Use statistically based audits to zero in, periodically by provider and procedure, on data quality in areas of highest cost.

Even when mechanisms are in place to ensure quality, employers need to be careful about drawing conclusions from data. Accuracy only means that the first test of usability has been passed. The next test is to ensure that the data being collected pass a sanity check in terms of reasonableness. A high number of claims per individual employee or provider for a limited time period indicates a higher potential of fraud or excessive treatment. When such situations are recurring and widely different from normal patterns, action needs to be taken through appropriate channels.

Ensuring data quality does not mean that usable information has been produced. This next step in the use of data is often the most difficult for employers and third-party managers. Translating data into quality information requires a basic understanding of statistical inference and sampling techniques. Some of the related issues include:

- The time period analyzed may be too short for drawing conclusions about problems and trends (e.g., a wellness program is deemed unsuccessful after a limited trial).

- The sample size may be too small to be representative of normal activities (e.g., two "bad" outcomes on two heart cases in one quarter may not tell the whole story when six "good" outcomes occurred in the other three quarters).

- The sample may not be a reliable indicator of the general population (e.g., two "bad" outcomes in treatment at one provider may only indicate that the provider is inferior or unlucky, not that all providers doing similar treatment will produce the same results).

Instead of spending time and money on the latest program solutions, employers need to focus on the providers and third-party managers achieving the best and worst results on current health, health care, and disability programs. Clinical issues do not escape the logic of statistics. Obtaining quality data and then applying that data to create usable information underpins a quality system and effective health and disability strategy.

Establishing Information-Based Controls— Quality Assurance

Once data quality is ensured, organizations can stand back and look at health and disability in broader systems terms. The tendency, however, is to zero in periodically on claims-related problems, not to develop a system of controls that is sustainable and fundamentally quality driven.

One of the biggest problems is the self-limiting nature of a system viewed only as health care or workers' compensation transactions. Claims themselves are retrospective and do not provide insight into the vast range of health activities taking place daily, often translating into productivity gains or losses. For this reason, a system of controls requires a much broader view. To achieve this kind of system, employers should take the following steps:

1. Ensure the data collected objectively represents the benefit of the transaction (e.g., signing up for a health program is not the same as true participation).

2. Ensure that the data sample is comprehensive and that there are not disincentives to complete reporting (e.g., that deductibles are not limiting the sample because small claims are not reported).

3. Ensure controls over who can submit a claim or report an activity (e.g., a well-defined credentialing process in a managed care network).

4. Whenever possible, eliminate quarterly adjustments in reasonable and customary rates in health care coverage and place control over the use of settlements in workers' compensation cases.

5. Identify areas of potential conflict of interest in advance (e.g., self-referral patterns in care activities) with a focus on high-cost specialty care. Alert third-party managers to this issue and develop a history of problems.

6. Use statistically based control limits on high-volume transactions to identify problems, and use statistically based audits periodically to trace the flow of claims and cases from a control standpoint, focusing on areas of highest cost.

7. Develop a connection between claims data and broader measures of health and productivity for the covered population.

The lack of system-based controls is evident in coordinaton of benefits procedures in health care coverages. Unpaid amounts exceeding reasonable and customary allowances are commonly viewed as cost savings to employers. In reality, they are further evidence that the system itself is not controlling provider rates. Whether the excess charges are actually borne by the employee and dependent is often an issue for negotiation. Even copayment amounts are sometimes negotiated away.

Similar control problems exist in workers' compensation claims. Settlements are often common practice providing little incentive for employees to change claims behavior. Insurance companies may promote a sign-off on the liability, but to stop a treadmill of future claims, employers must still manage their costs. Only by defining a system of control and ensuring data quality can employers establish quality assurance on a systems basis. Value will truly be obtained when employers control activities through more than spending. Some of the key quality assurance points for management include:

- Participation rates in health and safety programs.
- Adherence to personal health programs.
- Adherence to individual care plans.
- Readmission in acute medical treatment.
- Regression in rehabilitation.
- Relapse in substance abuse.

These quality assurance mechanisms can be used to maximize the investment made in health programs and activities and in health care itself.

Setting Targets and Measuring Performance

Health and disability did not traditionally offer a large opportunity for management based on performance accountabilities. Health care coverage was commonly viewed as a total program with an emphasis on requoting and rebrokering. Workers' compensation coverage had more connection because of individual claims experience and related modification ratings, but even then insurers often settled claims or established their own reserves. Regardless, premiums were often dependent on the vagaries of insurance market cycles.

Performance has taken on a whole new light with managed care networks and specialized services, and with the advent of experience rating and levels of self-insurance. Employers now have an opportunity to develop comprehensive cost and quality management based on performance measurement. Accountabilities can move well past the generalized program level to managed care services, providers, procedures, and types of cases. Most importantly, accountabilities can be defined for both internal and external participants in a wide range of health and disability activities as well as in care activities.

Performance can be viewed at many levels. Organizations are concerned with managing total costs, but control and leverage over costs requires setting targets and measuring performance at the following levels:

- Individual employee and related dependents.
- Line supervisors and line management.
- Functional management.
- Total department as a group.
- Total facility or region as a group.
- Total division as a group.
- Providers and third-party managers.
- Total organization.

The type of targets set at each level will vary, stressing a combination of cost, quality of care, and health status measures. There is no reason why significant performance improvements cannot be tasked. For the individual, health itself is the most powerful personal goal. Organizations can tap into employee and dependent self-interest by providing information, training, and supports in a wide range of health issues such as health and safety risks at home and work and self-care and health programs.

When a health culture is developed among employees, the targets set at the management levels have more chance for success. Line supervisors and line management can be measured against performance targets in such areas as workplace accidents, absenteeism, time out of work, return to work success, and many different types of productivity costs. These goals need to be both comprehensive to gain line attention as well as directly related to specific causal factors under line control when a cooperative relationship exists with employees.

Performance targets among employees and dependents need to be tangible and realistic. Concrete actions which benefit both the individual and the immediate group require emphasis. As goal setting moves to broader groups such as facility, division, or total organization, the targets can become progressively oriented toward costs and quality of care, and less directed toward health status measures. Goals such as lost work days due to accident or workplace health issues, group progress in reducing health risks and costs, and participation rates in preventive care and health programs are powerful organizational tools to reinforce personal behavior. These measures will have a positive influence when employees and line supervisors are working together to manage personal and group productivity. Even quality of care will benefit when feedback is solicited from employees and dependents and line supervisors about various health, health care, and disability programs.

As performance measures are developed for larger organizational units, there is a need to promote the Managing Forward approach in all activities. The organizational bias needs to be toward accountability and action, rooting out wasteful delays. Measurement can thus be identified across the health continuum, as part of the systems framework employed in this book.

Results can be achieved through the following methodology with some specific employer actions listed as an example:

1. Systematic reduction in the underlying causes of costs.
   —Hiring practices upgraded for the third shift.
   —Health and safety training program instituted for new employees.
   —Auto driving safety stressed with all sales staff.
2. Cumulative and continuous improvement among a range of cost-saving activities while managing total health and disability costs.
   —Outside legal counsel for disability issues to be reduced by 75%.
   —Emergency room utilization to be reduced by 50%.
   —Chiropractic care to be reduced by 50%.
3. Investments in a portfolio of activities and related programs to reduce risks and costs.
   —Information for employees on health and safety risk factors.
   —Videos for employees and dependents on home safety.
   —Self-care program for backs.
   —Biking helmets made available for employees and dependents at company picnic for $10.00 each.

These activities have been selected to show small discrete areas for improvement, rather than to address major health and safety programs described in the next part of the book. None of the cost improvements targeted relate to cutting spending per se. Measurement of results needs to be in terms of specific cost savings and the probability of certain health and safety risks, while controlling total costs. Activities are often interrelated. For example, better driving practices could be reducing back related aggravation while at the same time back self care is having tremendous participation rates within a company, reducing the need for chiropractic care. Excellence in primary care will also reduce chiropractic utilization in both health care and workers' compensation. Similarly, the health and safety message could be made available for dependents through such visible signs as biking helmets and the availability of videos. Emergency room utilization is thereby addressed proactively and positively along with the serious issue of brain injury.

Many opportunities exist to reduce risks and to reduce costs, but usually no one is empowered to take action. Information, training, and supports are the key. Does it cost money to address many of the targets or is it more a matter of organizational attention and commitment? Isn't focused information often more important than new programs? Do employers need to rush into detailed health risk screening? Wouldn't they benefit first from information about the impact of health and safety risks on personal and family health? If 30 areas are targeted across an organization, won't at least 20 of them be achieved without much expenditure? And couldn't these be some of the highest ROI opportunities available within an organization?

What is needed is a commitment of organizational time at many levels to empower individuals and teams. And most critically, there is a need for line supervisors and line management to legitimize health as an organization concern. The bias needs to be toward action, with inaction penalized, not promoted.

Through broad based measurement and defined accountabilities performance can be defined across the total system to benefit senior management's understanding of a large portion of its organization's cost structure. Systematic management of specific cost improvements and risk reductions is very much like an early warning system. True control comes from having everyone within an organization alerted to the threat of health and safety risks and unnecessary costs, but with personal responses benefitting the collective whole. Predictability of future costs is thus enhanced. This Managing Forward approach to the use of information is described as a "Senior Management Dashboard" as shown in Table 7.2.

The measures on the Senior Management Dashboard can also include some clinical outcome measures and a wide variety of the costs making up the total cost of Health and Disability. Managing performance over time

Table 7.2   Senior Management Dashboard for Health and Disability

Population Profile	Prior Year Qtrly. Avg.	Prior Year 4th Qtr.	1st Qtr. Actual	2nd Qtr. Actual	Year End Target
Coverage (%)					
Employees covered for health care	.92	.90	.88	.93	.92
Covered employees covering dependents	.67	.70	.71	.73	.70
Dependent/employee ratio	2.0	2.1	2.1	2.2	2.1
Cost Index (%)					
Weighted average of regional health care costs	1.30	1.35	1.30	1.25	1.20
Weighted average of regional workers' compensation costs	1.40	1.40	1.35	1.30	1.20
Total Cost ($)					
Cost of health care per employee (annualized)	3,890	3,950	3,850	3,750	3,700

Table 7.2   *(Continued)*

Population Profile	Prior Year Qtrly. Avg.	Prior Year 4th Qtr.	1st Qtr. Actual	2nd Qtr. Actual	Year End Target
Total cost of health and disability per employee (annualized)	8,550	8,650	8,500	8,250	8,000
Managing Health (%)					
Employees in health programs	.25	.28	.35	.42	.50
Employees utilizing primary care (annualized)	.40	.40	.45	.50	.65
Employees utilizing specialty care (annualized)	.35	.35	.30	.25	.20
Employees in high-risk status	.20	.20	.18	.14	.10
Managing Care					
In network care	.50	.60	.65	.70	.80
Center of excellence on high-risk, high-cost cases	.50	.75	.75	1.00	1.00
Case management on high-risk, high-cost cases	.75	.50	.75	.90	1.00
Number of cases over $50,000	3	2	3	1	2
Readmission on cases over $50,000	—	—	2	—	—
Managing Productivity					
No. of work accidents	5	3	2	3	—
Return to work ratio	.60	.50	.75	.75	.90
No. of return to work cases (health care)	3	3	2	2	2
No. of return to work cases (workers' comp.)	4	3	2	1	1
Duration in months of workers' comp. cases	6	4	3	2	1
Lost work days—health care	250	300	200	200	200
Lost work days—workers' comp.	300	250	200	100	100
Absenteeism	.06	.07	.05	.05	.04
Cost of settlement	$30,000	—	—	$10,000	—

can be best achieved by establishing benchmarks to understand relative performance and the areas of greatest improvement potential. The cost and quality benchmarks that can be used include:

Internal Performance
- Prior year's results.
- Current year's targets.

External Performance
- By other employer organizations.
- By program, provider, procedure, or case.
- By population characteristics—health and safety risk incidence.

All these benchmarks can guide management of health, care, and productivity, but it is important to realize that external information combines today's undermanaged health and disability cost and quality results. Employers should strive to achieve excellence and to be the best in their class by exceeding the common performance benchmarks.

Managing Uncertainty—
The Truest Test of Management

As employers implement a comprehensive framework for managing the cost and quality of health and disability, performance measures help them understand the significance of their information and the effectiveness of all involved parties. Another need remains to be answered, however: systematic control of the factors determining performance.

The greatest consistency in health and disability cost and quality performance is achieved by pairing management of cause and effect with a reduction in the number of interdependent variables in health activities and the uncertainty related to each. For example, rehabilitation currently may be a low priority after certain specialty care. Instead, an employer or third-party manager might develop a predefined network of excellence which is fully communicated to health care plan participants.

In this way, patients with a serious problem such as brain injury are transferred directly from high-quality medical centers to a predefined rehabilitation program with identified outcome targets such as return to work and independent living skills. Employers thus eliminate the cost exposure from wide variances in performance on a costly form of treatment while minimizing the costs inherent in poorly coordinated and delayed transfers. Wide application of this center of excellence approach is essential in developing systems solutions.[5, 6]

When employers implement systematic management of the health system involving all participants, performance management extends into a fuller understanding of trends over time and an increased ability to project going forward. The following two examples show the importance of these issues:

Example   A good year of claims experience results in the Risk Manager and CFO increasing a company's self-insured financial risk from $100,000 to $200,000 per claim. In the following year, three claims totaling $175,000 each severely impact the company's cost experience causing 40 percent of the year-to-year cost increase. One of the claims trails into a subsequent policy year for another $150,000.

Example   A good year of claims experience results in lower realized claims than the budgeted accrual. The Vice President Human Resources and the Benefits Manager have a choice of accepting praise for the health care program or in maintaining the need to carry over some of the unused accrual into the next year. The CFO believes certain plan design features are benefiting costs and wants to reverse the accrual to improve fourth quarter and full year results.

These examples point out the importance of managing uncertainty and the potential pitfalls of partially self-insured financial risks. Increasing the financial risk exposure without addressing the underlying health and safety risks and related program management issues is an invitation for cost disasters. Employers need to be good, not just lucky.

Even in a fully insured world, uncertainty was never insured away. Insurers only absorbed the financial risks for one year at a time with the uncertainty returning with a vengeance in the next policy year. Now employers have an opportunity to fundamentally reduce the level of uncertainty in their health and disability costs. Systematic management of costs utilizes the techniques in earlier chapters and also considers the issue of uncertainty. The trade-off between overall program exposure to levels of financial risks can be weighed against the costs of coverage labeled as the financial risk premium. This cost variable identifies the importance of anticipating normal cost fluctuations and consolidating an employer's financial risk. This framework can also be used for workers' compensation program total costs with variables added for income supports, settlements, and legal costs.

$$\begin{matrix} \text{Health Care} \\ \text{Program} \\ \text{Total Costs} \end{matrix} = \text{Utilization} \times \begin{matrix} \text{Cost} \\ \text{Levels} \end{matrix} + \begin{matrix} \text{Management} \\ \text{and Administration} \\ \text{(Internal and} \\ \text{External)} \end{matrix} + \begin{matrix} \text{Financial} \\ \text{Risk} \\ \text{Premium} \end{matrix}$$

The preceding equation provides clues for answering the dilemmas in the two earlier examples. Bottom-up analysis of a program's cost structure is necessary for determining the appropriate level of self-insured risk or accrued expense to cover potential future claims. All too often, the analysis is done incrementally, based on new programs and perceived benefits.

Utilization is the cost driver. The amount of utilization and the intensity of treatment embedded in utilization are the most critical cost factors. Analyzing and understanding utilization provides the basis for projecting future utilization and ultimate health care costs. Information is essential for Managing Forward in this manner. The groundwork is thus established for understanding and projecting future performance based on continuous improvement.

This approach can manage and reduce uncertainty. Projecting cost performance and cash funding strategies in self-insured health care and workers' compensation programs requires the following three approaches:

1. A prudent level of self-insured financial risk can be established based on probability of future large dollar claims derived from risk probabilities for types of utilization.

2. The amount of accrued expense can be established based on a forecast of normal annualized utilization of high-cost specialty care. A good year may be only a timing issue with the next big claim hitting in the first month of the new year.

3. Conversion from premium-based coverage to self-insured coverage presents an opportunity to benefit in the first few months from the time lag on claims submission and processing. A cash gain approximating three months of prior premiums is generally realized. This cash benefit, however, is sometimes confused as a cost decrease by employers who have yet to change from annualized management. Accrual of this runoff liability in internal performance measures reflects good management practices while creating a baseline for assessing future costs.

Performance is no small matter when it comes to management of health and disability. With direct, indirect, and hidden costs equalling a substantial portion of operating costs for most organizations, what was once a minor benefits issue has become a matter of strategic importance. Understanding true cost performance is essential. Underrecognition of future liabilities can mask inherent program weaknesses. Sudden surprises in costs are the bane of operating and financial management and are unnecessary with systematic management of health and disability as part of corporate strategy.

Making Decisions Based on Return on Investment

The need for measures of cost-effectiveness and quality are widely recognized in health care and workers' compensation. No one seems to be arguing against such performance measures anymore. Many clinical professionals have trouble, however, when performance moves to the next level—return on investment. It can sound as numbers driven and calculating as Wall Street itself.

Return on investment has floundered as a decision-making tool, not because of an inherent conflict with human values, but because of the following structural deficiencies in the traditional cost-based care model:

- Health care plans underwritten for one-year periods provided little investment incentive to insurers.
- Insurers and third-party managers have mostly managed costs as a current period issue only, not as an investment with cost savings potential in future periods.
- Fully insured coverages removed the incentives for employers to make investments.
- Providers have commonly viewed cost savings as directly reducing care.

With today's focus on quality at the provider level, an awareness is developing about the costs of poor quality. For example, a poor surgical outcome can result in readmission for resetting a bone while necessitating more involved rehabilitation. Thus, clinical professionals are starting to realize that an investment in quality translates into cost savings that enhance human values, not degrade them. In this context, ROI is a positive force for allocating resources toward improved quality levels.

Reducing costs by eliminating obvious waste and inefficiencies in the care system is compelling to most everyone. The conflict occurs when clinical professionals continue their relentless drive toward improving care through increased technology. Whether the culprit is costly equipment or drugs, this is where ROI seems to fall by the wayside. And employers and third-party managers are at a loss in enforcing cost/benefit discipline over such sensitive human issues.

Solving this most difficult dilemma requires a new paradigm: The fundamental human issue is not care; it is health. To optimize cost and quality performance, employers must establish health as the primary goal and ultimate outcome of all activities. Technology is only beneficial when it enhances human health. In this context, ROI directed toward health provides the means to rank the human value of all care activities in cost/benefit terms. Using this measure will fully identify the value of preventive care. For example, the measure of a new diagnostic testing device's value is its cost savings in care activities and prevention of productivity losses. A rate of return in this context is not a coldhearted method to deny people care; rather, it is a way to determine the relative values of diagnostic testing devices and the most effective use of funds for addressing human needs.

Return on investment moves cost management out of being a current period issue only. Health and related care and productivity issues can be balanced between each other and between current and future periods. Various projects can be ranked against each other in selecting the most beneficial projects. The full benefits of health-based ROI as a decision-making criterion are as follows:

1. Cost/benefit assessment of health programs.
2. Ranking of current and prospective health programs.
3. Cost/benefit assessment of early management interventions and treatment interventions such as diagnostic testing and rehabilitation.
4. Ranking of current and prospective early health interventions.
5. Cost/benefit assessment of relative outcomes by provider and procedure.
6. Cost/benefit assessment of extra services and/or time in treatment versus levels of outcomes achieved.

Investment itself is very much part of a systems approach to problem-solving because Return on Investment analysis built into management decision-making can anticipate the range of options available in all types of management interventions. Apart from anticipation, a portfolio of actions can be undertaken to reduce underlying health and safety risks and to enhance the performance of individual health, safety, and disability programs. Resources can thus be optimized based upon available information with forward movement strategically built into the system of management. Continuous improvement at the operational level can then complement ROI put in place at the strategic level.

Leveraging the System through Limited Information

Health and disability is beginning to move away from industrial-age medicine toward information-age health. Access to claims data represents only the starting point to developing information as an integral element of an employer-specific health and disability strategy. Information is the greatest source of potential leverage over both costs and quality and, more fundamentally, over the actions and behaviors of all participants. Information feedback permits continuous management of the accountabilities that have been identified up front.

While access to a broad range of information is essential, employers need to approach information in a strategic context. The challenge is to apply the greatest leverage over costs and quality, by defining a limited amount of information at every level of use. The variables defined for each employer are most beneficial for all participants and the organization when mechanisms are in place to ensure understanding of use, ongoing integrity, timely availability to support decision making, and timely review by senior management. The starting point for such information based management lies

Table 7.3 Return on Investment Combining Strategic and Information Leverage

Cost Management Techniques	Investment		Cost Savings	
	Health Programs and Activities	Management and Information	Cost of Care	Cost of Productivity
Managing the Financial Risk (Chapter 2)				
Avoidance	—	$	$	—
Levels of self-insurance	—	$	$	—
Consolidation of programs	—	$	$	—
Developing a Quality System (Chapter 3)				
Program need and effectiveness	—	—	—	—
Management effectiveness, internal and external	—	—	—	—
Managing Health (Chapter 4)				
Health and safety risks	$$	$$	$$$	$$$
Proactive utilization management based on risk management	$$	$$	$$$	$$$
Health programs	$$$	$$	$$$	$$$
Primary care	$$$	$	$$$	$$
Managing Care (Chapter 5)				
Value-based approach to care providers	—	$	$$$	$
Case management on high-risk, high-cost cases	—	$	$$$	$
Managing Productivity (Chapter 6)				
Value-based approach to rehabilitation	—	$	$$	$$$
Closure on cases (e.g., disability management)	—	$	$$	$$$
Operations issues (e.g., employee turnover)	—	$$	$$	$$$

in some of the leverage points common to all organizations as shown in Table 7.3. This analysis extends the strategic cost management framework developed in Chapter 4 to identifying investment as consisting of health programs and activities and internal and external management with cost savings derived in the costs of care and productivity.

Table 7.3 integrates the leverage points identified in the beginning of Part One with various return on investment approaches. The key points are that health is an investment which needs to combine all health, safety, and disability programs. Programs can be assessed against each other and further analyzed by activities within an individual program. In addition to health efforts, management and information is another critical investment that needs to be made systematically within operations and in functional accountabilities, only then involving third party managers.

The challenge for senior management is to translate this broad framework into an individualized strategy for their organization. Within each cost and quality leverage point, there are a number of activities that can be undertaken. What kind of health programs should be considered and what are the most effective alternatives based on other's success? How should disability management be structured to bring a 24-hour perspective to line management? How can legal exposures and legal costs be systematically reduced, particularly in workers' compensation? How does information fit into all of these activiities? These are just a few of the leverage points that can be encompassed within an individualized health and disability strategy based on the organization's operating profile.

When reviewing their options, employers will probably find that the best source of information lies outside traditional reporting. Getting at the sources of costs requires investigation into activities, not just claims review. The following examples demonstrate the importance of strategically focused information.

Example   An employer suffers a twenty percent increase in the costs of its self-insured health care program, about double what was budgeted and accrued for the first nine months of the fiscal year. In response, severe cost sharing with employees is being considered for the next policy year.

The VP Human Resources and CFO undertake a detailed review of health care, workers' compensation, and disability issues. Analysis shows return-to-work experience on both health care and workers' compensation cases to be extremely poor compared with some industry leaders.

Excess costs are being incurred in drawn-out care, high legal costs, settlements and disability income supports, and staff replacement costs. Reducing these costs by 50 percent to only the industry average would save $1 million or 50 percent of the cost increase. In addition, a review of health care claims shows three high-cost cases that have all been completed.

Instead of increasing cost sharing, the company initiates an education and training program on disability and workplace health, entitled "Managing for Health and Productivity." In addition to this program for functional and line management and employees, new incentives are introduced, and major changes are made in off-site disability and wellness efforts that more directly tie into the organizational health commitment. Next year's cost goals for health and disability are finalized at a 20 percent reduction without changing benefits or increasing cost sharing.

Example An employer, in probing into its high health care costs, detects a number of utilization patterns: extensive testing, long-term treatment, and long-term use of medications. What makes the information so compelling is that these patterns are much more intensive in one operating region than in others. Very high utilization is also identified among new employees. The employer presents this problem to the national managed care network that manages the self-insured program. Follow-up analysis shows the problem is confined to two group practices. The managed care group's medical director then takes action and puts continuous review in place.

Utilization is further addressed through an on-site education and training program in managing personal health and accessing health care. A physician from the managed care group who advocates an empowered consumer reinforces the message at the problem facility. Line management makes an ongoing commitment to this effort by allotting time monthly for participation in the program and for discussion of workplace health and safety issues. In addition, the management team has been tasked by the company's CEO to address a serious employee turnover problem which is impacting health care utilization, workers' compensation claims, and productivity in general.

Information has been generally underutilized in addressing health and disability costs at the root cause level—within operations and among employees and dependents themselves. Consistent with the Managing Forward concept, the power of information can orient all activities toward a health intervention approach. The key elements for using information this way are:

- Focus information early in the health continuum.
- Design information to meet the user's needs.
- Identify how the information will benefit the user's self-interest.
- Reinforce the information message continuously.
- Concentrate on a limited number of critical issues.

- Contain the cost of information by making it relevant and understandable.

When information is applied to critical activities, organizations have the means to link an individualized strategy with a systems framework for major cost and quality gains. Even then, information itself needs to be highly focused based on the following techinques:

- Identifying only the most critical data.
- Ensuring that an objective, not subjective data measurement is employed.
- Ensuring that an interdependencies between data elements are understood and controlled.
- Reducing the variability of key data.
- Ensuring that quality data are obtained through standards backed by periodic audit.
- Linking the data into the issues of control, performance, and investment for relevance to an organization's cost and quality goals.
- Reporting the data in an understandable manner to meet the specific needs of various management users.

Integrating the Health System through Information

Information is essential for developing strategy-based solutions to current health and disability cost and quality problems. Yet information itself often creates a self-limiting framework for management. The split between health care and workers' compensation claims is a natural example. Although claims are administered separately, management of causal factors and the quality of activities behind the claims can be identified through both common and different data and then addressed in an integrated manner. To obtain strategy-based solutions, employers need to stand back from current reporting and reports, and instead assess health and disability from an integrated systems standpoint.

Information is the essence of strategy, yet to be operationalized, it must extend into management systems and even into culture. Consequently, the behavior and motivations of employees and line management need to be continuously addressed as part of the health system. Part One of this book has brought these elements together in a health and disability context, as originally identified in the Health Triangle.

The previously missing piece of information for employers has been that health itself needs to be managed. Health is the functional equivalent to quality, applied to personal issues. When viewed in these terms, information takes on a different meaning. All participants—employees, dependents, line managers need education and training on health and care issues, not just after a health event occurs, but in advance of care. This forward-directed approach to health and disability creates a focus on health interventions backed by involved management at every level instead of just treatment interventions. Communications about health, optimal access of care, and productivity is essential, particularly if the full benefit of incentives and risk sharing is to be realized.

When employers assess information in terms of the universe of involved parties, the importance of an employer-centered approach becomes evident. Health, a missing assignment in today's care delivery system, can be best achieved through joint employer–employee accountabilities. As shown in Figure 7.2, only the employer stands as the intermediary for the worlds of work, home, and care while absorbing all types of health and disability costs.[7] Human interconnections occur much more frequently between work and home, than between work and care, and between home and care. And only the employer translates health and care into a direct economic value in terms of productivity. As a result, proactive management of workplace health and disability can produce major productivity benefits for individuals, organizations, and the nation.

This three-way linkage among health, care, and productivity creates a need for regular information. When managed simultaneously, continuous improvement can obtain excellence in both cost and quality. Information provides the means for employers to control health and disability activities within their own operations while supporting employees in managing personal and family health. It also is the means for systematically obtaining value from care providers and third-party managers. The key to gaining these results is an individualized health and disability strategy identifying the following key issues:

- Where to focus through performance measures.
- Where to control.

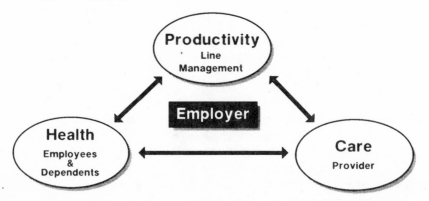

Figure 7.2   An Expanded Health Triangle: Managing the Total Health System

- Where to exert leverage.
- Where to invest.
- Where to provide incentives and share risk.

By Managing Forward, employers can reduce the risks of future health events through activities taken today and can control costs through the cost management techniques presented throughout the chapters of Part One. Integral to this approach is the concept of managing risk, not just financing it. Risk as a cost management opportunity can thereby supplement risk as a liability exposure.

In the end, health care and workers' compensation involve human issues. For too long, prescribed coverages and predefined methods of management have undermined the value of care and created the wrong incentives. When employers utilize an information-driven approach to solutions, they can operate through value-seeking methods that reduce cost and improve quality. In this way, human values are enhanced even as organizations achieve newfound, lasting success in managing health and disability as a part of mainstream organizational priorities.

References

1. Webb, J. 1992. Commercial Corporation Fitness Management Program, California Polytechnic State University at San Luis Obispo.
2. Foster Higgins Health Care Survey of 2,448 large- and medium-sized employers, March 1993, Freudenheim, M., *New York Times,* Study Sees Rise in Medical Costs, March 2, 1993, D1, 20.
3. Hammer, M. July–August 1990. Reengineering work: Don't automate, obliterate. *Harvard Business Review,* pp. 104–112.
4. Roberts, N. V. September 1992. Data collection and analysis. *Presentation to Midwest Business Group on Health.*
5. Marshall, M., & Perry, S. February 1990. *Centers of excellence: A definition and policy proposal for the Assistant Secretary of Planning and Evaluation.* U.S. Department of Health and Human Services, Contract No. HHS 100-88-0029.
6. Christensen, L. June 1991. Change of hearts centers of excellence concept, *Business & Health,* pp. 18–26.
7. England, M. J. View from the top. *Visions,* 3(2): 3, 19.

Resources

Boland, P. (Ed.) 1990. *Making managed healthcare work: A practical guide to strategies and solutions.* New York: McGraw-Hill.
Roberts, H. V., & Sergesketter, B. F. 1993. *Quality is personal: A foundation for total quality management.* New York: The Free Press.

PART
TWO

MANAGING
ORGANIZATIONAL
CULTURE

Operational execution is critical to controlling health care, workers' compensation, and disability costs. Although strategy and management systems provide essential direction and tools, optimal results are possible only when these are also translated into operational capabilities and actions. Alignment with operations makes management systems practical and concrete and greatly expands the number and effectiveness of stakeholders working to accomplish the employer's goals. Effective operational execution also allows employers to exploit the full potential for improvement in health-related costs, quality, and productivity.

The Health Triangle introduced in Chapter 1 illustrates the importance of this synergy between strategy, systems, operations, and incentives. Health and disability strategy and optimizing managed care, discussed in Part One, provide the strategic direction and management systems necessary for reducing cost and improving quality in health and disability. Managing organizational culture, discussed in Part Two, provides the operational programs and practices that influence manager and employee daily behavior to accomplish those goals. Incentives, which come from all three core elements of the model, support continued adherence and motivation among all system participants.

Because the influences within the health and disability system are complex, employers require this type of integrated approach to gain lasting control over health and disability costs.

The key role of the organizational culture is as a linking and alignment mechanism that ensures continuity in the transition from strategy and systems to daily operations. This transition can be difficult because it requires buy-in from line management, employees, and staff organizations, each of which may have different needs and agendas. Activities and programs can proliferate with little coordination or accountability for results. If not managed effectively, the transition from strategy to operations results in fragmentation, redundancy, rework, and increased costs.

Organizational culture therefore needs to be the glue that connects all health-related activities and ensures they add value to the employer's bottom line. Employers must seek synergy across programs such as wellness, safety, or employee assistance and must frame them in ways that produce demonstrable cost and health results. Information, training, and management practices must be delivered to support the same organizational goals and to motivate the desired behaviors among employees. As the culture reinforces the employer's health message in multiple ways, continual awareness and expectations for health results must become ingrained in daily procedures. Management of health and disability must become an integrated and continuous process, supported by the organizational culture and owned by line managers and employees, as well as by health-related staff functions.

The changing profile of modern health and disability risks provides a compelling rationale for employers to increasingly utilize their operational capability in managing health. Advancing medical technology has created greater risk for expensive cases, with a larger number of survivors who need longer term care and rehabilitation. Technology has also improved information access for managers and employees to help reduce that risk through early identification and better management. Illness, injury, and disability are increasingly subjective, including psychological and perceptual factors, and are the result of cumulative risk rather than a single incident. External parties such as health care providers, attorneys, and the media compete with employers to shape the health-related behavior of employees.

Changing workforce and workplace demands also require a different type of organizational response. Because there are more single-parent, two-earner, and single employees, there are often fewer natural home supports to help with illness or disability. Employee lifestyle both on and off the job is an increasingly important and controversial issue in controlling health and disability costs. Employees are working longer hours for less relative pay and are experiencing more stress and disruption due to rapid organizational change. In most organizations, there is greater diversity among employees resulting in a wider array of health and disability needs.

Because these risks are subjective, individualized, and change frequently, they require a dynamic and tailored approach which is best delivered in the context of daily work. Reducing these risks also requires the cooperation of employees and line managers and supervisors, supported through effective information and resources. Employers that manage health and disability solely through fragmented programs and staff functions will always be in reactive mode, spending resources where not essential and missing opportunities for significant impact. By contrast, employers that involve line mangers and employees in anticipating and managing these issues in daily operations can be proactive in reducing costs and in improving employee health and productivity.

The programs and management practices of the culture, in conjunction with strategy and management systems, must break down barriers that limit operational solutions to health and disability costs, including the barriers between:

- Health, health care, workers' compensation, and disability.
- Functional managers in human resources, safety, risk management, and occupational health and wellness.
- Line and functional management.
- Management and employees.
- The employer and dependents.

Employers using a systems orientation within their organizational culture can address two goals simultaneously: (1) integration of multiple stakeholders toward the employer's health strategy, and (2) concrete operational actions that reduce costs and improve health. As described in this part, this process requires identifying and prioritizing the greatest sources of risk, increasing the skills and accountability of line managers, increasing the effectiveness and accountability of health and disability programs, and involving employees throughout. Progress also requires an on-going change management process that builds buy-in among those affected and allows continuous improvement and learning.

Identifying and prioritizing the greatest sources of risk serves both purposes of integration and concrete action. The organization learns cross-functionally as it acts concretely to reduce the 10 percent of claims that account for two-thirds of costs. Similarly, line manger accountability and skill-building leads directly to teamwork and increased use of operational settings to attack costs. Health and disability programs become more integrated and cost effective as they are evaluated and held accountable to meet organizational objectives. As employees are involved throughout this process, the organizational culture builds buy-in, skills, and risk improvement capabilities among those most directly responsible for improving health.

Senior management plays a particularly important role in shaping the organizational culture to achieve significant and stable improvements in health and disability performance. Establishing clear goals and accountability for improvement is the first step in this process, as a necessary foundation for focusing attention and motivating teamwork toward desired outcomes. Yet even with common goals, active support from the top is needed to promote integration and cost-effectiveness across health programs and organizational boundaries. Senior managers must therefore reinforce expected results and values on an on-going basis.

The second key role for senior managers is that of champion, raising awareness and enthusiasm throughout the organization for the goal of health. Stories and statistics about health and safety lend themselves to employee and management meetings, since improving health and reducing costs is a win-win situation for all parties. In several leading organizations, senior managers open each weekly staff meeting with health and safety as the first agenda item, while others are visibly involved in health-related events and activities. Other senior managers use organizational vision statements or communications to reinforce health as a key organizational value that promote employee wellbeing as well as organizational productivity and cost control. The combination of on-going attention and accountability by senior managers exerts significant influence on the priority health and disability receive in the organizational culture.

Employers must pace their efforts effectively, since changing an organization's culture requires both action and timing to achieve optimal results. Over the past several years, many organizations have expended considerable effort to build continuous quality improvement into their culture, making quality truly everyone's job and not something separate from regular work. Lessons from the quality improvement effort are helpful in determining how to build a culture that delivers excellent health and disability results:

1. *Be Results-Focused.* Concentrate on accomplishing key objectives rather than performing activities or offering programs. Foster a sense of urgency for achieving specified results by specified dates.

2. *Harvest Quick Hits.* Capitalize on opportunities to get quick results from areas with clear cost improvement potential. This builds enthusiasm and allows further improvement to be cost self-sustaining.

3. *Consider Radical Re-Engineering Selectively.* For opportunities with sufficient strategic importance, examine whether the broad business process can be completely overhauled, especially by capitalizing on new technology or if continuous improvement would provide too little impact.

4. *Continuously Improve and Learn.* Capture key learnings from improvement efforts and share them widely. Leverage each set of learnings to continuously enhance future improvement efforts.

5. *Stay the Course.* Show consistent commitment to enhancing the effectiveness and integration of the system, always working to improve its alignment and results.

6. *Manage Change Proactively.* Provide visible and active sponsorship, focused on areas with the lowest levels of readiness for change. Champion change through multiple methods and walking the talk.

Managing the organizational culture to improve health and disability results offers employers not just cost reductions, but enhancements to productivity, quality, and general management effectiveness. The energy, concentration, and working capacity of a healthy workforce positions an organization to execute all its performance goals. Similarly, both performance and health work from an underlying foundation of management practices, values, and employee ideas, supported by the organizational culture. A highly effective culture is integrated vertically, in terms of common goals and objectives, and horizontally, through streamlined processes and practices that cut across the functions of the organization. Such a culture offers an additional competitive advantage which, unlike a new product, is difficult to duplicate.

8

Addressing
High-Risk Behavior

Managing forward to reduce health and disability costs requires emphasizing the prevention of the particular high-risk behaviors that are responsible for the majority of the organization's health and disability claims. By identifying and more closely managing these factors, employers can shift from simply avoiding risk to actively preventing it. This key move allows them to take control of the root causes of cost for their particular situation and tailor interventions that will yield a maximum payback for their time and investment.

Managing high-risk behavior is crucial because a relative minority of claims are responsible for the great majority of total costs. Several studies show that, in general, the most expensive 10 percent of employees account for nearly 70 percent of an organization's total health and disability cost.[1] Such costs often exceed $100,000 per person. A single case may cost 100 or even 500 times as much as the cost for a typical employee.

Phoenix-based U-Haul International, Inc., for example, had 18,600 employees and dependents in 1989, generating nearly $19 million in health care expenses: A mere 392 people accounted for $7.7 million of that total.[2] The Travelers Company in Hartford, Connecticut, studied health care costs over a four-year period for a sample of 752 employees: 72 high-risk employees accounted for over $220,000 in costs, whereas the remaining 648 employees generated $111,000 in costs.[3] In health and disability, high risk translates to large expenditures and a disproportionate share of total expense.

Understanding and managing these risks can significantly reduce health and disability costs by allowing the employer to prioritize the sources of cost and apply preventive measures—such as wellness, mental health, alcohol/drug, or safety—to the areas where they are most likely to impact those costs risks. This prioritization is the essence of proactive health risk management.

Again, in many ways, this experience with health and disability mirrors that from quality improvement. The efforts of many organizations have shown that for most business processes, a critical few root causes are responsible for a disproportionate share of quality problems, and focusing on these root causes produces the biggest return on investment. Similarly, to reduce health and disability costs, employers must identify the critical few root causes of risk that underlie the majority of cost. This focus allows organizations to achieve maximum management leverage for their health investment dollar.

Identifying and managing those key risk factors, however, requires insight and skill. Executives and managers have achieved quality improvement only through hands-on involvement and detailed understanding. Applying this logic to health and disability leads to the following four conclusions:

1. Many factors can affect health and disability risk, and the risk profile is different for every organization.

2. Employers fail to optimize (and sometimes waste) their health investment dollar when they buy generic health programs rather than tailoring approaches to their particular risk profile.

3. Managing risk information and incentives properly will achieve lower costs and healthier behavior by employees and dependents, and will increase employee commitment.

4. Improper management of risk information and incentives will generate lawsuits, poor morale, and counterproductive behavior by employees and dependents.

Addressing high-risk behavior is therefore a priority item for management. Combining this focus with a systematic approach will often lead to surprising insights and significant cost reductions. This approach can also empower employees and dependents, who are much more likely to actively manage their own health effectively when supported by risk information and incentives.

Steps to Manage High-Risk Behavior

Successful management of high-risk behavior requires a clear and systematic methodology or set of steps. Following these steps will prevent health and disability problems and reduce an organization's total cost of health. Two guidelines are necessary, however, in applying this methodology. First, the very term *risk* implies uncertainty, and the management of high risk should not assume a false level of precision. Second, using a differentiated management approach to tailor risk reduction efforts does not translate to targeting individuals.

By their very nature, health and disability include a significant element of chance. Although risk levels differ, everyone is vulnerable to unexpected health problems. The RAND Corporation found that nearly one in six Americans (41 million in 1989) suffers some economic loss each year from a non-fatal accidental injury (falls, motor vehicle accidents, household accidents). These accidents result in 200 million lost workdays each year, about one-third of all sick days.[4] Similar statistics for illness show that a large proportion of the population generates some health and disability cost each year through unexpected health care. Thus, while high-risk behaviors have the greatest probability of generating high costs, organizations also need to manage risk for the entire covered population.

At the same time, organizations should not use risk information to discriminate against individuals. In addition to being illegal, such discrimination is often ineffective. A better approach is to analyze the root causes of risk and develop overall solutions for all managers, employees, and dependents who might be affected. An axiom of quality improvement is that people's behavior is driven much more by the systems or processes within the environment than by individual characteristics. Preventive health and disability management should therefore target the causes of risk within the system, rather than try to target individuals.

To take an extreme example, an organization could manage high-risk behavior by simply identifying the most costly employees and dependents from the previous year and then firing them or removing their health insurance. Such a tactic is obviously illegal and would generate expensive lawsuits. More importantly, this approach assumes firing the "bad apples" would eliminate the root causes of risk. But since risk is more like a time bomb, present to differing degrees in all employees and dependents, it is most effectively managed by focusing on its root causes in the entire covered population.

Starting from this broader context, the management approach should include three phases: gaining understanding, sharing understanding, and targeting behavioral change. The following seven steps (described in more detail throughout the remainder of the chapter) highlight how each phase can be achieved:

Gaining Understanding

1. Study the organization's existing results from health care, workers' compensation, and disability. Gain an in-depth knowledge of the types of claims that are generating most of the costs.

2. Study the risk factors associated with the organization's unique employee population. Do this in terms of four risk characteristics: demographic/geographic, physiological, lifestyle, and employee perception/personality.

3. Study risk factors related to three organizational characteristics: type of work, management style, and existing health and disability programs.

Sharing Understanding

4. Share these results as appropriate with managers and employees to achieve widespread awareness of the organization's highest risks. Frame this sharing as a "win–win" opportunity that capitalizes on everyone's personal benefit in reducing health and disability problems.

5. Present risk results to individual employees, dependents, and managers in a meaningful framework. Break results out by work area, by demographic group, and by individual employee (through confidential health screening or individual health risk appraisal) to capitalize on intrinsic interest in reducing risks for co-workers, family, and self.

Targeting Behavioral Change

6. Explain which key risk areas are a particular priority and why. Explain the internal and external resources that are likely to be most effective in reducing these risks, including management and employee action, company programs, and community programs. If relevant, discuss the company's position regarding any legal issues (e.g., Americans with Disabilities Act) or confidentiality concerns.

7. Establish accountability and incentives at the lowest level possible to continually monitor and reduce these risks. This includes cost chargebacks to individual divisions or departments based on their unit's cost experience as well as incentives to employees and dependents for reducing their personal and work-related level of health risk.

Organizations differ in the characteristics of their highest risk cases. Thus, each employer must analyze and manage risks based on its unique employee and dependent population, type of work, and organizational culture. Even in the same industry, various employers often differ in their primary sources of risk and in the management approaches that will work best to reduce health and disability costs.

Studying the Root Causes of Costs

Many organizations make a key error in focusing attention only on overall costs or the average cost per claim. They manage costs and risk as if they are standardized and evenly distributed across the employee population. Implicitly, this approach treats each employee, employee group, or department as being equally likely to produce high health and disability costs. Table 8.1 illustrates the fallacy of this approach by showing how total health care costs of $300,000 might typically be distributed in an organization with 100 employees.

Table 8.1 Distribution of Health Costs in Example Company

Number of Employees	Average Cost per Employee	Total Cost
20	$ 100	$ 2,000
60	500	30,000
15	3,000	45,000
5	44,600	223,000

As shown in Table 8.1, the most expensive five employees account for a total of $223,000, almost three-quarters of the total health care cost expenditure. Among these five employees, the care for one was responsible for $95,000; for another $67,000; and for the other three, just over $20,000 each. In this example, the average cost per employee is $3,000. Yet simply looking at the overall total or the average cost obscures much of the information about this company's experience.

What factors contributed to the most expensive cases? What characteristics do people in the lowest cost categories share? What could have been done to prevent or to intercede in the limited number of cases that account for the great majority of cost? Managers can use these questions to address key causes of health and disability costs, the importance of which is not apparent by looking only at the overall total or the average cost.

A study at Liberty Mutual in 1990 of nearly 100,000 back injury claims initiated in 1986 showed that total costs were $673 million, an average of $6,800 per workers' compensation claim. Yet only 25 percent of these cases accounted for 95 percent of the $673 million total cost.[5] Many of these expensive claims differ from the average claim because they are very lengthy and typically involve multiple treatment approaches and extensive lost time. Again, average or total cost is of little help in understanding how to reduce these most expensive claims.

Similarly, birth-related costs at Levi Strauss & Co. for extremely premature babies (born in the seventh month or earlier) averaged nearly $28,000 each from 1984 through 1988, compared with only $500 per infant born at full term (see Figure 8.1). Levi Strauss found that these premature babies accounted for nearly three-quarters of total newborn costs.[6] Lumping all newborn costs together to determine overall or average cost obscures the most important cost information available.

In improving quality in other parts of the business, executives have learned that they cannot rely on overall results alone when they analyze the business process. Instead, in-depth investigation is necessary to clarify the problems and opportunities. Likewise in health and disability, managing high-risk behavior requires gathering information to understand the employer's unique risks. Otherwise, predicting areas of risk can be more difficult than predicting the stock market—there's already enough uncertainty even with full information.

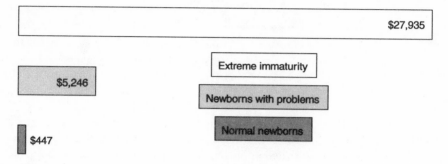

AVERAGE BENEFITS PAYABLE, 1984-1988

$27,935

$5,246

Extreme immaturity

Newborns with problems

Normal newborns

$447

Source: Levi Strauss & Co.

Figure 8.1 Health Care Cost Differences by Type of Birth (Reprinted from BUSINESS & HEALTH, March 1992. Copyright 1992 and published by Medical Economics Publishing at Montvale, NJ 07645-1742. All rights reserved. None of the content of this publication may be reproduced, stored in a retrieval system, or transmitted in any form or by any means (electronic, mechanical, photocopying, recording or otherwise) without the prior written permission of the publisher.

The root causes of health and disability costs can generally be found by examining three sources: (1) existing health and disability data, (2) employee and dependent risk factors, and (3) organizational risk factors. Each of these sources offers a different perspective on likely sources of future high costs. Each also increases the organization's ability to manage risk proactively—to use prevention and early intervention rather than costly and extended care.

Existing health and disability data are valuable because these results represent actual experience, hard dollars that have been paid out. Employee and dependent risk factors suggest likely future problems based on the demographic, health, and personal characteristics of the covered population. Finally, organizational risk factors identify workplace or cultural characteristics that may influence the kinds of claims filed and suggest preventive management action. These three areas of easily available data provide a complete picture of the root causes that management needs to attack.

Health and Disability Data

The biggest payoff from health and disability data comes from the questions it can answer. What kind of claims are the most expensive for this organization? What are the similarities among the most expensive claims over the past three years? If they are pregnancy related, what kind of prenatal care did the mothers receive and when? Are older or younger mothers more at risk? Are mothers who work in certain jobs more at risk? These questions can be applied to health care, workers' compensation, or disability results.

Because these data are based on real cases, they allow in-depth investigation that can lead to root cause and can suggest future management action. For example, using the data can help pinpoint when in the health continuum most of the utilization has been occurring: Is it for prevention, early intervention, or for expensive treatment of a serious illness or injury that could have been addressed earlier? These data allow organizations to use the utilization value index (see Chapter 4) to improve the cost-effectiveness of health and disability dollar expenditures.

The data can also provide invaluable insight into the areas where health interventions are likely to be most effective. For example, one midwestern manufacturer found that spouses accounted for 35 percent of all health care claims; other dependents, 25 percent; and employees, 40 percent,[7] suggesting that health messages and resources should encompass family members as well as employees. Other organizations have found that male employees generate much higher cancer treatment costs because they do not visit the doctor until much later in the disease. Male employees may therefore need a different intervention approach that better fits their attitudes and lifestyle. These insights have major implications for management direction and health programs.

In addition, data can assist managers in the following ways:

- Providing quantitative information, such as costs, length of disability, or number of visits.

- Providing qualitative information, such as patient perceptions of care received or reasons the patient did not follow a doctor or supervisor's recommendation.

- Identifying the experiences of actual employees, not hypothetical scenarios.

- Allowing historical comparisons such as trends or changes over time.

Although all organizations receive health and disability data, the kind and volume of information varies widely depending on the company's insurance status and the structure of its health care, workers' compensation, and disability programs. Managers and executives interested in investigating data in more detail may need to ask for additional information from their insurer or from their internal risk management, safety, or human resources staff. In some cases, additional data gathering will be necessary to fully represent the company's health and disability status.

Organizations have multiple options for enhancing and analyzing their existing health and disability data including interviews, focus groups, cross-functional teams, quality improvement techniques, and statistical analysis techniques. Each method can help fill in the picture begun with the basic data. This analysis produces additional understanding and an action plan for addressing root cause that delivers lasting cost reductions.

Interviews and focus groups with employees and dependents about their experience with health and disability services can be particularly helpful. For example, an excellent way to find the problem spots in an organization's return-to-work program is to interview previously injured employees about their experience. A focus group with employees who have been treated for cancer lends great insight into the best way to facilitate early recognition and intervention of this disease. Focus groups can also be used to determine what incentives will motivate people to be more involved in health and safety behaviors.

Having cross-functional teams look at data can provide insight that would be lacking if viewed only by staff specialists in safety or human resources. Such a team might include both line managers and front-line employees, representing differing ages, work units, and levels of experience with the organization's health and disability system. Some of the ideas and perspectives these teams can supply include:

- How health and safety data are used in their work unit (e.g., ignored, taken seriously).
- Why co-workers may engage in high-risk behavior.
- How to tailor health interventions to meet the needs of employees and dependents.

These teams can provide another angle on the data and insight into how to use it for more effective management.

Finally, analytical techniques from both quality improvement and statistics can usually aid data understanding. Techniques such as fishbone and pareto analysis from quality improvement are routinely used to determine root cause from a diverse set of data.[8] They could easily be applied to health and disability. Statistically, researchers have developed techniques such as "percentage of high cost cases" that are specifically intended for data in which there are extreme cases and the average cost is misleading.[9] Managers or cross-functional teams can easily use these techniques to better understand the critical causes of claims.

The key with using health and disability data is to keep an open mind and use multiple perspectives and analytical techniques to discover the most important cost improvement opportunities. Managers sometimes go into this process thinking they already know the root causes and don't need to gather data and do analysis. Typically, they are surprised by how much more effectively they can structure their management efforts based on the insights they gain. The best understanding comes from active involvement by people who are directly affected, not from cursory analysis or delegation to outside third parties.

Employee and Dependent Risk Factors

An organization's health and disability results often change somewhat from year to year. One year, back injuries may be driving the bulk of workers' compensation cost; the next year, carpal tunnel claims are the problem. A company might have two very expensive brain injury cases in one year and then not have another for five years. Because risk is widely distributed in the employee and dependent population, actual results will always vary somewhat over time simply by chance.

What this means is that employers should not look exclusively at past results to understand future health and disability risks. Instead, past results (particularly results for the past several years) should be used in conjunction with information about future risk. Analyzing the organization's employees and dependents is an excellent way to identify that risk. As discussed earlier in the chapter, information about employee and dependent risk can be organized into four categories:

1. Demographic/geographic.
2. Physiological.
3. Lifestyle.
4. Employee personality and perceptions.

Many organizations have information in each of these categories, but that information is seldom integrated and applied to predicting root causes of future health and disability costs. For example, human resources may collect demographic information to monitor affirmative action progress, but that same information is not used in better management of health. Similarly, many organizations conduct employee surveys about perceptions of the employer and job, but again they do not use this information in health management. A big part of the challenge, therefore, is simply to utilize available data in the health arena.

Demographic information, such as age, gender, and race, is perhaps the most traditional way to show differential health risk. For example, at Liz Claiborne, Inc., the New Jersey-based clothing manufacturer, 74 percent of the 3500 employees are women and the majority of them are in their child-bearing years. These demographics clearly show pregnancy risks as a key health area for management.[10] At Coors, Inc. in Golden, Colorado, the average age of female workers is 41, so Coors focused its health management efforts on early detection of breast cancer.[11]

Geographic or job status information can also show differences in activities that relate to the level of risk. For example, facilities in different parts of the country, urban and rural facilities, or blue collar and white collar operations may have somewhat different risk profiles. Workers' compensation climates vary by state. The health orientation of providers (i.e., prevention vs. treatment and use of expensive technology) also varies geographically. These differences exert a powerful influence on the behaviors of employees and the resulting organizational risk.

Physiological, lifestyle, and employee attitude measures also add depth to an organization's risk profile. As shown in Figure 8.2 (data taken from a midwestern manufacturer), each of these factors can significantly differentiate between high- and low-risk employees and dependents. Smokers in this organization generate health care costs $228 per year higher than nonsmokers. Those with low life satisfaction have costs $425 per year more than those who are satisfied with their life.[12]

Independent results from the Du Pont Company, show a similar profile. Excess illness costs per person at risk were calculated at $960 for smokers,

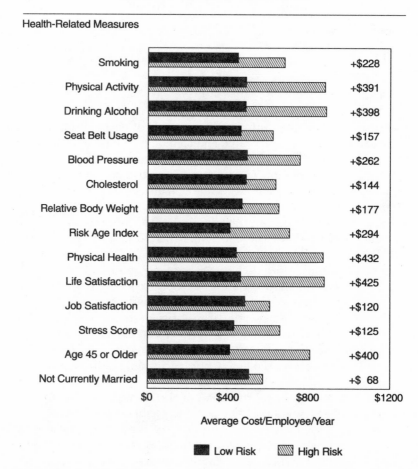

Figure 8.2   Health Care Costs for Low Risk vs. High Risk Behaviors

$401 for overweight, and $272 for inadequate seat belt use. Du Pont conservatively estimates that excess illness costs the company $70.8 million annually.[13] Such data can effectively target areas for future behavioral change and accompanying cost reductions.

Physiological measures such as blood pressure, cholesterol, or body weight can often be collected through a health fair, a health screening booth at work, or a health risk appraisal questionnaire. Family history of these risk factors can also be important. The key to using physiological measures effectively is to focus particularly on the people at greatest risk (who may also be least interested in participating). Employers can use management support for health, peer pressure, and ease of access to health screening to increase rates of participation and create a risk profile to target health efforts at the organizational as well as individual level (see Chapter 10).

Lifestyle characteristics have received much more attention in recent years, based on data suggesting that 51 percent of disease is lifestyle related.[14] Smoking, physical activity, drinking alcohol, and seat belt usage are all lifestyle behaviors that can affect health and costs. Like physiological measures, lifestyle patterns of employees and dependents can be targeted for change at both organizational and individual levels based on information from health fairs, screenings, or questionnaires.

The fourth category of risk, employee personality and perceptions, includes such indicators as job satisfaction, workplace stress, and the dependent's view of the employer. These perceptions are important for health and disability in two ways. First, psychological factors can affect physical health, and second, these perceptions affect behavior related to health, such as speed of return to work or cooperation with company health programs. Many organizations collect data through employee attitude surveys or communication meetings that could be used to predict risk areas.

Boeing, Inc., the Seattle-based aircraft manufacturer, recently worked with the University of Washington Medical School to investigate the importance of these employee perceptions on the risk for long-term back injuries (that keep employees off work for six or more months). Approximately 3000 uninjured employees were tested with a battery of both physical and psychological measures. Three years later, the researchers went back and compared the profiles of employees who had sustained serious back injuries with those who had not. By far the best predictors of future serious back injury were psychological measures, such as job satisfaction, life stress, and "locus of control" (whether an individual views events as being under personal control vs. being a matter of chance). These psychological factors were better predictors of long-term disability than were physical measures such as lifting strength or flexibility.[15]

Similarly, a large body of research suggests personality characteristics can significantly affect an individual's risk for health and disability problems. Personality characteristics such as impulsiveness, locus of control, and resistance to stress have been shown to predict an employee's level of safety performance.[16] A person's vulnerability to environmental illness appears to be related to personality characteristics such as neuroticism and anxiety.[17] Persons with Type A personality typically delay seeking medical care initially, but once sick, are also more likely to be impatient for early recovery.[18]

These employee and dependent risk factors—demographic, physiological, lifestyle, and attitudinal or personality—often have their greatest value in combination. Most injuries and illnesses have multiple causes. A person's or an organization's level of risk is typically an aggregate of many of these factors. Figures 8.3 and 8.4 illustrate the importance of viewing risk in this aggregated fashion. Figure 8.3 shows that the more risk factors a person has, the greater the likelihood he or she will be a high-cost case.[19] Figure 8.4 shows that the annual cost per employee increases systematically with the number of risks as measured by a health risk appraisal (HRA).[20] Both of these trends hold regardless of age and sex.

Examining risk across these categories of data can show the root causes of claims that need the most attention. Sometimes, a simple demographic analysis that fits well with health and disability claims results will show the primary risk areas for intervention. In other cases, organizations will want to gather and consider additional information related to geography, employee and dependent lifestyle, physical status, and attitudes. Interviews, cross-functional teams, and quality or statistical tools can provide insight into risks and suggest how to achieve health improvements and cost reductions.

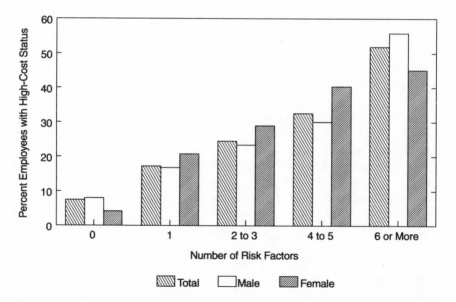

Figure 8.3 Comparisons of High Cost Status by Number of Risk Factors (*Source: American Journal of Health Promotion*, Yen, Edington, & Wittig, 6(1), 1991. Used with permission.)

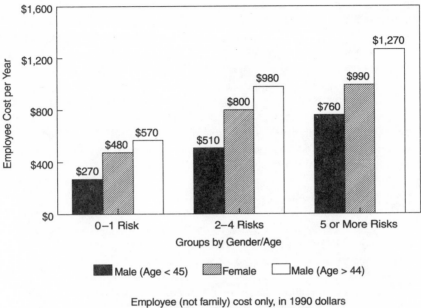

Figure 8.4   Risk-Related Employee Health Care Costs

Organizational Risk Factors

The final source of information related to health and disability risk comes from organizational factors such as the type of work performed, the management style or culture, and the present health and disability programs. Such factors as workload, physical hazards, management attention to health and disability, and access/support for health initiatives often have as much to do with the level and type of claims as do the risk factors of the employees and dependents. The following organizations show that managing these risk factors can dramatically lower health and disability costs.[21]

| Example | **Johnsonville Foods**   Johnsonville Foods, Inc., which self-insures, had total health care costs (claims and administration) of $1900 per employee in 1991, a figure nearly half the national average. Interestingly, the workplace environment at Johnsonville is also different from the national average. Teams make all decisions about schedules, performance standards, assignments, budgets, quality measures, and capital improvements. CEO Ralph Stayer says: "For the last five years, my own aspiration has been to eliminate my job by creating such a crowd of self-starting, problem-solving, responsibility-grabbing, independent thinkers that Johnsonville would run itself." |

Example   **W. L. Gore and Associates**   At W. L. Gore and Associates, a Delaware-based manufacturing firm, employee health care costs have been consistently below national averages. In 1991, per employee cost was $2,558, just 71 percent of the national average. Gore attributes its success to its workplace environment, in which the only job titles are president and secretary/treasurer (required by law). Everyone else is an associate, working on projects, teams, and functions by voluntary commitment. The company places a premium on open and direct communication, encouragement, trust, and the task-force approach to problem solving. Gore has followed this management philosophy since 1958.

Example   **North American Tool and Die, Inc.**   At North American Tool and Die, Inc., in California, their workers' compensation experience modification factor has dropped from 1.61 in 1989 to 0.88 in 1990, to 0.57 in 1991, to 0.54 in 1992. Company president James Bradt reports: "We created a culture where employees feel safe and wanted." Employees own 30 percent of the company stock, those on the shop floor have the right to shut down an operation they feel is unsafe or of poor quality, and all workers receive cross-training for a wide variety of tasks.

These examples illustrate how organizational conditions can strongly impact health and disability costs. Thus, assessing the physical environment, the psychosocial (or management) environment, and current health and disability programs can add significantly to understanding the root causes of health risks.

For the physical environment, many organizations today focus on ergonomic and environmental illness issues because of their rapid growth in the 1990s. This might include a high-level ergonomic audit to identify those jobs in which repetitive strain is a particular risk. It might also include an environmental illness audit focused on chemicals or workplace conditions of concern to employees. In the office environment, video display terminals (VDTs) and workstation design are candidates for sources of risk (see Chapter 13).

On the psychosocial, or management, side, organizations should look for job factors that contribute to high employee stress and a desire to escape, such as lack of control over job responsibilities or excessive demands. Risk assessment might also include more global organizational characteristics such as the level and type of change, the degree of job uncertainty, the level of employee involvement, or the effectiveness of communication. Often, existing employee survey or focus group information can be adapted for analysis as a contributor to health and disability claims (see Chapter 12).

Finally, organizations should also examine their existing health and disability programs as a point of comparison for the risk information generated in other areas. Some common measures of these programs are participation, comprehensiveness, and impact. Perhaps the greatest value of such an audit, however, is to identify the potential synergies among diverse program efforts. Are the safety, employee assistance, and wellness programs all working in complementary ways? Do they share data so they can see where they are and are not being effective? How closely aligned is the company's management strategy with the values espoused for health and disability? The real opportunities for attacking costs become apparent through these kinds of integrative questions.

Organizations have a wealth of valuable information to identify and manage root causes of health and disability costs—claims data, employee and dependent risk data, and organizational risk data. The goal, however, is not to overload on data, but to sample selectively from the many sources available. This approach will ensure balanced and well-informed management actions. Often, the greatest insight is obtained by gathering appropriate information from all these sources and having a cross-functional team of managers and employees analyze it simultaneously. With these results in hand, the organization can implement actions that will yield both immediate and long-term cost reductions.

Sharing Results

The beauty of a health and disability strategy is that it truly is a win–win proposition. When health is improved and injury or illness is avoided, all parties benefit. The organization saves money, making it more competitive and profitable. The executive or manager achieves better results, in productivity, quality, and the employee morale and well-being. The employee and dependents achieve better health and lower personal costs for health and disability as well.

Since there are no losers in a scenario of better health, there are few reasons to withhold information about health and disability risks. Rather, there is significant incentive to share risk information quite broadly to involve multiple parties in risk reduction collaboration. Yet in many organizations, few people are aware of the root factors driving up health and disability costs. All they know is that the costs keep going up, and the burden is increasingly difficult to bear.

This is a tremendous opportunity, especially for organizations that have done some work to identify the root causes of cost. Sharing this information is an excellent way to begin enlisting managers, employees, and dependents in the plans for health improvement. It is also a positive message for the organizational culture, since it promotes values such as empowerment, responsibility, trust, and caring for the organization's stakeholders. Sharing risk information broadly is a key way to move away from managing care and toward managing health.

Sharing this information is also a powerful way for the employer to improve the partnership with health and disability suppliers. Health care providers, third-party administrators, insurance companies, and assorted service providers can be linked in during the risk collection and analysis phase or can be brought into the loop once the results are complete. In either event, the risk information forms the basis for a more systematic and optimized relationship with suppliers than would otherwise be possible. For the supplier, it is often a welcome opportunity to tailor their services to better meet the employer's needs.

The risk information should be structured to be meaningful and actionable for the particular audience. An employee's view of risk is far different from that of the chief financial officer. This means messages that go to employees should clearly differentiate between the personal risk to their or their family's quality of life versus the financial risk to the organization. Sara Lee, Inc., the food products company, found that the corporation saves $66,000 for every case of colon cancer detected early.[22] To an employee, however, that $66,000 is insignificant in comparison with the life and lifestyle threat from the disease. Sara Lee therefore provides education that emphasizes the personal value to employees of early detection.

Example   **Coors, Inc.** Coors, Inc., the brewing company, found that the cost of a late detected case of breast cancer averaged over $150,000. Coors developed a program called "Talk to a Friend" to help spread the word among female employees about early detection of breast cancer. Seventy women were designated as communicators who, after training, scheduled luncheons and coffee breaks with small groups of other women. The resulting increase in preventive mammograms has helped Coors save an estimated $1.5 million in direct and indirect costs.[23]

Each organization must determine the most meaningful ways to develop and communicate its risk information. Some information should be common to all communications, such as how health and disability fit into the organization's philosophy and goals and why it is sharing these findings now. Beyond this general message, risk results are most powerful when tailored to the particular audience. What is important for the manager of a department may be boring for that manager's employee or for his or her spouse. What is of great interest to young women may be of little interest to older men.

Sharing risk information is an ongoing process of developing and enhancing procedures to communicate with and involve all stakeholders. This process is truly continuous improvement, as the organization builds a better and better baseline and an increasingly effective response to managing its health and disability risks. Like quality improvement, the methods themselves are fairly straightforward. What produces superior results is the energy from management and the on-going determination to do better.

Targeting Behavioral Change

Sharing risk information and the organization's analysis of root causes is the first step in attacking the minority of risk factors that account for the majority of health and disability cost. It is also the first step in gaining commitment to achieve behavioral change. Yet it is not enough for everyone to know what the root causes of risk are. To reduce risks dramatically, people must also change their behavior.

Example **Liz Claiborne, Inc.** When Liz Claiborne, Inc. found that 74 percent of its employees are women and that half of them are of childbearing age, management became actively involved by partnering with the March of Dimes "Babies and You" program. They arranged for recurring five class cycles of prenatal education and encouraged all employees and spouses to attend. To sweeten the deal, Liz Claiborne awards a free child car seat to all employees who attend at least four of the five classes.

Example **First National Bank of Chicago** First National Bank of Chicago joined with "Babies and You" after they experienced two or three childbirth cases that cost over $100,000 each. First National not only actively promotes the program, they also provide a waiver of the $300 deductible for the newborn's first year if the parents will begin attending "Babies and You" classes before the fourth month of pregnancy. Of the Chicago-area employees in the company's self-insured plan who delivered in 1989 or 1990, 50 percent attended the prenatal classes. The attendees averaged $6581 per delivery, whereas those who did not attend averaged $9815. Only 12 percent of attendees had Cesarean deliveries, compared with 25 percent for those who did not attend.[24]

The workers' compensation study of Michigan employers (see Chapter 1) compared the management strategies of the Michigan companies with the best and the worst workers' compensation results. The best companies were much more likely to use cost chargebacks to individual departments based on their own workers' compensation results. In other words, the best companies created a strong incentive for individual departments to become aware of the factors contributing to their costs and to manage them at the local level.[25] Accountability such as this also reinforces an awareness of the total cost of health and disability, including productivity and quality costs resulting from injured workers.

Targeting behavioral change to reduce health and disability risks includes three parts:

1. Encouraging managers, employees, and dependents to develop a local strategy for risks pertinent to them.

2. Developing or publicizing the organizational and community resources available to help them reduce their risk.

3. Establishing accountability and incentives for them to continually monitor and reduce these risks.

In the case of Liz Claiborne and First National, employees and dependents developed their risk reduction strategy through the education they received during "Babies and You." Their companies supported them by arranging the classes with the help of March of Dimes and by offering incentives such as car seats, deductible waivers, and management encouragement. In a somewhat different setting, the best Michigan employers motivated their managers to develop a local (departmental) strategy to control workers' compensation costs. They then encouraged them to get support from the company's safety professionals and gave them a financial incentive to keep costs under control. In all three cases, the employer empowered the managers, employees, and dependents to address the root causes of health and disability problems and supported their efforts.

As described in the next five chapters of this book, a multitude of specific management practices and programs can be successfully applied to reduce health and disability costs. The starting point, however, is to understand and focus on the very highest sources of risk. These sources of risk are where the action is, since it has been shown repeatedly that a minority of risks account for a majority of costs. Employers that identify and publicize these risks and involve all stakeholders in reducing them will contribute significantly to the competitiveness of their organizations and the welfare of their people.

References

1. Edington, D. W., & Yen, L. 1992. Is it possible to simultaneously reduce risk factors and excess health care costs? *American Journal of Health Promotion,* 6(6): 403–409.

2. Woolsey, C. February 17, 1992. Employers monitor lifestyles. *Business Insurance,* pp. 3–6.

3. Lynch, W. D., Teitelbaum, H. S., & Main, D. S. 1992. Comparing medical costs by analyzing high-cost cases. *American Journal of Health Promotion,* 6(3): 206–213.

4. Hensler, D. R. April 10, 1991. Compensation for accidental injuries in the United States. *RAND Publications.*

5. Webster, B. S., & Snook, S. H. 1990. The cost of compensable low back pain. *Journal of Occupational Medicine,* 32(1): 13–15.

6. Zicklin, E. March 1992. Prenatal teamwork fosters an employer/employee partnership. *Business and Health,* pp. 36–40.

7. Edington, D. W., & Yen, L. 1992. Is it possible to simultaneously reduce risk factors and excess health care costs? *American Journal of Health Promotion,* 6(6): 403–409.

8. Scholtes, P. R. 1988. *The team handbook: How to use teams to improve quality.* Madison, WI: Joiner & Associates, Inc.

9. Lynch, W. D., Teitelbaum, H. S., & Main, D. S. 1992. Comparing medical costs by analyzing high cost cases. *American Journal of Health Promotion,* 6(3): 206–213.

10. Zicklin, E. March 1992. Prenatal teamwork fosters an employer/employee partnership. *Business and Health,* pp. 36–40.

11. Baker, A. December 1991. An ounce of prevention. *Business and Health,* pp. 30–37.

12. Edington, D. W., & Yen, L. T. 1992. Is it possible to simultaneously reduce risk factors and excess health care costs? *American Journal of Health Promotion,* 6(6): 403–409.

13. Bertera, R. L. 1991. The effects of behavioral risks on absenteeism and health care costs in the workplace. *Journal of Occupational Medicine,* 33(11): 1119–1124.

14. McGinnis, J. M. 1990. *Half of premature deaths caused by lifestyle.* Washington, DC: U.S. Office of Disease Prevention and Health Promotion.

15. Bigos, S. J. et al. 1991. A prospective study of work perceptions and psychosocial factors affecting the report of back injury. *Spine,* 16(1): 1–6.

16. Hansen, C. P. 1990. Personality characteristice of the accident-involved employee. *Journal of Business and Psychology,* 2, 346–369.

17. Rosenberg, S. J., Freedman, M. R., Schmaling, K. B., & Rose, C. 1990. Personality styles of patients asserting environmental illness. *Journal of Occupational Medicine,* 32(8): 678–681.

18. Alemagno, S. A., & Zyzanski, S. J. 1991. Health and illness behavior of Type A persons. *Journal of Occupational Medicine,* 33(8): 891–895.

19. Yen, L. T., Edington, D. E., & Wittig, P. 1991. Associations between health risk appraisal scores and employee medical claims costs in a manufacturing company. *American Journal of Health Promotion,* 6(1): 46–54.

20. Edington & Yen. Is it possible to simultaneously reduce risk factors.

21. Lefkoe, M. June 1992. Unhealthy business. *Across the Board,* pp. 26–31.

22. Baker. An ounce of prevention.

23. Ibid.

24. Zicklin. Prenatal teamwork.

25. Habeck, R. V., Leahy, M. J., Hunt, H. A., Chan, F., & Welch, E. M. 1991. Employer factors related to workers' compensation claims and disability management. *Rehabilitation Counseling Bulletin,* 34(3): 210–226.

Resources

The Resources sections of Chapters 10 to 13 list many nonprofit and professional organizations that provide information related to reducing particular types of health and disability risks. In addition, various trade and industry groups such as the following organizations can supply resources related to general risk identification and management:

American Society for Quality Control
611 E. Wisconsin
Milwaukee, WI 53201
(414) 272-8575

Offers information, training, and assistance related to the use of quality improvement techniques in organizations.

National Association of Manufacturers
1331 Pennsylvania Avenue, N.W., Suite 1500 North
Washington, DC 20004
(202) 637-3000

Coordinates information exchange and discusson on a range of broad-based business issues, including health care, workers' compensation, and disability.

Risk and Insurance Management Society, Inc. (RIMS)
205 E. 42nd Street
New York, NY 10017
(212) 286-9292

Provides professional education, conferences, and information related to effective management of the risk and insurance needs of employers.

Self-Insurance Institute of America
P.O. Box 15466
Santa Ana, CA 92705
(202) 828-5021

Seeks to advance cooperation and information exchange among users of self-insurance services and self-insured organizations.

U.S. Chamber of Commerce
1615 H. Street, N.W.
Washington, DC 20062
(202) 347-7201

Coordinates information exchange and discussion on a range of broad-based business issues, including health care, workers' compensation, and disability.

Washington Business Group on Health and U.S. Public Service
National Resource Center on Worksite Health Promotion
777 North Capitol Street NE, Suite 800
Washington, DC 20002
(202) 408-0325

9

Supervision for the New Health Issues

Significant improvement of organizational performance is rarely possible without substantial involvement of line management. Companies successful with quality, for example, entrust the majority of responsibility to line managers. Staff functions such as quality assurance or quality control provide many useful support services, but the bottom line for raising the quality of performance rests with the people who manage daily operations.

This lesson is also true for health and disability management. Currently, many organizations treat health and disability as an issue to be handled mainly by staff units (e.g., human resources or safety). Line supervisors and managers in these organizations are often not aware of their unit's health and disability performance and take little action to reduce risk and cost levels. As a result, the people with the most opportunity for impact on cost—the supervisor and the employee—are those with the least involvement in managing it.

To achieve long-term success in controlling costs, those who understand and manage day-to-day operations must take increasing responsibility for health. Like quality, managing health must be integrated into work as an expected area of performance. Prevention and early intervention can then be truly emphasized in real time. Such a dynamic and meaningful response to health-related behavior is seldom possible if health remains strictly a staff responsibility.

The payoff is evident in organizations where line management has achieved this ownership of health and disability. In fact, line management involvement in health and disability is a trademark of organizations with the best results.

Large employers such as Johnson & Johnson (see Chapter 10) and Du Pont (Chapter 13) as well as small organizations such as All Plastics

Molding (Chapter 13) and Quad Graphics (Chapter 12) have all achieved outstanding health and disability results through line management involvement. These companies report that the key factor in cutting their costs has been the visible and personal involvement of managers and supervisors in keeping health a high-priority issue.

The Critical Role of Supervisors

Why are supervisors and managers so important in improving employee health and controlling health and disability costs? Some interesting insight comes from surveys measuring organizational climate and employee satisfaction. These surveys indicate:

- The best predictor of employee satisfaction is the number of useful one-on-one discussions employees have with their immediate supervisor (more powerful, for example, than number of training classes or level of pay).
- Employees' preferred source of communication is their immediate supervisor (preferred to newsletters, videos, executive management speeches, etc.).
- The level of employee satisfaction with an immediate supervisor is difficult for other organizational factors to overcome (if negative, hard to compensate for; if positive, makes up for many other limitations).

In short, supervisors play an integral role in the perceptions and satisfaction levels of employees. Supervisors actually set the culture for their immediate work area through the way they interpret organizational policies and the emphasis and tone they use. They are often the most frequent administrators of organizational rewards and punishment, both monetary and nonmonetary. It is difficult for any organizational initiative to be effective without support from line managers and supervisors.

From a health and disability perspective, supervisors are especially critical. They are often the first in management to know when an employee has a potential health or disability problem. Supervisors must decide, often with imperfect information, how to respond to employee health requests or health-related behaviors. They are therefore the most important organizational influence for moving employee utilization forward toward prevention and early intervention and away from expensive medical treatment. Also, the relationship between the supervisor and employee may be the most important predictor of whether the employee and his or her family members will cooperate with organizational health policies and programs.

The following examples illustrate the critical role of the supervisor:

Example John, a previously dependable employee, has recently been preoccupied, has had trouble remembering details, and has missed work four times in the past month. When asked about the situation, John becomes evasive. He says he hasn't been feeling well and has been having some problems at home. He doesn't seem to want to talk about the situation, but John's supervisor is concerned the situation could become more serious. It could be a physical health problem for John, a psychosocial problem within his family, or even a drug/alcohol problem that is just beginning to get out of control. John's supervisor would like to prevent any of these scenarios from becoming severe but doesn't want to get involved in something outside the company's business.

Example Sue has previously had trouble with soreness and swelling in her wrist and forearm that she says is related to repetitive movement in her keyboard operating job. The first time this became a problem, her supervisor encouraged her to take a few days off with pay to rest her arm. The supervisor also arranged for some arm support pads to reduce the strain of working on the keyboard. Now, Sue says that the problem has gotten worse and her doctor thinks that surgery is the only thing that will return her arm to full functioning. Her supervisor is afraid that if Sue has the surgery, recuperation will take a long time and it will be difficult to reintegrate her into her work unit. This situation might even give other keyboard operators the wrong idea if it's not handled right.

Example Bill has previously been hospitalized for hypertension that is aggravated both by his weight and his tendency to get upset about problems at work and home. When Bill returned from his most recent hospital stay, he told his supervisor he was going to keep his weight down and try to take things more in stride. Recently, however, Bill's weight has been climbing and he's had a very short fuse. His supervisor, although basically satisfied with Bill's work performance, is concerned about Bill's health and is afraid Bill will have a major heart attack one of these days.

In service delivery, incidents like these are sometimes referred to as "moments of truth." These moments of truth involve responses to an immediate situation that have a far-ranging effect. For example, the way an employee deals with a customer's complaint or special request will determine whether the customer thinks the company provides high-quality service. If the employee does not respond suitably in the moment of truth, the customer assumes all service from the company is poor.[1] This same concept can apply to health and disability, based on the response of supervisors to an employee's health crisis.

As shown in the examples, supervisors face these difficult health and disability moments of truth on an ongoing basis. The right thing to do is not immediately clear in most situations. Supervisors must consider both productivity and health, must balance short-term needs against long-term costs and benefits. The distinction is blurred between the health and the work situation, and the true cause of the problem may not be obvious. The supervisor, in dealing with these complex psychosocial, ergonomic, and medical issues, may play a major role in the employee's behavior and the ultimate health and productivity cost.

These examples also point out just how much the role of the supervisor has changed and expanded in the 1990s. Entirely new health issues—stress, ergonomics, substance abuse, wellness—now confront supervisors on a daily basis. They also continue to be responsible for safety and disability management, both of which have become more complex and potentially litigious. Organizations have become flatter, supervisors have larger spans of control, and employees have higher expectations and increased autonomy. Finally, many supervisors receive little training or organizational support for dealing with these modern health issues.

Connecting Supervisors with Organizational Goals

To function effectively as the first line of influence on employee health and disability behavior, supervisors must clearly understand the organization's goals, strategies, and priorities: They must be familiar with key health and disability targets; they must understand the payoff to the organization and to themselves; and, they must believe that managing health will yield important spinoff benefits to both quality and productivity. Gaining this understanding and commitment among line supervisors begins with senior managers, who are the most significant influence on the speed and level of supervisory buy-in. If they delegate this responsibility entirely to staff personnel, progress will be short-term and limited to supervisors already oriented toward management of health. Senior managers must therefore be personally involved in the following key behaviors:

- Establishing health as an organizational priority and increasing supervisor commitment to organizational health goals.
- Helping supervisors understand the link between employee health and organizational quality and productivity.
- Including supervisors in the organization's health, disability, and risk management strategy.
- Tying supervisory performance to the total cost of health.

- Providing information and accountability to supervisors for ongoing management.

Senior managers can raise the priority of health and disability management in numerous ways, both formal and informal. Formally, senior management can include employee health as a priority in statements about the organization's vision, business direction, or objectives. Executives can include health and disability measures as key performance indicators. Some employers have developed significant health programs such as wellness or safety that reflect an important commitment to health and disability management. Another useful approach is to develop supervisory training sessions that explain how to manage health and disability effectively.

Senior managers can also influence supervisor commitment informally. At Du Pont, for example, safety is always the first agenda item in management meetings.[2] At the Air Force Strategic Air Command, senior officers jog regularly on the base running track and post the number of miles they run. Executives who ask their supervisors knowledgeable questions show they understand and monitor health and disability performance. This day-to-day commitment to health and disability by senior managers is often as important as the formal goals and procedures.

Tying health and disability to other organizational priorities can also be extremely powerful in gaining supervisory understanding and commitment. Many supervisors may not have thought about the tremendous effect of health and disability on productivity and quality. Senior managers can provide this perspective by offering examples and statistics that show the significant impact on all aspects of the bottom line. At General Motors, senior managers cite examples of how ergonomic improvements in car design have reduced manufacturing costs, improved quality for customers, and lowered health and disability risk all at the same time.[3] Similarly, executives can explain how quick return of injured workers to the job can improve productivity and quality (by reducing reliance on inexperienced or temporary workers) while reducing workers' compensation costs.

As supervisors increasingly appreciate the organization's need for effective health and disability management, senior managers should involve them in shaping strategy. Gaining supervisory involvement in strategy pays off in two ways. First, many supervisors can offer valuable insight into the direction and operational procedures that health and disability strategy should contain. Second, the process of involvement increases supervisory commitment and the likelihood that strategy will become action.

Over time, supervisory performance can be increasingly linked to the total cost of health within the supervisor's work units. The first step in this process is charging back costs to individual departments to increase awareness and accountability of direct health and disability costs (e.g., workers' compensation costs, costs for lengthy disabilities). This simple procedure has been shown repeatedly to significantly influence supervisory attention to health and disability. Additional aspects of the total cost of health (e.g., productivity impact, workers unavailable due to illness or injury) can also be measured and provided to supervisors as opportunities for continuous improvement of their health and disability management.

Providing information and accountability to supervisors not only helps reinforce the organization's priorities toward health but also equips supervisors to work effectively with their employees. Although most supervisors support the goal of improved health, they often lack information and organizational support for changing procedures or for involving employees at a more significant level. When senior managers make this priority concrete through accountability and sharing of information, supervisors will usually do their best to transform the organization's goals into workable solutions at the unit level.

Preparing Supervisors to Promote Health

Organizational commitment and support are the foundation for motivating supervisor involvement in health and disability. Yet this commitment must also be translated into practical knowledge and tools that allow supervisors to effectively manage the health issues of the 1990s. These tools must include the following four key components:

1. A broader understanding of the changing role of the supervisor in managing health and disability issues.
2. A set of coaching skills for working with employees on health and disability.
3. Access to information for dealing with the issues that supervisors face and for maintaining focus on the critical risk areas.
4. Incentives that reinforce supervisors for making health and disability a priority.

Supervisors must understand the broader implications of health and disability to perform effectively in a role that has changed rapidly over the past several years. They must also have good coaching skills to achieve the interpersonal relationship with employees that is at the core of managing health behavior. Access to information helps supervisors stay focused on key priorities and effectively utilize outside assistance when appropriate. Finally, supervisors need incentives because promoting health is a difficult enterprise that deserves reward for accomplishing organizational goals.

Again, the goal is to prevent health and disability problems—to intervene in situations early in the health continuum and thereby minimize the expensive treatment and rehabilitation phases on the back end. Supervisors are the best mechanism for accomplishing this goal because of their proximity to and relationship with employees. The integration of understanding, skills, information, and incentives allows supervisors to fulfill this role and help reduce health and disability costs.

Training Supervisors in the New Health Issues

Because of the rapid evolution of health and disability during the past ten years, many supervisors are unaware of developments that, if understood, would significantly improve their management effectiveness. Many other supervisors have never received training in health and disability management, even though it is a key influence on cost, productivity, and quality. For these supervisors to respond effectively to employee moments of truth, they will need to develop knowledge and skills. Training these supervisors is an excellent organizational investment.

Training should combine content information and discussion of the supervisory role in influencing employee health behavior. Suitable subjects include the following:

- Understanding the employee perspective on health.
- Viewing disability as a social, environmental, and economic issue, not just as a physical condition.
- Obtaining increased productivity through the flexible support of health needs.
- Becoming appropriately involved in a way that respects confidentiality yet motivates personal health management and self-care (health interventions).
- Removing the stigma from getting help.
- Interacting effectively with regulatory requirements, health professionals, and lawyers.
- Acting as a reference and referral source for information and professional help.

Employee Perspectives

Understanding the employee's perspective about health issues can often help supervisors avoid problems and increase rapport with their employees. Health is an important personal issue, and this understanding is essential when supervisors seek to influence employee health behavior. The supervisor who displays understanding and empathy for employee perspectives will avoid alienating employees or appearing to be patronizing or uncaring.

Perhaps the greatest asset in working to promote employee health and safety is that good health is in the employee's self-interest. This allows the supervisor to emphasize "win–win" partnerships that are good for the employee as well as the organization. To capitalize on these opportunities, the supervisor must understand what aspects of health translate into good care and good quality of life for employees. For example, a white-collar employee in her 30s may look at preventive care very differently from a blue-collar employee in his 50s. A wellness orientation may be attractive to an employee who wants to achieve a more balanced lifestyle, but it could be threatening to an employee who has been happily overweight for years.

Supervisors must also consider the need to involve dependents in health issues and interventions, since dependents generate an estimated 60 percent of total health costs.[4] Dependents take on special significance because the spouse or someone other than the employee may make family health decisions. Employee perspectives may also be heavily influenced by informal employee leaders whose knowledge or opinions influence co-workers. Thus, a discussion of the influences on employee health perspectives can help prepare supervisors to modify employee behavior successfully.

Disability

Training should emphasize the strong influence of supervisors on length of employee disability. In fact, response to disability is probably the aspect of health supervision with the largest cost and productivity impact. Supervisors who manage disability effectively can save the organization thousands of dollars in disability payments while increasing total productivity. Effective management of disability can also produce tremendous loyalty from employees, since the supervisor's response comes at a time of great employee need and vulnerability.

Disability should be framed as a set of choices and decisions in which the employee's physical condition is often less important than social, environmental, and economic factors. For example, an ill or injured employee will typically consider the financial implications of staying off work, the attractiveness of the workplace as a source of self-esteem and belonging, and the messages he or she is receiving from the supervisor, co-workers, and family members. Will the employee be welcomed back and placed in a manageable and positive job situation? Or will the employee be isolated or ridiculed if unable to function 100 percent from the moment he or she walks in the door? Will the supervisor work flexibly with the employee's family and home situation to accommodate the employee's transition back to full functioning?

The upshot of disability training is that supervisors are not helpless in reactively waiting for 100 percent recovery from the physical injury. Instead, through flexibility and caring, they have a significant opportunity to influence the speed and effectiveness with which injured or ill employees return to work. Evidence shows that even a few supportive phone calls from supervisors to employees can dramatically improve the speed of return to work.[5] Returning these workers quickly, even on a limited basis, benefits both employee and employer by notably reducing the risk of long-term or permanent disability.

Many supervisors find it helpful to use case studies to examine the productivity payoff available through flexible support of disability or general employee health needs. These case studies can help supervisors trade off the short-term productivity costs of encouraging preventive health care versus the long-term productivity costs of a serious illness that could have been avoided. Another application would be to examine the productivity implications of returning a brain-injured employee who is functioning at 80 percent versus using a temporary worker who lacks experience working for the organization or in the particular job. Case studies can also focus on working with employees in situations that involve dependents. Such real-life examples help supervisors develop responses that optimize and integrate health, productivity, and quality.

Appropriate Involvement

A difficult issue for many supervisors is the appropriate degree of involvement in promoting employee health. How should a supervisor treat an employee who smokes heavily, taking frequent breaks to smoke outside the building? Should the supervisor encourage a heavily overweight employee to change eating habits and participate in company wellness activities? What can the supervisor do to encourage employees' safe behavior, both on the job and off? How important is the supervisor's own health and safety behavior? Discussions and case studies can help supervisors understand the organization's policies and goals, as well as develop skills for handling these situations.

Training should address how supervisors can remove the stigma for employees of seeking help early for health and disability issues. Many employees are reluctant to participate in wellness activities, to seek preventive health care, or to contact the employee assistance program because they fear being regarded as weak or undedicated. Yet employees will only improve their health and minimize total costs through active involvement in these low-cost, prevention activities. Supervisors can thus learn how to promote these proactive health behaviors while minimizing abuse or negative reactions from co-workers.

Dealing with External Agencies

Because health and disability issues are potential sources of litigation, supervisors should be familiar with acceptable supervisory practice. This might include the Americans with Disabilities Act, Occupational Safety and Health Administration (OSHA), personnel law and other regulations, as well as company policy and compliance with federal and state regulations. Many supervisors benefit from learning how to work effectively with rehabilitation and health care providers. They might also discuss how to respond if attorneys become involved in an employee's health and disability case. Making supervisors more comfortable with legal and regulatory requirements allows them to act aggressively within these parameters to promote health and disability goals.

Supervisors should not be expected to be health and disability experts, so reference and referral information is essential including an orientation to the internal resources of the company such as safety, wellness, employee assistance, and human resources. Often, supervisors are unaware of the services offered by other departments, as well as by community agencies. Many employers put together handy referral listings that supervisors can use to help solve an employee or workplace health problem.

For many organizations, health and disability training overlaps with management training in general. Managing quality improvement, for example, requires data and root cause analysis, listening and teamwork skills, and an orientation toward front-end prevention. Managing diversity in the work force requires treating employees as individuals, respecting confidentiality, and promoting empowerment to capitalize on employee uniqueness. All these skills are also important in health and disability management. Thus, health and disability training should build on existing supervisory training to promote integration across the many applications of good management behavior.

Coaching Skills

Supervisors are the coaches of the workplace. Like all good coaches, they are out to win: to get the job done on time, on budget, and with high quality. Successful coaches accomplish their goals by keeping everyone on their team physically healthy, mentally focused, and emotionally committed toward key objectives. Unfortunately, being a good coach does not come naturally to most people. Most supervisors need both training and experience to become effective. In particular, most supervisors need to develop people management skills, the so-called soft skills that are actually the hardest part of improving both performance and health. And supervisors must develop these skills in terms of their own unique style.

Consider, for example, Vince Lombardi, Tony La Russa, Joe Paterno, and Bobby Knight—they are all winning coaches, but each has a different style. Their success underscores that there are several winning coaching styles and not just one best way. To be effective, supervisors need to develop and use a coaching style that is both comfortable and flexible, with enough options to be effective with different people and situations. Table 9.1 shows six coaching options that supervisors can use to build a style that will promote healthy employee behavior and reduce health and disability costs.

Teacher

The *Teacher* style is particularly effective for explaining and demonstrating how to perform or behave in a safe and healthy way. This style works well when the supervisor is experienced and knowledgeable and when the

Table 9.1   Successful Coaching Styles

Style	Advantages	Requirements
Teacher		
Explains, demonstrates, and gives feedback on safe and healthy behavior	Allows supervisor to be proactive in building knowledge and commitment to health	A motivated learner; a knowledgeable and committed teacher
Authoritarian		
Expects employees to do exactly what they are told; disciplines/criticizes them if they don't	Can produce a quick response; may be needed for situations in which health or safety is threatened	Fairness and good judgment; must be used in combination with other styles
Counselor		
Uses questions and listens to employees to reduce resistance and increase motivation	Helps to manage the difficult employee or sensitive health situation; respects employees as adults	Supervisory patience; strong questioning and listening skills; knowledge of referral agencies
Monitor		
Observes employees; asks employees and others about health and safety behavior; gives feedback	Can identify health or safety problems early, before a crisis; puts action behind management commitment to health	Consistency and fairness; good judgment in when and when not to give feedback
Goal Setter		
Establishes objectives for individuals and teams; gives feedback on progress toward goals	Focuses attention on key goals and objectives; increases motivation; positive approach	Sufficient knowledge and information to set effective goals; ability to achieve employee buy-in to the goals
Champion		
Praises employees publicly and enthusiastically when they do well; gives them opportunity and support to achieve their goals	Builds employee loyalty and motivation; helps support lifestyle or behavior change; influences peer norms	Praise must be genuine, fair and consistent; supervisor must role-model desired behavior

worker is motivated to learn or to change. For example, this style works well when employees want to know how to operate their equipment without causing soft tissue or ergonomic problems. The Teacher style is also a good fit for employee meetings about healthy lifestyles and ways to prevent the most common health and safety problems.

Example   Frank convened a meeting of his employees to talk about questions and complaints he had heard regarding wrist and hand pain. He used a diagram to show how this kind of pain could develop from repetitive motion in certain jobs. Frank then demonstrated several ways to minimize repetitive motion and explained some resources employees could use if they experienced problems. Back on the job, Frank periodically had informal discussions with employees about how to reduce their risk for this disability.

Teaching is inappropriate when employees know how to perform the behavior but are not motivated to do so.

Example One of Phil's employees has had frequent illnesses and absences caused by what the employee describes as persistent fatigue. Phil thinks the problem is poor eating habits, so he asked the employee to meet with him for an hour so Phil could explain some helpful information about proper diet. Unfortunately, the employee became very offended by this suggestion and said Phil was invading her private life. She even threatened to file a complaint or a lawsuit charging harassment. Phil now realizes that teaching was probably not the right approach in this situation.

Authoritarian

The *Authoritarian* style involves giving orders and then punishing or criticizing employees if they do not follow orders. This style can be effective in communicating expectations, but should always be combined with other coaching styles. It is best used when quick decision action is necessary.

Example Gwen is the new supervisor in a work unit that has had rapidly increasing workers' compensation costs over the past two years. She recently talked with her employees about the need to dramatically improve safety. When Gwen discovers that three employees were involved in a flagrant violation of safety policy, she calls them into her office, informs them that this serious violation will result in a written reprimand in their files, and says she will be monitoring their performance closely in the future. She makes it clear that they will be fired if they continue to display unsafe behavior.

The authoritarian style can backfire if employees believe it is being used simply to "show who's in charge" or if it is used when the situation doesn't warrant that approach.

Example Three employees in Chuck's work unit are smokers who have to smoke outside the building because of company policy. Chuck tries to time exactly how long they take for lunch breaks, makes sarcastic remarks about how stupid smokers are, and keeps stressing the smoking issue in employee meetings. Chuck has made the smokers so angry, they will continue smoking just to irritate him.

Counselor

The *Counselor* style uses questioning and listening to understand the employee's point of view and to reach agreement on what the employee will do to address the health or safety problem. This style treats employees as adults who can participate in solving the problem, especially if they are otherwise resistant. It works best when the supervisor can be patient in dealing with the problem and has strong questioning and listening skills.

> **Example** One of Al's employees has recently gained a lot of weight and has let his personal appearance and general performance slip. Al meets with this employee and asks him if everything is all right. By listening carefully and asking perceptive questions, Al ultimately gets the employee to agree that there has been a marked change in behavior. Al and the employee brainstorm what to do about the problem, and Al sets up a meeting for one week later, when they will document a formal plan (with dates) that the employee agrees to follow.

The counseling style is difficult with an employee who has a history of problems or a supervisor who does not have the time or the questioning skills to make it work.

> **Example** Judy tried to counsel an employee with a history of alcoholism-related absences and performance problems. She would leave each meeting feeling they had really made progress, but the problems always recurred. Finally, Judy realized that she had to limit her role to performance management and refer the employee to outside assistance for help with these deep-seated problems.

Monitor

The *Monitor* style is one of the best ways for supervisors to influence health- and safety-related behavior of their employees. Monitoring can be done by directly observing behavior, by questioning employees, or by obtaining information from other involved observers. This allows supervisors to give effective feedback to employees and deal with risk behaviors before they create a crisis.

> **Example** One of Bill's employees hurt his leg badly in a car accident and was initially unable to work. Bill contacted the employee regularly, however, to check his progress and encourage his recovery. When the employee returned to a modified job, Bill still monitored his capabilities and talked with him about what he expected to be able to do and when. Bill maintained this monitoring and feedback until the employee was completely recovered, resulting in much faster rehabilitation and a message of caring to employees.

Although useful in most situations, monitoring and feedback should not be the first choice when the health issue involves confidentiality, the employee is sensitive about the situation, and the supervisor does not have an adequate health background to deal with the problem.

> **Example** Kay supervises an employee with a history of depression. The employee does not really want anyone to know about this illness and only informed Kay because of needing time off to see a counselor. Kay, who had taken a freshman psychology class in college, decided to observe the employee closely and give her feedback. This attention intimidates the employee, and she sometimes stays home from work, not because of depression but to avoid Kay.

Goal Setter

The *Goal Setter* style relies on the principle that people will always work harder and more effectively when trying to reach a goal. Goals are an excellent way to build commitment and energy around health and disability.

> **Example** When Mickey's company decided to make a concerted effort to reduce health and disability costs, she decided to set concrete goals for her work unit. With the help of several employees, Mickey charted a baseline of present costs and the areas of greatest improvement opportunities. Mickey then called an employee meeting to determine the goals for the next year and the methods for achieving them, which ensured employee buy-in.

The goal-setting style is almost always useful but can be limited by a lack of information or barriers to employee buy-in.

> **Example** Carl wanted to set a goal related to healthy blood pressure levels among his employees as a way to improve overall health. Unfortunately, no information was available

about present blood pressure levels, and not all employees were interested in participating. Carl decided instead to organize a health fair and try to build enthusiasm for health risk screening that could in turn be utilized for later goal setting.

Champion

Champion, the final coaching style, involves praising, recognizing, and rewarding employees—treating them as if they are "champions." Health and disability is an excellent area for the champion style because good health is an accomplishment that everyone can easily celebrate.

> **Example**   Tom's work unit has remained free of accidents for five straight months, remarkably better than a year ago. In addition, the employees have helped a previously injured employee successfully return to work three months ahead of schedule. Tom reinforces this success as widely and as often as possible, citing both the financial payback and the employee benefit as proof. His unit's success has been written up in the company newsletter, and the CEO stopped by to congratulate the employees. Their accomplishment has greatly added to the unit's morale and teamwork.

Like monitoring and goal setting, the champion style is appropriate for almost all settings. The praise must be warranted, however, and should be fair and consistent across all employees.

> **Example**   Joan has been assigned to lead a work unit with a poor health and disability history, in an area of the company that she knows little about. Joan would like to recognize and praise her employees, but she knows that premature recognition will seem forced and artificial. She plans to use the champion style after she learns more about the unit and they build some success together.

Effective Coaching—Style and Substance

The preceding examples show that supervising today's health problems demands a natural yet flexible coaching style. Successful supervisors usually draw on all six styles—teacher, authoritarian, counselor, monitor, goal setter, and champion—to deal with the diverse issues and situations that make up health and disability. Employers can use this listing of styles to assess skills and determine whether training is needed to improve coaching ability.

Yet, effective coaching for health and disability is not only a question of style. The substance underlying the style must be the supervisor's genuine commitment to the health and well-being of his or her employees. This commitment is the reason employees place so much trust in their supervisor and consider the supervisor a semiproxy for the organizational culture. Supervisory influence is strongest when employees believe in the supervisor's genuine concern and fairness in setting expectations and responding to behavior.

Supervisory commitment to employee welfare is also important because many health and disability problems can involve confidentiality. When injured or ill, employees are often concerned they will be labeled or judged as weak, lazy, or lacking in character. They may also be concerned that personal information will be shared with co-workers. Supervisors can only be effective in dealing with these situations if the employee trusts the supervisor to show discretion and good judgment.

The effective supervisor is not on a witchhunt to identify and stigmatize employees with health and disability problems. Every worker faces health issues at some point, and the goal is a positive approach that emphasizes prevention and early use of interventions. Effective supervisors, who are Managing Forward, recognize that this early investment of time and attention will reduce back-end cost and rehabilitation. They also understand that the payoff for good employee health is not only reduced cost, but also improved quality, productivity, and employee commitment.

In choosing and training supervisors, the organization sends an important message about its values for promoting health and increasing prevention because competent supervisors are the best proof that these stated values are an operative reality. Such supervisors are also among an organization's most effective weapons for reducing health and disability costs.

Access to Information

Supervisors who understand and support their employer's health and disability strategy still need two types of information to help them focus and monitor their management efforts: (1) baseline data about the health and disability progress of the unit, and (2) solutions or referral data that can be used to solve health and disability problems. Current and easy availability of this information is critical since most supervisors and managers will make time to manage health and disability only if they have regular reinforcement and convenient access to solutions and guidance.

Regular feedback about the unit's performance should include the status of both existing claims results and projected future risks. Supervisors should receive periodic reports about their unit's health care, workers' compensation, and disability results as well as regular information about the ongoing risk levels among their employees. Results shared must appropriately protect individual confidentiality, and help supervisors target root causes, not individual employees.

Reports to supervisors should be simple and meaningful and should reflect an ongoing baseline. Supervisors will achieve the best results by concentrating on a few key indexes and observing their unit's progress over time. For example, in workers' compensation, supervisors might focus only on the number of lost workday cases or the number of lost workdays from each case. Keeping it simple and focused also helps the supervisor to motivate employees with results charts and progress comparisons from month to month or quarter to quarter.

In managing health and disability issues, supervisors will sometimes need access to expert guidance and technical information. For example, they may need help in solving ergonomic problems or may need to refer an employee with psychological problems to an outside counselor. Supervisors cannot and should not be expected to be health and disability experts, but are most effective when they provide expectations, focus, and resources—and then coach employees to behave effectively within those parameters.

Supervisors can access health and disability expertise from multiple sources. Many organizations have internal capabilities or formal affiliations in a variety of health areas, such as employee assistance, wellness, and safety. Often, these professionals are happy to work with supervisors to prevent health problems. In addition, a large number of community, nonprofit, and government agencies provide free or low-cost health assistance to supervisors by supplying educational materials, speakers, and on-site consulting. Resources include local hospitals, universities or community colleges, and nonprofit local and national organizations such as the American Heart Association, the National Head Injury Foundation, or the National Safety Council. City, state, and federal agencies are another excellent source of assistance. The Resources sections at the end of Chapters 10 through 13 provide a good starting point for accessing these agencies.

Incentives

A final way to support supervisors in management of health and disability is to provide incentives and rewards for good performance. Even with an effective coaching style and access to health and disability information, supervisors still need a reason to make employee health a priority. Health and disability can get lost in the shuffle if not explicitly included in supervisory recognition and rewards. Recognized leaders in health and disability management, such as Johnson & Johnson or Du Pont, have for many years made health and safety a key accountability for managers.

Employers involved in quality improvement have found two aspects of incentives to be particularly important to motivating supervisors and managers. First, incentives must be integrated with the performance management system and overall culture of the organization. They will fail if announced at the beginning of the year and then never mentioned again or if they conflict with the way daily work is usually done and are the only counterbalance to established procedures and norms. Second, the nonmonetary rewards for the desired outcome are at least as important (perhaps more important) than the monetary rewards. To influence supervisory commitment to health and disability, incentives must therefore include both monetary and nonmonetary recognition.

On the monetary side, some organizations reward supervisors through annual, semiannual, or quarterly bonuses for achieving health and disability goals. Separating health and disability as a bonus item may give it a higher profile than merging it with several other areas of supervisory performance. Other organizations, however, view health and disability as a key performance area, along with cost, revenue, and production, and reward it through annual performance and salary review. This approach emphasizes that promoting health is an expected part of everyday work.

Nonmonetary recognition is also handled in numerous ways such as the following:

- A special dinner with members of top management to recognize the unit champions of health and safety.
- Plaques or trophies awarded to the supervisors whose units achieve the best health and disability performance.
- Personal visits by top management to healthy and safe work units to thank and recognize employees and supervisors.
- A paid day off to supervisors and employees who achieve their unit health and disability goals.
- Picnics, outings, and celebrations to honor health and disability accomplishments.
- Lapel pins, jackets, or T-shirts as visible signs of units with outstanding health and disability performance.
- Informal praise and recognition during meetings or on the job for the efforts of employees and supervisors to promote health.

Both monetary and nonmonetary rewards reinforce the importance of health and disability. Monetary rewards show that the organization's commitment is serious, that it "puts its money where its mouth is." Nonmonetary rewards show the organization's emotional commitment, reinforcing health and disability in ways that are memorable, fun, and personally meaningful. Together, they give supervisors a powerful incentive to emphasize the prevention behaviors that keep costs low and that keep employee health a priority.

Ultimately, success in controlling costs depends on an ability to integrate health priorities into daily operational decisions and practices. Supervisors are an organization's best mechanism for making this transition, moving employee health from a concept or program to a "real world" reality. Supervisory involvement and effectiveness moves health and disability from being a staff issue to a line issue and marshalls employee attitudes and behaviors toward health. Preparing, supporting, and rewarding these supervisors is key to improving the organization's health and disability results.

References

1. Carlzon, J. 1987. *Moments of Truth*. Cambridge, MA: Ballinger.

2. Tompkins, N. C. January 1992. America's leaders in safety management. *Occupational Health and Safety*, pp. 29–32.

3. General Motors Corp. 1992. *Proact Plant Safety*. Detroit: GMC.

4. Edington, D. W., & Yen, L. T. 1992. Is it possible to simultaneously reduce risk factors and health care costs? *American Journal of Health Promotion*, 6(6): 403–409.

5. Akabas, S. H., Gates, L. B., & Galvin, D. E. 1992. *Disability Management*. New York: AMACOM.

Resources

General training in supervision is a staple in the products and services of many management firms, as suggested by the following list. Supervisory training tailored particularly to health and disability is available from many of the organizations listed in the Resources sections of the next four chapters.

American Management Association
135 West 50th Street
New York, NY 10020
(518) 891-0065

Career Track
3085 Center Green Drive
Boulder, CO 80301-5408
(303) 447-2300 Seminars
(303) 440-7440 Tapes

Fred Pryor Seminars
A Division of Pryor Resources, Inc.
2000 Johnson Drive
P.O. Box 2951
Shawnee Mission, KS 66201
(800) 255-6139

National Seminars, Inc.
P.O. Box 2949
6901 West 63rd Street
Shawnee Mission, KS 66201-1349
(800) 258-7246

National Educational Media (NEI)
A Britannica Training and Development
  Company
310 South Michigan Avenue
Chicago, IL 60604
(800) 554-9862

Nightingale-Conant Corporation
7300 North Lehigh Avenue
Chicago, IL 60648
(800) 323-3938

10

An Integrated Approach to Employee Wellness

Chief executive officers (CEOs) are generally very busy people and yet, according to a survey by the American Health Fitness Institute, 64 percent of them exercise regularly—roughly six times the participation rate for American adults at large.[1] These executives make time for exercise because they know the health and productivity benefit it provides to them personally.

Similarly, many progressive organizations have active wellness or health promotion programs because they know the health and productivity payoff for their employees, based on studies that document improved health care costs, absenteeism, and employee attitudes. The following examples show this success can be achieved in companies with 30,000, 3,000, or 300 employees, and in both the private and public sector.

The Benefits of Wellness Programs

Example **Johnson & Johnson** At Johnson & Johnson, the wellness effort began in 1978 with an offer to employees to be "the healthiest in the world." Johnson & Johnson hired behavioral scientists, epidemiologists, and health promotion experts to develop a comprehensive health promotion program known as "Live for Life." Designed to improve employee health by encouraging healthful lifestyles, the program offers health screening and education to employees, supported by company policies, management feedback, and communications and follow-up that promote health.

The program began as a pilot in a few company plants and was then marketed to management of additional plants. Programs are offered to employees free of charge, and participation is voluntary. At present, Live for Life has grown to become an integral part of the corporation's personnel benefit and health care cost containment activities, available to over 30,000 company employees across the United States.

Results from the program show it has had a positive impact in at least five key areas: employee lifestyle behaviors, employee health, health care costs, absenteeism, and employee attitudes. During the study period, employees at plants participating in Live for Life showed the following compared with matched controls at nonparticipating plants:

- A 10.4 percent increase in fitness levels across the entire employee population.
- A 22.6 percent rate of smoking cessation compared with the general population average of 4 to 5 percent.
- A 61 percent increase in seat belt use compared with two years earlier.
- A 50 percent lower rate of growth in health care costs than the control group.
- A 33 percent lower rate of absenteeism.
- Significantly greater employee satisfaction and organizational commitment.

Thus, the Johnson & Johnson program is one of the most successful wellness programs in the country.[2, 3, 4]

Example **Standard Telephone** Standard Telephone is an independent phone company with 375 employees, located in Cornelia, Georgia. Standard began its wellness program in 1984 because claims for heart disease, diabetes, and stress were rising dramatically. In fact, an in-house medical screening of employees found that of 242 employees monitored for heart rate at that time, 178 were categorized as "needing immediate attention." Standard responded to the situation by setting up a separate department that would deal primarily with employee heath care. Annual employee testing was established for cholesterol levels, body fat, blood pressure, and cardiac capacity, and to motive employees to set self-improvement goals.

Over time, Standard built a number of self-help and physical fitness options for employees, including a walking track, educational classes, aerobics workouts with videotaping available, and gift certificates to encourage participation. Standard also sends a monthly health newsletter and a self-care medical reference book to its employees' dependents. To control program costs, Standard takes advantage of the many free or low-cost community resources available for wellness. Finally, the company asks employees to personally review the medical bills they generate—this helps identify costly errors and also raises employee awareness of cost.

Standard's payback has been remarkable. In 1984, the national average was 7.9 percent of payroll spent on health insurance, and Standard spent 9.1 percent. In 1989 (the most recent year with data available), the national average had climbed to 13.6 percent, whereas Standard spent only 8.0 percent of its payroll on health insurance. Thus, Standard actually reduced its health care expense during the same period the national average increased by over 50 percent.[5]

Example   **City of Birmingham**   At the City of Birmingham, Alabama, interest in wellness also stemmed from a significant concern about cost. From 1975 to 1984, health care costs had risen from $1.5 million to $7.6 million—an annual average increase of about 19 percent, or almost twice the national average. At that rate, the city's expenses for health care were projected at $70.5 million for the five-year period from 1986 to 1990 and $31.3 million just for the year 1992. The city elected to make a number of changes in both managed care and wellness programs.

Birmingham began wellness with a pilot project that involved health risk screening, employee education, the opening of a fitness center, and interventions for people with particular health risks such as smoking or overweight. The city then successfully applied for a National Institutes of Health (NIH) grant that allowed them to monitor and modify their existing programs and conduct an in-depth assessment of the impact of the wellness program. A condition of the grant was that *all* employees were required to participate in the health screening, which was done annually throughout the five-year period.

As opposed to the $70.5 million projected for health care costs in the second half of the 1980s, Birmingham actually spent $39.3 million. Average medical cost per employee rose by only $28 between 1985 and 1990. This savings was due in part to Birmingham's adoption of a health maintenance organization (HMO) and slightly higher employee contributions, but the wellness effort also played a significant role. Major improvements were achieved in smoking, cholesterol, and blood pressure, even among male, blue-collar employees, who are traditionally a tough audience for health promotion. In total, Birmingham estimates it saved about $10 for every dollar the city and NIH invested in wellness.[6]

These examples illustrate that wellness programs can work. Like the 64 percent of CEOs who exercise regularly, however, employers can accomplish these results only through integration and commitment. The executive committed to maintaining good health and productivity integrates exercise into his or her lifestyle, just as these successful organizations integrated a wellness program into their organizational culture. It is this integration and commitment that is the secret to achieving long-term success with wellness.

The Need for Integration

Often, the best insight into a wellness program comes from informal remarks heard in the hallway or at meetings:

- We tried wellness and it didn't work.
- Our employees just aren't that interested in running and weight lifting.
- We offered some noontime speakers and nobody came.
- Some people were interested at first, but it really died out.

Routine comments such as these highlight the need for integration. Wellness programs typically fail when perceived narrowly (e.g., as only a physical fitness program), as intended for some other audience (e.g., people who only eat lettuce and carrots), or as a short-term option that lacks ongoing management support (e.g., an occasional speaker on health). By contrast, successful wellness efforts are multifaceted, can be tailored to all employees' needs, and are reinforced by management as an important and stable aspect of maintaining an effective organization.

In fact, the concept of wellness is in many ways like the concept of quality. Both are broad, desirable states of being. Both are positive, prevention oriented, and have a simple, intuitive appeal. Wellness is more than just the absence of sickness, as quality is more than just the absence of defects. Also like quality, wellness or health promotion has brought together knowledge from several disciplines such as occupational medicine, exercise physiology, nutrition, training, and development. This has created an integrated and dynamic approach for maximizing the desired outcomes.

Achieving wellness, like quality, is an ongoing journey that senior management leads to build broad commitment and desired behavior throughout the organization's stakeholders. Actions to improve wellness affect not only the immediate goal of lower health cost, but also influence the employees' perception of the entire organizational culture. Employees who feel committed to and valued by the organization are much less likely to engage in litigation, absenteeism, and work slowdowns. They are more open to suggestions about managing health care for themselves and their family members. Health promotion can therefore play a key cultural role in developing commitment and promoting healthy behavior both personally and organizationally.

Finally, as with quality, not all companies have been equally successful with wellness. Many companies have generated some pilot wellness activity with few measurable results. After a year or two, these programs have typically died out. By contrast, the most successful companies have achieved a broad range of significant results from wellness by making it an integrated part of daily work life. They have set aggressive improvement targets, developed tailored programs that were likely to have impact for the employees, and have then actively managed these programs to ensure they met predetermined goals.

Successful wellness programs may include all or only some of the health interventions discussed in the remainder of this chapter. The key, however, is that they must be managed, supported, and held accountable in the same way as any other organizational investment. With this integrated view, both employer and employees will be more serious in their commitment to wellness.

Potential Health Interventions for an Integrated Wellness Program

1. Organizational philosophy and objectives.
2. Employee health screening.
3. Health education and promotion.
4. Increasing employee participation.
5. Personal counseling and follow-up with employees.
6. Use of financial incentives or penalties tied to health behavior.
7. Use of cost-effective community resources.
8. Program evaluation.
9. Retiree and family health promotion.

Organizational Philosophy and Objectives

An effective and well-managed wellness program begins with a statement of the organization's philosophy and objectives that serves as a touchstone for employees and managers, providing a context for understanding the employer's direction and expectations related to wellness. This statement should be targeted at three levels: (1) broad organizational values, (2) specific operational policies, and (3) measures for evaluation and continuous improvement. Each of these plays an important role in ensuring the wellness effort achieves desired results.

Organizational values should provide rationale and focus for how wellness will contribute to the employees and employer. For example, the philosophy statement might say that good health is critical to a full and productive life for employees and to effective performance and cost management for the organization. The philosophy statement should also reinforce the value of managing wellness from the perspective of the total cost of health and disability, including productivity, quality, and employee commitment, as well as direct costs. It should emphasize the importance of Managing Forward in the health continuum to increase prevention and early intervention.

Specific operational policies of the wellness program must also be decided, especially the concepts of "voluntariness" and "confidentiality." The policy on voluntariness might say that services will definitely be offered repeatedly to all employees in the target population, and that employees are free to participate either initially or at a later time. Such an arrangement guarantees that services will be available and provides positive inducement without coercion.[7] Alternatively, the organization may specify that certain behaviors such as health screening are required as a condition of participating in the organization's health coverage. For confidentiality, employees might be guaranteed that the company will not share any worker's health information without the employee's written authorization.

To ensure the wellness program meets the needs of employees and the organization, the philosophy must also specify the measures that will be used for ongoing evaluation and improvement. Possible measures for use include:

1. Health behaviors such as smoking or seatbelt use.
2. Health outcomes such as premature births or emergency room use.
3. Health cost outcomes such as health care costs or lost time due to illness.
4. Employee satisfaction with program as measured by participation rates and surveys.
5. Organizational outcomes such as turnover, absenteeism, and employee satisfaction.

As discussed later in this chapter, evaluation of health promotion impact can be complex and, in extreme cases, can cost more than the program itself. The organizational philosophy should therefore establish general guidelines for performing essential evaluation and measurement in a manner that makes good business sense.

Developing the organizational philosophy and objectives should involve input from multiple parties because of the sensitivity of certain health issues. For example, many employers today are debating whether to tie financial incentives or penalties to health-related behavior, such as assessing a $10 monthly insurance surcharge to employees who smoke. Similarly, there can be controversy over such issues as coverage for employee mental health or whether to invest in a company fitness center. Input from management, labor, legal, health and safety, and employee benefits representatives can ensure a policy that is balanced and reasonable.

The payoff is a coherent and integrated response to health issues with large cost and management climate implications. Senior management should personally direct or participate in the development and evolution of the wellness philosophy, policies, and measures. It may also be appropriate to have a standing wellness committee, composed of representatives from all segments of the work force, to monitor and support organizational wellness efforts on an ongoing basis.

Employee Health Screening

Work-site screening and early detection of health and life risk factors has grown rapidly during the past several years. According to the first National

Survey of Worksite Health Promotion Activities in 1988, approximately 30 percent of private sector firms with 50 or more employees offer some type of health risk assessment to their workers. Of these, 77 percent offered health or physical examinations; 15 percent offered cancer screening; and 43 percent did blood pressure screening.[8] In larger firms and those with some experience in employee wellness, the availability of screening for health risks is increasingly routine.

The rising popularity of health screening is closely tied to the numerous benefits that screening can provide. First, screening helps to identify employees at high risk for serious health problems and to arrange early intervention. Second, screening establishes a personal baseline that employees can use to chart their health progress. Third, many employees are interested in the results of health screens, providing an excellent way to motivate healthy behavior. Finally, as shown in the following examples, health screens can be an important focus in educating or counseling employees for health improvement.[9]

Example   **City of Birmingham**   At the city of Birmingham, health screening includes measurement of a variety of physiological indexes (e.g., blood pressure, percentage of body fat) as well as a computerized health risk appraisal. All participants receive confidential copies of their medical screens and appraisal results, and a copy is sent to their personal physician. Birmingham initially found that 13 percent of those screened had such abnormal findings that they were referred immediately to a physician. Results are also used on an ongoing basis to help educate, motivate, and measure progress as employees adopt healthier lifestyles. This screening is a key part of Birmingham's tremendous savings in health care costs.[10]

Example   **Coors, Inc.**   At Coors, the Colorado-based brewer, cardiac health screening has been a key element of the company's efforts to reduce heart attacks and related problems. For employees who have already suffered or are at high risk for heart attack, Coors performs treadmill stress tests and other physiological screens, as well as measures of diet, mental health, and lifestyle and Type A behaviors. This screening information is used in education and progress assessment and for making decisions about job placement and future health needs. Coors estimates it saved $1.39 million in the first six years of operation of this cardiac wellness program, $4.2 million in its first 10 years.[11]

Example   **Steelcase, Inc.**   Researchers working with Steelcase, the Michigan furniture manufacturer, have followed the medical costs and health habits of 1832 workers for eight years. Health care costs for employees with positive health behavior were $67 to $778 lower per year than those of workers with high-risk health behaviors.[12] Again, identifying these health problems through screening and then motivating employees to change their behavior could yield significant payback for both the employee and employer.

The payoff from health screening can also be enhanced by including aspects of the employee's work environment rather than personal lifestyle alone. Among employees for a large New England manufacturer, workplace conditions such as excessive noise and unpleasant working conditions were at least as important as employee lifestyle in predicting injuries, mental health problems, and absenteeism. When both job risks and life risk information were combined (double jeopardy), the accuracy of prediction increased. Employees in the high-risk group were three times as likely to be injured, twice as likely to be absent, and 5 times more likely to have psychological symptoms as employees in the low-risk group.[13]

Health Education and Promotion

For many organizations, health education and health promotion events are central to their wellness programs. Classes offer information on topics such as cholesterol, nutrition, warning signs of cancer, or the relationship between lifestyle and disease. Promotional events include health fairs, screening booths, contests, and health days. Both education and promotion increase employees' knowledge and reinforce the notion that the organization is committed to good health.

> **Example** **General Electric Aircraft Engines** General Electric Aircraft Engines in Cincinnati uses these two approaches in helping workers to lose weight. In October through January, the program is called "Slim Santa," and in March through June, it is known as "Reach the Beach." Seminars at various times, on different days of the week, discuss weight-loss techniques. Employees receive checklists that suggest requirements for the weight-loss program, but they are responsible for completing requirements on their own. Prizes are offered to encourage participation, and a weight reduction support group is also available. General Electric reports that claim costs for employees who participate in the company's fitness programs are $184 less per year than for nonparticipants.[14]

Structured classes and events appeal to a certain segment of the work force but may not meet the needs of those with busy schedules or those who are reluctant to deal publicly with a health problem. To reach these employees, some organizations use workbooks, audiocassettes, or personal assessments for guided self-help interventions. Another alternative is to identify employees with a particular health concern (e.g., previous heart attack, arthritis) and conduct formal sessions tailored specifically to that audience.[15]

Over time, health risk screening, education, and promotion can lead to a greater awareness of health and more effective use of health care. At Johnson & Johnson, a survey of more than 18,000 employees showed that they were significantly more likely than the national average to have their blood pressure checked (86%), receive a Pap smear (94% of all female employees) and a breast examination (81% of women), and receive other forms of sound preventive health care. Such rates of preventive care show that employees are increasingly taking personal responsibility for their health and incorporating what they know about health into their lifestyle.[16]

Increasing Employee Participation

How good is the best wellness program if it is used only by employees who are already oriented toward health? And, how much value does the program have for an employee who loses 20 pounds in a weight loss program but then gains it all back six months later? As these questions show, participation and adherence are key factors in ensuring that wellness programs go beyond mere activity to produce important employee and organizational results. Experience and research suggest the following conclusions:

- It is generally more difficult and also more valuable to achieve participation among the highest risk employees.
- At least 50 percent of employees will have difficulty in maintaining a lifestyle change and will need follow-up.
- The single most important influence on participation and adherence rates is the quality of the wellness program; it is more important than demographics of the work force.
- Management practices and personal follow-up with employees can also improve participation and adherence.

In most organizations, participation in wellness activity is voluntary, and participation rates range from 20 to 80 percent. In general, those who participate in wellness tend to be nonsmokers, are more concerned about their health, are more knowledgeable about the benefits of exercise, and are younger in age. In addition, they tend to use fewer health services and have lower absenteeism and turnover rates.[17] For example, Travelers Insurance in Hartford, Connecticut found that employees who joined their "Taking Care" wellness program had been absent in the prior year 10 to 20 percent less often than those who didn't join the program. Thus, the employees who joined were somewhat healthier (fewer absences) than those who didn't join, even before the program began.[18] On the other hand, these differences between participants and nonparticipants are not always large. At a facility of Northern Telecom (a telecommunications equipment company) in North Carolina, a comparison found no significant differences in employee health status and health habits between those who joined the health promotion program and those who didn't.[19] It seems likely that all wellness programs contain some very healthy employees who choose to participate because it fits their lifestyle and some less healthy employees who participate because they feel they need to.

Still, the employees the organization is most concerned about are the least healthy 10 to 20 percent including employees who drink excessively, are long-term smokers, are significantly overweight, or have high blood pressure or a high-risk family history. Because many of these employees may be embarrassed or sensitive about their health status, they are difficult to motivate to participate in wellness activities.

In addition, many employees who participate in wellness activity will fail to maintain their initial progress. As shown in Figure 10.1, most people participating in a wellness activity (smoking cessation, weight control, exercise, alcohol abstention) will maintain the desired behaviors for the first several weeks, but adherence drops significantly over time, until bottoming out at around 30 to 40 percent. Most people do not change their lifestyle permanently on the first or perhaps even the second try.[20]

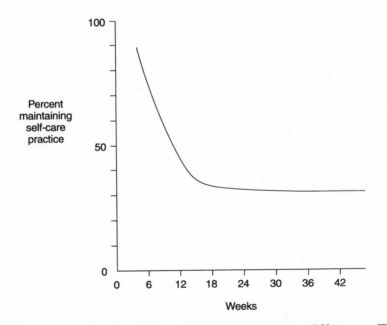

Figure 10.1   Percent Employees Maintaining Wellness Effort over Time

The upshot of these participation and adherence results is twofold. First, it takes a special effort to gain the desired rate of participation and adherence, especially among the highest risk employees. Second, organizations should expect stable improvement in health and lifestyle for no more than 30 to 40 percent of those who do participate, at least in their first or second participation. Achieving this improvement for a third of the participants is not a trivial accomplishment, since a stable improvement in health and lifestyle will pay benefits for many years to come. For the remaining 60 to 70 percent who failed to maintain the desired behavior, the investment may have been (1) a complete loss, (2) a partial success because some lifestyle improvements occurred, or (3) a learning experience for the employee that increases the odds for success the next time.

Organizations interested in improving participation should begin by ensuring the program meets employees' needs. At Northern Telecom, employee perception of program effectiveness was the only variable that significantly predicted participation rate. There were no significant differences in participation by age, sex, importance of health, or job satisfaction. Those who rated program effectiveness highly participated 30 percent more than those who rated it low.[21] These results show how delivering a wellness program that meets the needs of employees can increase participation, which in turn increases the program's impact.

In fact, at Travelers Insurance, those who participated most frequently in the "Taking Care" health promotion program showed the greatest reduction in absenteeism. Employees who utilized the corporate fitness center three times a week were absent half as often as nonparticipants, while those who used it once a week had absenteeism rates about one-quarter less than nonparticipants. Overall, a 2-year comparison of 2000 employees who participated in corporate fitness programs versus employees who didn't showed that participants reduced absenteeism by an estimated 2400 days annually.[22]

Organizations can tailor wellness programs to employees' needs in the following ways to improve participation rates:

1. Offer a range of wellness options to appeal to employees with varying interests/motivation.
2. Involve employees in program design.
3. Ensure program accessibility and convenience (schedule, location).
4. Hold programs on work time.
5. Provide personal warmth, concern, and contact from program personnel.

In addition, management practices and personal follow-up with employees can markedly increase participation. Communication and support from management and supervisors about the importance of wellness activities can be especially important for reluctant employees. This support may include time off to attend sessions, encouragement, and personal participation as a role model. These follow-up techniques include goal setting, contracting, individual counseling, and tailored interventions.

Example   **Michigan State University**   At Michigan State University, an exercise program for employees that incorporated several of these methods for enhancing participation achieved extraordinary results. Over a six-month period, only 9 percent of participants dropped out, and 98 percent of nondropouts adhered to the program regimen. This included exercising aerobically for at least 30 minutes four times a week on their own time. The results were attained by preparing a personalized exercise regimen, developing a personalized behavioral contract and system for monitoring, and using group support and team competition for additional motivation.[23] These results show that careful program design can enhance participation rates.

Personal Counseling and Follow-Up

As mentioned earlier, personalizing the wellness program may be the most effective approach for ensuring that wellness makes a stable, long-term difference in employee health. Each individual has a different health and lifestyle situation and is likely to change it only for compelling reasons and with ongoing support. This is particularly true for the highest risk employees, who are reluctant to become involved.

Researchers at the University of Michigan Worker Health Program, one of the leading such programs in the country, have studied extensively the impact of this personal attention. As shown in Table 10.1, they believe it is the key to what makes wellness work.[24]

Table 10.1   The Value of Personal Contact in Increasing Participation

What Works	What Doesn't Work
Health screening conducted in-person, on a one-to-one basis	Self-administered health risk appraisals, with no personal contact or advice
Signing "eager" employees up on the spot for appropriate wellness activities	Depending on media or mailings to get employees to sign up on their own
Aggressive phone and personal outreach to sign up high-risk employees	Continued reliance on media or mailings to get to high-risk employees
Offering a range of options to employees that allows them to personalize activity	Offering only health improvement classes (and only when enough employees sign up)
Continued outreach and follow-up, plus tailored strategies for high-risk employees	Depending on health improvement classes with little to prevent dropout or relapse

In many ways, changing health behavior is like selling: The more personalized you can make the program, the greater the likelihood of a sale. Thus, personal contact and tailoring are excellent techniques for increasing participation and changing long-term behavior. Among these techniques are personal planning (developing a list of activities, a schedule, and goals for the individual), behavioral contracting (formalizing the employee's agreement to meet these goals), and ongoing follow-up (discussing barriers and giving suggestions and praise). Another powerful personal technique is group support, either as part of a team working to accomplish a health goal or a support group offering each other encouragement.

The greatest limitation to personalized techniques is that they can take more time and effort, particularly if supported only by wellness staff personnel. Therefore, wellness program designers should work to get as much involvement and support as possible from others—family members, supervisors, co-workers, or team members. This support can be built into the employees' goals and behavioral contracting. For example, employees might choose to have their children help monitor progress and might use a family day at an amusement park as a reward for achieving their goal. Not only does this make the process more fun, it greatly increases participant motivation to live up to their self-imposed standards.

Use of Financial Incentives or Penalties

For some companies, a voluntary approach to wellness is not enough. Many of them are now pursuing the same goal through mandatory policies and financial incentives and penalties. This shift appears to be gaining momentum as shown in these quotations from the 1992 annual meeting of the National Association of Health Underwriters, an association of life and disability insurance carriers:

> The bottom line is the consumer does not want to be financially burdened by the excess cost of health care because of voluntary, dysfunctional health habits like tobacco use, alcohol abuse, and drug abuse. . . .

> Americans lead the most reckless lifestyle of any nation on earth. [The public] calls for the health care system to fix [the resulting disease] with little interest in better lifestyles. . . .

> The alcohol epidemic is killing the health insurance industry. If we are going to properly price individual and small group risks, we need to place emphasis on the health habit factors.[25]

Example   **Hershey Foods Corporation**   In 1991, Hershey Foods Corporation, based in Hershey, Pennsylvania, introduced a pilot program to 600 of its management employees that adjusts the portion of health care costs employees pay, based on the risk factors shown in Table 10.2.

Employees who do well in all five categories can save $30 on their monthly premium, while those who "fail" all five would pay an extra $117 per month. Hershey limited the maximum extra fee to $50 per month during the pilot period. Employees can also avoid the extra fee if they are following a treatment plan for the condition under a doctor's care.[26]

Although the preceding example is more comprehensive than practices at most organizations, a 1991 survey found that 12 percent of 135 large employers (more than 5000 employees) either offer a discount or impose a surcharge on employee contributions to life or health care coverage based on health behaviors. The majority of these programs are strictly reward oriented, offering rebates, coupons, or prizes for healthier behavior. Many of these programs are also loosely administered today, with liberal health criteria and honor systems for reporting.

The use of incentives or penalties to change health behavior is still more an art than a science. While many employers believe incentives motivate desirable health behavior they have a number of questions about when and how to use them including:

- What size and type of incentive is effective in different situations?
- How does an organization monitor and enforce use of incentives?
- How does an organization handle associated ethical or legal questions?

Table 10.2 Health Costs Charged to Employees, Based on Risk Factors

Risk Factor	Measure	If Yes	If No
Smoking	Do you abstain from smoking?	Pay $11 per month less	Pay $32 per month more
Blood Pressure	Is your blood pressure reading below 140/90?	Pay $5 per month less	Pay $35 per month more
Physical Exercise	Do you work out aerobically at least three times a week?	Pay $8 per month less	Pay $8 per month more
Weight	Are you within 120% of your ideal weight (defined by standard tables)?	Pay $4 per month less	Pay $32 per month more
Cholesterol	Is your cholesterol level 240 or lower?	Pay $2 per month less	Pay $10 per month more

- Is there sufficient knowledge of all health risks to tie precise dollar figures to them?
- At what point does the administrative burden of using incentives outweigh the benefit?

Incentives can vary in their ability to encourage employee participation. Georgia Pacific Corporation, the forest products company, experimented with adding a small incentive (a flashlight or a picnic cooler) in a cholesterol screening and intervention program. They found the incentive sometimes improved cost-effectiveness, but the impact varied for different study groups.[27] A group of 68 automobile dealerships in New York state tried a low-cost prize drawing to improve recruitment rate for a work-site smoking cessation program. The prize had no impact on participation rate, even though participation rates varied from 0 percent to 40 percent at different dealerships.[28] As these examples show, the same incentive can vary in its impact for different individuals, and success may require tailoring of the size and type of incentive offered.

Monitoring and enforcing health behaviors associated with incentives can be difficult logistically and also raises legal and ethical issues. How does an organization determine whether an employee is smoking during time away from work? How does the organization respond to an employee's high blood pressure if it reflects genetic predisposition rather than lifestyle behavior? Approaches to dealing with these questions often have their own limitations. Health surcharge and incentive policies must balance the expected benefit against the administrative and legal/ethical impact on the employer and employees.

In addition, not all health and lifestyle risks are the same. There is more evidence for the negative cost and health impact of smoking than for the cost of eating a poorly balanced diet. Also, these risks often work in combination, so it is hard to tease out the independent cost of only one risk factor in a person with several high-risk behaviors. An organization can easily produce a false level of precision in incentives or surcharges by identifying and isolating too many risk factors. Ultimately, these questions are a matter of cost versus benefit and value for productivity, employee morale, and health—interpreted in the total cost of health and disability framework.

Employers seeking to use incentives effectively should keep it simple. One alternative is to offer incentives only for the one or two key health behaviors that are known to be a problem for the organization (e.g., smoking). A second alternative is to focus on the total number of risk factors rather than to offer separate incentives for each one. For example, an organization could identify 10 potentially important risk factors measured in its health screening. Incentives for an employee or work team could then be based on the number of those risk factors currently at acceptable risk levels. Organizations could also establish the first unacceptable risk factor as "free," since it may be due to factors outside an employee's control. This approach provides flexibility to the use of incentives and targets the overall level of risk.

A final option for motivating employees to change health behaviors is to make certain activities mandatory. As mentioned previously, the city of Birmingham was required to institute mandatory health screening for all employees to comply with a National Institutes of Health grant. The city now reports that such screening has proven to be one of the best ways to identify high-risk employees who will not voluntarily join a wellness program. Birmingham accomplished the mandatory requirement by making screening a prerequisite for coverage under the health plan.[29]

Use of Cost-Effective Community Resources

Most organizations today are interested in focusing on their core competencies and reducing or outsourcing noncore staff and services. A related trend from quality improvement is the move toward closer business partnerships with a smaller number of key suppliers. From both of these perspectives, community health and nonprofit organizations are an attractive option. They often possess more expertise than the employer in specific health areas and typically are motivated to partner with employers to provide cost-effective wellness services.

Nearly every community in the United States has numerous governmental, educational, and nonprofit organizations with the explicit mission of improving the population's health and reducing disability. These agencies like to partner with employers because access to and support in the workplace helps them reach large numbers of people effectively. Many of these organizations can deliver excellent low-cost programs for the workplace. The following are three examples of such programs:

1. "Babies and You," the March of Dimes prenatal education program.
2. "Freshstart," the smoking cessation program of the American Cancer Society.
3. "Heart at Work," the cardiovascular health program of the American Heart Association.

Each of these targeted programs is well suited for use with employees and dependents. Many other similar programs deal with health issues such as nutrition, weight loss, substance abuse, stress management, safety, and cancer prevention as well as disabilities such as brain injury or spinal cord injury. Other integrated programs combine information and assistance across a broad spectrum of health concerns. (For listings of useful agencies, see the Resources sections at the end of Chapters 10 through 13.)

Employers interested in utilizing community resources for a wellness program should consider two issues. First, promoting employee use of community resources will still take some organizational resources for coordinating activities such as health screening, education, or promotional events conducted by the community agency. It might also mean maintaining a current and effective referral service that employees could access for their health concerns. Second, the employer is entrusting the agency to present content or philosophy that reflects organizational values and needs. The employer might, for example, have strong ideas about how wellness fits in the management plan for the total cost of health and disability.

Both these issues reinforce the need for true partnership if community resources are to meet an employer's objectives. With up-front clarification of roles, values, and areas of expertise and interest, community resources often represent a cost-effective and high-quality solution for many of an employer's wellness needs.

Payoff of Program Integration

Of these many approaches to wellness—policy, screening, education, promotion, personal counseling, financial incentives/penalties, community resources—which are the most important? Does an organization need to offer all of them? How can they be integrated to achieve substantive and stable program impact? Does cost-effectiveness increase or decrease when they are used in combination?

Perhaps the best answer to these questions comes from experience at four large automobile manufacturing plants in southeastern Michigan, employing nearly 10,000 workers. In a carefully designed study, Plant 1 served as a control site in which only health risk screening was performed. At Plant 2, screening was supplemented by health education of several types. In Plant 3, follow-up counseling by wellness coordinators was added to the screening and education. Finally, Plant 4 received screening, education, follow-up counseling, and a variety of organizational activities to make wellness involvement more socially acceptable. Costs per employee were approximately $3 at Plant 1, $18 at Plant 2, $31 at Plant 3, and $38 at Plant 4.

Cost-effectiveness results showed a clear advantage for Plants 3 and 4. In fact, Plants 3 and 4 were from 5 to 10 times more cost-effective, both in getting employees to participate and in improving health and reducing relapse. Spending the extra money up front for follow-up and organizational support definitely was the most cost-effective choice. At Plants 1 and 2, where organizational follow-up and support were not provided, the screening and education were far less effective. These results show that simply offering a program can be an ineffective use of health dollars, providing little impact in improving worker health without the follow-up and support utilized at Plants 3 and 4.[30]

Virtually all organizations that have achieved important bottom-line results from wellness have utilized multiple lines of support (screening, education, follow-up, management practices). City of Birmingham, Coors, Standard Telephone, Johnson & Johnson—all have wellness programs with significant management commitment and several diverse but supporting program elements. Their success is based in large part on the synergy and additional accountability created when wellness touches employees in multiple ways. These diverse approaches also hasten the rate at which health and wellness become an integral part of the organizational culture.

The key to successful wellness integration differs among organizations. Some may feature a network of partnerships with community organizations. For others, the anchor of the program may be personal contact and follow-up. As with quality improvement, one isolated approach is unlikely to achieve the cultural change needed to strongly influence employee and manager behavior. Wellness programs that offer one-dimensional and half-hearted approaches for behavioral change are likely to have impact only with those who need it the least, the already healthy employees.

By contrast, strong and integrated wellness programs can produce benefits for several related aspects of organizational health. Involved and knowledgeable employees are better consumers of health care, thereby saving money on treatment costs as well as through prevention. An effective wellness program benefits rehabilitation, facilitating quick return to work and reducing high workers' compensation costs. This kind of synergy can also be achieved with the employee assistance and safety programs, through sharing of information and mutual promotion of broad employee health.

Example   **Northern Telecom** The power of integration is evident in the experience of Northern Telecom, the world's largest supplier of telecommunications equipment. Since the mid-1980s, Northern Telecom has pursued a six-pronged continuous improvement strategy to manage employee health. This cross-functional effort, encompassing the Finance, Benefits, Employee Relations, Legal, Internal Communications, Facilities, Operations, Management Development, and Health, Safety, and Environment functions, has included prevention and primary care, health care coverage changes, educational outreach to employees, and extensive data analysis and reporting.

Through this effort, Northern Telecom has accomplished the following:[31]

- Reduced its adjusted rate of hospitalization from 95.9 per 1000 in 1984 to 73 per 1000 in 1988.

- Reduced its adjusted cost per claimant by 18 percent over the same period.

- Significantly reduced case rates for several key health care outcomes including heart attack and inpatient and outpatient treatment of substance abuse.

- Reduced workers' compensation frequency by 40 percent and total lost work days by 43 percent.

Like Northern Telecom, companies with an integrated and cross-functional approach to improving employee health will significantly decrease health and disability cost.

Program Evaluation

Over the past several years, a great deal of attention has been devoted to studying the true economic impact of wellness programs. Organizations interested in wellness evaluation should consider the following conclusions:

- Wellness efforts can have impact on multiple health and organizational indicators, some of which are fairly direct and others quite indirect.
- There is often a gap between documenting improvements in measures of employee health versus documenting resulting cost improvements.
- Health improvements can have a very long tail; payoffs or costs may not show up for years.
- The true cost-effectiveness of wellness programs is complicated by turnover, cost of replacement workers, age of work force, inflation, discounting, and a host of other economic and personnel factors.
- Because rigorous scientific evaluation of a program can be so complex, most organizations will want to use a simplified business analysis.

The most direct impact of wellness efforts is often on physiological and behavioral measures such as blood pressure, aerobic capacity, or percentage of employees who smoke. Through improvement in these indexes of employee health, employers can expect to reduce their health and disability costs as well. Equally important, such improvements translate into many other aspects of total organizational costs, including reduced absenteeism, inexperienced replacement workers, and increased employee morale and productivity.[32]

Unfortunately, the true measurable impact of some of these health improvements may not show up for years. For example, a well-known study of cardiac mortality showed significant results in a 10-year follow-up that were not significant at 7 years.[33] Thus, an employee who changes lifestyle may avoid a costly stroke several years later, but this improvement shows up today only in improved behavior and physiological functioning, not in reduced cost. Some of the employee's health improvement may impact cost in the first year or two following wellness involvement, but the overall impact of wellness is likely to be underestimated because longer term cost savings have not yet been harvested.

On the other hand, employee turnover, participation rates, and economic opportunity costs can cause impact estimates to be overstated, or at least difficult to estimate properly. For example, a 10 percent turnover of the employee population in a year, can reduce the impact of the wellness investment over time. It is also possible that those who turned over were nonparticipants in wellness anyway, so the level of investment lost was minimal. Or perhaps the more important question is, "What would have been the return if the time and money invested in wellness had been spent on other opportunities?" These are just a few of the confounding factors that limit accuracy of wellness impact estimates based on a strict scientific evaluation model.[34]

Considering all these factors could push the cost of evaluating the program beyond the cost of the program itself. Thus, many organizations have used straightforward business analysis to estimate their program's effectiveness. One approach to performing this analysis is simply to make historical comparisons, such as those mentioned earlier for Northern Telecom. The results of these comparisons can then be interpreted in light of other changes that may have affected them, such as economic downturn or introduction of a new medical technology. To ensure the analysis includes productivity and quality impact, evaluations should use the total cost of health approach described in Chapter 4.

A second approach is to use the results of direct physiological measures to estimate indirect cost measures. For example, there is a known relationship between smoking and lung cancer, and costs associated with treating lung cancer are also known. Using such data, an organization can estimate fairly accurately the economic value of each improvement in direct health or lifestyle measures. These estimates can also be adjusted by making some assumptions about employee tenure or other relevant factors. For example, wellness programs are likely to have their greatest economic impact in organizations with an older, highly productive, difficult to replace employee group.[35]

In evaluating impact, the important lesson is not the analytical niceties, but management accountability. The reasons for program evaluation are to identify root causes of program success and failure, and to ensure that managers continually act on this information to improve wellness performance. Many types of information, both direct and indirect, can accomplish these purposes. Participation rates and relapse rates establish one type of management accountability but ultimately, evaluation must also demonstrate impact on direct cost results.

Retiree and Family Health Promotion

Although the traditional focus in wellness has been on employees only, retirees and family members represent extremely important potential audiences for health improvement and cost control. Health promotion is especially beneficial for retirees because:

- Their health status is poorer and they generate higher costs.
- The adverse events prevented would likely have occurred sooner for seniors.

- The population of retirees is growing rapidly.
- Seniors may be especially motivated to pursue health promotion because of their available time, interest in health, and risk aversiveness.

Example   **Bank of America** To capitalize on this opportunity, Bank of America recently conducted a health promotion campaign for nearly 5700 retirees living in California. The goal was to use a low-cost health intervention to motivate behavior and lifestyle change. For study purposes, the retirees were randomly divided into three groups: Group 1 received the full intervention, Group 2 the health questionnaire only, and Group 3 was unaware of the program, thus serving as a control.

The full Group 1 intervention included a lifestyle questionnaire administered at 6-month intervals, serial personal health risk reports, individualized recommendation letters, quarterly newsletters, and a book entitled "Take Care of Yourself." A letter from a senior Bank of America official introduced retirees to the intervention. They received health risk appraisal reports and specific personal recommendation letters that showed both initial and change scores over time (developed by computer for each participant from the information the respondent provided). Personal letters, provided over a physician's signature, identified the retiree's special health risk problems and provided suggestions on how to correct those problems.

Results showed significant improvement over the 12-month study period for the members of Group 1. Estimated direct costs decreased by 22 percent in Group 1, whereas they increased by 12 percent in the combined Groups 2 and 3. Per person claims paid decreased by $74 from baseline in Group 1, whereas they increased by $266 for the combined Groups 2 and 3. In addition, Group 1 members experienced 6 to 14 percent improvements in self-reported health habit and health status results. Bank of America estimated a cost–benefit ratio of $5 saved in direct costs for every $1 expended in the program. Total cost of the full intervention was $30 per participant per year.[36]

The success of this approach with retirees could also be easily extended to employees' family members. In many companies, family member health care costs represent 40 to 60 percent of total costs. Thus, companies such as Standard Telephone have outreach programs to improve wellness among this critical audience. The Standard program for dependents includes monthly newsletters on health and a medical reference book stressing self-care. Perhaps because of increased employee awareness of health, 65 percent of Standard's employees recently reported that their families overall health improved over the past year.[37]

Another way to involve family members is to include them in health promotion events and services. Several organizations, for example, make families a big part of company health fairs. Booths and attractions dealing with a broad range of family health issues are specifically designed for children, senior citizens, and spouses. Company representatives explain the health benefits program so that spouses better understand how to obtain quality care for themselves and their children. This can be particularly important for female spouses, since they are often significantly involved in medical decision making within families. Another way to promote health among dependents is to invite family members to use company-operated fitness centers or to participate in educational programs.

Efforts to optimize retiree and family member health with a company wellness outreach can reduce costs in a population that often receives little or no health attention or management. In addition, this approach yields a spin-off benefit to employees by reinforcing the company's wellness message and reaffirming positive values of health and commitment to those who have served the organization effectively in the past.

Health Promotion in Small Businesses

According to the National Survey of Worksite Health Promotion Activities, an estimated two-thirds of U.S. private sector organizations with 50 or more employees offer at least one form of health promotion activity.[38] If this is true, many small businesses are using at least some wellness activities to improve the health of their work force. Yet the media and literature about work-site wellness say relatively little about how small organizations might adapt the approaches used successfully in large concerns. This is particularly unfortunate since small businesses actually account for over half of the total American work force.[39]

Yet wellness technology has been shown to work as effectively in firms as small as a five-person gas station as in organizations with thousands of employees. This includes health risk screening, referral to treatment for high-risk employees, availability of a menu of wellness interventions, and personal follow-up. In one investigation, employees in a 77-person aircraft repair and maintenance company experienced a 40 percent decrease in high-risk cholesterol levels, 50 percent decrease in high-risk blood pressure, 50 percent decrease in number of cigarette smokers, and a 23 percent decrease in excessive levels of body fat. Similarly, at the five-employee gas station (where quantitative results were not reported because of the small sample), employees were enthusiastic about the wellness program and used their co-workers as a natural support group for sharing health status information and motivating health improvement.[40]

Many small organizations have achieved similar positive results on a less formal scale. In fact, it may be easier for them to make wellness successful because small numbers allow smoother coordination and more personal support and motivation. In addition, a number of nonprofit, governmental, and community organizations are now making a concerted effort to promote wellness within small businesses and to tailor techniques to their unique situation.

Organizations of any size or industry can access the cost savings and health improvement benefits of wellness by having their employees and managers integrate these approaches into several aspects of the workplace culture and support them by personal contact with individual employees. The field of wellness or health promotion has matured and moved away from one-shot programs with little staying power. Instead, employers who have built wellness into the everyday workplace experience have shown how this integrated focus can lower costs and improve employee health.

References

1. Gavin, D. July 30, 1992. How to cut your risk of heart attack by 50%. *Bottom Line*.

2. Breslow, L., Fielding, J., Herrman, A. A., & Wilbur, C. S. 1990. Worksite health promotion: Its evolution and the Johnson & Johnson experience. *Preventative Medicine*, 19: 13–21.

3. Holzbach, R. L., Piserchia, P. V., McFadden, D. W., Hartwell, T. D., Hermann, A., & Fielding, J. E. 1990. Effect of a comprehensive health promotion program on employee attitudes. *Journal of Occupational Medicine*, 32(10): 973–978.

4. Jones, R. C., Bly, J. L., & Richardson, J. E. 1990. A study of a work site health promotion program and absenteeism. *Journal of Occupational Medicine*, 32(2): 95–99.

5. Lombino, P. February 1992. An ounce of prevention. *CFO*, pp. 15–22.

6. Whitmer, R. W. March 1992. The City of Birmingham's wellness partnership contains medical costs. *Business and Health*, pp. 60–66.

7. Heirich, M. A., Erfurt, J. C., & Foote, A. 1992. The core technology of work-site wellness. *Journal of Occupational Medicine*, 34(6): 627–637.

8. Fielding, J. E., Knight, K. K., Goetzel, R. Z., & Laouri, M. 1991. Utilization of preventive health services by an employed population. *Journal of Occupational Medicine*, 33(9): 985–990.

9. Heirich, Erfurt, & Foote. The core technology of work-site wellness.

10. Whitmer. The City of Birmingham.

11. Henritze, J., & Brammell, H. L. 1989. Phase II cardiac wellness at the Adolph Coors company. *American Journal of Health Promotion*, 4(1): 25–31.

12. Connors, N. March 1992. Wellness promotes healthier employees. *Business and Health*, pp. 66–71.

13. Walsh, D. C., Jennings, S. E., Mangione, T., & Merrigan, D. M. 1991. Health promotion versus health protection? Employees' perceptions and concerns. *Journal of Public Health Policy*, 12(2): 148–164.

14. Siegelman, S. November 1991. Employers fighting the battle of the bulge. *Business and Health*, pp. 62–73.

15. Heirich, Erfurt, & Foote. The core technology of work-site wellness.

16. Fielding, et al. Utilization of preventive health services.

17. Lovato, C. Y., & Green, L. W. 1990. Maintaining employee participation in workplace health promotion programs. *Health Education Quarterly*, 17(1): 73–88.

18. Lynch, W. D., Golaszewski, T. J., et al. 1990. Impact of a facility-based corporate fitness program on the number of absences from work due to illness. *Journal of Occupational Medicine*, 32(1): 9–12.

19. Strange, K. C., Strogatz, D., et al. 1991. Demographic and health characteristics of participants and nonparticipants in a work site health promotion program. *Journal of Occupational Medicine*, 32(4): 474–478.

20. Lovato & Green. Maintaining employee participation.

21. Strange, K. C., Strecher, V. J., Schoenbach, V. J., Strogatz, D., Dalton, B., & Cross, A. W. 1991. Psychosocial predictors of participation in a work site health promotion program. *Journal of Occupational Medicine*, 33(4): 479–485.

22. Lynch, Golaszewski, et al. Impact of a facility-based corporate fitness program.

23. Stoffelmayr, B. E., Mavis, B. E., Stachnik, T., Robinson, J., Rogers, M., Van-Huss, W., & Carlson, J. 1992. A program model to enhance adherence in work site based fitness programs. *Journal of Occupational Medicine*, 34(2): 156–159.

24. Erfurt, J. C., & Holtyn, K. 1991. Health promotion in small business: What works and what doesn't work. *Journal of Occupational Medicine*, 33(1): 66–73.

25. Mulcahy, C. June 15, 1992. Health insurers will focus more on lifestyle risks. *National Underwriter*, p. 2.

26. Friedan, J. November 1991. Hershey's newest nonfat product: Wellness. *Business & Health*, pp. 56–60.

27. Wilson, M. G., Edmundson, J., & DeJoy, D. M. 1992. Cost-effectiveness of work site cholesterol screening and intervention programs. *Journal of Occupational Medicine*, 34(6): 642–649.

28. Emont, S. L., & Cummings, K. M. 1992. Using a low cost, prize drawing incentive to improve recruitment rate at a work site smoking cessation clinic. *Journal of Occupational Medicine*, 34(8): 771–773.

29. Whitmer, R. W. March 1992. The City of Birmingham's wellness partnership contains medical costs. *Business and Health*, pp. 60–66.

30. Erfurt, J. C., Foote, A., & Heirich, M. A. 1991. The cost-effectiveness of work site wellness programs for hypertension control, weight loss, and smoking cessation. *Journal of Occupational Medicine*, 33(9): 962–970.

31. Dalton, B. A., & Harris, J. S. 1991. A comprehensive approach to corporate health management. *Journal of Occupational Medicine*, 33(3): 338–347.

32. Harris, J. S. 1991. The cost-effectiveness of health promotion programs. *Journal of Occupational Medicine*, 33(3): 327–329.

33. The Multiple Risk Factor Intervention Trial Research Group. 1990. Mortality rates after 10.5 years for participants in the multiple risk factor intervention trial. *Journal of the American Medical Association*, 263: 1795–1801.

34. Shephard, R. J. 1992. A critical analysis of work site fitness programs and their postulated economic benefits. *Medicine and Science in Sports and Exercise*, 24(3): 354–370.

35. Patton, J. P. 1991. Worksite health promotion: An economic model. *Journal of Occupational Medicine*, 33(8): 868–873.

36. Leigh, J. P., Richardson, N., Beck, R., Kerr, C., Harrington, H., Parcell, C. L., & Fries, J. F. 1992. Randomized controlled study of a retiree health promotion program. *Archives of Internal Medicine*, 152: 1201–1206.

37. Lombino, P. February 1992. An ounce of prevention. *CFO*, pp. 15–22.

38. Fielding, J. E., & Piserchia, P. V. 1989. Frequency of worksite health promotion activities. *American Journal of Public Health*, 79: 16–20.

39. U.S. Department of Commerce. 1990. *County Business Patterns*. Washington, DC: Bureau of the Census.

40. Erfurt & Holtyn. Health promotion in small business.

Resources

Organizations

American Cancer Society
Freshstart
599 Clifton Road NE
Atlanta, GA 30329

A free smoking cessation program with training, administrators, films, pamphlets, and Freshstart kits provided by the American Cancer Society.

American Heart Association
Heart at Work
7320 Greenville Avenue
Dallas, TX 75231
(214) 373-6300 or call your local office

A lifestyle program designed to reduce cardiovascular disease. The program concentrates on high blood pressure, smoking cessation, exercise, nutrition, weight control, and early detection.

American Institute for Preventative Medicine (AIPM)
19111 West 10 Mile Road, Suite 101
Southfield, MI 48075
(800) 345-AIPM
(313) 352-7666 (Michigan)

Conducts wellness programs for the public and provides training and technical assistance to organizations.

American Lung Association (ALA)
Freedom from Smoking
1740 Broadway
New York, NY 10019
(212) 315-8700

Helps individuals quit smoking and also aids organizations in setting up a smoke-free work environment.

Association for Fitness and Business
310 North Alabama
Suite A 100
Indianapolis, IN 45204

A professional association designed to help health promotion professionals promote employee health and fitness.

Center for Health Promotion and Education
Centers for Disease Control
1600 Clifton Road NE
Atlanta, GA 30329
(404) 639–3311

Offers technical assistance and expertise in health promotion and health education.

Combined Health Information Data-Base
National Diabetes Information Clearinghouse
Box NDIC
Bethesda, MD 20892
(301) 468-2162

An on-line, publicly accessible database [(800) 345-4277] that includes these sub-files: AIDS, school health education, arthritis, diabetes, health education, health information, high blood pressure, kidney diseases, and Veterans Administration education.

National AIDS Information Clearinghouse
P.O. Box 6003
Rockville, MD 20850
(301) 762-5111

Provides referral, information, educational materials, and services on AIDS-related organizations.

National Center for Health Promotion (NCHP)
3920 Varsity Drive
Ann Arbor, MI 48108
(800) 843-6247

A lifestyle management program targeting weight control, smoking cessation, stress management, and fitness.

National Cholesterol Education Program
Information Center
4733 Bethesda Avenue, Room 530
Bethesda, MD 20814
(301) 951-3260

Provides information on cholesterol to health professionals and to the general public.

National Dairy Council
6300 North River Road
Rosemont, IL 60018-4233
(312) 696-1860

A nonprofit organization devoted to nutrition research and education.

National High Blood Pressure Education
Program Information Center
4733 Bethesda Avenue, Room 530
Bethesda, MD 20814
(301) 951-3260

Provides information on the detection, diagnosis, and management of high blood pressure to consumers and health professionals.

National Wellness Institute, Inc.
1319 Fremont Street-South Hall
Stevens Point, WI 54481
(715) 346-2172

Provides wellness information, services, and products to organizations and communities.

National Women's Health Network
1325 G Street, NW
Washington, DC 20015
(202) 347-1170

A nonprofit organization that provides a clearinghouse of information on women's health and wellness.

ODPHP National Health Information Center
P.O. Box 1133
Washington, DC 20013-1133
(800) 336-4797
(301) 565-4167 (in Maryland)

A health referral organization linking those with health concerns and their appropriate counterpart.

Washington Business Group on Health and U. S. Public Health Service
National Resource Center on Worksite Health Promotion
777 North Capitol Street NE, Suite 800
Washington, DC 20002
(202) 408-0325

Maintains a database of companies that offer wellness programs to employees. It provides information on successful worksite programs, with special emphasis on reaching high-risk employees.

Weight Watchers International, Inc.
Weight Watchers at Work
Jericho Atrium
500 North Broadway
Jericho, NY 11753-2196
(516) 939-0400

Provides a comprehensive, action-oriented approach to losing weight. Employees can attend "on-site" meetings either before work, during lunch hour, or after work.

WELCOA
Wellness Councils of America
7101 Newport Avenue, Suite 311
Omaha, NE 68152
(402) 572-3590

Provides nationwide support services to community-based wellness councils.

Publications

American Journal of Health Promotion
746 Purdy Street
Birmingham, MI 48009
(313) 258-3754

A bimonthly journal that discusses health promotion interventions, applications, and research.

Business and Health
680 Kinderkamck Road
Oradell, NJ 07649
(201) 262-3030

A monthly magazine that discusses programs used by employers to reduce health and disability costs and improve employee health.

Journal of Occupational Medicine
428 East Preston Street
Baltimore, MD 21202-3993
(800) 638-6423
(800) 638-4007 (in Maryland)

A monthly journal with research articles about current findings related to improving health at the work setting.

11

Fighting the War on Substance Abuse

Employee substance abuse has been a highly visible issue for at least the past 10 years in part because incidents involving pilots, captains of ships, physicians, train and subway operators, and long-haul truckers among others have received a great deal of publicity. Most employers have had personal experience with employee problems related to alcohol or drug abuse.

A 1992 survey of 32,000 Americans by the National Institute on Drug Abuse found that 66 percent of those reporting current illicit drug abuse—at least one usage in the past month—are employed. An estimated 15 percent of the working population is addicted to either alcohol (10%) or drugs (5%). An additional 10 percent regularly use alcohol or drugs before or at work. Among workers aged 18 to 34 years, 20 percent report using marijuana at least once in the past month; 30 percent used it in the past year; and 12 percent used cocaine in the same 12-month period.[1]

A study conducted for the U.S. Department of Health and Human Services, released in November 1990, estimated the total costs of alcohol and drug abuse in the United States at $144 billion per year—$86 billion for alcohol abuse and $58 billion for drug abuse.[2] Costs include lost productivity, absences, mistakes, health and disability costs, and indirect costs such as employee turnover. Although these estimates seem staggeringly high, they are consistently high across studies, whether done by economists or social scientists, by researchers or practitioners. Employee substance abuse also continues to be a very strong contributor to costs for health care, workers' compensation, and disability. For a typical employer, alcohol/drug abuse increases health and disability costs by several hundred dollars per employee per year.

Substance abuse affects health and disability cost at all levels of the system. First and most important, substance abuse is a long-term health and safety risk factor that greatly increases the odds that employees will become ill or injured. Second, recovery from illness or injury is significantly delayed when employees are substance abusers, contributing to short and especially long-term disability. Third, treatment for employee substance addiction represents an important percentage of total health care costs.

Each of these three factors independently adds cost. They also can work in combination. For example, employees with a drinking problem stand a much greater chance of experiencing a number of major illnesses, including heart disease, hypertension, and liver problems. These employees will also be slower to recover from illness, partly because of physical deterioration and partly because they use alcohol as a primary means of coping with problems. If an employer or afflicted employee finally recognizes the problem and substance abuse treatment is arranged, the employer may also be responsible for the costs of treatment (although this approach at least addresses the core problem, not its effects).

The same pattern applies to accidents and employee disability. Research shows that substance abusers are significantly more likely to be involved in a workplace or vehicular accident, usually due to impaired concentration and slower reaction time. Their substance abuse complicates rehabilitation and recovery from injury, since they often use alcohol or drugs to cope with the anxiety and pain of recovery and do not participate actively in rehabilitation. Some employees begin abusing multiple medications in addition to alcohol or illegal drugs, which is especially problematic for subjective kinds of injuries such as back problems. And again, substance abuse treatment may be necessary to return the employee to full functioning.

Fortunately, professionals have learned much about dealing with employee substance abuse over the past 10 years, both from the practical experience of trying different methods and the research findings of government and academic agencies. Employers can now access significantly better guidance in the following areas:

- How and how much substance abuse contributes to costs for health care, workers' compensation, and employee disability.
- The strengths and limitations of various approaches, in particular drug testing, for minimizing substance abuse.
- The tradeoffs for various methods of substance abuse treatment.
- The need for better answers about value for cost incurred in all aspects of prevention, intervention, and treatment.
- How substance abuse policies and programs fit into the corporate culture.

Each of these is discussed in the remainder of this chapter.

Better Estimates of Substance Abuse and Cost

As mentioned, substance abuse can contribute to health and disability costs in three main ways: (1) as a health and safety risk factor, (2) as a barrier to rapid recovery, and (3) as a cost for treatment. Over the past several years, several studies have begun to develop hard numbers for each of these categories. The following descriptions of some of these studies illustrate the impact of substance abuse on objective, measurable indexes of health and disability costs.

Substance Abuse and Workplace Accidents

A thorough study by an economist with the National Council on Compensation Insurance[3] found that a 10 percent reduction in alcohol consumption would have reduced U.S. workers' compensation costs by approximately $2.5 billion in 1989. $1.85 billion of that total would have been saved through fewer claims, and the remaining $675 million through lesser severity (per claim cost) of the claims that did occur.

This study included data from 27 states over a 20-year period, 1964 to 1984. A variety of sophisticated analyses were used to simultaneously examine alcohol consumption rates, economic and demographic factors, and workers' compensation results. The findings showed that in the five states with the highest per capita alcohol consumption, workers' compensation costs were 33 percent higher than in the five states with the lowest rate of alcohol consumption. This study clearly documents an extremely high relationship between levels of alcohol consumption and workers' compensation costs.

Similarly, accident rates are often significantly higher among employees who test positive in drug tests versus those who don't. For example, Utah Power & Light, a public utility, compared a group of employees who had tested positive for illicit drugs (primarily marijuana) with a similar number of co-workers in a matched control group. They found that those testing positive were five times more likely to be involved in an accident than those in the control group. Utah Power also found that accident and motor vehicle rates, which had increased between 1983 and 1985, decreased significantly in 1986 and 1987 after the company began their drug and alcohol program in late 1985.[4]

Spinal cord injuries or closed head injuries are among the most serious accidents, since they often lead to significant and permanent disability. Studies suggest somewhere between one-sixth to one-half of these injuries involve people who were legally intoxicated at the time of injury. Many of the injuries come from motor vehicle crashes in which substance abuse has played a major role.[5] Evidence also shows that a substantial number of spinal cord injury victims have lengthy histories of substance abuse before the injury occurs.[6]

Finally, research also links alcohol use to increased risk of being killed in workplace and auto accidents. Three different investigations found that between 10.7 percent and 13.3 percent of occupational fatalities involved employees who had measurable levels of alcohol in their blood.[7] This finding is consistent with research showing a demonstrated link between alcohol consumption and fatal auto accidents. For example, the National Safety Transportation Board reported in 1989 that 33 percent of truck drivers killed in "over-the-road" accidents in a one-year period tested positive for illicit drugs and/or alcohol.[8]

Health Care Utilization among Substance Abusers

In addition to workplace accidents, substance abusers are also at risk for poorer health and increased usage of health care. In fact, three large independent investigations have shown substance abusers to have health care costs approximately double that of nonabusers. Georgia Power Company, in comparing the health care usage of employees who were referred to the Employee Assistance Program or who entered treatment for substance abuse with a sample of matched controls for the year prior to referral/treatment, found that abusers produced almost double the health care costs of nonabusers. They also were absent 1.5 times as often and filed more than twice as many workers' compensation claims.[9]

A review of all health care claims filed with Aetna Life and Casualty Company from 1980 to 1983 found a similar pattern. The four-year average monthly health care costs for families with an alcoholic member were $209.60, or almost twice the comparable costs for families with no apparent alcoholic members ($106.54). On the average, these alcoholics incurred gradually increasing health care costs that rose dramatically in the six months prior to treatment (not including any costs for substance abuse treatment).[10]

McDonnell Douglas, the St. Louis-based aircraft and defense manufacturer, studied health care costs prior to substance abuse treatment for both employees and family members. Alcoholic employee medical costs prior to treatment were found to be twice the company average. Employees later diagnosed as both alcoholic and drug dependent had costs triple the company average. Health care costs were also approximately 50 percent higher among the abusing employee's family members in the year prior to the employee's treatment.[11]

Substance Abuse and Length of Disability

When substance-abusing employees are injured or ill, the abuse often slows recovery and lengthens the period of disability. In fact, substance abuse is sometimes part of a self-defeating syndrome that retards recovery because the employee is using alcohol and drugs as a coping mechanism for a wide range of problems. The illness or injury may increase feelings of isolation or depression, leading to further abuse of prescription drugs as well as alcohol or illegal drugs. This weakens motivation to participate actively in rehabilitation and regain previous ability to function on the job, which in turn leads to further isolation and depression.

A study at a large Midwestern manufacturing firm compared chronic alcohol abusers (for short and long-term disability and workers' compensation) with employees who did not have alcohol problems. Over the period 1974 to 1987, the alcoholic group had payments about twice that of the nonalcoholic group ($1272 per year per capita vs. $671). The great majority of this difference between the two groups was in short- and long-term disability that was nonoccupational (i.e., not directly the result of a workplace injury or accident). Alcoholic employees were also absent about twice as often.[12] Other studies have shown significant effects on this disability syndrome following workplace-related injuries and illnesses.

Treatment Costs for Substance Abuse

In contrast to other costs related to substance abuse, treatment is an investment in the employee that reduces or eliminates the source of abuse-related costs. Successfully treated employees often have lower total health and disability costs on an ongoing future basis. Still, substance abuse treatment costs are a significant part of an organization's total health care expenditures. Treatment for substance abuse and mental health has represented between 9 and 12 percent of total medical costs over the years 1988 through 1991.[13]

The evidence clearly documents that substance abuse contributes significantly to health and disability costs, raising costs at each step in the system. And these direct costs are only part of an organization's total cost from substance abuse, since absenteeism, productivity, and quality are also strongly affected. Effective management can make a difference in these costs. As with other areas of employee health, the key is not to develop a huge array of management programs but to ensure that management strategies are targeted toward the greatest needs of the covered population and the greatest cost-effectiveness for the health investment.

Prevention, Monitoring, and Intervention

Organizational approaches to reducing substance abuse might be grouped into three general categories, as shown in Table 11.1. Since each of these has its own strengths and weaknesses, many companies use them in combination. Each method can be effective or ineffective depending on how it is implemented and whether it fits the employer's needs.

The first category—policy and prevention—attempts to forestall substance abuse problems. These proactive Managing Forward approaches deter potential abuse, reduce related risks, and promote health. Organizations combine awareness, education, and company policy in encouraging employees to avoid drugs and use alcohol responsibly. Preemployment drug

Table 11.1   Possible Management Approaches for Reducing
Substance Abuse

Formal Policy and Prevention

Formal written standards and philosophy regarding substance abuse.

Communications, signs, or other methods for reinforcing the policy.

Education of employees and managers about the dangers of substance abuse.

Preemployment drug tests to prevent hiring of substance abusers.

Monitoring

Supervisor observation of workers with performance or behavior problems.

For-cause or random drug testing.

Undercover workplace investigations of suspected employee drug dealers or abusers.

Performance testing of employees to assess readiness to work.

Intervention and Treatment

Employee assistance programs to provide counseling and referral.

Alcohol or drug treatment programs to facilitate recovery.

On-site support groups for recovering substance abusers.

Off-site community and support agencies for employees and dependents.

screening is also a preventive device because it seeks to identify persons who would abuse drugs and alcohol as employees. All these approaches are often part of a drug-free workplace program.

The second category—monitoring—assumes that some substance abuse is likely to occur but aims to catch it in its early stages. The goal of monitoring is to prevent a crisis, in which an employee's substance abuse behavior becomes an expensive personal and organizational problem. Supervisor observation of impaired job performance is the most traditional monitoring approach. Performance testing is a relatively new alternative that focuses on an employee's "readiness to work." The most controversial monitoring methods are random drug testing and undercover workplace investigations, which some employees view as an unwarranted invasion of privacy, and possible grounds for conflict, grievances, and lawsuits.

Finally, the third category—intervention and treatment—comes into play when the substance abuse problem is recognized and requires professional assistance. Employee assistance programs provide counseling and referral to employees with substance abuse or other personal life problems. Inpatient and outpatient treatment programs help employees face their addiction and develop a new lifestyle including abstention from drugs and alcohol. Some employers offer recovery support or aftercare groups such as Alcoholics Anonymous to assist recovering substance abusers in maintaining their sobriety. Also, many community agencies such as Al-Anon or Adult Children can serve as resources for employees and their family members. The goal of these programs is to help substance abusers regain full functioning and support them in maintaining a drug-free lifestyle.

Popularity of various management approaches for dealing with substance abuse appears to vary mostly by the size of the organization. A 1988 survey of 7500 firms by the Bureau of Labor Statistics found small organizations more likely to emphasize methods that cost less money. For example, of companies with 100 to 250 employees, 17 percent were using drug testing, 29 percent had an employee assistance program, and 50 percent had a formal written policy about substance abuse. By comparison, companies with more than 5000 employees reported that 60 percent were using drug testing, 83 percent offered an employee assistance program, and 83 percent had a formal written policy.[14] Some of this difference may be attributable to larger organizations seeking more aggressively to comply with government contract regulations and the Drug-Free Workplace Act.

Drug testing in particular appears to have grown in popularity. The American Management Association reports that 21.5 percent of firms surveyed were doing drug testing in 1987. This number has grown dramatically to 75 percent who report using drug tests in the 1992 survey (1200 firms responding). Among firms with annual sales in excess of $500 million, 85 percent test either job applicants and/or employees.[15]

Yet the popularity of various approaches is not the same as evidence of their impact. A method may be widely used but deliver little real value to the organization and its employees. Unfortunately, several of the approaches are very difficult to evaluate formally, particularly prevention programs such as policy, communication, and education. It is also difficult to gauge the impact of supervisory monitoring, undercover investigations, and certain treatment approaches such as support groups. Organizations use these methods largely because they seem to make sense and reinforce a message management wants to convey.

Although the direct impact of these approaches will always be difficult to pinpoint, organizations can measure some aspects of program effectiveness. For example, employees and managers can be surveyed about their attitudes toward drug and alcohol use, the company's substance abuse policy, and the frequency of drug and alcohol use among co-workers. Another useful measure is the number of employees referred to the employee assistance program or to outside treatment resources. Two substance-abuse approaches receiving the most systematic evaluation are drug testing and employee assistance/substance abuse treatment. Evidence shows that both these methods, when used appropriately, can reduce substance abuse and related costs.

Drug Testing

Drug testing has been a growth industry over the past several years, increasing to an estimated $350 million in annual revenues. This growth has been fueled by several organizational objectives: governmental compliance, desire to deter drug abuse, and desire to identify drug abusers before they cause major problems. In evaluating drug testing, most organizations have focused on the latter two objectives. Several studies have also explored the accuracy of drug tests and employee attitudes toward drug testing in their organizations.

With regard to deterrence, results indicate that the threat of drug tests has been a factor in reducing drug abuse among current employees and job applicants. This trend is shown in Figure 11.1. Of 2.2 million job applicants and employees tested in 1991 through SmithKline Beecham, a major drug testing company, just 8.8 percent were positive. The number of positive drug tests was down significantly over each of the past five years.[16] These results are consistent with findings in numerous companies, such as Southern Pacific Railroad[17] and Dow Chemical's Texas Operations.[18]

Several organizations have also found drug testing to be effective in identifying drug abusers before they cause problems. This is especially true when tests are used with job applicants and in a "for-cause" situation with current employees. For example, two high-quality studies performed with applicants for the U.S. Postal Service investigated the predictive power of a preemployment drug test (the results of the test were not used in the hiring decision). Over a year later, job performance was compared among those hired, contrasting the employees who had earlier tested positive (i.e., marijuana and cocaine users) with those who had tested negative.

In both studies, the employees who tested positive at hiring had rates of absenteeism and turnover (both voluntary and especially involuntary turnover) that were 50 percent to 100 percent higher than for those testing negative. The Postal Service could presumably have avoided these absenteeism and

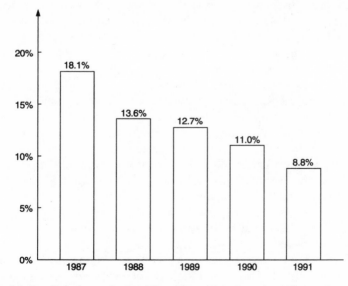

Figure 11.1 Decreases in Positive Drug Test Results (*Source:* Institute for a Drug-Free Workplace. Used with permission.)

turnover problems by not hiring the positive-testing applicants in the first place. On the other hand, results were mixed for disability. One study found those testing positive to be involved in 50 to 80 percent more accidental injuries, but the other found no significant difference between the two groups.[19, 20] It is possible that more of a difference would have been found if the two groups had been tracked over a longer period.

As mentioned earlier, drug testing of current employees at Georgia Power showed that substance abusers had been generating significantly higher health and disability costs. In the year prior to testing positive, drug-using employees averaged $1377 in health care usage compared with $163 for the control group and $590 for the companywide average. Two years prior to detection, employees who tested positive had averaged $264 in workers' compensation claims, compared with $25 for the control group and $197 for the general work force. The predismissal rate of absenteeism for 198 employees dismissed after a positive drug test was approximately four times that of the control group. Similar positive reductions in health and disability outcomes have been documented at Southern Pacific Railroad and Utah Power and Light following the implementation of drug testing.

The overall cost benefit analysis at the U.S. Postal Service shows that drug testing would have saved the Postal Service $162 per applicant hired, based on a 12 percent prevalence of drug use among the applicants screened and a cost per test of $49. Savings to another organization could be higher or lower depending on the type of applicants and the cost of testing for them.[21] Georgia Power estimates total savings of between $294,000 and $1.7 million by discharging and replacing the 198 employees who tested positive between 1983 and 1987. Overall, the evidence clearly shows that testing can be effective in identifying substance-abusing employees or applicants and reducing organizational costs, particularly in jobs and industries in which such abuse is prevalent.

The accuracy of results from laboratory analysis of drug tests is seldom questioned today. This accuracy has increased markedly over the past several years, with the implementation of National Institute of Drug Abuse (NIDA) certification procedures. Still, results from a 1990 study of samples submitted through Rockwell International suggests drug tests are not perfect in detecting abusers. When commercially prepared samples containing various drugs were submitted to several reference laboratories, error rates of 2 percent false positive and 20 percent false negative were obtained. This suggests that a person being tested for drugs would rarely be falsely accused of drug abuse, but perhaps a fifth of those who are abusing drugs would go undetected.[22]

Survey data show that many current employees willingly accept drug testing, especially if they feel it is appropriate to their company and handled fairly. This includes an explanation of what, where, and why testing is being used, an opportunity to voice concerns or an appeal, and effective procedures to deal with positive results. Employees recognize the costs of a substance abuser on co-workers and the public in terms of increased risk to them and an inability to rely on the abuser for safe and effective performance. A Gallup survey of employees commissioned by the Institute for a Drug-Free Workplace found that the great majority of employees think drug testing is a "good idea." As shown in Figure 11.2, this response ranged from 94 percent supporting testing for airline pilots to 61 percent supporting it for office workers.[23]

Drug tests appear to be a useful tool in reducing risk for substance abuse and associated health and disability problems. They provide both a deterrent effect and the opportunity to identify abusers before they cause problems to themselves and the organization. In some industries and parts of the country, drug testing is expected, based on governmental requirements,

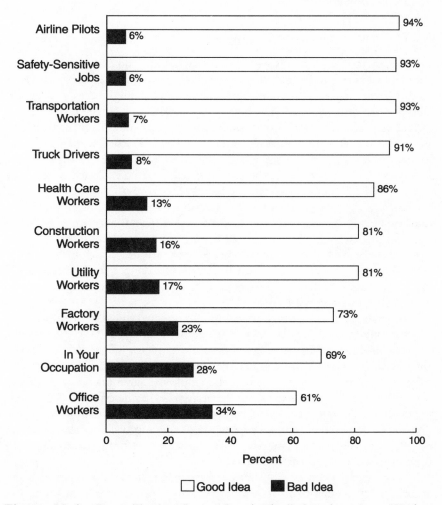

Figure 11.2 Drug Testing Is a "Good Idea" Say American Workers (*Source:* Institute for a Drug-Free Workplace. Used with permission.)

the safety sensitivity of the work, or the perceived characteristics of the available work force. Preemployment and for-cause testing are the most widely used and evaluated approaches.

On the negative side, some factors limit the applicability of drug testing. First, drug testing often does not include testing for alcohol, even though alcohol is by far the most significant contributor to health and disability problems. Second, drug testing can be expensive and disruptive to employee relations, especially if the base rate of illegal drug use among those tested is low. Finally, a positive drug test shows only that the employee has at some point in the recent past used drugs—it does not necessarily mean the employee is an addict or even a poor performer. Careful implementation of the drug testing program can mitigate these concerns, or the company can opt for a nontesting approach.

The Performance-Testing Option

What organizations generally want to know when they do drug testing of current employees is whether the employee is "ready to work." In other words, is the employee impaired in some important way that might create a health, safety, or performance risk? If an employee is positive on a drug test, employers take that as a sign that the person's use of drugs could likely reduce his/her ability to perform the job safely and effectively. By itself, however, a positive drug test simply means there is the chemical metabolite of a drug in that person's system. For example, the person may have used cocaine the previous weekend and all its effects except the metabolite wore off days ago.

Critics of drug testing argue that decisions about employees should be based on current readiness to work, not the presence or absence of metabolites from off-the-job behavior. In addition, some employees who don't use drugs may not be "ready to work" because of fatigue, health problems, or stress. They might pass a drug test but are still a danger to themselves and others because of these nondrug factors. Performance testing addresses these two important criticisms.

Performance testing, which is still in its infancy, typically involves a simple psychomotor task similar to a video game. Employees take the test numerous times to establish a personal baseline of performance. Whenever the employer wants to assess the employee, such as at the beginning of work or before beginning an overtime shift, the employee again takes the test. The employee's performance shows immediately whether he or she has the concentration and hand–eye coordination to perform at an acceptable level, relative to the personal baseline. Proponents of this approach say that it is perfect for assessing performance readiness in jobs that range from pilot and surgeon to crane operator and bus driver.

It is too early to know whether performance testing will prove to be an important replacement for or adjunct to drug testing. It is a different and broader approach with some distinct advantages, but it has not yet been widely used. For health and disability, its main applications are in reducing the risk for on-the-job accidents and in identifying when an employee's substance abuse or other health problem is impairing his or her ability to perform.

Ensuring Value from Treatment

Many executives are concerned about the value they are receiving for money spent on employee and dependent substance abuse treatment. As mentioned earlier, these costs have skyrocketed over the past 10 years. Nationally, substance abuse and mental health treatment accounts for between 9 and 12 percent of total health and disability costs, and is markedly higher in some organizations and industries. In addition, there has been a long-standing controversy about how much treatment is enough and when inpatient care is justified. Fortunately, answers about obtaining optimal value from substance abuse treatment investment are beginning to emerge.

Major recent studies at General Electric, McDonnell Douglas, and CATOR (the nation's largest database for effectiveness of chemical dependency treatment) suggest the following four core conclusions for managing substance abuse treatment:

1. A major key to assessing value in substance abuse treatment is relapse. Value can only be assessed when relapse costs are considered along with treatment costs.
2. Treatment that prevents relapse results in better health and reduced cost for the treated employee or dependent.
3. Certain patients need more treatment than others, based on their substance abuse condition and history.
4. Treatment is most effective when there is accountability and incentive for success. The person's motivation is at least as important as the treatment used.

Value and Relapse

The traditional tradeoff in substance abuse treatment has been between upfront treatment costs (which are known and easy to monitor) and resulting outcome effectiveness (for which monitoring and determining hard dollar costs is more difficult). In the 1970s and early to mid-1980s, this balance was heavily in favor of 28-day inpatient treatment. The popular wisdom at the time was that intensive up-front treatment produced significantly better outcomes and thus better value.

By the mid-1980s, however, two trends dramatically changed this balance. First, inpatient costs had become prohibitive, with increased utilization and per patient fees as high as $10,000. Second, a number of independent reviews found little evidence that the more intensive, 28-day inpatient approach yielded any better results than much less costly outpatient treatment programs. Given this lack of evidence and strong cost pressure, many employers quickly moved to adjust their health care coverage to limit inpatient treatment. Saving money on the front end was assumed to yield better value.

Yet both the growth and the decline of inpatient treatment have occurred without a sound understanding of value from the treatment investment. This has sometimes resulted in shortsighted decision making and a failure to weigh the costs and benefits of various treatment options. Companies must take this value perspective to get the most for both their dollars and their employees. Value for both an organization and an employee includes three components:

1. *Outcomes Have Much More Leverage Than Treatment Costs.* This is true for organizations because outcomes include the productivity, quality, health and disability costs, retraining costs, replacement costs, and numerous other costs that result from successful or unsuccessful treatment. The differences in payoff for successful versus unsuccessful outcomes far outstrip differences in costs for treatment. Similarly for the employee, the payoff of recovering a stable and productive existence far outstrips the cost in time, motivation, or co-pay needed to achieve successful treatment.

2. *Value Depends on Maintaining the Success of Treatment.* Treatment of any type does not deliver good value if it only works for six months. This is particularly true for expensive treatments but is also the case for less costly treatment approaches. Inexpensive treatments do not deliver good value if they work for a few months when a more expensive treatment option would have worked for 10 years. Value can only be optimized by maintaining successful outcomes over an extended period.

3. *Value Means Optimizing the Treatment Approach for Each Individual.* If for employee A, a moderate-cost treatment and aftercare program can yield and maintain good outcomes, this approach yields better value. For employee B, however, the less expensive program may not be sufficient to achieve desired outcomes. Better value might be achieved by spending more on treatment and aftercare monitoring to obtain lasting results. Tailoring the treatment to the individual person and situation is essential to optimizing value.

The McDonnell Douglas, General Electric, and CATOR results suggest that no one type of treatment is always best, yet type of treatment can in fact make a difference. A key part of understanding that difference is to look at relapse, a key part of value.

Figure 11.3 shows number of hospitalization days for two large groups of patients treated for chemical dependency. These results come from CATOR, the nation's largest database on substance abuse treatment effectiveness. The group of patients on the right (about 60 percent of the sample) remained abstinent from alcohol for the two-year period following treatment. The members of the group on the left relapsed at some point during the two-year follow-up (although about half were abstinent for at least one year during the study period).

As shown, both groups of patients reduced their hospitalization rate somewhat following treatment. Patients who relapsed after treatment, however, show a different pattern from those still in recovery (abstinent). The hospitalization rate for relapsed patients was never as low as for recovering patients. In other words, patients that relapsed were higher cost from the start. Also, rates for the relapsed patients began to climb to their old levels within two years of treatment. The recovering group, by contrast, attained a lower rate from the beginning and was successful in maintaining that lower rate.[24]

As shown by the group that did not relapse, substance abuse treatment has the potential to return an abusing patient to a more normal level of functioning and associated cost. Other CATOR data (see Table 11.2) also show dramatic improvements following treatment in such areas as hospitalizations, missing or being late for work, not finishing work, conflict with boss, and driving violations. These data are from one-year follow-up of 4541 persons who received inpatient treatment and 1026 who received out patient treatment.[25]

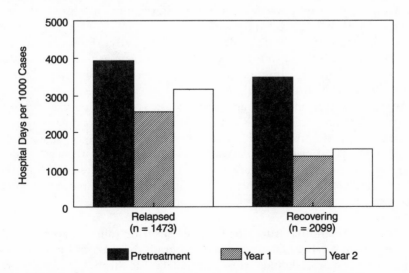

Figure 11.3 Increased Hospitalization Rates for Alcoholics Who Relapse (*Source: Journal of Addictive Diseases,* 12(1), The Haworth Press, Inc. Used with permission.)

Table 11.2 Percentage of Employees with Work/Health Problems before and after Substance Abuse Treatment

Measure	Inpatients Before	After	Outpatients Before	After
Hospitalizations	21	10	16	7
Missing work	41	7	25	4
Late to work	33	7	24	7
Completing work	22	5	16	5
Confict w/boss	26	14	24	12
Driving violation	14	11	23	9

These results show that patients can be salvaged—they can recover their previous level of productivity and health and can be restored as an effective member of the organization and society. However, this only works if they don't relapse. With relapse, their health and disability costs quickly begin to increase, their performance goes down, and the employer's investment in their health produces much less value.

Similar results are found in the General Electric and McDonnell Douglas investigations. In both of these high-quality studies, the majority of patients did improve their performance, reliability, and health following treatment. At General Electric, strongly alcoholic workers who were close to losing their jobs prior to treatment were followed up regularly for two years after treatment. Supervisors now rated 76 percent as excellent or good performers, and the percentage of those with warning notices had dropped from 33 percent before treatment to under 5 percent during the two-year follow-up. Significant improvement in drinking habits was observed.[26]

At McDonnell Douglas, employee health care costs were tracked for four years following treatment. Costs declined each year after treatment, including costs directly related to substance abuse treatment as well as for health care costs unrelated to substance abuse. Costs for family members' health care showed a similar decline.[27]

At the organizational level, an employer can receive good value even if treatment for some employees is not fully successful. For example, if 10 employees receive treatment and three relapse, the company's intervention may still be a good investment. Nevertheless, the value lost through relapse of those three employees significantly reduces the total return from the treatment investment. As important, the three relapsed employees slipping back into substance abuse pay a large personal price that may be impossible to recover.

In the treatment literature, the term for ensuring value is "cost offset." An effective substance abuse treatment program should offset much if not all its direct costs and should return additional value through increased productivity and quality. It should be an investment in a valued employee or family member that allows the person to return to or even improve a previous level of health and performance. It should reinforce organizational values of health, accountability, and caring and should send a strong message

throughout the organization. But again, the value of the treatment investment depends strongly on the ability to prevent relapse.

Some Patients Need More Than Others

The McDonnell Douglas and General Electric studies were primarily designed to test the cost-effectiveness of differing approaches to treatment.
McDonnell Douglas compared the costs for employees who received treatment through the company's employee assistance program (EAP) with
costs for employees who obtained treatment through non-EAP means. The
General Electric study randomly assigned those needing treatment to inpatient treatment, compulsory attendance at Alcoholics Anonymous (AA), or
an employee choice from several options. Both studies found that some
treatment options produce better results than others.

McDonnell Douglas found substantially better results when treatment
was coordinated through the company EAP. Initial substance abuse treatment costs were approximately $4000 per employee (in 1988 dollars) for
those working through the EAP versus $8000 per person for the non-EAP
group. In addition, the EAP employee group had markedly lower medical
costs over the next three years than the non-EAP group. These results are
shown in Figure 11.4.

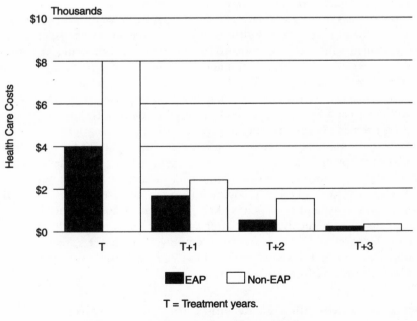

Figure 11.4   EAP Referral Helps Reduce Health Care Costs (*Source: Almacan*. Used with permission.)

McDonnell Douglas attributes the success of its EAP approach to its ability to tailor treatment to the needs of the individual patient. The EAP offered skilled clinicians who made differential diagnoses and ensured each patient received the treatment that would be most effective for him or her. This included inpatient, outpatient, Alcoholics Anonymous, and various combinations of follow-up monitoring and support.

For General Electric, inpatient treatment yielded the best results for this group of seriously addicted alcoholics. The "choice" group (who selected their form of treatment themselves from a list of options) did next best. The group that only attended Alcoholics Anonymous meetings did least well. All groups showed progress, especially in improved performance at work, but inpatient treatment was significantly more effective in maintaining sobriety over the two-year follow-up period. In fact, 63 percent of the Alcoholics Anonymous group eventually required hospitalization for treatment, which basically eliminated the earlier cost advantage of avoiding inpatient care. Those employees who were abusing both cocaine and alcohol made significantly better progress with inpatient treatment.

For General Electric, the results again fit the model of tailoring treatment to the individual. Because those treated were seriously addicted alcoholics, the more intensive inpatient approach worked best. Also, the biggest advantage for inpatient treatment was among employees who were abusing multiple substances, typically a more difficult patient to treat. General Electric's results indicate that inpatient treatment should remain an option, especially for long-term or severe substance abusers.

It is too early in the treatment debate to say unequivocally that one or another treatment approach will ultimately be the final answer. Still, maximizing treatment value usually seems to involve individual tailoring. A patient who has been drinking heavily and abusing drugs for the past 20 years will not usually respond in the same way as someone whose use has been sporadic and recreational for the past two years. The best response to an employee or dependent's need for treatment will likely be to tailor a treatment plan reflecting the person's and the organization's particular situation.

Many patients may respond very effectively to outpatient treatment and regular monitoring and support. A minority of seriously dependent abusers (those who are motivated to overcome their addiction) will require some inpatient treatment because recovery will be more difficult for them. By contrast, no treatment approach is likely to prevent relapse among those patients who lack the motivation or internal resources to succeed in recovery. The goal, therefore, is to structure an employer–employee agreement that is supportive but that also makes the individual responsible for the benefits and losses resulting from progress in recovery.

Increasing Success through Accountability and Incentives

A quite consistent finding in treatment evaluation is that a motivated patient often achieves success regardless of treatment modality. In fact, the Institute of Medicine concluded in 1989 that "the best predictor of patient outcome was the patient."[28] Achieving value for chemical dependency treatment must therefore include a focus on maximizing patient motivation for long-term recovery.

Numerous sources of motivation can contribute to high treatment success. Researchers at General Electric observed that one reason for their positive treatment results was the desire of those treated to keep their jobs. Professional licensing boards often use the threat of license revocation to motivate substance-abusing physicians or lawyers. The threat of losing family members and friends can be a highly effective motivation for many abusers. Finally, the greatest motivation may come directly from the patient, who recognizes the toll substance abuse has taken in his or her life.

Employers can contribute to improved patient motivation in three ways:

1. The organization should ensure that its substance abuse referral system includes the ability to diagnose each case individually and tailor a high-value treatment plan.

2. This treatment plan should result in a formal contract with the abusing employee, spelling out expectations and contingencies if the contract is not followed.

3. The organization should support recovery through supervisors, aftercare, anticipation of family needs, and support groups such as Alcoholics Anonymous.

Substance abuse referral systems come in many different forms including employee assistance programs, managed mental health care, and for smaller employers, less formal local relationships. Structuring this system can be quite detailed, but should in general emphasize professional evaluation and a treatment plan that recognizes the individual patient's motivation and risk for relapse. Factors to consider include the employee's history of chemical abuse, his or her desire to continue working for the organization, and any family relationships or aspects of lifestyle that could enhance or impede recovery.

Based on this analysis and resulting treatment plan, the employee should be asked to sign a contract that identifies expectations and contingencies for behavior following treatment. The contract might specify random drug and alcohol testing for the next two years and what would happen should the employee test positive. It might also identify goals for absenteeism, tardiness, and warning notices, again indicating the consequences of not meeting the goals. The objective of the contract is to provide a fair but firm understanding that increases employee motivation to recover and that also specifies the organization's future response.

The contract could include financial considerations to increase the employee's commitment. For example, the employee could be asked to make a significant co-pay up front and asked to also pay for all continuing care. Then if the employee meets the goals of the contract (such as clean drug tests and regular attendance at aftercare for a specified period), this money will be rebated back to the employee. In this way, the organization can ensure that it is not throwing its money away on ineffective treatment, and the employee has a strong additional incentive to meet the terms of the contract. Such an arrangement may seem harsh, but if used properly, it is actually much more humane than many alternatives (firing the employee, refusing to pay for treatment at all, showing no interest in the employee's needs and progress).

A final way to increase patient accountability and motivation is through ongoing support. Supervisors, in particular, play an important role in providing flexibility and acceptance to the recovering employee while at the same time monitoring the performance indicators in the contract (e.g., tardiness, absenteeism). Supervisors will themselves need training and support to make this happen effectively. The organization should encourage treatment providers to involve the family in treatment and aftercare planning, since family member support is crucial to maintaining sobriety. Finally, the organization can also support recovery through such activities as sponsoring a local chapter of Alcoholics Anonymous and providing aftercare counseling through an employee assistance program.

An organization's approach to ensuring value from substance abuse treatment should, in many ways, resemble its approach for general management. First, the organization must establish a system that can tailor its response to the needs of the individual and situation. Next, the system must establish the goals for the individual, the payoffs or penalties for all parties if the goals are or are not achieved, and the specific measures to evaluate progress. Finally, to accomplish these goals, the system must minimize barriers and maximize motivation. As each of these steps becomes more concrete and systematic, value from the investment in treatment will increase for both the patient and the employer.

Substance Abuse and Corporate Culture

Over the past 10 years, societal responses to substance use and abuse have changed significantly in the United States. For example, there are now much tougher laws about drunken driving, and there is more education for children about resisting drug abuse. The changes show that the previous norms about substance abuse were exacting too heavy a cost on the country, and a different kind of behavior is now being encouraged.

All the components of an organization's approach to substance abuse—education, communication, testing, treatment—present a message to employees. One such message could be, "We do not tolerate substance abuse in this organization and will strongly punish anyone who fails to comply." Another message could be, "We believe substance abuse is an illness, and employees need our support for their recovery." The differing messages say something not only about the employer's approach to substance abuse but also about the kind of behavior that will fit into the organizational culture.

Executives and managers should carefully consider this cultural impact as they make decisions about substance abuse programs and policies. For some organizations, a tough, businesslike approach may play best for the kinds of employees in the work force and the company's history in working with them. For others, the approach must be more participative to achieve the buy-in of managers and employees. The message should fit the traditional expectations of the culture or should offer alternatives and a rationale if it represents a change.

This is especially true when employers communicate the meanings of programs and policies to employees. For example, one company sent out a memo to all managers saying that alcohol should no longer be served at any company functions or meetings because of the liability risk. This angered many of the managers because they felt that these get-togethers were one of the few opportunities they had to "blow off steam" with their co-workers. The policy was interpreted by many as another expression of the company's lack of trust in employees, willingness to cut the things that employees valued, and concern solely for finances.

By contrast, the memo could have explained the company's concern about both people and financial risk, offered managers some guidelines, and asked them to use good judgment. It could have offered some alternatives to heavy drinking that would still help build camaraderie at company meetings. Behavior change could still be strongly encouraged, but in a way that shows respect and confidence for the managers and their employees. Even more powerfully, company leaders could model the desired behavior when they attend these meetings.

Senior managers today have a significant opportunity to shape organizational norms about substance use and abuse. Employees and society in general are increasingly open to reexamination of appropriate types of substance use behaviors. The message for alcohol and drugs should be one of health and personal responsibility—strong and positive underlying values that fit well into the organization's culture without bordering on private lives and standards. Senior executives must also ensure this message applies to its managers as well, not just to employees. The more closely the organization's response to substance abuse is tied to these overall cultural norms, the more effective will be its impact on changing employee behavior and reducing health and disability costs.

References

1. National Institute on Drug Abuse. December 19, 1991. *National Household Survey on Drug Abuse.* Washington, DC: NIDA.
2. Rice, D. P., Relman, S., Miller, L. S., & Dunmeyer, S. 1990. *The economic costs of alcohol and drug abuse and mental illness.* San Francisco: University of California Institute for Health and Aging.

3. Durbin, D. 1989. *Alcohol consumption and workplace accidents.* New York: National Council on Compensation Insurance, RD-89-3.

4. Crouch, D. J., Webb, D. O., Buller, P. F., & Rollins, D. E. 1989. A critical evaluation of the Utah Power and Light Company's substance abuse management program. *Drugs in the workplace: Research and evaluation data,* pp. 169–193. Washington, DC: NIDA.

5. Rohe, D. E., & DePompolo, R. W. 1985. Substance abuse policies in rehabilitation medicine departments. *Archives of Physical Medicine and Rehabilitation,* 66: 701–703.

6. Heinemann, A. W., Donahue, R., & Schnoll, S. 1988. Alcohol use by persons with recent spinal cord injury. *Archives of Physical Medicine and Rehabilitation,* 69: 619–624.

7. Alleyne, B. C., Stuart, P., & Copes, R. 1991. Alcohol and other drug use in occupational fatalities. *Journal of Occupational Medicine,* 33(4): 496–500.

8. National Transportation Safety Board. 1989. *Truck driver fatalities and substance abuse.* Washington, DC: NTSB.

9. Sheridan, J., & Winkler, W. 1989. An evaluation of drug testing in the workplace. *Drugs in the workplace: Research and evaluation data,* pp. 195–216. Washington, DC: NIDA.

10. Holder, H. D., & Blose, J. O. 1986. Alcoholic treatment and total health care utilization and costs. *Journal of American Medical Association,* 256(11): 1456–1460.

11. McDonnell Douglas Corporation & Alexander & Alexander. August 1989. McDonnell Douglas Corporation's EAP produces hard data. *The Almacan,* pp. 18–26.

12. Holder, H. D., & Blose, J. O. 1991. A comparison of occupational and non-occupational disability payments and work absences for alcoholics and non-alcoholics. *Journal of Occupational Medicine,* 33(4): 453–457.

13. Foster Higgins. 1991. *1991 health care benefits survey.* Princeton, NJ.

14. U.S. Department of Labor, Bureau of Labor Statistics. 1989. *Survey of employer anti-drug programs* (Report 760). Washington, DC: U.S. Government Printing Office.

15. American Management Association. 1992. *1992 AMA survey: Workplace drug testing and drug abuse policies.* New York, NY: AMA.

16. SmithKline Beecham Press Release. February 10, 1992. *SmithKline Beecham index shows drug use decline for fifth straight year.*

17. Taggart, R. W. 1989. Results of the drug testing program at Southern Pacific Railroad. *Drugs in the workplace: Research and evaluation data,* pp. 97–108. Washington, DC: NIDA.

18. Tolley, L. 1991. Random testing program effective at Dow Chemical's Texas Operations. *The Drug-Free Workplace Report.* Washington, DC: IDFW.

19. Zwerling, C., Ryan, J., & Orav, E. J. 1990. The efficacy of preemployment drug screening for marijuana and cocaine in predicting employment outcome. *Journal of American Medical Association,* 264(20): 2639–2643.

20. Normand, J., Salyards, S. D., & Mahoney, J. J. 1990. An evaluation of preemployment drug testing. *Journal of Applied Psychology,* 75(6): 629–639.

21. Zwerling, C., Ryan, J., & Orav, E. J. 1992. Costs and benefits of preemployment drug screening. *Journal of American Medical Association,* 267 (1): 91–93.

22. Knight, S. J., Freedman, T., Puskas, A., Martel, P. A., & O'Donnell, C. M. 1990. Industrial employee drug screening: A blind study of laboratory performance using commercially prepared controls. *Journal of Occupational Medicine,* 32(8): 715–721.

23. Institute for a Drug-Free Workplace. 1991. *What employees think about drug abuse.* Washington, DC: IDFW.

24. Hoffmann, N. G., Rode, S. S., & Fukerson, J. A. 1993. Recovery status and cost offsets for chemical addictions treatment. *Journal of Addictive Diseases,* 12(1).

25. Hoffmann, N. G. June 1991. Treatment outcomes from abstinence based programs. *36th International Institute on the Prevention and Treatment of Alcoholism.* Stockholm, Sweden.

26. Walsh, D. C., Hingson, R. W., Merrigan, D. M., Levenson, S. M., Cupples, L. A., Heeren, T., Coffman, G. A., Becker, C. A., Barker, T. A., Hamilton, S. K., McGuire, T. G., & Kelly, C. A. 1991. A randomized trial of treatment options for alcohol-abusing workers. *New England Journal of Medicine,* 325(11): 775–782.

27. McDonnell Douglas Corporation & Alexander & Alexander. 1990. *McDonnell Douglas Corporation employee assistance program financial offset study, 1985–1989.* St. Louis, MO.

28. Institute of Medicine. 1989. *Prevention and treatment of alcoholism: Research opportunities.* Washington, DC: National Academy Press.

Resources

Al-Anon Family Group Headquarters
(800) 356-9996
(212) 245-3151 in New York and Canada

Provides printed materials on alcoholism specifically aimed at helping families deal with the problems of alcoholism. Service hours: 24 hours, 7 days a week. Al-Anon also provides fellowship meetings for relatives or friends of alcoholics; consult the yellow pages for information about meetings in your community.

Alcoholics Anonymous
General Services Office
P.O. Grand Central Station
New York, NY 10163
(212) 686-1100

Provides printed materials on alcoholism and fellowship meetings for individuals to support their abstention from alcohol. Consult the yellow pages for information about meetings in your community.

American Council for Drug Education
204 Monroe Street
Rockville, MD 20850
(301) 294-0600

Publishes substance abuse educational materials for managers, employees, and their families.

Institute for a Drug-Free Workplace
1301 K Street NW
East Tower, Suite 1010
Washington, DC 20005
(202) 842-7400

A nonprofit coalition of businesses and business organizations that seeks to influence national drug abuse policy. The Institute also provides information, research and referral to businesses regarding drug testing and other drug abuse issues.

National Association for Adult Children of Alcoholics
P.O. Box 3216
Torrance, CA 90505
(213) 534-1815

Provides printed materials and information for individuals who grew up with alcoholic parents. The Association also provides fellowship groups; consult the yellow pages for information on meetings in your community.

National Council on Alcoholism and Drug Dependency
(800) NCA-CALL

Refers to local affiliates where substance abusers can obtain help; also provides written information on alcoholism. Service hours: 24 hours, 7 days a week.

National Institute on Drug Abuse (NIDA)
Drug-Free Workplace Helpline
(800) 843-4971

Offers information, publications, and referrals to organizations on developing and implementing drug abuse policies and programs.

National Institute on Drug Abuse (NIDA)
Drug Information and Treatment Referral Hotline
(800) 662-4357

Provides referrals to local facilities where adolescents and adults can seek help. Service hours: 9 A.M.–3 A.M. daily.

U.S. Office for Substance Abuse Prevention
P.O. Box 2345
Rockville, MD 20852
(800) 729-6686

National clearinghouse for all requests for printed or audiovisual substance abuse information.

12

Managing Stress and Employee Mental Health

In California, newspapers carry classified ads that read "Stressed at work? Call me for a consultation about your employee rights." In national surveys, nearly half of employees report feeling burned out. Researchers are prominently featured on TV talk shows, discussing the stress of modern life and its negative impact on health. Many employees and managers say they "need to get away" or "have to have some time off."

For many American workers, issues of stress and mental health are a primary and daily source of concern. The problems may not originate in the workplace—they might be due to the poor health of a parent or problems with finances—but they show up in the workplace anyway. And increasingly, the health and disability costs associated with these problems have become a major issue for employers.

Stress and employee mental health problems have been among the most rapidly growing sources of health and disability costs for American organizations over the past 10 years:

- During the 1980s, costs for mental health and substance abuse treatment grew at four times the rate of the overall consumer price index.
- Mental health and substance abuse costs went up at twice the rate of total health care costs and now represent approximately 10 percent of total health care costs.
- So-called stress claims became among the most rapidly growing categories of workers' compensation claims.
- Mental health and substance abuse inpatient admissions increased 85 percent from 1982 to 1989, and the corresponding number of available beds increased from 58,000 to 96,000 in the same period.

- Adolescent inpatient mental health admissions nearly tripled, even though the adolescent population (demographically) decreased by 10 percent during this period.

- Stress-related disabilities more than doubled from 1982 to 1990 and were significantly more difficult to rehabilitate than disabilities in general.

- Research reinforced a spreading belief that many health and disability claims that are not specifically mental health in nature nevertheless include an important mental health component.

The cost explosion from stress and mental health crosses virtually all segments of health and disability costs.[1,2,3] These increases are related to health care, workers' compensation, and disability; and they come from employees as well as from family members. There are also good reasons to expect stress and mental health to be an important long-term concern for organizations.

Reasons for the Increase

Both societal and economic factors have driven this rapid growth in mental health-related claims. Societal pressures include greater awareness and acceptance of stress and mental health problems, as well as greater ambiguity and tension in modern lifestyles. Economically, employers have had to deal with changes in government regulation and market conditions, combined with increasing financial strains on employees and their families.

Greater awareness and acceptance in many ways go hand in hand, since greater understanding about stress and mental health often leads to a more open and tolerant attitude on the part of society. During the past decade, extensive research linking mental and physical health has reinforced this trend. For example, there is now solid evidence that prolonged, excessive stress reduces the body's immune function and its ability to fight disease. Organizations such as the National Institute of Mental Health have widely publicized research showing that many people (not just a tiny minority) suffer from depression, anxiety, and burnout at some point in their lives or have significant difficulty coping with a stressful work or family problem. Stress and mental well-being increasingly are viewed as legitimate, mainstream health issues.

The growing complexity, uncertainty, and demands in life itself have also enhanced societal awareness and acceptance. Downsizing, mergers, and restructuring have added to significant existing pressure at work. Changing lifestyle norms and a faster pace have strained personal lives as well. Previously taboo mental health problems such as those stemming from child abuse or poststress trauma are now more openly discussed. All these pressures of modern life have received extensive media attention.

In response to this new awareness and acceptance of stress and mental health problems, legislatures and courts have broadened criteria for tort liability, punitive damage awards, and bad faith claims. Similarly, health care providers are more likely to recognize a wider range of mental health problems and to provide care for them. More people receive care and financial compensation for their mental health injuries, and the costs have gone up correspondingly.

Economically, the increase can be attributed in part to two changes in government regulations that affect the health care market. First, there has been a gradual shift over the past decade to move mental health coverage responsibility from the public to the private sector. Second, the advent of diagnosis-related group (DRG) regulations inadvertently augmented the incentive for mental health and substance abuse treatment, while dramatically reducing the number of beds in health care facilities that were dedicated to surgical and physical treatment cases. These changes made mental health and substance abuse treatment a key advertising and marketing target for health care facilities in the mid to late 1980s.

At the employee level, economic conditions have made it more difficult for most families to maintain the same standard of living without taking on additional employment. Two-earner families, second jobs, grown children living at home, and economic pressure to support aging parents have all increased. This financial pressure raises stress levels and risk for mental health problems, as many people work harder for less relative wages. Financial uncertainty also contributes to the risk for disability.

Thus, for both societal and economic reasons, costs for stress and mental health have risen dramatically. Inpatient mental health and substance abuse treatment costs grew from $19 billion in 1985 to $50 billion in 1990.[4] There was also rapid growth in a new kind of workers' compensation and disability claim, the so-called stress claim.

Stress Claims

For many years, physical pain, illness, or limitation was the core basis for the great majority of workers' compensation and disability claims. It was recognized that mental factors could play a role in producing or aggravating the physical complaint, but they were tangential to the physical basis required for a claim to be seen as meritorious. This general position was supported in written legislation, case law, and professional practice.

Throughout the 1980s and into the 1990s, however, the clarity of this distinction slowly eroded. Legislatures, courts, and health care professionals became more willing to see a mental injury as being just as valid as a physical injury. An employee's anxiety about the hazards of a workplace chemical or an employee's depression resulting from a corporate restructuring became a serious basis for claims. This was particularly true in cases involving a particular traumatic event that precipitated the emotional injury.

In workers' compensation, the results of the trend can be seen by examining the three categories into which stress-related claims have traditionally been divided:[5]

1. *Mental-Physical.* A mental cause produces a physical health problem (e.g., a police officer who has developed an ulcer as a result of a stressful job).
2. *Physical-Mental.* A physical cause produces a mental health problem (e.g., a workplace accidental injury that has physically healed, yet leaving the victim with significant anxiety requiring treatment and time off).
3. *Mental-Mental.* A mental cause produces a mental health problem (e.g., an employee who has received harassment from his/her supervisor that results in clinical depression).

Traditionally, all 50 states have considered the first two categories of claims to be compensable under workers' compensation. Because these two categories intertwine the physical and mental, it is difficult to determine whether stress contributes to more of these claims today than years ago. Some case law suggests that courts interpret the mental-physical and physical-mental categories more liberally today, but good statistics are not available on the question.

For the third category, mental-mental, state laws differ significantly, and the responses in individual cases or courts may also differ as well. Overall, the number of paid mental-mental claims has grown considerably both nationwide and in certain states. The National Council on Compensation Insurance reports that mental-mental claims are an increasing source of occupational disease claims, posing extraordinary problems of both causation and measurement of disability and offering unparalleled opportunities for fraud.[6]

In California, mental-mentals climbed from 4,000 claims in 1979 to 30,000 in 1987, resulting in legislative action in both 1989 and 1991 to curb the rise. Workers in that state received an estimated $380 million in 1989 for stress claims related to problems such as headaches, depression, and sleeplessness. The average cost per claim was over $13,000 in 1987, although individual claims varied considerably.[7]

Disability insurers such as Northwestern National Life in Minneapolis report that stress-related disability claims more than doubled from 1982 to 1990. These cases represented 13 percent of all disability cases in 1990, compared with 6 percent in 1982. Northwestern also reports these disabilities are more difficult to rehabilitate, with an average success rate of 50 percent versus 75 percent for disabilities overall. For a stress-related disability, Northwestern typically reserves over $73,000 per case.[8]

In addition to workers' compensation and disability, stress claimants can pursue other legal remedies through the tort system including (1) intentional infliction of emotional stress, (2) defamation, (3) breach of good faith, and (4) implied contract. Such venues might be used most often by employees who feel their mental health has suffered as a result of personnel actions, such as demotions or unwanted job changes.

It is still too early to predict the ultimate standards that will be applied to the stress claim. Should an organization be held just as liable for injuries to its employees' mental well-being as to their physical well-being? If so, is the employer just as liable for the employee's depression if some of it is the result of factors outside the workplace (i.e., the employee's personal life and genetic/family history)? Can distinctions like this be made today, given the limited knowledge of what causes someone's state of mental health? These difficult societal questions are slowly and inconsistently being worked out across the country.

What is certain, however, is that societal awareness and acceptance of stress and mental injury have translated to a rapidly increasing general exposure for employers that could appear in a variety of lawsuits as well as in health and disability costs. Because this exposure parallels the growth in health care costs directly related to mental and emotional problems, it gives employers an additional incentive to manage the stress and mental health issues effectively.

Limiting Benefits

Because of the explosion in mental-health-related costs, many organizations acted in the late 1980s and early 1990s to place limits in their health care benefits plan on mental health care coverage. The most common of these limitations pertain to inpatient treatment and apply to (1) the maximum lifetime dollar amount, (2) the maximum number of days per year, or (3) the maximum dollar amount per year.

Employers took this action because many had previously been using the same cost ceilings across both physical health and mental health coverage. For example, there may have been a ceiling of $1 million or even $100,000 that made sense for an area such as heart surgery but that did not make sense for mental health care. Organizations therefore put restrictions on mental health coverage to limit exposure to severe abuse of treatment benefits that could otherwise occur. These benefit ceilings often have their greatest impact on inpatient treatment.

By itself, however, limiting benefits has its own limitations. First, it is an end-of-the-line standardized approach rather than being prevention-oriented and tailorable to the person and situation. Second, it is a one-dimensional solution to a complex problem, offering no opportunity to understand and manage the root causes that may result in other types of health and disability claims or losses in productivity and quality. Third, limited benefits may communicate an "uncaring" message to employees if not supplemented by other organizational messages about employee stress and mental health. Fourth, it fails to address the crucial question of value from treatment—whether the organization and employee or dependent are receiving a treatment outcome that is worth the cost expended.

As discussed with substance abuse, this question of value is central for the management of stress and mental health. Like substance abuse, mental health treatment decisions should seek to optimize the value received in comparison with the costs expended. This broader approach places more emphasis on the quality of outcome, the length of time the outcome is maintained, and the appropriateness of the treatment for the particular individual. A lack of orientation to value sends the message that stress and mental health issues are fads or trivial concerns that do not warrant serious business scrutiny. In contrast, a focus on value encourages an organization to think more systematically about its stress and mental health goals and to design more integrated and long-term solutions.

Limiting benefits is one part of an effective solution. If it is the only solution, however, its effectiveness will be like pushing in one side of a balloon. Gain will be achieved in controlling excessive cost among abusers of the benefit plan. The unsolved underlying problem will reappear, however, in other aspects of the total cost of health and disability. Employees will get sick, file lawsuits or workers' compensation stress claims, skip work, or perform poorly when properly targeted assistance could have solved the root problem at far less cost.

The mental health of the work force is a key factor in organizational productivity and competitiveness. Therefore, spending resources to reduce stress and improve mental health can be an excellent investment. This investment pays off only if it is part of an integrated approach that is focused on obtaining good value. Organizational approaches that emphasize prevention and early intervention of mental health problems can increase value while also reducing the pressure on treatment to be the total solution.

Leading companies such as Wells Fargo Bank, Hewlett-Packard, Johnson & Johnson, Chevron, and Quad Graphics have established strong efforts to deal directly with employee stress and mental health. Examining their different approaches shows the range of management options available for promoting good value from a mental health investment. An organization can emphasize assessment, education, health/wellness, assistance/treatment, reduction of sources of stress, or any combination of these. Each of these proactive approaches is discussed further in the remainder of the chapter.

Determining the Prevalence of Mental Health Problems

Many organizations have little systematic evidence about whether stress/ mental illness is a significant health issue for employees and dependents. Instead, most employers have to rely on stories about employees who report these problems, statistics about those who have contacted the employee assistance program, or general costs associated with utilization of mental health care coverage. These sources of information say little about how the majority of employees may be dealing with mental health issues. The lack of information also makes it difficult to focus preventive mental health efforts.

Example **Wells Fargo Bank** Wells Fargo Bank, the San Francisco-based financial institution, found that gathering data from the employee population at large led to some very different conclusions than might otherwise have been reached. Wells Fargo's goal was to assess the prevalence of mental health problems among its employee population so that the company could focus and tailor management efforts to the mental health issues with the most potential for impact. To do this, Wells Fargo sent out an anonymous survey to a representative and random sample of nearly 1500 employees.

Results showed that about 10 percent of the respondents were experiencing significant levels of anxiety; 8 to 10 percent reported a moderate to severe problem with alcohol, and 15 to 20 percent had significant concern about family member's use of alcohol or drugs; 30 to 35 percent were experiencing a number of symptoms of depression, with 12 to 15 percent estimated to be clinically depressed. These figures, which resemble national statistics, identified the mental health problems that were most likely to affect employee productivity, absenteeism, and health and disability costs.

Responses also showed where people sought help for significant mental health problems:

Source of Help	Percentage
Trusted friend	71
Trusted relative	51
Supervisor	32
Did not seek help	21
Private physician	19
Personnel officer or professional counselor	11
Religious leader	10
Wells Fargo employee assistance program	5

Most employees, according to the survey, were not using the company's designated resource (the employee assistance program) to help with their mental health issues. In fact, about 45 percent of employees said they did not believe help offered through work could be completely private. This information helped Wells Fargo refocus its education, communication, and outreach resources to better meet the needs of its employees and dependents.[9]

Example **Westinghouse Corporation** At Pennsylvania-based Westinghouse Corporation, a study of mental illness among managers and professional staff also provided significant and valuable results for focusing future effort. The approximately 2000 managers and professionals who took part in the study were interviewed individually by University of Pittsburgh psychologists and social workers in a two-hour, face-to-face meeting, typically in the manager or professional's home. All participants were promised the results would remain completely confidential. (Funding for this study came in part from the National Institute of Mental Health.)

Interestingly, the interviews took place when Westinghouse was reducing its white-collar work force, a change that coincided with an increase in organizational workload, as measured by the number of service requests handled during the interview period. Thus, the mental health of these managers and professionals was determined during a time span that truly represented uncertain job security and "doing more with less."

Results showed that 9 percent of the men interviewed had been clinically depressed within the last year, 23 percent at some point in their lifetime. For the women, the rates were 17 percent and 36 percent, respectively. Alcohol abuse/dependence was found among 4 percent of the men within the year, 16 percent during their lifetime. These rates were 4 percent and 9 percent, respectively, for the women. Compared with national norms, these managers and professionals had higher rates of depression among men and higher rates of alcohol abuse/dependence among women.

Results also showed the characteristics that put employees at greatest risk for mental health problems. The three most important risk factors for depression were being female, separated or divorced, and having a family history of depression. For alcohol abuse/dependence, the most important risk factors were being male, unmarried, and having a family history of alcoholism. Managerial or professional status, length of employment, hours worked per day, and supervisory responsibility were not significantly associated with either depression or alcoholism. Thus, personal characteristics affected mental health status more than aspects of the job itself.[10]

Example **Johns Hopkins University Study** Some occupations, however, do have higher risk for mental illness than others. In fact, a Johns Hopkins University study found that people working in certain occupations are up to three times more likely to be clinically depressed than the general population. The study of approximately 12,000 people employed in a wide range of jobs identified the following high-risk occupations:

High-Risk Occupations for Depression	Odds of Depression
Lawyers	3.6 times higher
Sales Worker/Apparel	3.0 times higher
Educational Counselors/Special Teachers	2.8 times higher
Secretaries/Computer Operators	1.9 times higher

These results are intriguing because the high-risk occupations differ in many respects. Although the causes of depression may also be different across the occupations, they share two factors that have been shown to increase stress: (1) All four jobs involve high demand—demanding clients, problem students, high output expectations; (2) all four jobs can involve a lack of control over the type and pace of work that is expected. People in these occupations may have significantly more job stress caused by high expectations that change quickly, continuously, and without much input from them. Over time, this stress may put them at higher risk for depression.[11]

These three examples—the Wells Fargo survey, the Westinghouse interviews, and the occupational ranking of depression risk—show possible ways to develop an organization's mental health risk profile. Knowing these risk factors can help an employer tailor education and assistance efforts to the employee subgroups most likely to benefit from them. The focus of this assistance can be an occupational group (e.g., secretaries), a demographic group (e.g., gender or marital status), or a mental health problem (e.g., depression or family substance abuse).

Measuring Employee Stress

Highly related to the identification of mental health problems, stress measurement has emerged as an increasingly popular way to understand and focus management efforts for workplace mental health. Stress measurement is in many ways an evolution of the organizational climate or job satisfaction surveys that companies have used for years. Like climate surveys, stress measures broaden understanding of employee perceptions and encourage improved dialogue between employees and management. However, stress measurement also differs in three important ways:

1. Stress measurement is typically scientific, based on the extensive stress research of the past decade.
2. Stress measurement is focused on health, emphasizing areas with the greatest impact on mental and physical health (e.g., degree of control over work, opportunity for social support).
3. Stress measurement tends to be broad, including sources of personal life stress (finances, children, marriage or relationships) and an array of workplace conditions (ergonomics, humor in the workplace, company resources to promote health and wellbeing).

Two of the higher quality stress measures in current use were both developed through insurance companies interested in reducing this area of risk. Northwestern National Life, a life and disability insurer in Minne-apolis, and St. Paul Fire and Marine Insurance, a property/casualty insurer in St. Paul, have developed separate but complementary stress measures. The Northwestern National survey has been administered to a random, nationally representative sample to help raise awareness of stress-related risk for lengthy employee disabilities. The St. Paul survey has been used with St. Paul-insured organizations to help them individually reduce their stress-related risk for workers' compensation and liability losses.

Results from the Northwestern National survey show the following re-sults for 600 representative American workers, survey in 1991:[12]

Stressor	Percentage
Frequent occurrence of three or more stress-related conditions that could increase health and disability costs	72
Extremely stressful job	46*
Need to prove value to employer because of recession	40
Serious thought given to quitting job in 1990 because of workplace stress	34
Job considered to be greatest cause of stress in their life	27

* Up from 20 percent in 1985.

Lack of control and major workplace change are the two greatest sources of job-related stress.

Respondents to the Northwestern National survey also indicated that they expect their employers to take substantive action to address job stress, and they will hold them financially responsible for the consequences of such stress. For example, 82 percent said that victims of burnout are due disabil-ity pay. On the positive side, the rate of burnout reported was 50 percent lower in companies in which employees believe the employer is taking action to solve workplace stress.

St. Paul survey results are from a database of nearly 28,000 employees surveyed between 1989 and 1992.[13] The database includes a maximum of 500 employees from each of 215 of their insured organizations who re-sponded to the 124-item Human Factors Inventory. Although it is difficult to make absolute comparisons across the two surveys, the St. Paul results may be somewhat more positive since they come from employees in compa-nies that chose to participate in the survey and its follow-up consulting (i.e., more progressive organizations). Employees in these organizations re-ported a number of positive overall results:

Positive Factor	Percentage
Very satisfied with their job	80
Enjoy their work	85
Have maintained good health since joining company	84
Able to get help from co-workers when needed	87
Can easily talk with their supervisor about a problem	77

At the same time, these companies are far from stress-free, as shown in the following results:

Work Stressors	Percentage
Feel hurried or rushed to complete deadlines	64
Feel department is understaffed	47
Feel the company does not let employees make decisions that affect their work	50
Believe people are not rewarded for doing a good job	46
Would like their job to be more challenging	49

Personal Life Stressors (within the past year)	Percentage
Major or extreme problem with money or financial situation	46
Major difficulty with feelings and emotions (angry, upset)	33
Major problem dealing with illness or death of a loved one	32
Major difficulty in responsibilities related to care of others (children, parents)	31

Health and Performance Outcomes	Percentage
Feel burned out on their job	39
Feel tired out during workday	60
Believe productivity could be a lot better in their department	56
Are at least 10 pounds overweight	80
Think employees in their department seem to miss work a lot	62

Measurement of employee stress can provide great insight into the workplace and personal life problems affecting employee health. Especially when broken down by demographic group or work group, these results allow management to identify and manage the specific issues most likely to produce expensive health and disability losses. These stress results can be used separately or in combination with mental health related findings, as discussed in the previous section.

Managing Stress and Mental Health

Employers have several options for reducing mental health-related costs, based on an understanding of the key mental health and stress problems within the covered population. For example, education and employee assistance programs can be tailored and applied to achieve the best results for the organization's particular situation. In addition, significant progress in controlling these costs often comes from considering stress and mental health impact as part of operational management decisions. The ideal approach therefore includes both formal organizational programs and day-to-day management practices.

Workplace celebrations and recognition programs can be as important as an employee assistance program. Effective communication and a clear sense of vision can be more valuable than a curriculum of stress management classes. The most effective organizations are able to integrate stress and mental health goals with the organization's overall values and sense of future direction. Employee mental health then is seen as an integral part of the organization's mission, as important for organizational productivity and quality as for health and disability.

Example   **Hewlett-Packard**   For some organizations, one prong of this integrated, multipronged approach is education. Hewlett-Packard, for example, makes some type of stress management class available to all 56,000 of its employees through one of 17 vendors. Because of its decentralized culture, Hewlett-Packard allows each local entity to shape its program to its particular needs. This might include teaching coping skills for workplace and personal problems or educating employees about how to access community organizations that provide free or low cost mental health assistance. Hewlett-Packard also uses the education classes to explain its other mental health services such as the employee assistance program, the wellness program, and its extensive mental health benefits plan.[14]

By using education in this broad-based way, Hewlett-Packard not only builds skills, it also underscores its commitment to the well-being of its employees. This is particularly important in stress management education, since research shows that employees cope less well with worksite stresses than with stresses in other areas of life. Thus, stress management education may help employees improve parenting or marital relationships, which are more under their own control. At the workplace, however, it is not as easy for employees to change stressful organizational, social, and physical conditions.[15]

The most effective management of stress in the workplace usually comes from addressing root causes within the job and organizational culture. This might include the level of employee involvement, the amount of variety and control in work, or the frequency of recognition employees receive for their work. In a larger sense, the most important influences on workplace stress are the expectations and values employees experience in their daily work.

| Example | **Quad Graphics, Inc.** Quad/Graphics, Inc., a commercial printing company, is an illustration of the |

power of the workplace culture. At Quad/Graphics, press operators are given the freedom and responsibility to run their press the way they want to, to function more like partners in a law firm where each runs his or her part of the business. Company CEO Harry Quadracci seeks a mind-set in employees similar to that of clowns: "Unlike so many others, [clowns] are not wedded to conventional wisdom. They retain their childlike ability to be surprised, and the flexibility to adapt to or even thrive on change. I'd rather have 50 people out there thinking and working independently to develop an operating policy I can validate, than for me to sit up here from the top and say 'This is the way we're going to do it.'"[16]

This type of employee involvement and commitment generated by the culture of Quad/Graphics has significantly benefited the company's bottom line. Quad/Graphics total health plan costs per employee were $2350 in 1991, only 65 percent of the 1991 national average of $3605. These costs increased just 27 percent from 1988 to 1991, compared with the national increase of 53 percent.

Similarly, Leaf, Inc., a North American candy company, has reduced its workers' compensation costs by 35 percent from 1986 to 1991 during a period in which costs increased by 82 percent nationally. Leaf also has relied on involvement as a key strategy for both improving operations and employee commitment. Again, the cultural values encouraged by the organization have resulted in both increased employee satisfaction and improved employee health.[17]

Organizational cultures that encourage employee involvement and responsibility attack the root sources of stress and mental health problems in three important ways. First, employees gain a sense of control, a feeling that their efforts make a difference in improving problem areas. Second, the responsibility and self-esteem that go along with involvement at work can generalize to areas away from work, causing employees to function more effectively and reduce stress in all aspects of life. Third, employees in companies with effective cultures often feel a greater sense of belonging and of social support for their well-being, which contributes to sound mental health.

Managing the Constant of Change

Managing change is a key aspect of creating a workplace and culture that promotes positive employee mental health. The ability to manage change may be the most important mental health skill an employee or organization can possess. As mentioned, the Northwestern National Life stress survey found that workplace change and lack of control were the two biggest contributors to employee burnout. At the organizational level, workplace changes such as downsizing, mergers, or reorganization are among the most powerful influences on employee mental health.

As the term "managing change" suggests, the goal is not to stop or even totally to control change—it is a constant of modern work and personal life. The key is to manage or channel that change without losing perspective of the overall goals. For an organization, this means retaining the focus on key organizational values and objectives, even though day-to-day operations or relationships may change. For an employee, it means retaining the focus on personal values and objectives and developing ways to meet them in the new environment. Both organizations and employees should seek a broader context for understanding the change so that they can focus change-related energy in productive ways.

To take a simple example, assume that an organization decides to convert from its present computer equipment to a new model that many employees will need to master. The change is announced, and employees are immediately scheduled for training classes. The employer provides a brief explanation of reasons for the change, pointing out the technical superiorities of the new system. Exactly what the change means for employees is left more or less open to interpretation. Such an introduction fails to frame the change effectively making it likely that employees will resist the new equipment, feel stressed by the new procedures, and be open to suggestions of carpal tunnel or VDT (video display terminal) exposure from the new machines.

The organization, instead, could have used the following five simple steps to minimize employee resistance and increase the odds of accomplishing the change smoothly:

1. Explain why the change is beneficial or necessary, both for the company and the employee. If the change is important enough, explain how it fits with key company values or objectives.

2. Acknowledge the accomplishments and success of the past situation. In particular, honor the hard work and sacrifices employees have made under the past system.

3. Ask for employee input and involvement in implementing the change. When employees respond, actively involve them and support their ideas and actions.

4. Prepare for employee resistance. Work individually with the most resistant employees to understand their concerns and explain organizational expectations.

5. Reward employees for their efforts in making the change successful. Begin to establish a track record with employees that supports effective change management.

Applying these steps to the example of the new computer equipment would have changed several aspects of how the organization framed the change. First, the new equipment could have been described as an investment that provides employees with the best equipment and the most current skills. This will improve their job security and the company's ability to remain profitable. Second, employees could have been thanked for the hard work and high productivity they attained with the old equipment, perhaps emphasizing how they went the extra mile to get the old equipment to perform. Third, employees could have been involved in deciding which new equipment to buy, how to distribute the new equipment, and how to conduct the training.

As the new equipment is phased in, supervisors or co-workers could meet individually with employees having difficulties with it. This would give these employees an opportunity to vent their frustration and to problem-solve solutions. In addition, quick learners could be recognized and could help to establish a norm of using the equipment to improve performance.

Naturally, change management must be applied with more sophistication and follow-through for a departmental reorganization than for a change in a work procedure. Also, concurrent changes on many fronts must be linked together to reflect the organization's strategy and direction. One way to display this linkage is with a three-level categorization: (1) long-term strategic direction, (2) medium-term operational direction, and (3) short-term procedural direction. Organizations can then communicate and manage changes at any of these three levels by showing employees how the change fits into overall vision and values. Such clarifying frameworks become essential stress management tools for dealing with change in organizations.

Patricia Owen, Vice President of Hazelden Services, Inc., remarks, "Often when people say they are 'burning out,' they are saying that their work has lost meaning for them. They feel disillusioned, stretched too thin, or are starting to believe their investment may not be making a difference in the greater scheme of things."[18] Similarly, some employees interpret change as a personal attack because they have no other frame of meaning for the circumstance.

The employer's values and vision can provide an interpretation for change that promotes employee well-being. Articulating the solid reasons for changes allows employees to find renewed meaning and commitment in their work. This acknowledgment and involvement of employees can be one of the organization's most effective investments in their mental health.

Linking Wellness and Mental Health

Many people find that physical activity is an excellent individual technique for reducing stress. Exercise often helps clear the mind of frustrations and strains, while improving the body's capability to resist stress. Other wellness activities such as nutrition, weight control, and recreation also contribute to good overall health, a positive self-image, and an enhanced ability to deal with stress.

From the organizational perspective, linking wellness to mental health offers several advantages. First, it supports and broadens the cognitive coping skills acquired through stress management education. Second, it provides another medium (in addition to management practices and education) for reinforcing organizational values of health. Third, efficiencies and synergies can often be gained by coordinating wellness and mental health services across education, employee assistance or counseling, and communication and promotion of health messages. An integrated approach also helps organizations respond more effectively to the increasingly blurred line between physical and mental in health and disability claims.

Some organizations have used organizational structure to foster this wellness–mental health linkage. For example, employee assistance and wellness can be combined within the same department or can report to the same individual. A second possibility is to define roles for each with specific accountability for working together on such projects as education, health fairs, or employee outreach.

Employee Assistance versus Managed Mental Health

Despite all the preceding organizational efforts—assessment, education, managing stress, managing change, and wellness—some employees will need assistance and/or treatment for mental health problems. Employee assistance programs (EAPs) have for the past several years been the most widely used mechanism to supply these services. A 1988 survey by the Bureau of Labor Statistics found that 83 percent of companies with at least 5000 employees offered an employee assistance program, as did 29 percent of companies with 100 to 250 employees.[19]

More recently, however, an increasing number of organizations have also added managed mental health care to deal with utilization of mental health services. Campbell Soup Company in Camden, New Jersey, found that despite the presence of an EAP, 75 percent of its employees who used inpatient psychiatric care were self-referred, many of them being responses to ad campaigns by hospitals and substance abuse treatment facilities without professional guidance for appropriateness.[20] Because many employees did not contact or work through the EAP, it had been ineffective in fulfilling the referral and watchdog role.

This experience raises important questions about programs for managing employee mental health assistance and treatment. Does an organization need both an EAP and managed mental health care? What are the advantages and optimal role of each? Doesn't having both create additional bureaucracy— could their functions be combined? Are there other options to consider? To answer these questions, employers should consider the strengths and historical traditions of each option.

EAPs, which began as occupational alcoholism programs, have a strong tradition of patient advocacy. Many EAPs emphasize early identification of behavioral health problems and prefer involving the patient's whole family to improve long-term treatment effectiveness. At Chevron, Inc. (the petroleum company), EAPs have established a reputation of trust among employees, based on concern for the well-being of the patient and strict adherence to confidentiality. Chevron's EAP is also quite familiar with the jobs and history of people in the organization and can closely manage previously treated employees who are working in chemical or refinery jobs with significant risk of disaster.[21]

In contrast, managed mental health stems from utilization review and is oriented toward efficient use of treatment resources. Like utilization review in general, managed mental health seeks to curb expensive treatment by emphasizing preferred providers and alternatives to inpatient care. Managed mental health is also oriented toward mental health utilization of the entire covered population, regardless of how a particular patient chose to access treatment. With its financial orientation, managed mental health seeks to ensure that treatment is always cost-effective and appropriate. In general, therefore, EAPs focus on managing broad-based mental health, whereas managed mental health focuses on managing treatment aspects of care.

For organizations with both an EAP and managed mental health, these differences in traditions can lead to conflict and inefficiency or to optimal synergy. If the two do not work together, patients will receive inconsistent treatment and follow-up, be referred back and forth, and be the subject of extensive turf battles. Yet if the EAP and managed mental health do work together effectively, their advantages could complement each other for an optimal result.

There appear to be three main alternatives for resolving the question of EAP versus managed mental health. First, an organization could employ only one of the two approaches and try to compensate for the advantages of the other. Second, the two approaches could be combined into an integrated function. Third, the two could work out a partnership with clearly defined roles for each. Each of these options is viable, depending on the organization's situation.

Organizations that use only EAP or only managed mental health will want to supplement weak areas of the program with an appropriate benefit design and/or case management. For example, the benefit design could feature much more attractive benefits when the patient works through the EAP, minimizing the risk that employees will bypass the EAP with no checkpoint for appropriateness of care.

The importance of such a checkpoint is illustrated by research with the EAP at McDonnell Douglas, the St. Louis-based aerospace and defense firm.[22] Employees who received psychiatric treatment as clients of the EAP had markedly fewer lost days and medical costs than those whose treatment did not involve the EAP. As shown in Figure 12.1, employees treated through the EAP had a 25 percent reduction in lost days over the five-year period following treatment. Figure 12.2 shows that employee medical costs for EAP clients were nearly $4000 lower than non-EAP clients over the five-year period.

Organizations that choose to use only managed mental health care and not EAP might selectively add case management to provide the follow-up and personal attention available through EAP. Case managers closely follow high-risk cases where costs could climb to tens of thousands of dollars. Case management helps to avoid excessive fees, and it improves chances of effective recovery.

Organizations that use the second major option—combining the services of EAP and managed mental health with a single vendor—should guard against two dangers. First, can the single vendor truly provide all the services that the organization needs? Second, will the organization need to

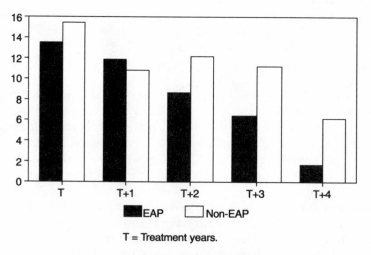

T = Treatment years.

T+4 = 4 years after treatment.

Figure 12.1 Impact of EAP Psychiatric Treatment on Lost Work Days (*Source:* McDonnell Douglas Corporation Financial Offset Study 1985–1989. Used with permission.)

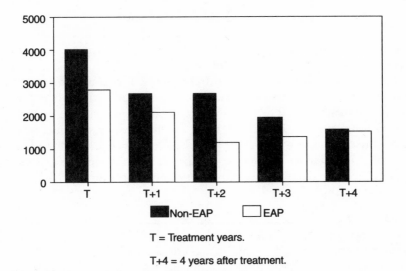

Figure 12.2 Impact of EAP Psychiatric Treatment on Health Care Costs (*Source:* McDonnell Douglas Corporation Financial Offset Study 1985–1989. Used with permission.)

take on a watchdog role (i.e., to ensure the single vendor does not abuse its exclusive access through preferential referral to "sister units")? If these questions can receive adequate attention, the single-vendor approach can increase efficiency and integration.

Organizations with both an EAP and managed mental health need to define each of these roles. Should the EAP be the gatekeeper for all outpatient treatment, while managed mental health handles all inpatient care? Or should the EAP function as an "information booth" directing employees toward appropriate care, while the managed care entity serves as the gatekeeper in deciding whether or not care will be covered? Again, this model can also produce integration and quality results, but only if the roles are clear and able to function cooperatively.

Virtually any of these models can work effectively to control costs and improve quality when tailored to the needs of the organization, as shown in the following example.

Example **Chrysler, Inc.** Chrysler, Inc., structured its benefit plan so that patients receive incentives for beginning with EAP; they are then referred to a closed panel of providers, successfully minimizing use of nonpanel providers. This program, by emphasizing early intervention and outpatient treatment, saved $20 million in the first year. Importantly for the culture at Chrysler, it also secured the support of the United Auto Workers, because the union wanted to oversee the EAP in every Chrysler plant.[23]

Ensuring Quality and Value

Organizations can use a variety of approaches—assessment, education, managing stress, managing change, wellness, employee assistance, and managed mental health care—to address causes of cost and improve employee mental health. These approaches are most powerful when part of the ongoing management practices of the organization, a reflection of the organizational culture. Returning again to the question of value, organizations must consider which approaches to emphasize and how to ensure they work together to provide optimal value. An example of assessing such value comes from the employee assistance program at McDonnell Douglas.

Example   **McDonnell Douglas**   In 1987, McDonnell Douglas spent $1.3 million to operate its EAP. The company estimates it saved $3.7 million by reducing absenteeism and employee and dependent health care claims. In 1989, McDonnell Douglas took actions to channel more employees through the EAP, resulting in expanded EAP caseloads and greater program costs at $2.3 million. However, the resulting reduction in absenteeism and employee and dependent health care costs was $6.0 million.[24]

This example shows that the relative success of outcomes typically has much more to do with value than with the level of up-front costs because the differences in payoff for successful versus unsuccessful outcomes are often larger than differences in program costs. Promotion of employee mental health can provide cost-effective outcomes by managing toward key objectives. Such programs are unlikely to be cost-effective, however, without ongoing organizational support and accountability identifying mental health as an important employer objective.

Because it is more difficult to develop and analyze information related to outcome success, it is tempting to simply limit the up-front investment and hope that the outcomes will fall within a reasonably acceptable range. An organization might, for example, limit its mental health benefits, try to offset the limitation with some occasional stress management classes, and wait to see what happens. This approach could cut costs in the short term but is likely to cause problems in the middle and long term. Worst of all, such an approach relegates management to a helpless position with little control over costs and even less understanding of how to manage the factors that impact cost.

In the late 1980s and early 1990s, many organizations have done well in limiting mental health costs by plugging the most obvious hole in the system: unmonitored and extended inpatient treatments. The challenge now is to achieve a better level of value for mental health investments throughout the system. Organizations can attain this value by taking a broader view of the payoff from mental health and by effectively targeting management approaches to involve and support employees. Cost and quality will improve at the same time when managers and employees actively pursue prevention, tailored support, and cost-effective treatment. The mentally healthy and committed work force that results positions the organization for increased productivity, higher quality, reduced lost time, and lower health and disability costs.

References

1. Sullivan, C. B., & Miller, J. E. June 1991. *The evolution of mental health benefits.* Washington, DC: Health Insurance Association of America, Policy and Research Findings.

2. Mangan, J. F. March, 1991. Stress-related claims: causes & controls. *Best's Review—Property/Casualty Insurance Edition,* 68–76.

3. Northwestern National Life. 1991. *Employee Burnout: America's Newest Epidemic.* Minneapolis: Northwestern National.

4. Berger, J. K. 1992. Controlling costs in mental health and substance abuse treatment programs. *13th Annual Conference of Public Risk Management Association.* Anaheim, CA.

5. National Council on Compensation Insurance. 1985. *Emotional stress in the workplace: New legal rights in the eighties.* New York: NCCI.

6. National Council on Compensation Insurance. 1992. *Issues Report.* Boca Raton, FL: NCCI, p. 22.

7. California Workers Compensation Institute. June 1990. *Mental stress claims in California workers' compensation: Incidence, costs, and trends.* San Francisco, CA: CWCI.

8. Northwestern National Life. *Employee Burnout.*

9. Lawton, B., & Carroll, R. 1989. *Problem prevalence rates and internal EAP utilization.* San Francisco, CA: Wells Fargo Bank.

10. Bromet, E. J., Parkinson, D. K., et al. 1990. Epidemiology of depression and alcohol abuse/dependence in a managerial and professional work force. *Journal of Occupational Medicine,* 32(10): 989–995.

11. Eaton, W. W., Anthony, J. C., Mandel, W., & Garrison, R. 1990. Occupations and the prevalence of major depressive disorder. *Journal of Occupational Medicine,* 32(11): 1079–1087.

12. Northwestern National Life. *Employee Burnout.*

13. St. Paul Fire and Marine Insurance Company. 1992. *Work and personal life stress: Results with the Human Factors Inventory.* St. Paul, MN: St. Paul Fire and Marine Ins.

14. Walker, C. K. September, 1991. Stressed to kill. *Business and Health,* pp. 42–51.

15. Heaney, C. A., & Van Ryn, M. 1990. Broadening the scope of worksite stress programs: A guiding framework. *American Journal of Health Promotion*, 4(6): 413–420.

16. Lefkoe, M. June, 1992. Unhealthy business. *Across the Board*, pp. 26–31.

17. Ibid.

18. Northwestern National Life. *Employee Burnout.*

19. U.S. Department of Labor. 1989. Bureau of Labor Statistics. *Survey of employer anti-drug programs* (Report 760). Washington, DC: U.S. Government Printing Office.

20. Connors, N. February, 1992. Do you need a managed mental health program? *Business and Health*, pp. 48–53.

21. McDonnell Douglas & Alexander & Alexander. 1990. *Employee assistance program financial offset study, 1985–1989.* Bridgeton, MO.

22. Special Report. 1991. EAP and mental health: Made for each other. *Business and Health*, pp. 14–15.

23. Bryant, M. August, 1991. Testing EAPs for coordination. *Business and Health*, pp. 20–24.

24. McDonnell Douglas & Alexander & Alexander. 1990. *Employee assistance program financial offset study, 1985–1989.* Bridgeton, MO.

Resources

American Institute of Stress
124 Park Avenue
Yonkers, NY 10703
(914) 963-1200

Provides materials and conducts free workshops and symposia on stress.

The EAP Association Exchange
4601 North Fairfax Drive
Suite 1001
Arlington, VA 22203
(703) 522-6272

Provides articles about EAPs and the EAP profession. Lists resources such as EAP professional services, films, and books.

Institute of Stress Management
United States International University
School of Human Behavior
10455 Pomerado Road
San Diego, CA 92131
(619) 271-4300

Provides information on stress management. The Institute seeks to further scientific, educational, and clinical endeavors on stress.

National Institute of Mental Health
Public Inquiries Branch
Office of Scientific Information
Parklawn Building, Room 15c-05
5600 Fishers Lane
Rockville, MD 20857
(301) 443-4513

Provides information on stress, stress management, and other aspects of mental health.

National Mental Health Association
Communications and Information Services
1021 Prince Street
Alexandria, VA 22314-2971
(703) 684-7722

Works to improve the public's understanding of mental health and mental illness. Provides information and help for the mentally ill, their families, school systems, and local governments.

13

Innovative Strategies for Workplace Safety

Workplace safety—once the stodgy domain of slide rules, arcane statistics, and cutesy posters—has emerged in the 1990s as a dynamic and multidisciplinary management approach that can reduce health and disability costs quickly and significantly. In fact, workplace safety and disability management has become one of the best ways to exert quick leverage on those costs. Using this approach, many organizations have reduced workers' compensation costs by as much as 50 percent within one to three years. Other organizations have maintained significantly lower cost structures over several years through effective safety and disability management. This progress has occurred against the backdrop of a safety and disability management field redefining itself to adapt to widespread change.

The changes and opportunities affecting safety and disability management today have raised the stakes for effective performance. Organizations performing poorly in safety and disability management are at a much greater competitive disadvantage today than in the past when compared with superior performers. The changes increase an organization's leverage for differentiating itself from competitors through improved safety and disability management performance. These changes come in many forms, including financial, legal, organizational, and physical.

Financially, rapid increases in workers' compensation costs in particular have placed a greater priority on effective action. Organizations have also become more aware of the total cost implications of injured and disabled employees, including productivity, quality, health care costs, and the organizational revenues necessary to compensate for these costs. An organization with $500,000 in annual workers' compensation costs and a 3 percent profit margin must realize $16 million in sales just to offset the costs of those injuries.[1] In an era of self-insurance and growing risk of expensive permanent disabilities, these financial realities make safety and disability management essential.

Legally, extensive litigation and government oversight have forced a more proactive orientation toward safety and disability management. Attorney involvement on workers' compensation lost-time cases increased nationally from 11 percent in 1981 to 17 percent in 1989. In California, 32 percent of indemnity claims were litigated in 1991, and 1990 litigation costs represented $1.5 billion out of a workers' compensation premium base of $9 billion.[2] The Occupational Safety and Health Administration (OSHA) and other government regulatory bodies have levied large fines and established required standards for safety and disability practices. The Americans with Disabilities Act (ADA) has also spurred organizations to reexamine their response to injured and disabled employees.

In addition, the implementation of safety and disability management has been affected by shifts toward flatter, more team-based, and more rapidly changing work structures. Managers in this environment need to promote an informed and active employee work force that can take more responsibility for safety and disability without compromising cost and quality. Simple and one-dimensional solutions that worked in the past are no longer appropriate. Safety and disability must adapt to team and quality improvement models to fit today's organizational climate.

The physical environment and results also present change and opportunity. The physically dangerous work environment of the past has been replaced by one in which repetitive strain and cumulative trauma are the watchwords. Workplace injuries are more subtle and require different management techniques. Safety of family members and the interplay between work and home safety are increasingly important. Environment is now much more than just the obvious physical hazards of the work area.

The net result is that an effective workplace safety program can provide tremendous leverage on health and disability costs. In fact, the beauty of safety and disability management is that employers can often harvest the return on investment quite quickly, particularly if they have average or poor health and disability results. Although typically exerting its strongest effect on workers' compensation costs, safety and disability management will impact an organization's total cost of health as well. Safety pays off by preventing workplace accidents and injuries and by creating a general awareness among employees that affects off-the-job health attitudes and behaviors. Because safety and disability issues are important to most employees, action in this area improves employee commitment while also enhancing financial results.

Corporate Leaders in Safety

Any organization, large or small, can use the kind of approach needed to excel in safety. One of the best things about safety and disability management is that remarkable payback is possible for any employer truly committed to making it work. This management commitment is always the key to improving safety and disability performance, even though particulars of the program may differ to fit each organization's needs.

Du Pont, Alcoa, and Dow Chemical are large companies that have achieved excellent results through long-standing safety traditions. Du Pont has been identified by the National Council on Compensation Insurance as the American corporate leader in safety. Fourteen Du Pont plants have gone more than 10 million hours without a lost workday, and two of these have gone more than 40 million hours without losing a workday. In 1987, 1988, and 1989, Du Pont's principal chemical operations enjoyed lost workday incidence rates of 0.05 per 100 workers, a rate that is 1500 times better than the national average of 78.7 per 100 workers.[3] Similarly, Alcoa and Dow Chemical have notably better safety results than their industry or national averages. For one Dow Chemical location, workers' compensation costs bottomed out at two cents per $100 of payroll.[4] Nationally, workers' compensation costs average between two and three dollars per $100 of payroll.[5]

How can these companies be so remarkably effective at safety? First, because safety is not an additional duty, but a key part of the culture and daily life. For Du Pont, this tradition began over 100 years ago when the company manufactured highly volatile black powder, and arranged for each employee to work alone in a separate area so that any explosion would kill only one worker. Later, as Du Pont began to manufacture dynamite, the plant superintendent and his family were required to live on the grounds of the factory to reinforce attention to safety. Even today at all three—Du Pont, Alcoa, and Dow—safety is an executive-level issue that receives continual top management attention.

Concrete and formal safety programs also reinforce the culture and management commitment of these companies. Key elements of these programs include:

- *Careful Tracking and Analysis.* Data concerning the rate and causes of accidents and injuries are broken down by location and by primary and root cause. This information receives careful management attention oriented toward future prevention.
- *Formal Organizational Structure That Supports Safety.* Safety is the first agenda item in management meetings and is a priority issue all the way up to the chief executive officer (CEO). Safety committees made up of both managers and workers actively review safety issues, participate in safety audits, and work in teams to review high-risk tasks or processes.
- *Emphasis Is on Employee Involvement and Behavior.* Employees receive thorough safety training and assume a great deal of responsibility in making safety a reality among their peers. Employee buy-in and peer pressure are key factors in reinforcing safe behavior.

- *Awards and Recognition Keep Safety Awareness High.* Recognition is not in large monetary awards, but rather through many forms of non-monetary recognition such as plaques, certificates, and awards. Safety is reinforced through personal recognition and appreciation of managers at all levels in the organization.

Overall, these three companies achieve outstanding safety results not only because of the preceding program elements but mostly because of the commitment with which they execute them. Much of safety success is not rocket science—it is the result of planning, persistence, and constant attention. Du Pont, Dow, and Alcoa have institutionalized these characteristics by building safety into the way they do business and by constantly enhancing or reenergizing their efforts with new initiatives tied to behavioral safety and to quality improvement. They have made safety a key part of their organizational culture despite differences across plants and facilities. Their success has resulted in a dramatically lower health and disability cost structure and in a considerable marketing and competitive advantage.

Successful Small- and Medium-Size Companies

The size and tradition of the corporate leaders should not suggest that safety success is only possible for huge employers working for many years. In fact, small- and medium-size companies may actually have the advantage because it is easier to change culture quickly in a small company than in a large one. Often, the combination of committed upper management and a highly effective safety coordinator can cut costs dramatically within one to two years.

Example   **Aspen Imaging International**   Aspen Imaging International, a manufacturer of computer printer supplies with 300 employees in Lafayette, Colorado, cut its workers' compensation costs from $600,000 in 1989 to $221,000 in 1991. The company accomplished this dramatic improvement by taking seven steps that built on suggestions from its new insurer:[6]

1. Established an executive committee to monitor the number and cost of injuries and to manage injury-prevention efforts.
2. Hired a full-time health and safety coordinator to work with employees, medical providers, and insurers on prevention and claim management.
3. Designed several new ergonomic tools to reduce repetitive strain, using the plant's industrial engineer and the insurance company loss prevention representative.
4. Gave employees safety and lifting training to minimize back strains.

5. Established an employee safety committee to review incidents, inspect the plant for hazards, and recommend improvements.

6. Developed a safety incentive system, such as free lunch for work teams without an accident for a specified period.

7. Emphasized returning injured employees to work quickly through the use of modified schedules or duties.

These steps, instead of requiring extensive direct expenditures or years of implementation, focused existing internal resources toward an organizational goal strongly supported by senior management.

Example   **HON Industries**   HON Industries, of Muscatine, Iowa, is an office furniture manufacturer with 5600 employees working in 23 facilities in 11 states. HON reduced its number of accidents 41 percent from 1990 to 1991 through five key steps:[7]

1. Implementing a safety infrastructure, in which safety is an agenda item at all management meetings. The CEO chairs the safety review board, and each facility has its own safety manager and review board.

2. Certifying all employees for job safety through an education and testing process about required safe procedures used in that job.

3. Certifying employees for safe operation on individual pieces of equipment such as the punch press.

4. Regularly reviewing the workplace and its equipment for hazards or ergonomic problems.

5. Encouraging all employees to report potential safety problems to their supervisor and to the safety director or review board.

The experience of a HON facility with primarily repetitive motion tasks shows how this works in practice. Previously, carpal tunnel had been a significant problem at this facility. Employees now start the day with calisthenics to warm up. They take a five-minute break every hour and rotate jobs every two hours. Because of these changes, employees are working 40 minutes less per day, yet production levels have increased from 65 percent of capacity to 95 percent. Reports of carpal tunnel syndrome have nearly disappeared.

Example   **All Plastics Molding**   All Plastics Molding of Dallas, Texas, is a custom plastic injection molder with 100 employees. In a one-year period from 1990 to 1991, All Plastics reduced its annual frequency of workers' compensation claims from twenty-five to nine. It also established a new company record of 156 consecutive accident-free days.[8] All Plastics accomplished these changes largely through increased employee involvement, focus on safety, and an effort to improve the overall culture of the organization. Strategies included:

- Using an employee stress survey to identify key issues affecting health and performance.
- Using team management and employee problem solving to address these issues in areas such as communication, safety, quality, and departmental activities.
- Implementing a new benefits plan and a 401K program, with employee input to design.
- Initiating a safety incentive program for achieving consecutive days without a plant accident.
- Enhancing communication between employees and managers and between departments through problem-solving sessions and a company newsletter.

For All Plastics, these changes represented an important shift in the overall company culture. The climate became more open, employees felt more involved and able to participate, and there was increased focus on improving safety as a team effort. All Plastics also reduced its rate of absenteeism, tardiness, and turnover through these integrated efforts.

Throughout each of these example companies, both large and small, management has been committed to making safety an integral part of the organization's culture. This commitment is evident in the time and attention devoted to safety as well as the open involvement of employees in making the safety program effective. Results of this commitment are dramatically reduced workers' compensation costs and improvement in productivity and employee satisfaction. These examples are typical of numerous employers who have shown that effective safety and disability management is a proven investment in company profitability.

Blending Old and New in the 1990s Organization

To strengthen safety and disability management, employers must somehow balance the traditional strengths of an industrial age safety approach with the emerging needs of the information age organization. Even though significant changes over the past several years have reshaped the urgency and application of safety and disability management, employers wonder if they should abandon techniques that have worked successfully for years. The answer is to blend the best of the old and new around a shared foundation.

As shown in Table 13.1, both the traditional and the modern approaches to safety and disability management revolve around four core capabilities:

Table 13.1 Traditional and Modern Approaches to Safety and Disability Management

Core Capability	Traditional Approach	Modern Approach
Safe physical workplace	Machine safeguards Steel-toed shoes	Ergonomic design VDT glare screens
Line manager involvement	Accountability/incentives Delegated responsibility	Accountability/incentives Hands-on coaching
Employee involvement	Safety representative Safety films	Quality improvement team Behavioral safety
Response to injury and disability	See the doctor Give us a call	Employer involvement We call you

(1) a safe physical workplace, (2) effective involvement of line managers, (3) effective involvement of employees, and (4) quick and appropriate response to injured employees. Both the traditional and the modern management techniques address these four capabilities, although in different ways.

Safe Physical Workplace

The traditional approach to securing a safe physical workplace was through protective devices that reduced the risk of harm from physically dangerous and demanding work environments. Machine safeguards, steel-toed shoes, and separate storage areas for hazardous materials are traditional applications that still make sense in many work environments. With the rise in light manufacturing and service or information jobs, however, employers need additional approaches. The most prominent of these are the ergonomic solutions, such as better design of equipment, more "people-friendly" work areas, and glare screens for users of video display terminals (VDTs).

Line Manager Involvement

The involvement of line managers has always been crucial to successful safety and disability management, and here the traditional and modern approaches are somewhat alike. Accountability and incentives have been used effectively for decades and continue to be a critical part of motivating line managers to make safety and disability a priority. But instead of simple delegation of responsibility, line management today requires hands-on coaching about goals, changes, and opportunities that encompasses both senior managers coaching their subordinates and middle managers and supervisors coaching their employees and teams.

Employee Involvement

Traditionally, employees became involved in the context of hierarchical structures, which often consisted of a departmental safety representative combined with safety education such as posters, films, and "toolbox talks." In today's flatter and more empowered work environments, employee involvement is much more active and responsible. This includes having employee teams attack safety and disability problems with quality improvement techniques. It also includes behavioral safety approaches that focus on creating peer- and self-monitoring behavior.

Appropriate Responses to Injuries

Response to injury and disability was traditionally the domain of the physician and other health care professionals, with the employer waiting reactively for the employee to be sent back to work. Today, employers need to be much more involved in multiple ways, especially in developing relationships with professionals who understand the employer's needs and goals. It also includes much more proactive contact with injured employees to encourage their speedy return and the establishment of flexible working conditions to enhance the quality and speed of their transition.

Cooperative Efforts

Working together, the traditional and modern approaches to safety and disability management can capture the strengths of what has worked well in the past while adapting to a different environment. Each of the four core capabilities also work together to reduce risk and to manage forward toward minimizing lengthy disability. An excellent example of this synergy is in avoiding the intervention of attorneys in workers' compensation cases.

A workplace with good ergonomic design can reduce attorney involvement because ergonomics reduces the number of cumulative trauma injuries and also shows employees the organization's commitment to their safety and well-being. Line managers further reduce the risk of legal complications by communicating concern for the safety of employees and especially by flexible and active support for effective return to work following injury. When the organization encourages employee involvement in safety and provides education about the workers' compensation system, employees do not need to seek out lawyers for assistance or support. Employer–physician partnerships also help ensure the employee is the beneficiary of a coordinated treatment and return-to-work plan that improves results and minimizes conflict. Each of these approaches is described in more detail in the remainder of this chapter.

Ergonomics

The growth in the field of ergonomics is ironic, since it is an unanticipated result of the move away from the industrial era. Experts had predicted that injuries would decrease as mechanization and automation lightened the physical workload. Instead, automated equipment in many jobs has increased the pace of work and has concentrated the demand on smaller elements of the anatomy such as the hands and wrists. Employees may have done more physically exhausting tasks decades ago, but the demand was often more variable and was distributed more evenly across different parts of the body.

As a result, modern jobs in such areas as construction, clerical, manufacturing, and services have produced a rapid increase in cumulative trauma disorders. In many organizations, cumulative trauma now is responsible for over half of occupational injuries including repetitive strain, carpal tunnel, certain types of back injuries, and a variety of other soft-tissue ailments. These injuries have multiple causes such as intense repetitive motion, awkward positions, and poorly designed tools. Most injuries develop over weeks, months, or years; symptoms include pain, swelling, tingling, loss of feeling or strength, and muscle atrophy.

Many of these injuries result from forcing employees to adapt to the physical requirements of the job, rather than ergonomically designing the job to accommodate human capabilities and preferences. Ergonomics is particularly important as the work force ages because it is more difficult for older workers to adapt to a higher pace of activity or to repetitive, awkward tasks. In addition, good ergonomic design will often improve productivity and quality at the same time it reduces the risk of injury. A better design can improve the speed and reliability of employee performance, while also reducing the physical strain in performing the task.

Example **General Motors Corporation** General Motors has developed a better design for a windshield wiper assembly that formerly required a worker to use a heavy mechanical wrench for attaching 10 different screws. The new wiper assembly is lighter, easier to attach, and is better integrated into the overall contours of the car. General Motors therefore gets higher productivity (easier and faster to install), higher quality (less wind noise for the customer), and reduced incidence of injury—all through a better ergonomic design.[9] This same multiple benefit has been repeated in many companies in all types of industries.

Organizations interested in improving the ergonomics of their work environment can access a wide variety of approaches, ranging from formal to informal and falling into three main categories:

1. Review and redesign of ergonomic problems.
2. "Design-in" of effective safety requirements from the beginning.
3. Employee exercise and education for prevention of cumulative trauma.

Review and Redesign

To review and redesign ergonomic problems in the work environment and in areas producing the greatest cumulative trauma risk, employers can take the following steps:

- Review of workstation design, machinery, methods, and conditions to determine points of strain.
- Personal observation and employee feedback about cumulative trauma hazards.
- Employee surveys to assess points of discomfort and pain on a body diagram.
- Formal job analysis to establish ergonomic standards.
- Equipment or workstation modifications to reduce strain.
- Ergonomic job aids such as supports, pads, or guides.

"Design-In" of Safety Requirements

In contrast to the ongoing review and redesign, "design-in" seeks to ensure good ergonomics from the very beginning. Design-in means that safety considerations are integrated with productivity and quality criteria at the earliest stages of developing or purchasing work environments and equipment. This approach minimizes retrofitting and fire fighting, but it requires close cooperation among multiple parties early in and throughout the purchase or development process. Examples of design-in include:

- Seeking feedback from line managers, employees, safety professionals, and engineers when purchasing and designing equipment, work areas, and procedures.
- Getting this involvement at the earliest stages of the process rather than after initial and irrevocable design decisions have already been made.
- Seeking designs that maximize safety while improving productivity and quality.
- Gathering ergonomic data from outside sources or pilot-testing designs before implementing equipment or procedures systems wide.

Exercise and Education

Employee exercise and education is the third factor in preventing cumulative trauma injuries, since even the best physical environment can be inadequate without ready and knowledgeable employees. In many work settings, injured employees have poor physical fitness, bad posture, a lack of self-care, and little understanding of the relationship between injury and their work and personal habits. Organizations can address these issues by positioning employees as "industrial athletes" who, like all athletes, require physical and mental preparation to perform safely. This might include:

- Educating employees about the cumulative trauma risks of their jobs and how to perform tasks in ways that prevent injury.
- Periodically rotating employees to limit time spent performing repetitive tasks.
- Encouraging regular stretching exercises before and during task performance.
- Promoting good self-care and early detection of cumulative trauma problems.
- Explaining how working together to prevent cumulative trauma injuries serves employees' self-interest and the interest of the employer.

Many organizations have used these three ergonomic approaches successfully to reduce cumulative trauma injuries quite quickly. One review cited over a dozen companies that reduced cumulative trauma claims by at least 50 percent, generally within as little as a year.[10] In addition, an organization's chances for success increase by focusing not only on the physical hazards but also on employee behavior and buy-in toward ergonomic guidelines.

The National Institute on Occupational Safety and Health (NIOSH) reports that the psychosocial aspects of cumulative trauma are often as crucial as the physical and ergonomic conditions.[11] An excellent way to address these issues is to involve employees in the process, perhaps through the safety committee or a special ergonomics team. Each of the preceding approaches can also be modified to strongly promote employee buy-in. When integrated into both the physical environment and the management environment in this way, ergonomics provides additional energy and support to existing safety efforts and prevents a critical and growing source of health and disability claims.

Employee Involvement in Safety

Employee involvement has been a traditional strength of a successful safety program, as evidenced by the strong peer pressure among co-workers in leading safety organizations. These employees believe safety is truly an important part of their jobs. Today, achieving this commitment and involvement of employees is particularly important to success. First, many employees today expect such involvement and will resist safety efforts if it is not present. Second, flatter organizations mean that employees must become more involved since there are not as many supervisors to pick up the slack. Third, organizational efforts with quality improvement have given employees numerous skills that transfer extremely well to the challenges of safety.

A starting point is to use techniques that encourage involvement in general. For example, a suggestion system for employee input on a variety of topics can be used for safety as well, allowing early reporting of problems and preventing them from becoming injuries. Most employee communication methods—focus groups, regular meetings, publications, posters, videos, or surveys—can also be applied to safety quite effectively. Many organizations have used these relatively traditional approaches successfully by showing a consistent commitment to gathering and using employee ideas. It is the way this input is used that tells employees their role in safety is important.

Improvement teams are a second method for involving employees. Such teams often use techniques they have learned in quality improvement and apply them to safety and disability. For example, a cross-functional team might study the causes of current ergonomic problems and use the results to make workplace improvements or develop training for co-workers. They might use quality tools such as flowcharting, Pareto analysis, and fishbone diagrams to better understand and improve their safety procedures and might develop a measurement scheme for making everyone aware of the unit's safety performance on an ongoing basis. In fact, organizations such as IBM Rochester and Federal Express have used such teams in improving their safety effectiveness on the way to winning the Baldrige Award.

A variant of the improvement team is the safety committee, which many organizations use to conduct safety audits and develop safety procedures. Dow Chemical has also developed a program called "Safe Working Styles" that encourages employee involvement through four interventions: (1) speaking up about a safety problem, (2) redirecting the work behavior of a fellow employee, (3) praising safe work practices, and (4) using reprimand as a last resort.[12] These teams, committees, and working styles help employees take responsibility for safety that might once have been handled only by a supervisor.

A third somewhat specialized approach to safety management is called behavioral safety. This technique combines elements of feedback, goal setting, and continuous improvement to secure employee involvement. The behavioral safety approach involves six steps:

1. With the help of employees, define which job behaviors are critical to safe performance.

2. For each of these behaviors, have employees identify observable indicators of whether it is performed safely or unsafely.

3. Develop a schedule for employees to sample/observe using this list, and to record the safety of behavior in their work area.

4. After sampling, the employee observer gives his or her co-worker immediate and specific feedback about the safety of the co-worker's behavior.

5. Aggregate results for the entire work unit in terms of percentage of safe behavior. Post the results publicly to show the trend over time.

6. Use the results and trend as a source for continuous improvement of unsafe behavior.

The preceding systematic approach—actually a hybrid of employee involvement, behavior modification, and quality improvement methodologies—is often useful when traditional efforts have hit a plateau. Behavioral safety gives employees ownership over the factors that cause unsafe conditions and ensures both buy-in and understanding of safe procedures. Most importantly, it directs attention to the most sensitive safety measure available—percentage of safe behavior. Safety risks are addressed in a preventive way that is not possible by looking only at outcomes such as accidents.

One more very important way to involve employees in safety is through education. Many employees are quite unaware of safety issues in their job and at home, and they often lack knowledge of the organization's safety goals and programs as well. When employees become ill or injured, their lack of knowledge of workers' compensation increases the chance they will retain a lawyer or will become frustrated and depressed during recovery. Educating employees about these issues is an excellent way to improve their own and the organization's safety effectiveness. Topics for education include:

- The organization's current level of safety performance, how it is measured, and what the goal is.
- The personal implications of the preceding information for employees (e.g., experience of injured co-workers, impact on company competitiveness, impact on family if injured).
- The greatest causes of accidents and injuries in the work unit and how to prevent them.
- The importance of safety at home and while driving, and the safety needs of family members.
- What to do about an observed safety hazard or a symptom of injury.
- The organization's role and responsibilities if an employee is injured.

Organizations will vary in the type of employee involvement that best fits their safety needs. An organization with few safety issues might use existing communication vehicles to hear employee safety ideas or concerns. Where safety is a larger or more complex issue, teams, committees, or behavioral safety approaches may be appropriate to achieve greater involvement. Education is always appropriate, with the length and delivery method tailored to the needs of employees. The outcomes of safety efforts directly affect employees, and involving them in safety is the best way to reduce the root causes of costly accidents and injuries.

Effective Response to Injured Employees

Despite an organization's best efforts to prevent accidents and injuries, some employees inevitably will become injured or will begin to suffer pain from cumulative trauma. The organization's response in these situations is critical. In fact, years of experience suggest that response to employee injury is the area of safety that produces the most dramatic and consistent return on investment. Organizations that do this well save hundreds of lost workdays and many thousands of dollars through targeted but relatively inexpensive effort.

Example **Weyerhauser, Inc.** Weyerhauser, Inc., the Washington-based forest products company, achieved significant savings through an effective return to work and disability management system. Health care costs at Weyerhauser have risen only 5 percent annually from 1982 to 1990 during a period when costs increased by 16 percent annually for the nation as a whole. In addition, Weyerhauser's workers' compensation costs have *decreased by* 51 percent from 1984 to 1990, as shown in Table 13.2.

Achieving these tremendous savings was the result of a concerted corporate effort to get workers' compensation costs under control. The program included several key elements:[13]

- Chargebacks for disability costs make individual departments directly responsible for the injuries in their area and give departments a strong incentive to return workers' compensation recipients to work.

- Cost reports are generated to show how much is being spent on employees who are off work.

- Part of supervisors' performance review includes managing disability and maintaining contact with injured workers to show concern and interest in their rapid return.

- Guidelines and regular monitoring are used to ensure high performance and cost-effectiveness from rehabilitation vendors.

- All external service providers are trained to understand Weyerhauser's corporate culture and return-to-work programs and goals.

- Weyerhauser worked closely with the unions to win their support.

The Weyerhauser example illustrates the importance of accountability, speed, and genuine caring in effective response to injury. Accountability is essential to maintain priority and motivation for injured employees' return to work. Departmental cost chargebacks and supervisor performance reviews are excellent ways to reinforce this priority as part of everyday management. Speedy response is also essential, since disability can often be avoided or greatly minimized if the organization becomes involved from the very beginning stages of treatment. Numerous studies show that the longer

Table 13.2   Total Workers' Compensation

Year	Costs	Costs per Claim
1984	$26,100,000	$2,640
1985	$24,900,000	$3,070
1986	$16,400,000	$2,170
1987	$15,100,000	$1,950
1988	$16,500,000	$2,300
1989	$13,500,000	$2,001
1990	$12,800,000	$2,161

the employee is off work, the less likely it is the employee will return. Finally, genuine caring is equally important, since it motivates the employee to work with the organization to achieve an effective solution. Educating and involving all players (unions, vendors, supervisors, etc.) helps build a shared understanding of their critical role in helping injured employees.

Creating accountability, speed, and caring within a return-to-work program takes planning and consideration of the types of jobs, supervisors, and barriers in the organization. For example, the organization needs to identify up-front jobs that might effectively accommodate employees returning from different types of injury. Supervisors need training in how to work effectively with injured employees, both immediately after the injury and throughout the transition of restoring impaired functions. Addressing barriers to effective return to work is essential—these are often more a mind-set than a true obstacle.

Two of the most common mind-set barriers are that job accommodation costs too much and that most employees are malingerers who do not want to return to work. Both of these are unequivocally false. Research shows that at least half of job accommodations for injured employees cost nothing, 30 percent cost less than $500, and only 8 percent cost more than $2000.[14] Accommodation success is more a function of organizational flexibility and creativity than of spending money. For example, some organizations have had recuperating employees telephone customers; this service provides valuable information for the organization and helps the employee transition back to the work environment. Other organizations have reorganized duties temporarily or adjusted a workstation to accommodate an employee's limitation. The barrier is almost always manageable if the employer is motivated to do so.

Most injured employees are also not malingerers, although employee attitude is a key variable in determining the length and severity of disability. Many injured employees begin to feel anxious and alienated toward their work if the employer does not encourage them. They may think they will no longer have the respect of co-workers and supervisors if they cannot immediately perform 100 percent as before. Organizations must therefore be proactive with early and consistent reassurance to avoid lengthy disabilities and expensive litigation. For the small minority of employees who are physically or psychologically unable to return to work, this early and consistent support still helps reconcile their situation more quickly and amicably and reduces the risk of lawsuit.

Two additional payoffs to employers make effective response to injury especially attractive. First, quick and compassionate response during a time of trauma builds tremendous employee loyalty to the organization. Effective response thus makes a strong contribution to the culture by reducing turnover or absenteeism and by fostering employee willingness to work hard and support company goals. Second, effective response is a core part of compliance with the Americans with Disabilities Act and the goal of maintaining the skills and knowledge of injured employees through rapid reentry into the work force. As shown by the example of Weyerhauser and numerous other organizations, these advantages can be obtained at the same time the employer is achieving dramatic reductions in health and disability costs.

Effective Measures for Safety and Workers' Compensation

Managers interested in charting the progress of their safety and workers' compensation efforts can choose from a range of measurements. Each of these supplies somewhat different information and can be valuable for understanding exactly where improvement opportunities are greatest. Unfortunately, these measures can also create confusion if not understood and used appropriately. The following are six of the most commonly used measures:

1. *OSHA Recordable Rate.* This is the number of injuries incurred that did not involve employee lost time. For example, a cut that is treated at the work site is a recordable. This statistic is often reported per 100 employees.

2. *Lost Workday Case Rate.* This is the number of injuries incurred that do involve employee lost time. For example, a carpal tunnel injury where the employee stays home for three days to rest his or her arm is a lost workday case. Again, this measure is often reported per 100 employees.

3. *Wage Loss Claim Rate.* This is the number of injuries in which the employee misses enough workdays for the claim to involve wage loss payments under the workers' compensation system (often after seven consecutive lost workdays).

4. *Lost Workdays per Case.* This is simply the number of lost workdays resulting from each lost-work-time claim.

5. *Lost Workdays per 100 Employees.* This is the total number of lost workdays for the organization, divided by the number of employees, and reported as an average per 100 employees.

6. *Workers' Compensation Losses per Employee.* This is the actual dollar costs to the organization of workers' compensation payments, reported as an average per employee.

Although each of these measures is related, the differences among them can be helpful in problem solving. A useful way to think about them is that measures 1 and 2 delineate frequency; 3 and 4, severity; and 5 and 6, overall impact on the organization. Thus, the first two measures indicate how often injuries are occurring (both without and with lost time). The middle two measures indicate how serious the injuries are (in terms of wage loss and number of days per case). The last two measures combine the impact of both frequency and severity in terms of cost for the organization.

Trends among each of these measures suggest somewhat different management approaches, especially when the results are considered as a total picture. For example, the recordable rate (measure 1) is the most sensitive of the six gauges, since it indicates how often injuries are occurring even if they do not involve lost time. An organization with a high recordable rate and low levels of lost time is usually doing an excellent job of surfacing injuries early and dealing with them before they turn into lost time cases. To further improve prevention efforts, this employer needs only to look for trends in the types of recordables reported.

By contrast, an organization that has low levels of frequency (measures 1 and 2) but a very high number of lost workdays per case (measure 4) needs to improve its response to injured workers. This pattern would indicate that safety is working well through low frequency of injuries, but once injured, employees are off work for a long time. The organization needs to strengthen its return-to-work program and consider the use of case managers for high-risk disability cases.

Organizations that monitor only the overall measures (5 and 6) can miss the information available from more specific frequency and severity measures that help direct continuous improvement. On the other hand, it is essential to monitor these overall measures to establish the bottom-line impact of safety and disability management efforts. Typically, all these measures are collected or easily retrievable and can greatly benefit the management of safety and workers' compensation.

Widely sharing results from these measures with line managers and employees helps them understand the organization's needs and goals. For simplicity, the organization might report only the one or two measures believed to have the most leverage on the safety and disability effort. Some organizations report only absolute numbers such as the number of lost workdays, without adjusting it per 100 employees. Adjusted numbers can cause complacency if the department or facility is better than average, whereas absolute numbers show the size of improvement still possible. Lastly, additional forms of measurement such as percent safe behavior and gauges of process safety management are now emerging in an attempt to better integrate diverse elements of safety at the operational level.[15]

Linking Safety On and Off the Job

Today's world of 24-hour exposure means that organizations cannot confine their safety efforts only to the workplace. Employees carry their level of risk and injury with them both on and off the job. Dependents represent a significant opportunity for safety intervention and reductions in health care and disability costs. Attitudes about safety from both employees and dependents affect overall health habits, driving practices, and lifestyles in general.

Emphasizing safety for family members and safety while away from work is particularly important because this message is often not communicated by health care providers. Many providers are not knowledgeable about safety or are oriented more toward care for the results of unsafe activities than toward prevention. Employers can help fill this gap by expanding the scope of their safety outreach to include key causes of off-work accidents and injuries. Two examples of this approach are driving safety and child safety.

Driving safety is a natural area of involvement for employers since driving is closely connected to work and is also a major source of accidents and disability. This importance is illustrated by results for traumatic brain injury, a major factor in long-term disability cases. Driving is the principal risk factor for these injuries, accounting for nearly half of brain injury incidents nationally (other than brain injury caused by stroke, anoxia, etc.):[16]

Risk Factor	Percentage
Car, motorcycle, and bicycle accidents	48
Falls and accidents at home	20
Industrial accidents	15
Assaults	7
Other	10

The preceding statistics are just one example of a wealth of evidence showing driving to be one of the most significant safety risks in modern life. Organizations can use such data in training and communications with employees and dependents to motivate them toward safe driving practices. A variety of national and community nonprofit agencies offer attractive and interesting information on driving topics such as the benefits of seat belt use or the dangers of driving while intoxicated. The employer can also reinforce these points through policies for driving company vehicles, through publicizing how many employees are wearing seat belts when they enter company parking ramps, or through lunchtime speakers from an organization such as Mothers Against Drunk Driving.

Extensive information is also available for child safety, another important issue affecting the whole family. Information about falls, accidents, poisoning, and walking or biking safety can be tailored to meet the needs of different parts of the employee population, timed for delivery at key points in children's development or activities. For example, information could be delivered to parents when children are first learning to walk, are starting school, or are about to begin summer vacation. Again, community resources and speakers are often readily available at little or no cost. Promoting the health and safety of children is a positive message to employees and an excellent way to prevent tragic and expensive injuries.

In addition to education and communication, organizations can also reinforce home safety through a variety of events and actions. Safety can be a key part of organizational health fairs, with exhibits or activities that highlight safety messages. Employers can also sponsor a family bicycling event and distribute free bicycle helmets to all participants. Some organizations offer free or subsidized child car seats to encourage safety or sponsor coloring contests for children around safety themes. Such actions involve the whole family and emphasize that a safe lifestyle does not begin and end at work.

Safety and a Culture of Health

Workplace and personal safety are an integral part of an organization's total health culture. Attitudes, behaviors, and lifestyle habits that employees acquire through involvement with safety often carry over into other areas of health, such as wellness, stress management, and drug and alcohol use. Another benefit is that supervisors often generalize lessons learned in promoting safety and disability management into promoting other areas of health. In addition, employees whose injury or disability is managed effectively and compassionately are often strong advocates of the organization's commitment and goals related to health.

In many respects, safety is the least threatening of an organization's health interventions. No one wants to be involved in an accident or injury, and most employees and family members appreciate an employer's concern for their safety. Perhaps because safety programs have been around for several decades, employees accept them as a legitimate arena for active employer involvement. Safety is in the best interests of all parties, since accidents or injuries negatively affect family members, co-workers, supervisors, and employees themselves. Most employees support the use of strong action to eliminate dangerous practices and conditions quickly.

Safety and disability management contributes to the economic well-being of all by providing an excellent record of return on investment, a return that has often been harvested through significant reductions in workers' compensation costs in as little as one year. Safety and disability management should therefore be a key element of an organization's total strategy for improving health and controlling cost. Linking safety efforts with other health promotion and management activities will strengthen the organization's health message to line managers and employees and will reduce the costs of health and disability as well as of workers' compensation.

References

1. Scannell, G. F. October 1990. OSHA's new safety initiatives. *Insurance Review,* p. 36.
2. Venter, G. G. September 21, 1992. Workers' compensation: Are there solutions? *National Underwriter,* pp. 45–62.
3. National Council on Compensation Insurance. 1991. *Issues report, 1991.* Boca Raton, FL: NCCI.
4. Venter. Workers' compensation.
5. Tompkins, N. C. January 1992. America's leaders in safety management. *Occupational Health & Safety,* pp. 29–60.
6. Morehouse, J. 1992. Safety programs help cut workers' compensation costs. *Business and Health,* pp. 72–75.
7. Ibid.
8. Kunz, L. 1991. All Plastics molds a healthier culture. *The Human Factor,* 3(3):4–5.
9. General Motors Corporation. 1992. *ProAct Plant Safety.* Detroit, MI: GMC.
10. Hebert, L. October 1992. Body at work. *Occupational Health and Safety,* pp. 48–58.
11. Millar, D. October 1992. Trends in the health and safety industry. *Occupational Health and Safety,* pp. 26–27.
12. Tompkins, N. C. January 1992. America's leaders in safety management. *Occupational Health & Safety,* pp. 29–60.
13. Akabas, S. H., Gates, L. B., & Galvin, D. E. 1992. *Disability Management.* New York: AMACOM.
14. Collignon, F.C. 1986. The role of reasonable accommodation in employing disabled persons in private industry. In *Disability and labor market.* M. Berkowitz & M. A. Hill (eds.), pp. 196–241. Ithaca, NY: ILR Press.
15. Kuritz, S. J. October 1992. A holistic approach to process safety. *Occupational Health and Safety,* pp. 28–37.
16. Galvin, D. E., Lipoff, E., & Carbine, M. E. September 1990. *Report from the Third Annual National Disability Management Conference.* Washington Business Group on Health, Washington, DC.

Resources

American Society of Safety Engineers
1800 East Oakton Street
Des Plaines, IL 60018-2187
(312) 692-4121

Provides information, networking, conferences, and professional education to those working in the safety field. Addresses a range of safety issues such as supervisor training, ergonomics, and physical hazard control.

National Institute for Occupational Safety and Health
Building 1, Room 3106
1600 Clifton Road NE
Atlanta, GA 30333
(404) 329-3778

Conducts research, provides education and communication, and acts as a government advocate for improved workplace safety and health. Possesses diverse expertise
including workplace stress and mental health, ergonomics, and workplace environmental hazards.

National Safety Council
444 North Michigan Avenue
Chicago, IL 60611
(800) 621-7619
(312) 527-4800 (Illinois)

Provides education, research, and advocacy related to increasing safety in all areas of
life, including home, driving, and family safety. Maintains statistics regarding the
level of safety in the United States.

University of Michigan Center for Ergonomics
1205 Beal, Room 172-IOE
Ann Arbor, MI 48109-2117
(313) 763-2243

Conducts research and provides education related to ergonomic improvements to
workplace safety, quality, and productivity. Addresses a wide range of ergonomic
issues in the workplace.

University of Southern California Institute of Safety and Systems
3500 South Figueroa Street, Suite 202
Los Angeles, CA 90007
(213) 743-6523

Provides professional training and conducts research related to safety systems and
factors affecting their performance. Emphasizes a systems framework for understanding safety.

Washington Business Group on Health and U.S. Public Service
National Resource Center on Worksite Health Promotion
777 North Capitol Street NE, Suite 800
Washington, DC 20002
(202) 408-0325

Provides information on disability management, return-to-work, and job accommodation for injured or disabled employees. Links employers together to share experiences and strategies for improving disability management.

14

Conclusion: Achieving the Full Promise of Strategy-Based Solutions

One person's problem is another person's opportunity. The same is true for organizations. Health care, workers' compensation, and disability costs have become a serious financial exposure, yet organizations addressing these costs on a systematic basis, that encompasses the cost of health and disability in operations as well, can achieve clear cost breakthroughs in their cost structure and health-related productivity.

This opportunity is great regardless of changes in state and federal public policies for health care and workers' compensation. Organizations that manage the root causes of health and disability will always have significant cost and employment advantages. Employers are directly connected to health and disability issues through health and safety risks in the workplace, return to work, and health-related productivity. The key is to develop a comprehensive view that proactively addresses the causes of costs. Involved line management and coordinated and integrated functional management are essential elements for developing management solutions.

The evidence of the ability of organizations to achieve superior results in managing health and disability costs comes in many forms:

- Two broad-based studies show disability cost experience to be more related to employer management practices than to macrohealth or industry factors.
- Significant cost dispersion between the high and low performers in disability management shows the cost leverage available from high performance due to good management practices.

- Documented results from leading organizations show the paybacks from effective health and safety programs. Even without broad-based and integrated health and disability management, some organizations have achieved continuing success in cost performance through proactive management combined with a limited group of focused programs.

Far greater leverage exists over costs than has been commonly applied. Many employers are already obtaining a more direct connection between risk and cost through experience rating and self-insurance. This connection increases the payback for capitalizing on the comprehensive and systematic approaches to cost management in this book. The issue is not one of capping costs at today's unacceptable levels. The organizational goal instead should be transformation in the level of health and disability costs based on an employer-specific health and disability strategy, as shown in Table 14.1.

These programs are some of the best in the country. The strategy-based, health system approach in this book targets workers' compensation and cost of health and disability in operations as well as health care. The cost–benefit

Table 14.1 Health as an Investment: Evidence from the Best Comprehensive Programs

Organization	Approach	Results
City of Birmingham, Alabama Medium-size public entity	Active, multifaceted wellness program combined with HMO	Health care costs were flat from 1985 to 1990, saving estimated $30 million from prior trend
Standard Telephone, Inc. Small telephone company	Active wellness and employee involvement in health	Spends 8% of payroll on health care costs compared with 14% nationally; per capita costs reduced
Johnsonville Foods, Inc. Medium-size meat-preparation company	Team-based, empowering environment with strong commitment to quality	1991 total health care costs of $1900 per employee, 50% lower than national rate
Quad Graphics, Inc. Medium-size printing company	Strong culture of encouraging employee involvement/responsibility	1991 health care costs per employee of $2350, 33% lower than national rate
Weyerhauser, Inc. Large-size forest products company	Very active safety, disability management and return to work programs	Workers' compensation costs reduced by 51% from 1984 to 1990 saving over $50 million
Leaf Inc. Small-size candy company	Strong employee involvement in quality and safety	Workers' compensation costs reduced by 35% from 1986 to 1991 versus a national average increase of 82%

ratio of an improved health and disability cost structure translates into enhanced predictability of future performance. Apart from profitability and cash flow gains, organizations with a solid health-oriented benefits package can finance faster growth and attract the best talent.

Employers have traditionally kept a low profile in health and disability matters. Despite funding most of the costs of health care and workers' compensation, they have tended to assume the role of agent between employee and provider, insurer, and third-party manager. Today's cost levels, everincreasing exposures, and the changed characteristics of modern health and disability issues now require more active employer involvement. Employers are also in the best position to do something about costs when they address the broader health system and the individualized needs of their covered population instead of limiting themselves to contracting with the care system. Operations issues are as important as benefits issues in this broader perspective.

Although counterintuitive in terms of past practices, employers can address health and disability in the same manner as other business issues by identifying the entire spectrum of health and disability activities as part of an employer/employee health system. When strategy links with a systems framework, employers are applying the highest value added in terms of management on the most critical health and disability issues for their covered population. The best health and care services can thereby be obtained over time, but even more importantly information can support management at every level. This approach emphasizes optimization—managing risk and reducing costs through focused investment—not minimization based on containing costs alone.

When organizations focus only on cost containment, a care perspective limits the potential for significant cost and quality breakthroughs. Prevention and rehabilitation remain unfunded or underfunded with major cost implications for employers because the emphasis then is on industrial age medicine, not information age health.

The new focus on quality by health care providers is important, but the basic system remains provider centered, not consumer centered. Fundamental health problems are being ignored, and no new management strategies for employers are being brought to bear. Achieving cost and quality breakthroughs requires the much broader strategies of a quality-based health system where the consumer role of employer and employee can be given appropriate balance and where total value can be emphasized in health and productivity, as well as in care.

Developing a Systems Framework

Health as a management issue is everywhere within organizations, yet it is nowhere. Health care and workers' compensation usually receive direct attention, rather than organizational health as the determinant of costs.

In broad systems terms, the care delivery system is only part of the overall health system. The worlds of work and home, not just the world of care, need full consideration to systematically address and manage the root causes of costs and the quality of activities by employees, dependents, and line supervisors, as well as by senior management, functional management, providers, and third parties.

All participants have a role in the health continuum that links health, health care, and disability. The emphasis on Managing Forward toward health through interventions often prevents the need for care, while promoting early treatment and outcomes when care becomes necessary. Optimizing utilization toward health interventions and away from treatment interventions is the goal. In addition, disability management can be linked into overall health and health care programs to support a return to individual functioning in both health care and workers' compensation cases.

Integrating health and disability at the line level is even more critical than doing so at the provider and third-party manager levels. In this way, health and disability become day-to-day accountabilities in the organization's culture. A health systems approach stresses the role of employees (and dependents) in managing personal health and the role of line supervisors in managing health-related productivity. Measurement, accountabilities, incentives, and risk sharing can all tap into self-interest when information is employed strategically.

By combining an individualized health and disability strategy with a health systems framework, employers not only can control costs, but can exercise considerable leverage to proactively reduce costs. This book identifies the following three-part management system to achieve this result:

1. *Managing Health.* An intervention approach.
2. *Managing Care.* A systematic approach to obtaining value for required care.
3. *Managing Productivity.* Integration of health and disability in the workplace to support health at the line level, while managing disability as a personal and organizational productivity issue.

This systematic approach for managing health and disability must be rooted in the characteristics of an individual organization, and so health itself needs to become part of the organizational culture. Success in managing health and disability costs will be greatest when employers emphasize health as a cultural value. Health is a natural complement to quality and productivity. And organizational health can be equated to an organization's financial health, while supporting an employee's personal and family health.

Development of a health culture is essential for achieving the full benefit of systematic health and disability management. Integration and staying power are derived through cultural influences. All too often, employers sow health programs and related financial incentives in barren organizational soil. These programs can accomplish little if employees lack empowerment, and line managers provide inadequate reinforcement in managing health and safety risks.

An organizational culture of health provides both formal and informal activities directly related to supervisory behavior, employee involvement, wellness, employee mental health, and safety. These activities take root in the broader context of culture[1] as follows:

- *Authority.* Formal and informal clout.
- *Values.* Beliefs or principles held in high regard.
- *Norms.* Standards of behavior.
- *Rewards.* Benefits of good behavior.
- *Sanctions.* Punishments and pressures used against anyone who violates the norms.

Many employers have failed to achieve full organizational effectiveness because they did not relate health to these cultural factors before developing health, health care, and disability programs. The power of a health culture is essential for success in controlling and reducing health and disability costs. Culture comes from senior management's vision and the shared experiences of an organization. The following areas provide direct expressions of culture:

- Relationship between management and employees.
- Sense of mutual responsibility between employees.
- Value of the individual as expressed by the organization.
- Individual's sense of self-worth.

These cultural influences allow organizations to achieve lasting results in health and disability issues. By stressing health in all activities, employers can reinforce the interconnections between participants in the health system at the most personal level without intruding into private matters.

Achieving Continuous Learning and Continuous Improvement

The cost breakthrough potential of health and disability strategy within a health systems framework relates to individualized strategy-based solutions. Organizations that tailor strategies and programs to their particular situation will achieve significant control and a lower health and disability cost structure than those operating with generalized programs. In addition, providing individualized health, health care, and disability at the employee level will obtain the best results. This focus on human values underpins the systematic management framework and program solutions in this book.

Relating management to the individual manager and individual employee changes the emphasis from control to learning, and dependency gives way to empowerment. There is no better area for a "Learning Organization"[2] than health—the most personal issue. Managers and employees can develop the techniques of learning-based management on an issue that directly affects them and their families. As workers develop these skills, they can apply them to products and services. In the meantime, the organization is addressing one of its most serious structural cost issues and obtaining related benefits in quality and productivity.

Learning is by definition a continuous information process involving all aspects of an organization. Just as employees need empowerment, management needs to provide leadership and direction. The starting point is to make health and disability a mainstream issue at the level of organizational strategy where it will demand greater management attention. This is only natural in view of today's cost exposures. Even more compelling are the cost opportunities related to the total cost of health and disability when all direct, indirect, and hidden costs are included.

Because this strategic cost target cuts across all organizational boundaries and encompasses key external relationships, it requires senior management leadership direction as well as a shared vision within the organization. Starting the learning process to gain this strategic advantage requires a call for action and change that reorients everyone's perspective toward personal and organizational health. This will establish a continuous learning and improvement process in health and disability at every level. The following 10 points identify the elements of a broad-based plan for accomplishing this strategic redirection:

1. Develop a health and disability strategy, integrated with separate insurance and benefits strategies. Identify health and disability as an accountability for regular review at the operating level as both an organizational cost and quality issue.

2. Identify improvement targets across the organization:

    Quality and health measures.

    A range of costs within the total cost of health and disability.

    Best opportunities for managing health and safety activities.

3. Develop an integrated management system encompassing the three management tracts of health, care, and productivity and tied to individual health, health care, and disability programs.

4. Develop or refocus formal and informal interventions that support health as a key aspect of culture including supervisory behavior, employee involvement, wellness, mental health, and safety.

5. Integrate and identify functional accountabilities between Human Resources, Benefits, Risk Management, Finance, Safety, and Health:

Develop an ongoing team effort, utilizing the management information system.

Closely manage the role of external consultants and third parties.

6. Involve line management in health and disability issues:

Identify health and disability as a direct accountability.

Identify measurable performance targets and related incentives.

7. Manage all third parties and providers directly:

Establish rigorous terms and conditions in all relationships.

Provide prospective, concurrent, and retrospective review.

Create incentives based on value criteria and risk sharing.

8. Connect employees and dependents directly in health and disability issues:

Encourage broad participation and personalization of a health culture.

Implement health incentives emphasizing organizational issues as well as personal ones.

Involve family members in health and safety activities.

9. Develop information as a key point of strategic leverage:

Provide up-front information and training to all participants.

Give continuous information feedback emphasizing control, performance, and investment.

10. Develop external relationships:

Consider employer coalitions.

Consider partnerships with providers and third parties.

Comprehensive and involved management is the key to lasting success in health and disability across all cost elements. Through continuous learning and improvement, management can move up the curve toward strategy-based, systems solutions, as follows:

Level	Management Issue	Strategy
1	Numbers	Cost containment and risk avoidance approaches
2	Plan	Annualized management of health care and workers' compensation
3	Processes	Continuous management of health and disability (structural issues)
4	System	Continuous management of health and disability (systems and cultural issues)

Moving from Level 2 to Level 3 represents a big change because management can no longer be annualized. Instead, root causes of costs and the quality of underlying activities need to be addressed. And when management moves from Level 3 to Level 4, the focus is on broader systems interconnection between all internal and external parties. The worlds of work, home, and care are fully connected through internal culture and external coalitions and partnerships. When operationalizing this type of involved management, small employers can effect change through cultural transformation faster than large employers with more complex environments.

Information both starts and stops the sequence of events. No one can diagnose a problem and related opportunity without information, but information will often be incomplete or will have to be partially estimated. Although such limitations can be addressed over time, there is really little difference in managing the uncertainties inherent in health and disability than in managing other organizational issues. The only reason information may be more limited is that no one previously focused on ensuring comprehensive, quality data. In fact, the starting level of understanding is usually low because the organizational attention span for health and disability has been similarly low. When employers continuously develop information for management, learning turns to understanding, the truest measure of effective management.

Managing Risk, Not Just Financing It

Movement toward a proactive role in health and disability by employers ultimately leads to the issue of risk. Unfortunately, the past practice of fully insuring risk as part of group-rated coverages has led to an exclusive fixation on risk in financial terms only. Organizations have typically financed risk as a cost of doing business rather than managing it systematically. Even loss control can result in a reactive, claims orientation unless rooted in an overall risk management strategy.

With the trend toward experience rating and self-insurance, organizations can manage underlying health and safety risks apart from financial risks. A continuous improvement approach to managing health and safety risks can occur simultaneously with a prudent program to anticipate highly uncertain large dollar claims through combined self-insured and insured financial risks. This integrated organizational effort is necessary in a world of changing health and disability exposures and advancing medical technologies.

An exclusive financial risk orientation characterizes the historical health care and workers' compensation system. Breaking free of traditional limitations requires management of risk based on a health system, not a care system. Table 14.2 shows the characteristics of this new form of risk management.

By just financing risk, employers take on the role of in-house insurers. Nothing may be done differently to manage the underlying health and safety risks. This book presents an integrated framework to implement a

Table 14.2   Contrasting Forms of Risk Management

Characteristics	Care System	Health System
Employer management	Underinvolved, reactive	Involved, proactive
Prime financial issue	Liability	Cost
Prime risk issue	Financial risk	Underlying health and safety risks, backed by prudent management of financial risks
Goal	Manage to obligation	Manage to outcome
Prime risk strategy	Avoidance	Prevention

new form of proactive risk management in all health activities, involving all participants. The emphasis is on Managing Forward along the health continuum to eliminate, reduce, and control the probability of injury, illness, reduced functioning, and disability, as well as the most intensive forms of care and threat of litigation. This approach addresses cumulative health and disability issues up front, while the health emphasis creates an important bond between management and employees.

Through systematic management of risk, employers can manage uncertainty in health and disability issues. They achieve more control and less uncertainty by taking action to reduce the frequency, severity, and duration of potential health and disability events. The probability of follow-up care also declines and the best possible outcomes are obtained when the number of transactions and their individual intensity decline.

The issue of managing, not financing, risk is an unappreciated opportunity for significantly reducing the costs of health and disability while improving health and the quality of care. Figure 14.1 shows risk as a range of probabilities. Health and safety risks fall along the risk curve, where the probability of human events and underlying activities are either under control or not under control. The extent to which control over risk exists is the degree to which activities are managed to the right on the curve. Control is obtained through the employees' management of personal activities and behaviors and through organizational management as well.

The risk curve points out a number of problems in today's care system:

- Individuals are not sufficiently informed and trained to manage health and safety risks in their lives, nor to understand the inherent uncertainties in treatment.
- Employers are not fully managing the health and safety risks within their operations.
- Providers are trying to control health and safety risks through facility-based environments and advanced technologies, not through systematic management.

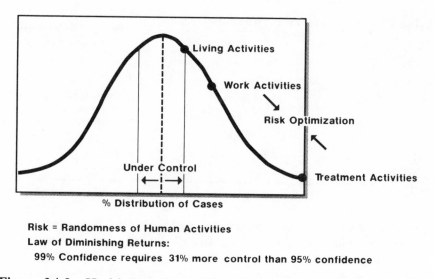

Risk = Randomness of Human Activities
Law of Diminishing Returns:
  99% Confidence requires 31% more control than 95% confidence

Figure 14.1 Health Risk Curve: The Management Opportunity (RHM Systems, Inc., 1993, Marlboro, MA)

- There is a need to coalign the understanding of health and safety risks by employees and dependents, employers, and providers.

The result of these problems is unmanaged and undermanaged risks that cause excessive costs. Through proactive risk management, employers can promote the role of employees and dependents in personally managing individual health and safety risks. Relationships between patients and physicians will change as patients become able to comanage their treatment, but more importantly, to manage their health in ways that make treatment unnecessary. Failure to involve employees and dependents fully in personal risk management is a primary reason for the limited success and staying power of many employer-funded health programs.

An informed and empowered consumer may present a challenge to physicians and clinical professionals, but it also represents a major source of opportunity for providers. By linking up with patients to manage risks individually as an underlying health and safety issue rather than collectively as a sole financial issue, providers can help reduce costs and improve quality of care. Traditionally, providers have also viewed risk in insurance terms. Management is thus geared toward limiting the possibility of an "incident," and if one occurs, to ensuring that in-place damage control mechanisms limit the financial exposure.[3]

Health care's inability to respond to the malpractice crisis is centered in this narrow, defensive view. Instead of managing risk, many providers have sought to eliminate it through technology. Management requires individualized treatment focusing on outcomes that identify the risk/reward trade-offs of diagnostic and treatment procedures for the patient's benefit. Instead, health care has emphasized generalized treatment rooted in processes, not outcomes, commonly applied in facility settings.

Risk as a probability measure can be expressed in relation to outcome, but it cannot be expressed in terms of process. This is a critical element in health care's malpractice exposure—risk often remains undermanaged because treatment fails to identify individual outcome goals and related risks of reduced functioning and disability in advance. Just as important is that the patient and related family members are not fully involved in risk decisions nor supported afterward when outcomes are not achieved.

Providers who capitalize on this new form of risk management[4] will gain some significant advantages:

- Consistency in diagnostic and treatment practices, thereby benefiting quality of care.
- Direct connection of risk/reward decision making to individual circumstances, thereby enhancing case documentation and creating improved customer service.
- Direct management of expectancies of patient and family members throughout treatment to control reactions and legal exposures.
- Reduction of costs by combining proactive risk management with absorption of levels of self-insured risks for professional liability exposures.

Today's malpractice costs are a sign that risks can no longer be managed as a damage control issue only, nor financed as a cost of doing business. The exposures were minimal in the old world of a family physician who acted as case manager. Little technology was available, and specialists or third-party managers were seldom engaged. The world has now changed profoundly. Legal exposures have increased because many parties are involved in every case and advanced technology has created the spectra of life and death decision making. In fact, attorneys are zeroing in on the poorly managed interconnections within the system while using the power of information to identify cases of unmanaged or undermanaged risks.

Disarming the attorneys requires managed risks. Employers are paying double, for undermanaged risks in their own workplace and for the passed-through costs of undermanaged risks in the provider world. What is surprising to most observers is that the interests of employers and providers merge when managed risk drives waste out of the system.

Developing a Level Playing Field

When employers adopt a systems view of health and disability, they can identify the activities and behaviors of all participants, apart from coverages, programs, and plans. Management can then focus on interconnections within the system rather than on isolated parts of the system. The quality of the interconnections between providers and between provider and home or work can be just as important as some treatment stages in between. Management of these interconnections within an individualized health system framework will minimize waste and litigation, while improving the quality of health and disability services.

Applying a systems view to the broader world of health, health care, and disability involving all employers presents a challenge. Excess health and disability costs are currently being incurred for the following reasons:

1. Claims by new employees and dependents who have delayed health care increase costs because the human body degenerates toward disease if health issues are not addressed in a timely manner.

2. Organizations with good benefits programs end up absorbing a higher than normal percentage of dependents for coverage because other employers are paying incentives to drop coverage.

3. Organizations absorb undermanaged health and safety risks from other employers in workers' compensation assigned risk pools and residuals and from community-rated and group-rated health care plans.

4. Organizations absorb shifting overall health care costs because of termination of employees or even health care coverage by other employers.

Apart from these potential costs, excess complexity has been created in the transfer of employees and dependents between coverages. Some employers provide immediate coverage and no preexisting condition limitations; others provide immediate coverage but have a preexisting condition limitation; and still others have a three- to six-month probationary period before coverage eligibility. At the same time, employees are fully covered for workers' compensation, even if not for health care. Employees in a fluid labor market fall through the cracks as a result—experiencing problems in obtaining coverage, in receiving care at the right time, and in having coverage for serious illness or injury.

These frayed interconnections within the broader health system combined with the transfer of excess costs between employers are a sign of risk avoidance running out of control. For every risk transferred to someone else, another is absorbed. Avoidance is now like a game of chicken. No one dares to stop. In the meantime, risk managers and benefits managers are preoccupied with financing or avoiding risk, not managing it through prevention strategies. Costs are thus increased through care needs delayed or unmet and unnecessary administration and legal costs.

On a systemwide basis and ultimately for every employer, current avoidance strategies are raising costs, not lowering them. Creation of a level playing field in terms of minimum coverages could actually lower costs for many employers. The key is to minimize the cost burden on small employers while eliminating the cost subsidies of organizations that are not effectively managing their internal risks. The requirements that employers could support for both insured and self-insured health care on a national basis include:

- Eliminate redlining or noncoverage by group insurers by requiring risk rating to encompass a risk-sharing element between employer and insurer even in the policy period.
- Eliminate all preexisting condition limitations.
- Create a common eligibility rule at time of hire.
- Establish common rules on dependent eligibility.
- Share dependent coverage exposure between employers.
- Require mandatory employee coverage—no opt out without coverage.
- Set minimum part-time standard down to 30 hours per week.
- Require coverage by current employer only.

The concept of employer-based health care needs to be approached as a health issue, not just a care issue. Employers are benefiting from an individual's productive capacity, therefore employee health is in an employer's self-interest. Coverage for all could be tied to an employer's health care program so that all employees and related dependents plus part-time employees and contract staff are eligible. This would provide access to almost all for whatever level of coverage they wanted to pay for.

At the same time, mandatory employer-paid coverage might be limited to full-time employees. It might also be limited to fully paid health features, preventive care, and major medical for catastrophic and chronic care, inclusive of rehabilitation and long-term care. This approach would create the proper health incentives, eliminate carte blanche subsidy of an illness, injury, and disability system, and provide better care for the most serious cases. It would also provide universal access and risk diversification within the context of an employer-centered health system.

Addressing a Major Social and Business Issue—
Serious Care Needs

One of the biggest challenges in creating a systematic solution to health and disability issues is to address the special problems presented by serious care needs. Major social questions are inherent in cases ranging from high-cost, advanced medical care to disability of a catastrophic and chronic nature to long-term care for the elderly. These cases have many dimensions for individuals and their families, including financial and health requirements as well as social issues.

An estimated 43 million persons in the United States have one or more disabilities. Disability may be related to a hereditary condition, but an important phenomenon is the rising level of functional and activity limitation by age, as shown in the following percentages:[5]

Age	Percentage of Functional and Activity Limitation
Under 18	3.7– 5.1
18–44	8.2–10.1
45–64	22.7–31.9
65 and over	28.0–58.7

This assessment of functional and activity limitation does not directly translate into inability to work. What it does show is the cumulative nature of acquired functional limitations as people age, and it acts as a barometer of workplace impact. The main causes are orthopedic impairments, arthritis, and heart disease, with hypertension and brain injury becoming increasingly important modern conditions.

The challenges to employers are threefold:

1. To manage health-related productivity among an increasingly aging work force.
2. To proactively manage both health and disability among current and prospective employees.
3. To respond to these human health needs without exposing an organization to financial ruin.

In a world of intense domestic and international competition, organizations cannot compete while being fully subjected to the financial exposure of random health events. An employee and/or dependent may have a hereditary condition or be the victim of random violence or an auto accident. These issues underscore the crucial need for a level playing field.

Government has a natural role among the elderly, the unemployed, and the most seriously disabled after employer-based supports are fully utilized. However, much more can be done to address the issue of serious care needs among the working population and their dependents. Financial liability might be defined to no-fault lifetime maximums of $1 million or $2 million spread between a coalition of employers or group-rated excess insurance above certain self-insured amounts. The continued definition of some level of self-insured financial risk creates the incentive to proactively manage controllable health and safety risks at the individual employer level.

Today's crisis with serious care needs is manifest in personal bankruptcies and unreimbursed health care to providers. Patients suffer when care does not include rehabilitation because of financial constraints and when disputes take place between insurers responsible for workers' compensation, health care, automobile, and liability policies. Complications are even greater when self-insured employers, primary and excess insurers, and reinsurers get involved at various levels of financial risk. And when all these dueling policies and coverage levels are threatened by real or potential litigation, cases stand still. Patients suffer and lawyers prosper. Legal costs are borne by all and contingency fees are collected. Meanwhile, persons with a disability often wait in limbo. When settlements are made, what may appear to be large sums to an individual or family can be quickly consumed by the serious health issues involved in a lifetime of disability.

Today's overwhelming focus on financial liability undermines optimal management of health for persons with a disability. Prescribed coverages are often licenses to spend on nonoptimal forms of care. Most of today's funding goes to acute medical treatment, continuing medical care, and long-term care facilities, not to home and community services for rehabilitation, and assisted and supported living. The implications for today's patients with impaired or limited functioning and related family members are limited choices that raise costs, not lower them, as follows:

- Transfer of a working-age adult into a skilled nursing facility when rehabilitation could enable the person to live at home.
- Inadequate funding for vocational rehabilitation in health care coverages preventing a return to work by employees with limited functioning after a surgical procedure.
- When non-goal-directed, rehabilitation can result in wasted funding. Once funding has been consumed, the patient may be returned home without having developed supports based on a long-term living plan.

The needs of those with a newly acquired disability relate to health, not just care. By focusing on individual functioning levels as the measure of health, patients, related family members, and employers could emphasize proactive management of health to optimize an individualized care plan.

As with this book's health system approach in general, the greatest opportunity for proactive management relates to segmenting the financial risk apart from the underlying health and safety risk. Cases might then no longer be managed toward reserve levels, but toward the best possible functional outcomes. This would optimize and potentially reduce costs instead of focusing on the maximum liability exposure. Worse than wasted spending on cases of serious care needs is the cost created by the funds not being spent and in a timely manner. Everyone wants to cap spending on the most expensive cases, but counterintuitively, these are often the cases where a small amount of additional spending can create the greatest incremental return on investment for an employer, if not for an insurer involved in a one-year policy.

Outcome-directed rehabilitation is the best form of prevention on the most costly and risky cases. Return to work always needs to be considered with today's information-driven support technologies. Even seemingly small outcomes, however, can create major financial and human benefits. A person with a severe disability who learns to turn him- or herself in bed prevents the need for 24-hour attendant care, creating annual savings of $100,000 per year for a lifetime. Productivity is also a personal issue as well as a workplace one. The quality of life gains from every small outcome are immeasurable.

Apart from optimizing funding decisions in terms of services provided and in the functional goals targeted, there is the issue of timing. It is essential to proactively manage disability by stressing health interventions, not just treatment interventions. Personal health issues come with a window of opportunity that needs to be seized, otherwise human potential is compromised. Functional rehabilitation requires a building-block process that follows up reacquisition of skills with reapplication of skills in normalized living and work environments. Integrated care plans involve coordinated transfers and goal setting between providers. Sending patients home and then providing a patchwork of outpatient services immediately or later is a prescription for poor outcomes and higher ultimate costs.

Bringing proactive management to the most serious care issues extends a quality-based health systems approach to the area of greatest cost exposure and human need. Comprehensive management of the financial risk combined with a health emphasis will drive considerable waste out of today's care system.

Achieving Even Greater Leverage— Employer Coalitions

Even as a level playing field is developed in broad system issues, employers can equalize the playing field on a strategic basis through employer coalitions. This is a key consideration for small- to medium-size organizations that want to access the advantages of self-insured risks. It is also a consideration for all employers who want to work as a group directly with providers and provider coalitions.

Leverage is an underlying theme in this book. Employers need to utilize their considerable leverage over the health system by taking control of the issues that affect their operations. The foundation for this leverage is attention at the line management level combined with an organizational culture creating employer–employee partnership centered on health. When this strategy-based management is in place, employers can negotiate as equals in the world of health and disability.

Archimedes said, "Give me a lever big enough and I will move the world," and the same is true with the potential power of employer coalitions. The purchasing power alone is immense. Employers spent $238 billion in 1991 on health care when all related taxes were included.[6] Self-insured employers' portion in health care and workers' compensation can be derived as approximately $100 billion in direct annual funding based on these 1991 totals. In addition, much of the funding through insurers is on a minimum premium basis. So where once the funds were retained by insurers, about $25 billion now remains in the cash balances and cash flows of corporations, with similar potential among municipalities, and other organizations. Even state and federal governments have the potential to similarly draw back funding for their own employees and use it for other purposes.

Coalitions are developing throughout the country in many forms:

- Regional coalitions focusing on limited health and health care issues such as wellness and the development of quality services.
- Broader regional coalitions focusing on major health and health care issues such as provider cost and quality levels. The best known efforts are in Cleveland and Memphis.[7,8]
- National coalitions focusing on health, health care, and disability policy issues.
- Employer groups supporting reasonably priced, prevention-oriented community services in poor and disadvantaged neighborhoods.
- User groups coalescing among employers to bring common concerns forward to an insurer or third-party administrator, supporting improvement of services.
- User groups focusing on information sharing about wellness, employee assistance programs, safety, and other health programs.

Coalitions are making significant contributions, yet their impact has only recently begun to develop. Even in the current national health care debate, attention is too often directed toward the old insurance model, not appreciating that "insurers" are mostly acting as third-party administrators. The role of employer as both payor and active participant continues to be downplayed.

When employers develop a quality-based health system, the value-added potential of coalitions is apparent at many levels. Linkage with fellow employers can occur in the following areas:

1. A financial risk pool among a group of employers for health care and/or workers' compensation coverages. This allows smaller employers to handle state bonding requirements and spread their financial risks among themselves.[9] A less involved approach is health insurance purchasing cooperatives in which employers rely on more traditional insurance coverage.[10]

2. Common development of health, health care, and disability programs among a group of regionally based employers, such as a combined program among local auto dealers. Economies of scale and negotiating leverage are the natural benefits.[11]

3. Development of value-added staffing, such as health and disability experts, among a coalition to support all employers.

4. Support of local value-added services including return-to-work job coaching and regional transportation for disabled persons.

A coalition approach requires senior management leadership and support, obtained by justifying the coalition in terms of health and productivity, as well as care issues. The first step is to recognize the seriousness of the health and disability problem and establish a commitment to achieving a solution. Next, linkages throughout a community and region need to occur at a senior management level on an employer-to-employer basis. Third, middle management must support the cooperative efforts, recognizing the potential opportunities for job enhancement and improved health and disability programs. Thus, organizations will be elevating health and disability to a major strategy issue with dedicated management systems and information feedback.

When employers separate health and disability strategy from insurance and benefits, the natural role for coalitions becomes more evident. Employers can maintain very different benefit features while still working cooperatively on core health, health care, and disability programs, and financial risk pools. And coalitions provide a significant opportunity for continuous learning and improvement through the sharing of information and benchmarking of performance.

Achieving Even More Value Added—Partnerships

Interconnections within the health care and workers' compensation systems are one of the sources of greatest waste, in terms of cost, poor quality, and unnecessary legal exposures. Care is often delayed or incomplete, while management follow-up is lacking. Gaining a comprehensive and integrated framework for managing the health activities of all participants is one of the advantages of a quality-based health system.

Obtaining strategy-based solutions requires integration toward common health and disability goals. Such integration is essential, first of all, at the employer level, particularly among employees and dependents, line management, and functional management. The next level of integration occurs among fellow employers based on coalitions. At the third level, there is a need for partnerships between employers and other involved participants.[12]

Partnership is essential because employer, employees and dependents, providers and third-party managers all have a role in health and disability solutions. Successful dialogue requires appropriate access to information based on the following conditions:

- Employer commitment to problem solving, not problem avoidance or transference.

- Employee and dependent accountability for personal health and cost-effective use of health care.

- Provider commitment and accountability for true cost discipline, for objective measurement of quality, and for optimization of care through flexible and interconnected services.
- Third-party manager accountability for delivering value added in terms of management or information services.

The term *partnership* does not imply financial arrangements or insider deals. Rather, it conveys a unified effort for achieving excellence in the cost and quality of health and disability. This effort pertains to development of programs, services, incentives, and information systems that attack the root causes of risk. Partnership also means an overriding continuous improvement approach centered on health. Ultimately, there is a need for developing consensus about standards in claims data, patient records, case documentation, and clinical practices such as diagnostic testing. The goal needs to be a drive toward best practice and away from today's regulatory-oriented minimum standards.

A particularly important example of such cooperation is in developing care services on an individualized and functional basis so they meet the needs of the work and living environments. Providers, employers, and family members can all work together to establish the best way for the ill or injured employee to regain functioning quickly and permanently. This example points up the need to better integrate technology with its human applications. Flexible care services must ultimately translate to health services if they are going to provide true value to employers concerned with optimizing health and productivity, as well as managing care.

Partnership is also important because cooperative employer–provider efforts can leverage off the specialized expertise of regional medical centers. Centers of excellence classification will be truly verified when partnership arrangements provide enhanced services. Regional achievements can then translate into a national matrix of excellence to draw on for the benefit of other regions.

Organizational Focus—Integrating Health into Management Priorities

Health and disability issues are demanding greater attention from senior management. This situation is not likely to change regardless of various reform efforts in health care and workers' compensation. A strategic and operational perspective in health and disability is necessary in both internal operations and external relationships to target lasting organizational solutions.

Although this increased level of commitment may appear at first to be a problem, in reality it presents a major opportunity. A commitment to health can be translated into a two-way set of mutual accountabilities between employer and employee. In addition to managing costs, employers can make gains in health-related productivity and quality that can form the basis for an improved cost structure, increased competitiveness, and a higher level of organizational effectiveness.

One of the continuing problems in managing for productivity is that a benefits orientation fosters a care culture. Employees expect to be taken care of whether the issue is financial or health related. Little accountability for personal and family health exists. Even senior management can confuse the issue of caring for employees with sustaining a care culture. The individual must always be accountable for personal and family health regardless of financial arrangements.

The advantage of health is that it expressly states that employees are an organization's number one asset. This is no small consideration in an information-driven world economy where the value-added use of knowledge and technology is increasingly the source of competitive advantage. Often the problem is to translate these "soft" people issues into a strategic context. By focusing on the total cost of health and disability and by managing health-related productivity, organizations can balance the "soft" and "hard" concerns. In fact, a win–win situation can be created in which risk sharing and incentives share improved organizational health and related financial health between all stakeholders.

This book has continuously stressed that employers, to utilize the full power of health, must integrate the management of health and disability into mainstream organizational issues. The following four critical measures are a natural offset of the three-part management system focusing on health, care, and productivity:

1. Health.
2. Productivity (health related).
3. Care—quality features.
4. Care—cost features.

In addition, the total cost of health and disability can be tracked and segmented at any required level of detail. An organization making new investments in health will require a higher level of accountability in these areas. The result is the "Balanced Scorecard"[13] for health and disability, shown in Table 14.3.

This scorecard summarizes the critical health and disability issues that require ongoing attention from senior management. This combination of process and results measures provides a high level of management control and leverage over organizational performance even while considering only a limited number of measures. Each measure can be related to internal and external benchmarks or targets to create a never-ending drive toward continuous improvement.

Table 14.3   Health and Disability Balanced Scorecard

Health		Productivity (Health Related)	
Goals	Measures	Goals	Measures
Optimize health activities	Utilization of value index	Optimize health interventions	Time and dollars invested in health activities
Reduce health risks	Health risks as portion of population	Minimize health-related productivity losses	Productivity ratio
Optimize effectiveness of programs	Cost–benefit analysis ROI for total health effort	Minimize lost workdays due to health and disability	Full and partial days Average length of case

Care—Quality Features		Care—Cost Features	
Goals	Measures	Goals	Measures
Provider excellence	Outcomes per procedure and per case	Minimize high-risk, high-cost cases	Number of cases over $50,000
Third-party manager excellence	Outcomes per case	Optimize management of high-risk, high-cost cases	Outcomes, including durability Cycle times at all stages
Program excellence	Employee satisfaction with programs Employee participation and adherence	Reduce need for specialty care	Frequency Severity Duration
System excellence	Assessment of system interconnections—coverages, programs, providers	Optimize payback on health interventions	Cost–benefit analysis ROI for individual interventions

The range of measures used will depend on the organization. Preventing and managing disability on both health care and workers' compensation cases may be a major priority for one employer, whereas absenteeism may be a priority for another. The measures will need adjustment as an organization achieves success in one area or confronts problems. Changes in an organization's operating profile, such as acquisitions and divestitures or growth in certain regions, will also create new health and disability issues.

The intent of the Balanced Scorecard is not to replace the need for detailed information on health and disability for line and functional management. Such information will be utilized on an ongoing basis and reviewed by senior management periodically. Quarterly review may be best when an organization's leader is driving change in health and disability management. As goals are reached, the frequency of review can be reduced even as the Balanced Scorecard provides ongoing visibility.

What is more important about the Balanced Scorecard is that it addresses organizational performance as an ongoing strategy. Balance between all the elements of performance prevents overemphasis of any particular aspect.

The full benefit of a strategy-based, health system framework is in its integrative capacity. Improved health will mean improved health-related productivity. Similarly, improved quality in care activities will benefit health and health-related productivity. And the measures used for performance—health, productivity, quality, and cost—all have a direct equivalent in the measures currently used by organizations. Even organizational health can be conceptualized as an equivalent of financial health. This translation of strategic and operational measures between health and disability and mainstream product and service issues draws health and disability more closely into general operations even as health becomes a new priority.

Many Paths to Strategy-Based Solutions

Health is the most personal human issue and organizational health is no different. Individualized employer circumstances demand flexible strategies, programs, systems, and management in general. Otherwise, waste and excess costs pervade an employer's cost structure. Bringing the power of information to bear on the activities of all participants can exert proactive risk management on an individualized personal and family basis. Employers can emphasize a cultural habit of managing health and safety risks throughout the health continuum to avoid unnecessary care and to restore individuals to health. Environmental issues in work and home can be similarly encompassed, creating comprehensive health-centered solutions that link disability to health.

Through the use of information at every level, strategy-based health systems can be developed for the individual, for a family, for an individual employer, and for a group or groups of employers. Strategies will develop over time, responding to individual and organizational needs and related life cycles. At the same time, a systems framework inclusive of a health culture ensures the optimization of cost and quality within an individualized solution. The key is for health to remain the primary goal and ultimate outcome of all activities.

Managing based on health requires the application of many of the management theories and tools developed in the information age. Value added, quality, excellence, culture, continuous improvement, empowerment, and continuous learning all converge in health as a point of organizational focus. Health is the best means to connect these management practices between the individual and the employer. The energy of organizations can thus become fully forward directed and human in its values.

Information infuses organizations with this new form of health-related energy. Accountability for performance can be created at every level: employees and dependents (managing personal health), line supervisors (managing health and disability issues and health-related productivity), and providers and third parties (managing with health-related best practices). The use and distribution of information can emphasize prevention, rehabilitation, and early intervention in broad-based health terms, not just medical terms. The human gains are potentially great, even as the return on investment potential looms large.

Health is a highly individualized matter, so the path for achieving strategy-based health and disability solutions will be unique for each organization. The starting point is to address critical exposures and the areas of greatest opportunity. The gains will come from putting in place the appropriate strategies, programs, systems, and management training on a building-block basis. Continuous learning and continuous improvement are essential.

The organizational potential of health merits a strategic and operational commitment. Transformation of both cost structure and productivity levels is possible. Empowering individuals in personal health has the same breakthrough management potential as empowerment has had in product and service quality. Those employers tapping into this double-barreled advantage will achieve unparalleled levels of organizational effectiveness. This is health's full promise and the benefit to organizations from strategy-based solutions.

References

1. Albrecht, K., & Albrecht, S. 1987. *The creative corporation*. Homewood, IL: Business One/Irwin.

2. Senge, P. M. 1990. *The fifth discipline: Mastering the five practices of the learning organization*. New York: Doubleday/Bantam.

3. Mosser, G. March 1987. Risk management through quality assurance. *Minnesota Medicine*, pp. 70, 149.

4. Carlson, J. G. 1993. Risk management, clinical and financial (Chapter 3). *The Shortest Distance: The Pursuit of Independence for Individuals with Acquired Brain Injury*, edited by McMahon, B. J., and Evans, R. W. Orlando, FL: Deutsch Press.

5. Pope, A. M., & Tarlov, A. R., Eds., Institute of Medicine. 1991. *Disability in America: Toward a national agenda for prevention*, p. 49. Washington, DC: National Academy Press.

6. Health Spending: The Growing Threat to the Family Budget. A Report by Families USA Foundation, December 1991, supported by a grant from the Henry J. Kaiser Foundation, p. 5.

7. Bogdanich, W. February 6, 1992. Clevelanders bet top health care will be cheaper. *Wall Street Journal*, B1.

8. Winslow, R. February 4, 1992. Local businesses get together to cut Memphis health costs. *Wall Street Journal,* pp. A1, 6.

9. Albertson, D. April 1992. Comp. self-insurance bands together like-minded companies for savings. *Employee Benefit News,* 6(4): 1, 18.

10. Enthoven, A. The Jackson Hole Initiatives, *Health Care Strategic Management,* February 1993, pp. 11–14.

11. Ritter, S., & Leclair, S. W. August 1990. The small employer disability management consortium as a case management and consultation alternative. *NARPPS Journals & News,* 5(4): 15–24.

12. Johnson, D. E. February 1992. Creating health delivery systems—A CEO Interview with Samuel T. Wallace. *Health Care Strategic Management,* pp. 8–13.

13. Kaplan, R. S., & Norton, D. P. January February 1992. The Balanced Scorecard—Measures that drive performance. *Harvard Business Review,* January-February 1992, pp. 71–79.

Resources

Albrecht, K., & Albrecht, S. 1987. *The creative corporation.* Homewood, IL: Business One/Irwin.

Belasco, J. E. 1990. *Teaching the elephant to dance: Empowering change in your organization.* New York: Crown.

Jacobs, G. 1990. *The vital corporation: How American businesses large and small double profits in two years or less.* Englewood Cliffs, NJ: Prentice-Hall.

Maurer, R. 1992. *Caught in the middle: A leadership guide for partnership in the workplace.* Cambridge, MA: Productivity Press.

Schaffer, R. 1990. *The breakthrough strategy: Using short-term successes to build the high performance organization.* New York: Harper Business.

Index

Absenteeism, 44, 121, 131, 142
Accountability:
  historically, 34
  integrated approach, steps for, 135
  Managed Care and, 26
  national system of, 54
  performance and, 105–109, 122
  in quality-based health system, 53
  rehabilitation issues, 141–142
  self-insurance and, 11
  utilization problems and, 82
Accreditation, quality of care and, 112
Activity-based cost, 44, 45, 58
Adult children, 249
Advocacy, 77–78
Aetna Life and Casualty Company, claim review
  by, 247
Aging, impact of, 74
Al-Anon, 249
Alcoa, 56, 292
Alcohol abuse, *see* Substance abuse
Alcoholics Anonymous, 249, 259–260, 262
Alignment, 59, 68–70
Allied Signal, involvement by, 56
All Plastics Molding, 197, 294–295
American Cancer Society, 231
American Heart Association, 213, 231
Americans with Disabilities Act (ADA):
  compliance with, 128–129, 305
  regulation by, 124
  supervisors' knowledge requirements,
    205
  workplace safety regulation, 291
Ancillary services, 110
Aspen Imaging International, workplace safety,
  293–294
Assessments, significance of, 148–149
Attorneys, dealing with, 323

"Babies and You" program, 193–194, 231
Balanced Scorecard, 332–334
Bank of America, 6, 237
Behavior patterns, 16–17, 78
Benefits strategy, development of, 46–47
Birmingham, AL:
  health screening program, 231–232
  strategic approach, 6
  wellness program, 218, 222–223

Boeing, Inc., study of back injuries, 187
Budgets, 96, 148

Campbell Soup Company, employee assistance
  program, 282
Cancer, impact of, 132–133, 235
Care culture, 78, 332
Care knowledge, 107
Care orientation, examples of, 134
Carpal tunnel syndrome, 280
Case management:
  claims and, 106–107
  five-point program for, 108–109
  qualification devices, 114
  of rehabilitation, 141
  role of, 114–115
  See also Third-party management
CATOR, 255–257
Certificates of need (CON), 103
Change, management of, 280–281
Chevron, Inc., 272, 283
Child safety, 307
Chrysler, Inc., employee assistance program,
  285
Cigarette smoking, impact of, 79, 121, 186,
  235
Claims management, 45, 106
Commitment, significance of, 21, 49, 64, 67,
  79, 88, 157
Communication, significance of, 126, 278,
  281–282
Community care, 99
Competition, 62, 332
Compliance, 128–130
Conflict resolution, 8
Consolidated Omnibus Budget Reconciliation
  Act of 1985 (COBRA), 127, 128
Continuous improvement:
  advantages of, 84–87
  continuous learning and, 317–320
  health continuum and 99
  performance measurement, 332
  plan design, 101
  workplace safety and, 301
Continuous learning, 59, 317–320
Continuous quality improvement (CQI), 110,
  174
Control, systems of, 92, 153–154

Coors, Inc.:
  demographics, 185
  health screening program, 223
  "Talk to a Friend" program, 192
  wellness program, 232
Cost, root causes of:
  employee/dependent risk factors, 185–188
  health and disability data, 182–184
  organizational risk factors, 189–191
  study of, 180–182
Cost-containment approach, 17–19, 29
Cost attribution, reporting, 34, 126
Cost/benefit assessment, 47–48
Cost management:
  comprehensive cost targets, 124–126
  elements of, 19
  opportunities for, 39–40
  value-based approach to, 109–110
Costs-only approach, limitations of, 60
Cost targets, 38–40, 124–126
Coverages:
  eligibility time lags, 43
  first-dollar, see Deductibles
  generally, 324
  plan design issues, 100–102
Cross-functional teams, as information source, 183–184
Culture, as influential factor, 78

Data, see Information, data
Deductibles, 66, 78, 81–82
Deming, W. Edwards, 49
Demographics, significance of, 45, 55, 179
Dependent health:
  coverage issue, 43
  education/training of, 36
  employees perspective of, 204
  as productivity issue, 130–132
  as risk factor, 182, 185–188
Diagnosis-related group (DRG), development of, 269
Direct access, 54, 64
Direct costs, 38–39, 125
Disability:
  costs, generally, 125
  environmental factors and, 137
  management of, generally, 8
  prevalence of, 132
Dow Chemical:
  Texas operation, 251
  workplace safety, 292, 301
Driving safety, 45, 302, 307
Drug abuse, see Substance abuse
Drug-Free Workplace Act, 250
DuPont:
  disability costs, 126
  health and safety programs, 201, 213
  line management involvement, 197
  risk profile, 186–187
  strategic approach, 6
  workplace safety, 292

Education/training, see Continuous learning
Emergency room, utilization of, 86–87, 156
Employee(s):
  education/training, 36, 55, 64, 66
  interests of, 60–63, 65–67
  involvement of, 63–65
  needs of, awareness of, 55
  participation of, 7–8
  population, impact of, 61, 179
  risk factors, 185–188
Employee Assistance Program (EAP):
  function of, 55
  vs. managed mental health, 282–285
  substance abuse and, 247, 249, 259
Employee health screening, 222–223
Employee interests, systems solutions, 65–67
Employee lifestyle, effect of, 67, 172, 187
Employee surveys, 66, 146, 187
Employer coalitions, 328–330
Employer involvement, 56–57
Employer self-assessment, 57–58
Employer-specific strategy, 54–56
Employment Retirement Income Security Act of 1974 (ERISA), 42, 128
Empowerment:
  of employees, 63, 67, 80, 107, 335
  performance and, 157
  in risk management, 31
Environmental illness, 190
Ergonomics, 190, 297–300

Family:
  health care costs of, 65
  as health and productivity issues, 130–132
  health promotion and, 235–237
  risk factors of, 187
  safety issues, 302, 307–308
Federal Express, workplace safety, 301
Feedback, significance of, 80, 99, 113, 155, 209, 212
Financial risk, 34–35, 41, 48, 62
First National Bank of Chicago, 193–194
Flexibility, significance of, 54, 67, 100, 124, 126
Flexible benefits, 130
Focus groups, as information source, 183–184
Fraud, 152
Funding, sources of, 103

General Electric, substance abuse treatment and, 255–256, 258–261
General Electric Aircraft Engines, weight-loss program, 224
General Motors Corporation, ergonomics, 201, 298
Georgia Pacific Corporation, health screening program, 230
Georgia Power Company, substance abuse treatment and, 246, 252

Hazelden Services, Inc., 281
Health care costs:
 assumption-testing of, 148–149
 bottom-up analysis, 149, 160–161
 factors of, 87–89
 increase in, 1
 sources of, constraints on, 149–150
Health continuum, 97–99
Health culture, design of, 79
Health and disability:
 data, 182–184
 performance accountabilities, 154
 strategy development, 47–48
Health and safety programs, 77–80, 107. *See also specific companies*
Health issues, awareness of, 120
Health Maintenance Organizations (HMOs), 35, 145
Health opportunity, defined, 73–74
Health orientation, examples of, 134
Health promotion, 235–238
Health risk appraisal (HRA), 188
Health risks, prevalence of, 74
Health screening programs, *see specific organizations*
Health Triangle, 19–23
Heart disease, impact of, 132
Hershey Foods Corporation, health care cost program, 228–229
Hewlett-Packard, 272, 278–279
Hidden costs, 38–39, 125, 131
High-loss organizations, factors of, 9
High-risk, high-cost cases, leverage on, 113–116
High-risk behavior, management of, 177–181
Home care, 99, 104–105
Home safety, 45, 74, 302, 307–308
HON Industries, workplace safety, 294
Hospitals, 86, 102–103, 110

IBM Rochester, workplace safety, 301
Incentives:
 effect of, 67–69, 76
 function of, 22, 171
 for supervisors, 213–215
Indirect costs, 39, 125
Industrial-age medicine vs. information-age health, 132–135
Information:
 availability of, 54
 benefits of, 147
 as communication tool, 146
 data, 150–152, 182–184
 focusing techniques, 167
 health system integration through, 167–169, 320
 limitations, leverage points, 163–164, 166–167
 management of, 79
 role of, 14–16, 146–147, 168
 sharing of, 191–192
 utilization of, 166

Information-age health vs. industrial-age medicine, 132–135
Insurance, 40–42, 46–47
Integration of plans, 63, 69
Intervention:
 attitude/behavior control and, 135
 cost/benefit of, 89–92
 early, 36, 41, 75, 136
 supportive, 76. *See also* Line management; Supervisor
 timing of, 107–108
Interviews, as information source, 183–184

Johns Hopkins University, mental health study by, 274–275
Johnson & Johnson:
 employee survey, 224
 health and safety programs, 213
 line management involvement, 197
 "Live for Life" wellness program, 218–219
 wellness programs, 272
Johnsonville Foods, Inc., strategic approach, 6, 189
Joint Commission on Accreditation of Healthcare Organizations (JCAHO), 110–111

Kaiser Permanante, 13

Leaf, Inc., strategic approach, 6, 279
Levi Strauss & Co., health care costs study, 181
Liabilities, recognition of, 161
Liberty Mutual, health care cost study, 181
Line management, *see* Supervisor
 as case manager, 141
 education/training of, 76
 as information source, 150
 involvement, issues of, 125–126, 197, 296
 productivity issues, 121–123, 143
 rehabilitation, role in, 141–143
 reinforcement by, 124
 workplace safety, involvement in, 296
Litigation:
 avoidance of, 76–77, 304
 stress claims, 270–271
 workplace safety and, 291
Liz Claiborne, Inc., 185, 193–194
Long-term care facilities, 103–104
Long-term disability, cost of, 4
Low-loss organizations, factors of, 9

McDonnell Douglas:
 employee assistance program, 284, 286
 health care cost study, 247
 strategic approach, 6
 substance abuse treatment program, 255–256, 258–260
Malpractice, cost of, 323
Managed care, 25–26, 31
Managed care networks, 60–63

Managing Forward approach:
accountabilities, 37
activities-based approach, 44–45
benefits of, 35–38
control levels, 106
employee control, 67, 72
goal of, 35
health interventions, timing of, 75
health and safety, 45
incentives and risk sharing, 67–68
information, role of, 75–76, 150, 161, 166
performance management, 157, 159
risk reduction, 169
substance abuse prevention, 248
supervisors, effective, 212
utilization, 72, 84–85
Managing Care:
accountability, 26
control in, 147
cost management, 109–110
health continuum and, 97–100
information, role of, 150
optimizing, 21
systems approach, implementation of, 96–97
value, levels of, 26–27
Managing Health:
control in, 147
health opportunity, defined, 73–74
information, role of, 150
strategic development, 71–72
Managing Productivity, see Productivity
care culture, 332
control in, 147
information, role of, 150
Manufacturing industry, quality and, 4–5
March of Dimes, 193–194, 231
Medical care models, 133
Mental health:
problems, 13, 14, 272–275, 278–282
promotion of, 286
resources regarding, 288–289
treatment, see Mental health services
wellness and, 282
Mental health services, see Employee Assistance Program (EAP)
cost of, 100, 267, 271–272, 286
coverage of, 100–101
utilization of, 101
value of, 272
Michigan State University, wellness exercise program, 227
Motorola, 4

National Council on Compensation Insurance, 292
National Head Injury Foundation, 213
National health insurance, support for, 325
National Institute of Drug Abuse, certification procedures, 252
National Institute on Occupational Safety and Health (NIOSH), 301

National Safety Council, 213
National Survey of Worksite Health Promotion Activities, 237
Network, 60, 105
Non-profit organizations, 46, 213
North American Tool and Die, Inc., strategic approach, 6, 190
Northern Telecom, Inc.:
health promotion program, 225–226
integration, cross-functional approach, 233–234
Northwestern National Life, 270, 276, 280
Nurse, as gatekeeper, 105

Occupational Safety and Health Administration (OSHA):
compliance with, 128
regulation by, 123–124
supervisors' knowledge requirements, 205
workplace safety regulation, 291
On-site testing, 91. See also specific corporations
Operations management, 27, 127–128
Organizational culture, 172–175, 317
Organizational strategy, 49–50
Outcome studies, importance of, 113
Out-of-pocket costs, 66
Outpatient care, 99, 103–104
Owen, Patricia, 281

Paid time off, effect of, 124
Pareto principle, 11–12
Partnerships, 203, 330–331
Part-time employment, 128
Paybacks, see Return on investment (ROI)
Performance:
benchmarks, 159
managing uncertainty, 159–161
measurement, 113, 154–159
return on investment and, 161–163
setting targets, 154–159
Pharmaceutical programs, 86
Portfolio management, 140
Pre-existing condition, 43
Preferred provider organizations (PPOs), 61
Primary care:
access to, 105
as gatekeeper, 60, 99
health integration with, 79
quality of care and, 79, 86, 105, 113, 156
significance of, 99
utilization of, 75
Process control limits, 75
Productivity:
accountability, 122
care culture, 78, 332
compliance issues, 128–130
comprehensive cost of, 124–126
cost of, 89
health-related, 120–122, 129
loss of, 119
management of, 120

Productivity *(Continued)*
  operations issues, 126–128
  optimizing, 123–124, 129, 142
  significance of, 119
  as value index, 120
  workplace health and disability, integration of,
    142–143, 168
Program effectiveness, measurement of, 80–82
Psychological factors, 187. *See also* Mental
    health

Quad/Graphics, Inc., 6, 272, 279
Quality assurance, information-based controls,
    153–154
Quality-based health system:
  components of, 28
  essence of, 53–54
  integration of, 68–70
Quality of care, 111–113
Quality improvement techniques, as information
    source, 183–184

Rand Corporation, high-risk behavior study,
    179
Readiness to work, 249, 254
Rehabilitation, 43, 136–142
Rehabilitation therapy, 103
Return on investment (ROI):
  decisions based on, 161–163
  health costs and, 87–89
  intervention approach, cost/benefit analysis
    of, 89–92
  rehabilitation and, 138–142
  significance of, 31
Return-to-work programs, 126, 142, 184
Revenue, generation of, 51
Risk avoidance, 41, 44, 81, 324
Risk curve, 321–322
Risk exposure, management of, 42, 44
Risk factors, 182, 185–191
Risk information, sharing of, 192–193
Risk management:
  advantages of, 323
  care services and, 107
  case management and, 116
  vs. financing risk, 320–323
  insurance and, 40–42
  prevention vs. avoidance, 42–44
  risk information, sharing of, 190–192
  significance of, 45
Risk profile, 185–186
Risk reduction, 156–157, 193–194
Risk sharing, 67–68, 76, 332
Risk triangle, 41
Rockwell International, drug testing study,
    252

Safety programs, 79. *See also* Workplace safety
Safety risks, 45
St. Paul Fire and Marine Insurance, 276
Sara Lee, health screening program, 192

Senior management:
  accountability, 332
  corporate culture, substance abuse and, 263
  decision-making, 31
  information-gathering, 164
  involvement of, 200–201
  organizational culture, development by, 173
  retribution and, 76
  risk management by, 51
  roles of, 67, 173–174, 331–332
"Senior management dashboard," 157–158
Serious care needs, 75, 141, 325–328
Services, development of, 104–105
Short-term disability, cost of, 4
SmithKline Beecham, drug testing results, 251
Southern California Edison, involvement of, 56
Southern Pacific Railroad, health screening
    program, 251
Staff, 115, 120
Standard Telephone, Inc., 6, 217–218, 232
Statistical analyses, as information source,
    183–184
Steelcase, Inc., health screening program, 223
Strategy-based health systems, 314–315,
    324–325, 334–335
Stress:
  benefits limitation, 271–272
  claims of, 13, 269–271
  effect of, 44
  increase of, 268–269
  managing, 278–280
  measurement of, 275–278
  prevalence of, 267
  prevention of, 133
  resources regarding, 288–289
  work-related factors, as source of, 190, 268
Substance abuse:
  absenteeism and, 121
  corporate culture and, 262–263
  cost of, 245–248
  coverage of, 100–101
  drug testing, 250–254
  growth of, 13
  health risks and, 86
  intervention, 249
  monitoring, 249
  performance-testing option, 254–255
  prevention of, 248–249
  resources, 265–266
  significance of, 245
  statistics of, 244, 267
  treatment, value of, 255–262
Success factors, 7–10
Supervisors, *see* Line Management
  coaching skills, 77, 206, 208–212
  critical role of, 198–200
  education/training of, 36
  health issues, training in, 203–207
  health promotion by, 202–203
  incentives and, 213–215
  information, access to, 212–213

Supervisors *(Continued)*
  moments of truth, 199
  organizational goals and, 200–202
  as support for recovering employees, 262
Supportive intervention, 76–77
Systematic care management, generally, 116
Systematic quality, 23–24, 92–93
Systems approach, 27, 28, 62
Systems framework, development of, 34–39,
    315–317
Systems solutions, 63–67

Technological advancement, benefits of, 11–13,
    33, 172
Third-party management:
  accountability, 107
  after-the-fact claims, assessment of, 106
  data translation by, 152
  qualification of, 114
  role of, 19, 28, 35, 44, 52
  selection of, 59
  standards development, 105
  value-added, 62
Total Quality Management (TQM), 28, 38
Travelers Company, health care costs study, 177
Travelers Insurance, "Taking Care" wellness
    program, 225–226
Turnover rate, 112, 127, 128
Type A personality, 188

U-Haul International, Inc., health care costs,
    177
Uncertainty, management of, 33, 159–161
U.S. Postal Service, drug testing study,
    251–252
Unity of purpose, 63
University of Michigan Worker Health Program,
    227
Utah Power and Light, 246, 252
Utilization:
  continuous improvement and, 101
  as cost factor, 161
  factors of, 73
  as health value index, 80–82
  preventive, 73–74
  root causes of, 82–84
  significance of, 71–72

Value, levels of, 26–27
Value-added management services:
  assessment/development, 57–59
  care goals, 105
  employer interests, 60–63
  employer involvement, 56–57

Video display terminals, as risk factor, 190, 280
Vocational rehabilitation, 102

Washington Business Group on Health, 61
Wellness programs:
  benefits of, 216–218
  community resources, 231–231
  effectiveness of, 56
  employee health screening, 222–223
  employee participation, increasing, 224–227
  evaluation of, 234–235
  health education, 223–224
  health promotion, 223–224, 235–238
  incentives/penalties, 228–230
  integration of, 219–220, 232–234
  organizational philosophy and objectives,
      220–222
  personal counseling/follow-up, 227–228, 233
  resources for, 240–243
  retiree health promotion, 235–236
Wells Fargo Bank, mental health program,
    272–273, 275
Westinghouse Corporation, mental health study,
    273–275
Weyerhauser, Inc., 6, 303
W. L. Gore and Associates, strategic approach,
    190
Workers' compensation:
  cost increases of, 1
  measurement of, 305–306
  performance accountabilities, 154
  stress claims, 270
  workplace safety and, 290–291
Workforce, stability of, 8, 42
Workplace safety, *see* Ergonomics
  behavioral safety, 301–302
  culture of, 308
  cooperative efforts, 297
  corporate leaders in, 291–293
  education regarding, 302, 308
  employee involvement, 296–297, 300–302
  health risks and, 74
  injuries, 296–297, 302–304
  line manager involvement, 296
  management of, 301
  old/new techniques, blending of, 295–298
  program effectiveness, measurement of,
      305–306
  resources for, 309–310
  safe physical workplace, 296
  safety programs, elements of, 292–293
  significance of, 13, 290–291, 308
  small/medium-size companies, 293–295
Workstation design, as risk factor, 190